DATE DUE

BROWSED

OFFENDERS WITH DEVELOPMENTAL DISABILITIES

WILEY SERIES IN
FORENSIC CLINICAL PSYCHOLOGY

Edited by

Clive R. Hollin
Division of Forensic Mental Health, The University of Leicester, UK
and

Mary McMurran
School of Psychology, Cardiff University, UK

OFFENDERS WITH DEVELOPMENTAL DISABILITIES

Edited by

William R. Lindsay
The State Hospital; NHS Tayside and University of Abertay Dundee, Dundee, UK

John L. Taylor
Northumbria University, Newcastle upon Tyne and Northgate & Prudhoe NHS Trust, Northumberland, UK

and

Peter Sturmey
Queens College and The Graduate Center, City University of New York, USA

John Wiley & Sons, Ltd

Copyright © 2004   John Wiley & Sons Ltd, The Atrium, Southern Gate, Chichester,
West Sussex PO19 8SQ, England

Telephone   (+44) 1243 779777

Email (for orders and customer service enquiries): cs-books@wiley.co.uk
Visit our Home Page on www.wileyeurope.com or www.wiley.com

This publication is designed to provide accurate and authoritative information in regard to the subject
matter covered. It is sold on the understanding that the Publisher is not engaged in rendering professional services. If professional advice or other expert assistance is required, the services of a competent
professional should be sought.

Other Wiley Editorial Offices

John Wiley & Sons Inc., 111 River Street, Hoboken, NJ 07030, USA

Jossey-Bass, 989 Market Street, San Francisco, CA 94103-1741, USA

Wiley-VCH Verlag GmbH, Boschstr. 12, D-69469 Weinheim, Germany

John Wiley & Sons Australia Ltd, 33 Park Road, Milton, Queensland 4064, Australia

John Wiley & Sons (Asia) Pte Ltd, 2 Clementi Loop #02-01, Jin Xing Distripark, Singapore 129809

John Wiley & Sons Canada Ltd, 22 Worcester Road, Etobicoke, Ontario, Canada M9W 1L1

Wiley also publishes its books in a variety of electronic formats. Some content that appears in print may
not be available in electronic books.

Library of Congress Cataloging-in-Publication Data

Offenders with developmental disabilities / edited by William R.
Lindsay, John L. Taylor, and Peter Sturmey.
      p.   cm.—(Wiley series in forensic clinical psychology)
    Includes bibliographical references and index.
    ISBN ISBN 0-470-85410-3 (cloth : alk. paper)—ISBN 0-471-48635-3 (pbk. : alk. paper)
    1. Offenders with mental disabilities.   2. Offenders with mental disabilities—Rehabilitation.
  3. Developmentally disabled—Rehabilitation.   4. People with mental disabilities and crime.
  5. Criminal psychology.   I. Lindsay, William R.   II. Taylor, John L. (John Lionel), 1961–   III. Sturmey,
  Peter.   IV. Series.

    HV6080 .O46   2004
    365'.66—dc22   2003021217

British Library Cataloguing in Publication Data

A catalogue record for this book is available from the British Library

ISBN 0-470-85410-3 (hbk)
ISBN 0-471-48635-3 (pbk)

Typeset in 10/12 pt Palatino by TechBooks Electronic Services, New Delhi, India
Printed and bound in Great Britain by Antony Rowe Ltd, Chippenham, Wiltshire
This book is printed on acid-free paper responsibly manufactured from sustainable forestry
in which at least two trees are planted for each one used for paper production.

CONTENTS

ABOUT THE EDITORS

William R. Lindsay, PhD, *Consultant Forensic Clinical Psychologist, The State Hospital, Carstairs; Head of Clinical Psychology (Intellectual Disability) NHS Tayside & Chair of Learning Disabilities, University of Abertay Dundee, Dundee, UK*

Bill Lindsay is Consultant Forensic Clinical Psychologist at the State Hospital, Head of Clinical Psychology (Learning Disabilities) in Tayside and Professor of Learning Disabilities at the University of Abertay, Dundee, Scotland. He is a practicing clinician, has over 150 publications, and has directed several major research projects.

John L. Taylor, DPsychol, *Head of Psychological Therapies & Research and Consultant Clinical Psychologist, Northgate & Prudhoe NHS Trust, Northumberland & Principal Lecturer in Clinical Psychology, Northumbria University, Newcastle upon Tyne, UK*

Since qualifying as a clinical psychologist, John Taylor has worked mainly in developmental disability and forensic services in community, medium secure, special hospital and prison settings in the UK. In recent years he has published work related to his research interests in assessment and treatment of offenders with developmental disabilities in a range of research and professional journals.

Peter Sturmey, PhD, *Associate Professor of Psychology in the Department of Psychology, Queens College and The Graduate Center, City University of New York & Research Associate at the Institute for Basic Research, Staten Island, USA*

Peter Sturmey has published widely on intellectual disabilities, especially in the areas of challenging behaviours, functional assessment, dual diagnosis and staff training.

His current research interests include restraint reduction, client preferences for staff members, mood disorders and dissemination of behavioural technology.

LIST OF CONTRIBUTORS

George S. Baroff

Formerly Director of the Developmental Disabilities Training Institute, and Professor of Psychology, University of North Carolina at Chapel Hill, North Carolina, USA

Nigel Beail

Consultant Clinical Psychologist and Head of Psychology Services, Barnsley Learning Disability Service, and Professor of Psychology, University of Sheffield, Sheffield, UK

Frank Caparulo

Board Certified Forensic Examiner, Professional Specialist, Connecticut Department of Mental Retardation, Hartford, Connecticut, USA

Michael C. Clark

Director, Kern Regional Center, Bakersfield, California, USA

Jennifer Clegg

Senior Lecturer in Clinical Psychology, Division of Rehabilitation and Ageing, University of Nottingham, and Honorary Consultant Clinical Psychologist, Nottinghamshire Healthcare NHS Trust, Nottingham, UK

Bruce T. Gillmer

Consultant Clinical Psychologist, Northgate & Prudhoe NHS Trust, Northumberland, and Honorary Clinical Lecturer, University of Newcastle, Newcastle upon Tyne, UK

Michael Gunn

Professor and Associate Dean, Nottingham Law School, Nottingham Trent University, England, UK

Susan Hayes

Head of Behavioural Sciences in Medicine, Faculty of Medicine, University of Sydney, Sydney, Australia

Anthony J. Holland

The Health Foundation Chair in Learning Disabilities, University of Cambridge, Cambridge, UK

Kathleen Kendall

Lecturer in Medical Sociology, School of Medicine, University of Southampton, Southampton, Hampshire, UK

Jacqueline Law

HM Prison Service, Edinburgh, UK

William R. Lindsay

Consultant Forensic Clinical Psychologist, The State Hospital, Carstairs, Head of Clinical Psychology (Intellectual Disability) NHS Tayside, and Chair of Learning Disabilities, University of Abertay Dundee, Dundee, UK

Edwin J. Mikkelsen

Associate Professor of Psychiatry, Harvard Medical School, Medical Director for The MENTOR Network, and Consultant to the Massachusetts Department of Mental Retardation, Boston, Massachusetts, USA

Raymond W. Novaco

Professor, Department of Psychology and Social Behavior, University of California, Irvine, USA

Gregory O'Brien

Consultant Psychiatrist, Northgate & Prudhoe NHS Trust, Northumberland, and Chair in Developmental Psychiatry, University of Northumbria, Newcastle upon Tyne, UK

Anthony F. Perini

Medical Director and Consultant Psychiatrist, Northgate & Prudhoe NHS Trust, Northumberland, UK

Vernon L. Quinsey

Professor of Psychology and Psychiatry, Psychology Department, Queen's University, Kingston, Ontario, Canada

Andrew H. Reid

Formerly Consultant Psychiatrist and Medical Director, NHS Tayside, and Senior Lecturer, Department of Psychiatry, University of Dundee, Dundee, UK

Jay Rider

Director of Clinical and Wellness Services, Kern Regional Center, Bakersfield, California, USA

Alison Robertson

Consultant Clinical Psychologist, Northgate & Prudhoe NHS Trust, Northumberland, and Honorary Clinical Lecturer, University of Newcastle, Newcastle upon Tyne, UK

Michael L. Slavkin

Assistant Professor of Education, University of Southern Indiana, Evansville, USA

Anne H.W. Smith

Consultant Psychiatrist, NHS Tayside, Dundee, UK

Mark Steege

Steege and Associates, San Antonio, Texas, USA

Peter Sturmey

Associate Professor of Psychology in the Department of Psychology, Queens College and The Graduate Center, City University of New York, and Research Associate at the Institute for Basic Research, Staten Island, USA

John L. Taylor

Head of Psychological Therapies & Research and Consultant Clinical Psychologist, Northgate & Prudhoe NHS Trust, Northumberland, and Principal Lecturer in Clinical Psychology, University of Northumbria, Newcastle upon Tyne, UK

Ian Thorne

Forensic Psychologist, Northgate & Prudhoe NHS Trust, Northumberland, UK

SERIES EDITORS' PREFACE

ABOUT THE SERIES

At the time of writing it is clear that we live in a time, certainly in the UK and other parts of Europe, if perhaps less so in other parts of the world, when there is renewed enthusiasm for constructive approaches to working with offenders to prevent crime. What do we mean by this statement and what basis do we have for making it?

First, by "constructive approaches to working with offenders" we mean bringing the use of effective methods and techniques of behaviour change into work with offenders. Indeed, this might pass as a definition of forensic clinical psychology. Thus, this might pass as a definition of forensic clinical psychology. Thus, our focus is application of theory and research in order to develop practice aimed at bringing about a change in the offender's functioning. The word *constructive* is important and can be set against approaches to behaviour change that seek to operate by destructive means. Such destructive approaches are typically based on the principles of deterrence and punishment, seeking to suppress the offender's actions through fear and intimidation. A constructive approach, on the other hand, seeks to bring about changes in an offender's functioning, or increased awareness of the pain of victims.

A constructive approach faces the criticism of being a "soft" response to damage caused by offenders, neither inflicting pain and punishment nor delivering retribution. This point raises a serious question for those involved in working with offenders. Should advocates of constructive approaches oppose retribution as a goal of the criminal justice system as incompatible with treatment and rehabilitation? Alternatively, should constructive work with offenders take place within a system given to retribution? We believe that this issue merits serious debate.

However, to return to our starting point, history shows that criminal justice systems are littered with many attempts at constructive work with offenders, not all of which have been successful. In raising the spectre of success, the second part of our opening sentence now merits attention: that is, "constructive approaches to working with offenders to *prevent crime*". In order to achieve the goal of preventing crime, interventions must focus on the right targets for behaviour change. In addressing this crucial point, Andrews and Bonta (1994) have formulated the *need principle*:

> Many offenders, especially high-risk offenders, have a variety of needs. They need places to live and work and/or they need to stop taking drugs. Some have poor self-esteem, chronic headaches or cavities in their teeth. These are all "needs". The need principle draws our attention to the distinction between *criminogenic* and *noncriminogenic* needs. Criminogenic needs are a subset of an offender's risk level. They are dynamic attributes of an offender that, when changed, are associated with changes in the probability of recidivism. Noncriminogenic needs are also dynamic and changeable, but these changes are not necessarily associated with the probability of recidivism. (p.176)

Thus, successful work with offenders can be judged in terms of bringing about change in noncriminogenic need *or* in terms of bringing about change in criminogenic need. While the former is important and, indeed, may be a necessary precursor to offence-focused work, it is changing criminogenic need that, we argue, should be the touchstone of working with offenders.

While, as noted above, the history of work with offenders is not replete with success, the research base developed since the early 1990s, particularly the meta-analyses (e.g. Lösel, 1995), now strongly supports the position that effective work with offenders to prevent further offending is possible. The parameters of such evidence-based practice have become well established and widely disseminated under the banner of *What Works* (McGuire, 1995). It is important to state that we are not advocating that there is only one approach to preventing crime. Clearly there are many approaches, with different theoretical underpinnings, that can be applied. Nonetheless, a tangible momentum has grown in the wake of the *What Works* movement as academics, practitioners and policy makers seek to capitalise on the possibilities that this research raises for preventing crime. The task now facing many service agencies lies in turning the research into effective practice.

Our aim in developing this Series in Forensic Clinical Psychology is to produce texts that review research and draw on clinical expertise to advance effective work with offenders. We are both committed to the ideal of evidence-based practice and we will encourage contributors to the Series to follow this approach. Thus, the books published in the Series will not be practice manuals or "cook books": they will offer readers authoritative and critical information through which forensic clinical practice can develop. We are both enthusiastic about the contribution to effective practice that this Series can make and look forward to it developing in the years to come.

ABOUT THIS BOOK

Developments in offender treatments over the past decade or so have, for the larger part, been aimed at white males with average intellectual abilities. The needs of people not in this category have been ignored to a great extent. Treatments designed to suit women, people with cultural backgrounds that are minority in our societies, and those with different abilities are few and far between. This text on the treatment of offenders with developmental disabilities takes us forward with at least one under-served group.

In working with people with developmental disabilities, some say that regular treatments may be adapted to suit and others say that altogether different treatments are needed. The answer to this matter lies in a comprehensive understanding of the prevalence, nature and development of offending by those with developmental disabilities. Basing treatment approaches upon theory and evidence is fundamental to good practice; anything else is simply taking a gamble on what might work. In this text, we are presented with an informed discussion of the knowledge base on which effective practice may be founded. Treatment cannot, of course, be planned effectively without attention to legal processes, treatment context and the professionals undertaking the treatment. Who is determined guilty by the criminal justice system and how do they go about this? How should services that offer treatment be configured? How do we ensure that treatment personnel are well trained, supported and supervised? Throughout all of these activities should run the thread of ethics; are our legal, clinical and management practices ethical? These issues are important in offender treatment in general, but take on an added dimension when working with people who may be less able to comprehend complex processes and assert their views in a domain that operates at a high intellectual level.

This book, admirably edited by Bill Lindsay, John Taylor and Peter Sturmey, addresses the issues raised. The editors have gathered scholarly contributions from eminent authors that undoubtedly place this text at the forefront of the field. We are delighted to include this important book in the Forensic Clinical Psychology Series.

August 2003   Mary McMurran and Clive Hollin

REFERENCES

Andrews, D.A. & Bonta, J. (1994). *The Psychology of Criminal Conduct*. Cincinnati, OH: Anderson.

Lösel, F. (1995). Increasing consensus in the evaluation of offender rehabilitation. Lessons from recent research synthesis. *Psychology, Crime and Law*, **2**, 19–39.

McGuire, J. (ed.) (1995). *What Works: Reducing Reoffending*. Chichester: John Wiley & Sons.

PREFACE

Research and practice developments concerning offenders with developmental disabilities have been growing apace over the past ten to fifteen years. Much of the published work in this field has involved descriptive and epidemiological studies, issues concerning individuals' competence to comprehend and participate in the criminal justice system, and treatment outcome case studies. While these types of studies have predominated, there has also been a steady, if gentle, flow of publications investigating the relationship between psychological variables and offending—such as work on the impact of mental illness, impulsiveness and other personality variables on offending, as well as studies on the assessment and evaluation of such behaviour. The impetus of this book has been to bring these developments together in one volume, not only to summarise and document these advances, but also to provide insightful and knowledgeable commentary from scientists and practitioners in the field. In the course of developing the book, contributors have also provided a wealth of new material for the interested clinician and researcher.

Those with developmental disabilities, and particularly those with lower intellectual functioning, have been overly identified with and blamed for disproportionate amounts of crime and delinquency in a most pejorative manner for more than a century. One only has to read of the outcry from suburban neighbourhoods when a group home for clients with intellectual disability is proposed in their vicinity to realise that these (mis)perceptions and prejudices are far from being historical phenomena. Yet generally these persons will be law abiding and peaceful neighbours. The thoughtful contributions in this book hopefully provide a counterbalance to some of society's persisting prejudiced views and attitudes concerning people with developmental disabilities and histories of offending.

As for the contributions themselves, they combine to provide a comprehensive overview of contemporary work in this field. The chapters begin by placing the topic in a historical and theoretical context and then go on to describe epidemiological, legal and ethical frameworks in which to consider later chapters on assessment, treatment and staffing issues. The reader will note that on occasions different contributors have differing, even opposing, views on particular issues, and sometimes incompatible interpretations of certain research findings. As editors we have decided to allow these differing perspectives, relying on each author to justify their position rather than insisting on uniformity of views. Consequently the reader is exposed to a range of differing views about particular issues that they then need to make their own minds up about. However, this approach emphasises that there can indeed be different interpretations of particular sets of data and other types of evidence. In this way we hope that we have produced a lively volume that will not only be helpful in the development of treatment and management endeavours but will also stimulate future research and inquiry.

We need to explain to readers the reasons for the choice of terminology used by the editors in the title and text of this book to describe the client group with whom we are concerned. In the United Kingdom the term "learning disability" is commonly used to describe people characterised as having (a) significant sub-average general intellectual functioning as measured on standard individual intelligence test, (b) more difficulties in functioning in two or more specified areas of adaptive behaviour than would be expected taking into account age and cultural context, and (c) experienced the onset of this disability before the age of 18 years. These criteria are broadly those included in the International Classification of Diseases (ICD-10), Diagnostic Statistical Manual (DSM-IV) and American Association on Mental Retardation (AAMR) diagnostic classification systems. The terms "mental retardation" and "intellectual disability" are commonly used in North America and Australia, respectively, to refer to the same syndrome.

We have preferred the term "developmental disability" in this book. It refers to the definition given in the United States Developmental Disabilities Assistance and Bill of Rights Act (2000) and is a broad concept covering the equivalent terms of mental retardation, learning disability and intellectual disability. In general terms developmental disability means a severe, chronic disability of an individual that (a) is attributable to a mental or physical impairment (or combination of mental and physical impairments), (b) is manifested before the individual attains age 22, (c) is likely to continue indefinitely, (d) results in substantial functional limitations in three or more areas of major life activity, and (e) reflects the individual's need for individualised and planned supports and assistance that may be of life-long duration.

In addition to mental retardation, the concept includes other conditions that do not necessarily involve significant sub-average intellectual functioning such as autism, epilepsy and some other neurological conditions. For these reasons we consider that the term "developmental disability" provides the best description of the population described in this volume. However, we have not insisted that individual contributors stick rigidly to this term, and some have preferred to use other terms with which they are more comfortable.

Inevitably in a volume comprising contributions from colleagues around the world, occasionally other minor cultural/language differences arise. For example, the word "disposal" has a particular meaning in the UK criminal justice system that relates to the type of sentence received following conviction for a crime. This does not translate in the same way in Australia or North America, where the word has connotations of getting rid of something, often something unpleasant.

A number of people at John Wiley have been helpful and patient while we produced this book. Notably Lesley Valerio and Dr Vivien Ward have all shown the patience of those who have the wisdom of experience. Dr Mary McMurran has been helpful, supportive and constructive throughout the process. Most of all we are extremely grateful to Charlotte Quinn who prepared the finished manuscript, a task that was well beyond the call of duty.

Bill Lindsay
John Taylor
Peter Sturmey

August 2003

PART I

THEORETICAL ISSUES

Chapter 1

NATURAL HISTORY AND THEORIES OF OFFENDING IN PEOPLE WITH DEVELOPMENTAL DISABILITIES

WILLIAM R. LINDSAY,* PETER STURMEY[†] AND JOHN L. TAYLOR[‡]

*The State Hospital, Carstairs; NHS Tayside & University of Abertay Dundee, Dundee, UK
[†]Queens College, City University of New York, USA
[‡]University of Northumbria, Newcastle upon Tyne and Northgate & Prudhoe NHS Trust, Northumberland, UK

This chapter reviews the natural history and theories about the development of offending behaviour in people with intellectual disabilities, and the extent to which current theories on the genesis of offending behaviour are relevant to this client group. If they are relevant, then what are the limits on this relevance and what other factors do we have to take into account because of intellectual disability itself? The first part of this chapter provides a summary of descriptive studies relating crime to intelligence and other potentially relevant factors. The second part investigates the various hypotheses about the development of offending behaviour such as genetic factors, familial influences, intelligence, environmental factors, peer group influences, the role of the media, developmental factors and the way in which criminal careers may develop in this client group. In the final section we provide an overview of this volume.

NATURAL HISTORY OF OFFENDING RELATED TO DEVELOPMENTAL DISABILITIES

Intelligence and Offending

History

There is little doubt that intellectual disability was seen as a prime factor in criminal behaviour in the late nineteenth century and the beginning of the twentieth century. Although the early and mid-nineteenth century were periods of relative optimism

Offenders with Developmental Disabilities. Edited by W.L. Lindsay, J.L. Taylor and P. Sturmey.
© 2004 John Wiley & Sons, Ltd.

about the educability of people with intellectual disability (Scheerenberger, 1983), Social Darwinism and the eugenics movement were major influences in the development of scientific and popular thought at the time as well as in the subsequent development of public policy.

In 1889 Kerlin put forward the view that vice was not the work of the devil, but "the result of physical infirmity" and that physical infirmity is inherited (Trent, 1994, p. 87). He went on to write that inability to perceive moral sense was like inability to perceive colour in the colour-blind and "the absence can not be supplied by education" (Trent, 1994, p. 87). Hence, Kerlin's views directly challenged the optimism of earlier authorities that viewed people with developmental disabilities as full of potential and remediable by suitable education. For the next 50 years Kerlin's views were dominant. Terman (1911), an author of one of the earliest IQ tests, wrote that "There is no investigator who denies the fearful role of mental deficiency in the production of vice, crime and delinquency... Not all criminals are feeble-minded but all feeble-minded are at least potential criminals" (p. 11). This quotation gives us an idea of the extent to which individuals who were lower functioning were considered a menace to society. Goddard (1921), author of *The Criminal Imbecile*, concluded that "probably from 25% to 50% of the people in our prisons are mentally defective and incapable of managing their affairs with ordinary prudence" (p. 7). Sutherland (1937) also concluded that the 50% of delinquents in prisons were feeble-minded.

Scheerenberger's (1983) *History of Mental Retardation* is replete with the historical association between intelligence and crime in the late nineteenth and first half of the twentieth century. At that time intellectual disabilities came to be viewed as part of a broader degeneracy, which included moral degeneracy, child abuse and neglect, criminality, drunkenness and sexual promiscuity. In Gallager's (1999) cameo of race politics and eugenics in Vermont in the early part of the twentieth century, we see that part of the menace of the feeble-minded in Vermont was their menace to respectable, White property owners, whose property might be stolen. Family trees of degenerate families duly noted the criminals, sex offenders and those incarcerated in correctional institutions alongside the blind, alcoholic, stillborn and feeble-minded (Gallager, 1999, pp. 88–9, 181). Thus, in the late nineteenth and early twentieth centuries criminal behaviour and intellectual disability were firmly linked in the ideology of the menace of the feeble-minded (Trent, 1994). Whereas institutionalisation, segregation of the sexes and community placement contingent upon sterilisation could be effective in protecting the Anglo-Saxon gene pool, other strategies were also implemented. This was continued during the Nazi era, when Jews, Romanies, people with intellectual disabilities or psychiatric disorders, homosexuals and *persistent criminals* were gassed or taken out and shot, in order to preserve the Aryan gene pool (Burleigh & Wippermann, 1991).

Research findings

In a review of the role of intelligence in the development of delinquency, Hirschi and Hindelang (1977) concluded that the relationship between intelligence and delinquency was at least as strong as the relation of either class or race and delinquency.

They also noted that in the 1960s and 70s this relationship was denied by many influential writers, in spite of the ample available scientific evidence. In a study of 9,242 juvenile males, Reiss and Rhodes (1961) found that the rate of referral to juvenile court for those boys with the lowest IQ was slightly over twice that found for individuals with the highest IQ. In addition, they also found that IQ and occupational status varied at around the same rate with delinquency. Hirschi (1969), in an examination of over 3,600 boys in California, found that IQ was a stronger predictor of delinquency than the education of the father or parental occupation. West and Farrington (1973) reported the results of a longitudinal study of 411 boys conducted over a period of 10 years. By comparing those boys with an IQ of over 110 with those who had an IQ of less than 90, they found that quarter of the former group had a police record while half of the latter group had such a record. Further analysis revealed that one in 50 of those with an IQ over 110 recorded recidivism while one in five with an IQ of less than 90 reoffended. West and Farrington concluded that "low IQ was a significant precursor of delinquency to much the same extent as other major factors" (pp. 84–5). This relationship has now been found repeatedly by a range of authors (e.g. Goodman, Simonoff & Stevenson, 1995; Kirkegaard-Sorenson & Mednick, 1977; Rutter, Tizard & Whitmore, 1970; West & Farrington, 1973).

The relationship between IQ and offending is a robust one. However, the main criticism of the hypothesis that there is a *causal* relationship between IQ and delinquency in that the data are correlational. Thus, some other variable or variables other than IQ *per se* may account for the relationship. For example, the relationship between socio-economic status (SES) and delinquency or social deprivation and delinquency may account for the correlation between IQ and delinquency (Simons, 1978).

Two carefully controlled studies, (Moffit, Caspi, Dickson, Silva & Stanton, 1996; Moffitt, Gabrielli, Mednick & Schulsinger, 1991) investigated the relationship between SES, IQ, parental disorder and delinquency. Parental disorder included schizophrenia, character disorder, psychopathic disorder and normal controls. In their first study of 129 males they found that offender status was significantly predicted by IQ *independent* of parental disorder or SES. In their second study, data from 4,552 males available from Danish birth cohort information were used (Schaie, 1965). They again found a small but significant correlation between IQ and delinquency, independent of the effect of SES.

In their prospective study of boys living in London, West and Farrington (1973) reported that 9% of multiple offenders had an IQ of 100 or greater while 28% of recidivistic delinquents scored below an IQ of 90. Therefore, the relationship between IQ and delinquency would seem to hold fairly firmly even while other major variables are controlled within the statistical design.

While a relationship between IQ and delinquency has been established, most of these studies are looking at predictive value or differences between groups at one or two standard deviations around the mean. It would be irresponsible in this volume not to consider the much smaller amount of available evidence investigating these relationships around and greater than two standard deviations below the mean. Chapter 2 by Tony Holland looks at this relationship in more detail, as do some other chapters throughout the book. However, it is interesting to note some more specific studies at this point. McCord and McCord (1959) evaluated an interesting early intervention study with 650 underprivileged boys in Massachusetts. The Cambridge-Somerville Youth Study was set up "to prevent delinquency and to develop stable elements in the characters of children" (McCord & McCord, 1959, p. 2). The boys were divided into 325 matched pairs and assigned to treatment and control conditions. There was a relationship between IQ and rates of conviction in that for the treatment group, 44% of those in the IQ band 81–90 had a conviction while 26% of those with an IQ above 110 had a conviction. However, the 10% of individuals in the lowest IQ group (less than 80) had an intermediate rate of conviction at 35%, that is *lower* than that recorded in the IQ band 81–90. Furthermore, of those in the higher IQ band who were convicted of crime, none went to a penal institution while the highest percentage going to a penal institution, 19%, were in the lowest IQ band. The results were similar in the control group, with 50% in the IQ band 81–90 convicted of crime and 25% in the IQ band less than 80 convicted (although numbers in the latter cohort were small).

Maughan, Pickles, Hagell, Rutter and Yule (1996) and Rutter *et al.* (1997) followed up children who had shown severe reading difficulties at school. It might be considered that a significant proportion of the children with severe reading difficulties had developmental and intellectual disabilities. Surprisingly, they found that the rate of adult crime among boys who had had significant reading difficulties was slightly lower than the rate of adult crime in the general population comparison group. This finding still held true independently of psychopathology or social functioning. Similarly, antisocial behaviour in childhood was less likely to persist into adult life when it was accompanied by reading difficulties. Therefore, while the relationship between IQ and delinquency seems firmly established, there is some evidence that this relationship may not hold when considering individuals 1.5 or more standard deviations below the mean.

The intellectual differences between high and low delinquency samples tends to be greater for verbal than non-verbal IQ (Hirschi & Hindelang, 1977). Kandel *et al.* (1988) identified high- and low-risk samples of men, based on accepted risk predictors for criminality. A cohort of individuals whose father had had at least one prison sentence had received 5.6 times greater a number of prison sentences themselves (39.1% versus 7%). These individuals were then further split into four groups: high risk with prison sentence, high risk with no record, low risk with prison sentence, and low risk with no record. For both high- and low-risk groups, individuals with a criminal record showed lower IQ scores than those with no record. The high-risk subjects with no criminal record had considerably higher verbal, performance and full-scale IQs. IQ differences between criminal and non-criminal cohorts were seen only in the high-risk group. There was no IQ difference between the low-risk criminal conviction ($N = 20$) and the low-risk no registration ($N = 24$) subjects.

Comment

The crude relationship between IQ and delinquency is robust. However, several caveats apply. First, when other factors such as SES are controlled for, the relationship is considerably attenuated. Second, because many studies have focused on the IQ range of 80–120 the relationship to intellectual disability can only be inferred in many studies. Indeed, the few available studies suggested that when the sample was extended to IQs below 80, there was no simple linear relationship to IQ. Third, no studies investigated criminal behaviour in people with severe and profound intellectual disabilities. Few people with severe and profound intellectual disabilities commit many criminal acts since acts of crime assume *mens rea*; if they do enter into the justice system they are presumably diverted to the mental health, intellectual disability or forensic mental health service system via the courts. Nevertheless, in their review of US penal institutions, Brown and Courtless (1971) reported that 1.6% of inmates had an IQ score below 50 and, remarkably, a tiny proportion of individuals fell below an IQ of 25.

A final limit on these data is that they have focused on delinquency rather than white-collar, corporate or government crime. Thus, the relationship between IQ and delinquency, focusing on limited kinds of readily observable criminal acts, may obscure any relationship between IQ and criminal behaviour more widely defined.

Social and economic factors and crime

That delinquency and crime are related to social circumstances and SES is undeniable. Schuerman and Kobrin (1986) reviewed demographic changes in areas of Los Angeles County. They compared areas which had moved from low crime rates to high crime rates over 20 years, those with gradually increasing crime rates over 20 years, and those with stable high crime rates over the same time period. They concluded that certain sociological factors were associated with increasing crime rates. These included multiple dwelling and rent or occupied housing, a rising proportion of minority ethnic groups, unattached individuals and single-parent families, and greater deprivation as measured by a range of SES variables. Correspondingly, McDonald (1986) reported the opposite trend in areas of emerging gentrification. McDonald (1986) studied 14 such areas in Boston, New York and San Francisco into which middle class individuals were settling. Analysis of crime rates between 1970 and 1984 were less persuasive than the data from Schuerman and Kobrin (1986), but did tend to suggest that crime rates might be falling over this period. Given that most individuals with intellectual disability (ID) are unemployed, unattached and come from lower SES groups, it is a reasonable hypothesis that these factors may have an influence on this population.

Race and crime

The associations between race and crime have interested criminologists for decades. The main comparisons have generally been with White, western society males. Crime rates in Japan have historically been recorded as relatively low, and rates among Black youths relatively high (Wilson & Herrnstein, 1985). That there are large differences between ethnic groups and convictions and imprisonment for crime is indisputable.

How to interpret these facts is controversial: ethnicity is confounded with many factors. The relative contribution of socio-economic status, education, criminal justice procedures, cultural differences in behaviour, differential access to legal services, affluence, child rearing practices, differential sentencing practices in courts and mandated sentencing practices that differentially affect different ethnic groups, such as the "three strikes and out" rule, may all be important factors that explain these observations.

What data there are in the literature on people with ID are meagre and weak. In Edgerton's *Cloak of Competence* studies he compared rates of drug use, including illegal drug use, in four samples including a group of White and African American subjects with mild mental retardation who had been released from institutions in the 1950s and the 1960s (Edgerton, 1967). He noted relatively low rates of illegal drug use compared to the general population in all samples and no clear pattern of illegal drug use between ethnic groups. In any case, the samples were small and not representative of any particular population and so no conclusions can be drawn from these data on this issue.

Pack, Wallander and Brown (1998) compared the rates of a variety of health risk behaviours in African American adolescent students with mild ID living in an urban area of the United States with those of White students with mild ID. They found that although the prevalence of alcohol consumption was lower in the African American students, their prevalence of binge drinking was higher. An additional concern was that many of both the White and the African American adolescents also had access to weapons and engaged in drunk driving and were thus placed in significant personal danger. However, like the data from Edgerton, these data were very limited because of high rates of sample attrition which means that it is not possible to know if these data are representative of either group.

Given the very limited and flawed data we have available on this issue, no firm conclusions of any kind can be made.

THEORIES OF OFFENDING RELATED TO INTELLECTUAL DISABILITIES

Genetic Theories

The main purpose of research in this area is to determine the extent to which biological mechanisms of inheritance effect the likelihood of criminal behaviour. Most studies of antisocial behaviour in children or criminal behaviour in adulthood note the relatively high frequency with which these variables are associated with similar problems in parents (Farrington, 1995). Kandel *et al.* (1988) compared the sons of 92 fathers who had received at least one prison sentence with the sons of 513 fathers who were not registered with the police. They found the risk of serious criminal behaviour was 5.6 times greater among the cohort whose fathers had been severely sanctioned than among the cohort whose fathers had no registration for any offence. Farrington, Gundry and West (1975) found that convicted teenagers in their sample tended to have fathers and mothers who also had convictions. They noted that only 5% of families in their sample provided half the convictions.

The obvious difficulty with these and similar comparisons is that environmental variables and genetic variables are confounded. There are so many confounding variables, such as socio-economic status, peer group influence, labelling by the criminal justice system and exposure to modelling influences that this kind of study does not provide a test of the hypothesis that criminal behaviour may have a genetic component.

Evidence from twin studies

When looking for evidence on the relative influence of genetic factors one always turns to well-designed twin studies. If there is greater concordance for a trait for identical than for fraternal twins, this is taken as evidence for the genetic basis of that trait. Silberg *et al.* (1996a, b) reported findings from the Virginia twin study on around 1,400 twin pairs. They found that in the 6% of the population who showed multi-symptomatic behaviour problems, including oppositional behaviour, conduct problems, reading difficulties, hyperactivity and emotional difficulties, variance was largely accounted for by genetic factors. In contrast, the group of children showing antisocial behaviour only, typified by conduct disorder in the absence of hyperactivity, variance was almost entirely attributed to environmental factors. The group of individuals with hyperactive behaviour and conduct disorder showed a mixture of the two with genetic factors predominating although not massively so. Genetic factors seem to be associated with a complex mixture of antisocial and hyperactive problems. Environmental factors seemed to be associated with antisocial behaviour reported by teenagers themselves rather than parents. Other researchers have drawn this distinction. For example, Moffitt *et al.* (1996) noted the difference between early onset antisocial behaviour, which was pervasive and highly persistent, and antisocial behaviour which emerged in adolescence, was associated with peer subcultures and was more transient. Christiansen (1977) analysed data on 3,586 twin pairs and found 52% concordance for criminal behaviour for identical male pairs and 22% concordance for fraternal male pairs. While many twin studies suffer from difficulties in sampling, this comprehensive study, with its large between-group differences, certainly suggests a role for genetic inheritance.

Adoption studies

A number of adoption studies have attempted to separate the effects of environment and genetics. Mednick, Gabrielli and Hutchings (1984) and Mednick, Moffitt, Gabrielli and Hutchings (1986) conducted studies on adopted twins within the context of the register of 14,427 Danish adoptees. The various results are both comprehensive and complex. The main results were that if neither the biological nor adoptive parents were criminal then 13.5% of their sons were criminal. If the biological parents were not criminal and the adoptive parents were criminal the figure was only marginally greater at 14.7%. If the biological parents were criminal and the adoptive parents were not criminal the figure then rose to 20%. Finally, if both sets of parents were criminal the figure was 24.5%. The results suggest that sons who have had no contact with their biological father are more likely to become criminal if their biological father was criminal. Of the full cohort 6,129 adopted boys were identified. The probability of a conviction for the boy rose with the number of convictions for the biological parent from zero to three or more. Economic depression, age of adoption, adoptive parents' knowledge of the biological parent's criminal record and whether the biological parent offended before or after adoption had no effect on the results. Bohman, Cloninger, Sigvardsson and Von Knorring (1982) in a similar study on a large Swedish population found similar results.

Extra Y chromosome and offending

It has been hypothesised that the presence of an extra Y chromosome in males might be associated with severe aggression. This hypothesis was derived from case studies and small case series. Witkin *et al.* (1977) in a study of 31,436 men born in Copenhagen found only 12 with an extra Y chromosome. Further, many of the crimes they had committed were trivial and not very violent. Thus, larger scales studies have failed to confirm this hypothesis. Therefore, the theory of chromosome abnormality as a cause of crime has been laid to rest (Thielgaard, 1983).

Gender and crime

The most obvious and pervasive biological factor relating to criminality is that of sex. Men are far more likely to appear at every stage in the criminal justice process from apprehension to conviction (Dobash, Dobash & Gutteridge, 1986). These findings are true for violent, acquisitive and drug-related crimes. Although these gender differences in criminal behaviour are robust, they shed little light on the question to hand. Specifically, it is unclear if these differences arise from biological or social factors. These issues will be dealt with in greater detail in Chapter 14.

Genetic theories and offending: a comment

The best evidence for a genetic basis to criminal behaviour comes from twin and adoption studies, which are suggestive that inheritance plays a role in criminal behaviour. This relationship must be qualified in a number of ways. First, the strength of the relationship may vary substantially between one kind of criminal activity and another. Second, even when the relationship is strong, these studies do not specify *what* it is that is inherited—faulty learning, propensities toward thrill-seeking etc. Third, these studies often miss the point that heritability is a characteristic of a specific population, *not an individual*. Thus, the heritability of a trait found in one population at one time, may not apply to another population or time. Neither is heritability an immutable characteristic. The heritability of a trait can be very high when there is little variability in relevant environmental variables. If the environment changes and there is much greater variability in some relevant feature of the environment, then the heritability of that trait may decrease.

Sociological Theories

Conforming to a delinquent subculture

Cohen (1955) suggested that boys entered into delinquency because they were conforming to the expectations and encouragement of their delinquent subculture. This view held that the material and vocational aspirations of all boys tended towards those of the middle classes. Boys from lower socio-economic groups were disadvantaged in competition towards these aspirations because they were less likely to be schooled in the skills of the middle classes. Faced with lower ability to achieve these goals using legitimate, middle class means, these individuals were more likely to use subcultural delinquent methods to fulfil these aspirations. While Cohen tended to concentrate on destructiveness, Cloward and Ohlin (1960) focused more on the role of the adoption of middle class values in explaining acquisitiveness. Again, they focused on the fact that certain subcultures might adopt illegitimate means to obtain these goals in the absence of an ability to employ accepted middle class abilities, such as facility with verbal reasoning, non-aggressive approaches, the ability to delay gratification and socially appropriate manners.

One of the main criticisms of this theory was the view that delinquency and crime were a result of lack of commitment to the conventions of society, rather than a disparity between middle class aspirations and perceived personal potential. As a result, delinquent individuals would no longer have these aspirations, leading to a general disillusionment with society and low personal aspirations among those who have become delinquent (Gibbons & Krohn, 1986).

Control theory

The established relationship between lower SES and higher rates of crime encouraged the development of sociological theories to explain this link. Control theory (Hirschi, 1969) paid attention to both the positive learning of criminal behaviours, through association with criminal subcultures, and also the development of self-control through appropriate social learning in being law abiding. Hirschi felt that the success of social training was dependent on four factors: attachments, commitment, involvement and belief. Attachments referred to the extent to which the individual identified with the expectations and values of others within society such as teachers and parents. Commitment invokes a rational element in criminality. Individuals make subjective evaluations about the loss that they will experience following arrest and conviction. Involvement simply points out that many individuals are engaged in ordinary activities such as work, education or other occupational activities and have little opportunity to consider delinquency. The less involved individuals are with the day-to-day activities of society, the more likely they are to engage in criminal activity. Certainly Schuerman and Kobrin (1986) felt that within any particular urban area the displacement of semi- and unskilled jobholders for individuals who had long-term unemployment and were no longer seeking employment was a major factor in the increase in crime in an area. Belief referred to the extent to which individuals accepted the laws of society.

There is a wealth of evidence consistent with this hypothesis. This evidence shows that negative attitudes to schoolwork and authority are indeed associated with delinquent and antisocial activity (Elliot, Huizinga & Ageton, 1985). This suggests that the disruption of attachments between children and authority figures, such as parents and teachers, results in a failure to internalise parental values and promote social conformity. Thus, control theory shares some similarity with Patterson's social developmental studies and theories (Patterson & Yoerger, 1997) although Patterson's theory is more detailed in describing the processes and mechanisms which explain the effects of parent–child attachments.

Criminal subgroups

The final group of theorists stressing the importance of social processes for the development of criminal behaviour are those who emphasise the importance of criminal subgroups in developing both attitudes towards criminality and the practical techniques for carrying out criminal acts (Sutherland & Cressey, 1974). For example, Haynie (2001) conducted a study employing the ADD Health Survey, which consisted of interviews with 90,000 school students who provided self-report responses on 14 different delinquent activities, including damaging property, shoplifting, use of weapons and assault. She found that an individual adolescent's delinquency was strongly associated with the delinquency of their peers. She also noted that very cohesive peer group relationships were particularly associated with delinquency in comparison to less cohesive relationships. Warr (1996) added to this argument when he found that the effect of delinquent peer networks influenced individual behaviour beyond the impact of any individual traits. In particular, the structure of the group, rather than an individual's attributes, affected which individual instigated delinquency. Interestingly, he also found that many delinquent offenders tended to belong to multiple groups, each with a different style and range of offending.

As an example of peer networks in the context of intellectual disability, Hugh, aged 17 years, had been brought up in a reasonably stable home. Following his parents' divorce when he was 8 years old, he lived with his father, who appeared very caring towards him and maintained regular contact with his mother. He did, however, suffer from extreme hyperactivity and was placed in a special school for disruptive boys from the age of 14 years.

He was seen by WRL following a series of car thefts. It was clear that the relationships he made in this school were close and enduring. All but one of the individuals in this close cohesive network had been charged with a series of car thefts. However, two of these individuals, who were also assessed by WRL, were assessed as having intellectual abilities in the normal range. Hugh still lived with his father and, unusually, did not abuse either drugs or alcohol. Here it would appear that a reasonably stable upbringing had been superseded by a cohesive delinquent peer group network.

Sociological theories: comment

From the point of view of people with intellectual disabilities these theories suggest a series of interesting hypotheses. Individuals with mild intellectual disabilities tend to come from lower socio-economic backgrounds (Murphy, Yeargin-Allsopp, Decoufle & Drews, 1995; Zigler & Hodapp, 1986). They are more likely to have parents who themselves have a degree of intellectual disability and are therefore less able to develop what Trasler (1973) might describe as effective child rearing strategies. Child rearing strategies and attachments are also salient in the control theory, in which individuals develop attachments and commitments to the values of society.

Another interesting aspect of control theory is that of involvement. It must be recognised that individuals with mild intellectual disability are far less likely to gain employment and become regularly involved with the day-to-day business of society than individuals without intellectual disability.

As an example, Ricky Don had lived in a rural community for a number of years. He was raised by his mother alone. Despite her ongoing drug problems he continued to live in the community doing well for himself. He was in special education and made reasonably good progress there. He hung around the local fire station, fascinated with the men who worked there, and all of their machines and activities. Although he was easily recognised as a person with intellectual disabilities by most members of his small rural community, he was treated well by many of them.

After Ricky Don set fire to a field, he broke in and entered his neighbour's house, intending to steal something. He was caught by the police because he remained in the house eating ice cream out of the refrigerator, instead of leaving the scene of the crime. The police became involved and he was committed to a developmental centre nearly 400 miles away from his home.

Initially he was eager to please staff. However, it became evident that he often instigated minor acts of aggression to his peers, stole and lied blatantly, but without skill. He was vulnerable to peer pressure to join a gang or commit acts of violence to less able peers. He got into mischief during periods of inactivity and when he missed his mother and his home town. For a few months he received prevocational training and an individualised token economy. His life really improved when he obtained a community workplace and earned a significant sum of money every week. He bought smart clothes, and many personal items that made his life better. He was placed in a group home in a community setting and continued to do well at two-year follow-up. He maintained contact with his mother, made periodic visits home for long weekends and continued to work in a sheltered community setting. Therefore it would appear that once there was significant involvement with society, his offending behaviour disappeared.

When considering the impact of peer group relationships one has to consider not only the effect of cohesive networks, but also the perception of a cohesive network. Other members of the subgroup may not reciprocate this, but the perception of membership of the subgroup may afford status and self-esteem to the individual with intellectual disabilities.

For example, WRL interviewed 17-year-old Kevin subsequent to conviction and prior to sentencing for violent assault. The assault had occurred along with several other delinquent youths, but Kevin was not prepared to divulge their identity. He gained self-worth from the fact that "I am grassing on nobody". However, he did appear somewhat remorseful for the assault and apprehensive about punishment.

One year later WRL was asked to assess Kevin once again for an appeal against the severity of his sentence. On this occasion, he was completely different. He was comfortable with prison, talked of his friends and relationships in prison, and now appeared completely lacking in remorse. Indeed, he now maintained he would do the same again under similar circumstances. Kevin was assessed as having a WAIS Full Scale IQ of 73. He was clearly being exploited financially while in prison. However, his own perception of a cohesive attachment to a valued group of peers seemed to have completely changed his presentation in the year following his conviction and was probably a factor in the commission of the original offence.

Developmental Theories

Patterson's model

One of the major developmental models for the onset of delinquency and criminal behaviour is that of Patterson and his associates (Patterson, 1986; Patterson, Reid & Dishion, 1992). In an extensive series of studies based on learning and reinforcement theories, they have found that from as early as 18 months, some families may promote a child's coercive behaviour such as temper tantrums and hitting because those behaviours have functional value in terminating conflict. With repeated transactions, these behaviours are strengthened and firmly established. In other families, children learn interactions that are quite distinct from those learned in distressed families. In non-distressed families, in which pro-social behaviours are reinforced, the child learns that interaction such as talking and negotiating are followed by a termination of conflict. In distressed families, not only are coercive behaviours promoted, pro-social behaviours may not be particularly effective in terminating family conflict (Snyder & Patterson, 1995). Therefore, as these boys develop they fail to learn pro-social behaviours, problem solving and language skills, but become highly skilled in antisocial behaviours.

The major parenting processes outlined by these authors are discipline, positive parenting, monitoring and problem solving. In early years, parental discipline is more important in determining the emergence of coercive and pro-social skills. In early to middle adolescence, parental monitoring emerges as a more salient variable. In distressed family interactions, parental discipline reinforces coercive child behaviour, pro-social interpersonal academic and work skills are encouraged less, and deviant problem solving is inadvertently taught, which leads to the development of coercive behaviours in the termination of conflict.

Patterson and Yoerger (1997) relate these theories to the development of early onset and late onset delinquency. In early onset delinquency, the combination of the emergence of coercive behaviours and a high frequency of conflict density within families accounted for almost half of the variance in the development of antisocial behaviour in boys as young as six or seven (Snyder & Patterson, 1995). In late onset delinquency, the pattern was very different. These boys were better adjusted and in possession of more pro-social behaviours by the time they reached early adolescence. However, while the late onset delinquent boys were better adjusted than early onset delinquent boys, they were not so socially skilled nor as well adjusted in interpersonal skills as non-delinquent boys. At this point, criminal peer subgroups have a major influence in their movement to juvenile delinquency. Correspondingly, parental monitoring plays a more important part in that the ability of parents to monitor the amount of time their son spends with deviant peers becomes crucial. Patterson and Yoerger (1997) make the important point that almost all adolescents have some contact with deviant peers. They hypothesise that the extent of the contact and the length of the time period is related to the intensity of training and reinforcement by the delinquent subculture.

Social learning theory (Trasler, 1973) also invokes the importance of parent–child interactions in promoting social conscience through punishment and modelling (Bandura, 1977). On the one hand social learning theory proposes that behaviours which are consistently censured or punished will be internally conceptualised as anxiety provoking or "wrong". Trasler felt that discipline based on the withdrawal of love in the context of warm consistent relationships was more likely to be effective. Consequently, the upbringing of individuals who went on to develop delinquency and criminal careers was typified by less effective child rearing techniques. Bandura (1973, 1977) developed these ideas to encompass observational learning. The effects of observational learning were that individuals would tend to adopt the behaviour patterns, attitudes and eventually the values of those whom they esteemed and with whom they had a close relationship, e.g. parents. Bandura's theories are complex and wide ranging but they stress the importance of observational learning, and vicarious learning and its subsequent internalisation for the development of social conscience and law abiding behaviour.

The effects of schooling

The effects of school disruption throughout childhood have also been demonstrated to have a significant influence on the development of antisocial behaviour in childhood and adolescence (Gray, Smith & Rutter, 1980). The associations found indicated that the developmental effects were from the school on the children rather than vice versa. Good classroom management, high expectations of pupils, consistency of school values, good models of teacher behaviour, shared activities between staff and pupils, and opportunities for children to exercise responsibility had positive associations with pro-social behaviour in children. Conversely, low levels of these characteristics were associated with truancy, fighting and disruption. Rutter et al. (1997) caution that the association between misbehaviour at school and delinquency is variable but note that the school effects on delinquency remain strong. In later years, the composition of the school intake played a greater role than the school ethos, indicating yet again that deviant peer subgroups play an important role in the development of delinquency.

Comment on developmental theories and the development of criminal careers

This developmental model is interesting in our consideration of offenders with intellectual disabilities. Some individuals with intellectual disabilities have parents who have intellectual limitations. The extent to which intellectual limitations affect parenting practices is only beginning to become understood (Feldman, Varghese, Ramsay & Rajska, 2002; Murphy & Feldman, 2002). The obvious subsequent consideration is the extent to which child rearing practices in parents with intellectual disabilities promote coercive and antisocial behaviour in children in the way that Patterson and his colleagues have demonstrated. One interesting finding reported by Rutter *et al.* (1997) shows that the child rearing association with antisocial behaviour in children was from hostile parenting rather than from parental personality disorder *per se*. This would lead to the hypothesis that parental intellectual limitations *per se* would not be a factor in the development of antisocial behaviour.

It would seem that parenting practices, school ethos and peer group influence are extremely important in the development of criminal careers. West and Farrington (1973) note that for some boys offending begins at the age of 8. It may be that there are predisposing factors of low intellectual ability, impulsiveness/hyperactivity and inconsistent disciplinary practices even from the age of 18 months (Patterson, DeBarsyshe & Ramsey, 1989). Steinberg (1986) reported that early adolescent boys who were not monitored closely by their parents were more susceptible to deviant peer pressure and subsequently engaged in a greater amount of antisocial and delinquent behaviour than boys who were under closer supervision.

Farrington (1983, 1995) found that delinquency in early adolescence was significantly associated with troublesome behaviour at 8–10 years, an uncooperative family at 8 years, poor housing at 8–10 years, poor parental behaviour at 8 years and low IQ at 8–10 years. Their study of crime and deviance in later years found that the best predictors were invariably previous convictions from 10–13 years. For example, convictions at 14–16 years were predicted best by convictions at 10–13 years. Having convicted parents, being rated as daring and being rated as dishonest had additional predictive effects. Convictions at 17–20 years were best predicted by convictions at 14–16 years. A boy's reported delinquency of his friends at age 14 contributed to the prediction of convictions at 17–20 years. Adult criminal convictions at 21–24 years were best predicted by convictions in previous age ranges. An unstable job record, low family income and a hostile attitude towards police at the age of 14 years also made additional predictive contributions to the probability of an adult criminal career. This cycle begins with troublesome behaviour, uncooperative families, poor housing, poor parental behaviour and low IQ at age 8. The higher the number of risk domains (families, childhood behaviour, schooling, etc.), the higher the probability of later delinquency and criminality (Stouthamer-Loeber, Loeber, Wei, Farrington & Wikstrom, 2002). These are variables which are clearly relevant to offenders with intellectual disability but the extent to which the relationships hold in the careers of those individuals is uncertain.

Dewane provides an illustration of some of these developmental issues. He was a 17-year-old African American teenager admitted to a developmental centre by court order for possession of marijuana. He had a WAIS Full Scale IQ of 66. He was a likeable young man who vacillated from hostility to any kind of authority to being needy of attention and approval from adults. He had been used by his family to buy marijuana for several family members and was encouraged by them to engage in minor criminal acts, such as trespass, breaking and entering, and minor theft. He was also very susceptible to peer pressure. When his peers modelled remorse or began to make progress at school or work he would work hard to get on. When new peers entered the group who modelling delinquent behaviour, gang-related conduct and defying authority he would join in with gusto, gaining great personal satisfaction and pride from this. He was considerably conflicted over his personal identity as intellectually disabled. He refused to ride to school on the handicapped bus and would rather ride on a bike in 95 degree weather. When a staff member stupidly gave his residence away to his girlfriend, he was mortified and aggrieved at this injustice.

After doing well at the developmental centre for a number of months his requests to spend weekends home with his family were honoured. Although he had been warned that urine tests would be performed for drug use when he returned, he tested positive for marijuana use and admitted that he had been smoking with his sisters after buying for them.

After two years he was placed in a small group home with one or two other peers with similar histories and disabilities. After a few weeks he was arrested because he had taken a knife to a peer's throat and threatened to kill him. After a number of months in jail, with little or no legal representation and no assistance from the learning disabilities services, he was again placed in another developmental centre 250 miles away from the first. He remained there for a number of years without prospect of community placement or family contact.

Kohlberg's stage theory of moral development

The theory of moral development elucidated by Kohlberg (1964) is clearly relevant in this context since it is a developmental theory which will be relevant to individuals who are delayed in this respect. The six stages of this theory are in three periods of two stages each.

The pre-moral period is one where moral behaviour is based on concrete rules typified by the maxim that breaking rules will result in being punished. Stage two of the pre-moral period is when the individual will follow their self-interest irrespective of the effect on other people. Therefore, the individual is unlikely to break laws since it will result in personal loss. The second period is one of conformity to rules for the reasons of social convention. In stage three people conform to rules because of the social censure that would result otherwise. During stage four this develops further with the individual having a respect for social and cultural expectations and social cohesion. During the third period—stages five and six—self-generated principles of morality develop within the context of universal principles of ethics and justice. In general these would conform to existing legal systems but may transcend them if they violate fundamental human rights or personal conviction.

Arbuthnot, Gordon and Jurkovic (1987) reviewed several studies comparing delinquents and control subjects on Kohlberg's theory of moral development. They concluded that most studies demonstrated delinquents to have attained a lower stage of moral development than non-delinquents. Delinquent subjects also tended to consider various offences more acceptable than control subjects. While there were some exceptions, with many individual delinquents found to be at higher stages of moral development than controls, there was broad support for the model.

This model has clear relevance for offenders with intellectual disabilities. It is likely that most offenders covered by this volume will be placed in stages one and two of Kohlberg's progression. However, the extent to which and the way in which they might differ from control groups of non-intellectually disabled offenders and non-offenders with intellectual disability is entirely unknown. The effects of any subsequent interventions or manipulation of moral development is similarly unknown.

CONCLUSIONS AND INTRODUCTION TO THIS VOLUME

The early chapters of this volume address broad issues such as epidemiology, legal matters, ethics and disposals available to the criminal justice systems. Tony Holland provides an introduction to emerging issues and themes in criminal behaviour and developmental disabilities, and he sets these within an epidemiological context. Legal issues are discussed in Chapter 3 by George Baroff, Michael Gunn and Susan Hayes from three distinct national perspectives—those of the United States, Australia and the United Kingdom. In Chapter 4 Susan Hayes discusses alternative disposals for offenders with intellectual disabilities and in the following chapter Jennifer Clegg provides fascinating ethical perspectives on some of the dilemmas with which we all have to grapple in this field.

The next group of chapters review issues related to assessment. Chapter 6 by Edwin Mikkelsen provides an overview of assessment issues as well as including methods which he himself has developed over several years. Vern Quinsey provides a detailed account of static and proximal dynamic risk assessment in Chapter 7, and Nigel Beail contrasts various approaches to evaluation in Chapter 8.

Treatment issues are described in the next group of chapters, with Bill Lindsay reviewing a variety of approaches to treatment in Chapter 9, and Michael Clark, Jay Rider, Frank Caparulo and Mark Steege describing several systems for the treatment of sexual offenders and abusers in Chapter 10. Subsequent chapters review treatment and management of anger and aggression (John Taylor, Raymond Novaco, Bruce Gillmer and Alison Robertson), fire setting (John Taylor, Ian Thorne and Michael Slavkin), dual diagnosis in mental illness (Anne Smith and Greg O'Brien), services for women (Kathleen Kendall) and personality disorders (Andrew Reid, Bill Lindsay, Jacqueline Law and Peter Sturmey) in offenders with intellectual disability. The final chapters in this volume address staff support and development (Tony Perini) and research and development (Bill Lindsay, Peter Sturmey and John Taylor).

This introduction has set a theoretical and developmental context for the chapters to follow. While the authors of these chapters do not use such a framework in which to set the information and studies, it is interesting to consider these boundaries and assumptions as one reads each chapter. The impact of intellectual and cognitive limitations, socio-economic status, societal engagement, upbringing, peer relations and moral development are all germane to each of the problem areas illustrated. There is little doubt that the field of offenders with intellectual and developmental disability is at a point where we have a good deal of disparate information which requires some integration and synthesis. Our hope is that this book is a starting point to such integration.

REFERENCES

Arbuthnot, J., Gordon, D.A. & Jurkovic, G.J. (1987). Personality. In H.C. Quay (ed.) *Handbook of Juvenile Delinquency* (pp. 139–83). New York: John Wiley & Sons.

Bandura, A. (1973). *Aggression: A Social Learning Analysis*. Englewood Cliffs, NJ: Prentice Hall.

Bandura, A. (1977). *Social learning theory*. Englewood Cliffs, NJ: Prentice Hall.

Bohman, M., Cloninger, C.R., Sigvardsson, S. & Von Knorring, A. (1982). Predisposition to petty criminality in Swedish adoptees. 1. Genetic and environmental heterogeneity. *Archives of General Psychiatry*, **39**(11), 1233–41.

Brown, B.S. & Courtless, T.F. (1971). *The Mentally Retarded Offender*. Publication number (HSM) **72**, 19–39, Department of Health, Education and Welfare. Washington, DC: US Government Printing Office.

Burleigh, M. & Wippermann, W. (1991). *The Racial State: Germany, 1933–1945*. Cambridge: Cambridge University Press.

Christiansen, K.O. (1977). A preliminary study of criminality among twins. In S.A. Mednick & K. Christiansen (eds) *Biosocial Basis of Criminal Behaviour*. New York: Gardner Press.

Cloward, R.A. & Ohlin, R.E. (1960). *Delinquency and Opportunity*. New York: Free Press.

Cohen, A.K. (1955). *Delinquent Boys: The Culture of the Gang*. Glencoe, IL: Free Press.

Dobash, R.P., Dobash, R.E. & Gutteridge, S. (1986). *The Imprisonment of Women*. Oxford: Blackwell.

Edgerton, R.B. (1967). *The Cloak of Competence*. Berkeley, CA: University of California Press.

Elliot, D.S., Huizinga, D. & Ageton, S.S. (1985). *Explaining Delinquency and Drug Use*. Beverley Hills, CA: Sage.

Farrington, D.P. (1983). Offending from 10–25 years of age. In K.T. Van Dusen & S.A. Mednick (eds) *Prospective Studies of Crime and Delinquency* (pp. 289–348). Boston, MA: Kluwer-Nijhoff.

Farrington, D.P. (1995). The development of offending and antisocial behaviour from childhood: key findings from the Cambridge study in delinquent development. *Journal of Child Psychology and Psychiatry*, **36**, 929–64.

Farrington, D.P., Gundry, G. & West, D.J. (1975). The familial transmission of criminality. *Medicine, Science and the Law*, **15**, 177–86.

Feldman, M.A., Varghese, J., Ramsay, J. & Rajska, D. (2002). Relationships between social support, stress and mother–child interactions in mothers with intellectual disabilities. *Journal of Applied Research in Intellectual Disabilities*, **15**, 314–23.

Gallager, N.L. (1999). *Breeding Better Vermonters*. Hanover, NH: University of New England Press.

Gibbons, D.C. & Krohn, M.D. (1986). *Delinquent Behaviour*, 4th edn. Englewood Cliffs, NJ: Prentice Hall.

Goddard, H.H. (1921). *Juvenile Delinquency*. New York: Dodd, Mead & Company.

Goodman, R., Simonoff, E. & Stevenson, J. (1995). The impact of child IQ, parent IQ and sibling IQ on child and behaviour deviance scores. *Journal of Child Psychology and Psychiatry*, **36**, 409–25.

Gray, G., Smith, A. & Rutter, M. (1980). School attendance and the first year of employment. In L. Hersov & I. Berg (eds.) *Out of School: Modern Perspectives in Truancy and School Refusal* (pp. 343–70). Chichester: John Wiley & Sons.

Haynie, D. (2001). Delinquent peers revisited: does network structure matter? *American Journal of Sociology*, **106**, 1013–57.

Hirschi, T. (1969). *Causes of Delinquency*. Berkeley, CA: University of California Press.

Hirschi, T. & Hindelang, M.J. (1977). Intelligence and delinquency: a revisionist view. *American Sociological Review*, **42**, 571–87.

Kandel, E., Mednick, S.A., Kirkegaard-Sorensen, L., Hutchings, B., Knop, J., Rosenberg, R. & Schulsinger, F. (1988). IQ as a protective factor for subjects at high risk for antisocial behaviour. *Journal of Consulting and Clinical Psychology*, **56**, 224–6.

Kirkegaard-Sorensen, L. & Mednick, S.A. (1977). A prospective study of predictors of criminality: a description of registered criminality in the high risk and low risk families. In S.A. Mednick & K.O. Christiansen (eds) *Biological Bases of Criminal Behaviour* (pp. 229–44). New York: Gardener Press.

Kohlberg, L. (1964). The development of moral character. In M.C. Hoffmann (ed.) *Child Development*. New York: Russell Sage Foundation.

Maughan, B., Pickles, A., Hagell, A., Rutter, M. & Yule, W. (1996). Reading problems and antisocial behaviour: developmental trends in co-morbidity. *Journal of Child Psychology and Psychiatry*, **37**, 405–18.

McCord, W. & McCord, J. (1959). *Origins of Crime: A New Evaluation of the Cambridge-Somerville Youth Study*. New York: Columbia University Press.

McDonald, S.C. (1986). Does gentrification affect crime rate? In A.J. Reiss & M. Tonry (eds) *Crime and Justice. An Annual Review of Research*, vol. **6** (pp. 163–202). Chicago, IL: University of Chicago Press.

Mednick, J.A., Gabrielli, W.F. & Hutchings, B. (1984). Genetic influences in criminal convictions: evidence from an adoption cohort. *Science*, **224**, 891–4.

Mednick, S.A., Moffitt, T., Gabrielli, W. & Hutchings, B. (1986). Genetic factors in criminal behaviour: a review. In D. Olweus, J. Block & M. Radke-Yarrow (eds) *Development of Antisocial and Pro-Social Behaviour* (pp. 33–50). London: Academic Press.

Moffit, T.E., Caspi, A., Dickson, N., Silva, P. & Stanton, W. (1996). Childhood onset versus adolescent onset antisocial conduct problems in males: natural history from ages 3–18 years. *Development and Psychopathology*, **8**, 399–424.

Moffit, T.E., Gabrielli, W.F., Mednick, S.A. & Schulsinger, F. (1991). Socio-economic status, IQ and delinquency. *Journal of Abnormal Psychology*, **90**, 152–7.

Murphy, C.C., Yeargin-Allsopp, M., Decoufle, P. & Drews, C.D. (1995). The administrative prevalence of mental retardation in 10-year-old children in metropolitan Atlanta, 1985 through 1987. *American Journal of Public Health*, **85**, 319–23.

Murphy, G. & Feldman, M.A. (2002). Parents with intellectual disabilities. *Journal of Applied Research in Intellectual Disabilities*, **15**, 281–4.

Pack, R.P., Wallander, J.L. & Brown, D. (1998). Health risk behaviors of African American adolescents with mild mental retardation: prevalence depends on measurement method. *American Journal of Mental Deficiency*, **102**, 409–20.

Patterson, G.R. (1986). Performance models for antisocial boys. *American Psychologist*, **41**, 432–44.

Patterson, G.R., DeBarsyshe, B.D. & Ramsey, E. (1989). A developmental perspective on antisocial behaviour. *American Psychologist*, **44**, 329–35.

Patterson, G.R., Reid, J.B. & Dishion, T.J. (1992). *A Social Interactional Approach*. vol. 4: *Antisocial Boys*. Eugene, OR: Castalia.

Patterson, G.R. & Yoerger, K. (1997). A developmental model for late onset delinquency. In D.W. Osgood (ed.) *Motivation and Delinquency* (pp. 119–78), Nebraska Symposium on Motivation, vol. **44**. Lincoln, NE: University of Nebraska Press.

Reiss, A.J. & Rhodes, A.L. (1961). The distribution of juvenile delinquency in the social class structure. *American Sociological Review*, **26**, 720–32.

Rutter, M., Maughan, B., Meyer, J., Pickles, A., Silberg, J., Simonoff, E. & Taylor, E. (1997). Heterogeneity of antisocial behaviour: causes, continuities, and consequences. In D.W. Osgood (ed.) *Motivation and Delinquency* (pp. 45–118), Nebraska Symposium on Motivation, vol. **44**. Lincoln, NE: University of Nebraska Press.

Rutter, M., Tizard, J. & Whitmore, K. (1970). *Education, Health and Behaviour*. London: Longman.

Schaie, K.W. (1965). A general model for the study of developmental problems. *Psychological Bulletin*, **64**, 92–107.

Scheerenberger, R.C. (1983). *A History of Mental Retardation*. London: Brooks.

Schuerman, L. & Kobrin, S. (1986). Community careers in crime. In A.J. Reiss & M. Tonry (eds) *Crime and Justice: An Annual Review of Research*, vol. **8** (pp. 67–100). Chicago, IL: University of Chicago Press.

Silberg, J.H., Meyer, J., Pickles, A., Simonoff, E., Eaves, L., Hewitt, J., Maes, H. & Rutter, M. (1996a). Heterogeneity among juvenile antisocial behaviours: findings from the Virginia twin study of adolescent behavioural development. In G.R. Bock & J.A. Goode (eds) *Genetics of Criminal and Antisocial Behaviour* (pp. 76–86). Chichester: John Wiley & Sons.

Silberg, J.L., Rutter, M.J., Meyer, J., Maes, H., Simonoff, E., Pickles, A., Hewitt, J. & Eaves, L. (1996b). Genetic and environmental influences on the co-variation between hyperactivity and conduct disturbance in juvenile twins. *Journal of Child Psychology and Psychiatry*, **37**, 803–16.

Simons, R.L. (1978). The meaning of the IQ delinquency relationship. *American Sociological Review*, **43**, 268–70.

Snyder, J.J. & Patterson, G.R. (1995). Individual differences in social aggression: a test of a reinforcement model of socialisation in the natural environment. *Behaviour Therapy*, **26**, 371–91.

Steinberg, L. (1986). Latchkey children and susceptibility to peer pressure: an ecological analysis. *Developmental Psychology*, **22**, 433–9.

Stouthamer-Loeber, M., Loeber, R., Wei, E., Farrington, D.P. & Wikstrom, P.O.H. (2002). Risk and promotive effects in the explanation of persistent serious delinquency in boys. *Journals of Consulting in Clinical Psychology*, **70**, 111–23.

Sutherland, E.H. (1937). *The Professional Thief*. Chicago, IL: Chicago University Press.

Sutherland, E.H. & Cressey, D.R. (1974). *Principles of Criminology*. Philadelphia, PA: Lippincott.

Terman, L. (1911). *The Measurement of Intelligence*. Boston, MA: Houghton Mifflin.

Thielgaard, R. (1983). Aggression and the XYY personality. *International Journal of Law and Psychiatry*, **6**, 413–21.

Trasler, G. (1973). Criminal behaviour. In H.J. Eysenck (ed.) *Handbook of Abnormal Psychology*, 2nd edn (pp. 67–96). London: Pitman Medical.

Trent, J.W. (1994). *Inventing the Feeble Mind. A History of Mental Retardation in the United States*. Berkeley, CA: University of California Press.

Warr, M. (1996). Organisation and integration in delinquent groups. *Criminology*, **34**, 11–38.

West, D.J. (1982). *Delinquency: Its Roots, Careers and Prospects*. London: Heinemann.

West, D.J. & Farrington, D.P. (1973). *Who Becomes Delinquent?* London: Heinemann.

Wilson, J.Q. & Herrnstein, R.J. (1985). *Crime and Human Nature*. New York: Simon & Schuster.

Witkin, H.A., Mednick, S.A., Schulsinger, F., Bakkestrom, F., Christiansen, E., Goodenough, K.O., Hirschhorn, D.R., Lundstein, K., Owmen, C., Phillip, J., Ruben, D. & Stocking, M. (1977). Criminality, aggression and intelligence among XYY and XXY men. In S. Mednick & K. Christiansen (eds) *Biosocial Bases of Criminal Behaviour*. New York: Gardener Press.

Zigler, E. & Hodapp, R.M. (1986). *Understanding Mental Retardation*. New York: Cambridge University Press.

Chapter 2

CRIMINAL BEHAVIOUR AND DEVELOPMENTAL DISABILITY: AN EPIDEMIOLOGICAL PERSPECTIVE

ANTHONY J. HOLLAND
University of Cambridge, Cambridge, UK

INTRODUCTION

The relationship between developmental intellectual impairment (learning or developmental disabilities) and the propensity to behaviour that results in contact with the criminal justice system is a complex and ethically problematic area of study. While sound prevalence studies and investigation of the potential risk and protective factors associated with such behaviour would seem essential for the purposes of policy and service development and for the design of preventive strategies, the undertaking and findings of such studies can lead to repressive policy developments. The political climate of the UK and of other developed countries is one in which the emphasis is on the public fear of crime and therefore the need for public protection. There is a real potential for particular groups such as those with mental disorders, developmental disabilities, or those seeking asylum becoming scapegoats for such fears.

History provides important lessons when it comes to investigating any apparent association between a rather ill-defined concept such as developmental disabilities, and similar vague concepts such as *challenging behaviour* or *offending*. As early as the 1300s people who were *idiots* were considered "not to blame" for crimes committed and these cases were referred to the monarch of the day (Walker & McCabe, 1968), and in the 1600s people were acquitted of crimes on the basis of their cognitive difficulties (see Walker & McCabe, 1968). In the 1900s a causal relationship between *feeble-mindedness* and criminality was seen as self-evident (Goddard, 1913; Fennell, 1996), and the social policies of segregation were justified on this basis. Scientific theories were used to bolster prejudices and preconceptions embedded in the moral climate of the times. The definitions used in legislation, such as the

Offenders with Developmental Disabilities. Edited by W.L. Lindsay, J.L. Taylor and P. Sturmey.
© 2004 John Wiley & Sons, Ltd.

Mental Deficiency Act (1913) included judgements about behaviour. Thus the use of these tautological definitions confirmed the presumed links between low intellect, destitution and criminality. This group of people came to represent one of the great concerns of the day, that of *moral degeneracy*. The solution of the time was one of segregation and isolation in what were then *colonies*. These later became hospitals. Halstead has reviewed the literature that considered how stereotypes of gender at that time also influenced policy and practice (Halstead, 2002). Men were being detained because of unruly behaviour and women because of their sexual behaviour.

Recent proposals for new mental health legislation put forward by the UK Government for England and Wales (Department of Health, 1999) illustrate that lessons from history have not been learnt, and that policy development in this field is driven by wider political concerns. The proposed new legislation is not based on established ethical or legal principles that apply to the treatment of physical disorders. The proposed Act includes a very wide definition of mental disorder, which, unlike the present Mental Health Act, has few exclusion criteria but, like the present Mental Health Act, still enables the overriding of a competent person's wishes (in contrast to case law on the treatment of physical disorders), and the emphasis of the legislation is on public protection rather than the right to, and potential benefits of, health treatment. Public safety is clearly a matter of legitimate concern but, in the absence of specific treatment, that is fundamentally an issue for the courts. The new proposals as they stand do nothing to reduce the stigma associated with mental disorder and it is likely that an increased number of people, including those with developmental disability, will meet criteria that potentially will render them liable to detention either by civil orders or through the courts. As was the case in the past, the present political climate is one whereby the results of research investigating any association between a particular group of people (in this case people with developmental disabilities) and offending may have unintended consequences. If such legislative changes were to become law, both private and NHS hospitals may again expand, much as detention centres are being established to contain those seeking asylum.

The process of classification that is necessary for legislation also underpins much of scientific methodology, bringing with it clear benefits. It is this process that can lead, for example, to the understanding of, and eventual treatment for, specific diseases. This is as true for psychiatric illnesses, such as Alzheimer's disease or schizophrenia, as it is for physical illnesses. Similarly, this approach has enabled some of the causes of developmental disabilities to be established. These advances cannot be ignored, and, as argued earlier, such information is necessary for policy and planning purposes. However, particularly when research is concerned with disadvantaged groups, the problem is how, in the broader sense, such knowledge is used, and who determines the policy. Equally, we cannot argue that, as the motive behind research is to gain knowledge, those doing the research are absolved of any responsibility for the policy outcomes. The process of research, the motivations behind it, and the use it is put to are inextricably linked.

It has been argued that this process of *objectification* of particular individuals, leading to classification and then to social division, has repeated itself over the centuries from the establishment of the leper colonies, to the madhouses, and to poorhouses, and also to segregated colonies for people with developmental disabilities (see Rabinow, 1991). This process of classification brings with it power that organisations and/or governments can then use, justifying their actions on the basis of presumed scientific theory (such as eugenics), or for the purposes of public protection, or for both. Those undertaking research into the relationship between two groups of already disadvantaged people—those with developmental disabilities and those who offend—are trapped between the wish to understand, the power that comes with that process, and the outcomes of such deliberations. As there is no clear distinction at the margin as to who does and does not have a developmental disability and as there would appear to be considerable discretion over whether someone with a developmental disability engaging in challenging behaviour is reported to the police and charged, there is considerable room for discretion (Lyall, Holland & Collins, 1995b). Thus, as subtle social forces exert their influences and political pressures develop and, as a result, the nature of legislation changes as described above, this discretion becomes squeezed into a more oppressive direction and the cycle of segregation and incarceration starts again. It is important to be aware of these pressures, and of the political implications and interpretations that might be placed on research concerned with the relationship between any form of mental disorder (including developmental disabilities) and crime.

This chapter provides an overview of some of the prevalence and related studies. The key message is not that many people with developmental disabilities offend but, rather, how few offend given the nature and characteristics of their individual and social circumstances. Research needs to move on from prevalence studies into the expertise of criminology and the social sciences. Studies are required of the processes, care pathways, and the influence of the complex dynamics that exist within society and within organisations, which in turn modify a process that at times seems inexorably to lead to social exclusion (Holland, Clare & Mukhopadhyay, 2002). Figure 2.1 illustrates this dynamic, which relates to both how developmental disability and offending are defined and also to legislation and policy that establishes the political and societal context within which we currently work.

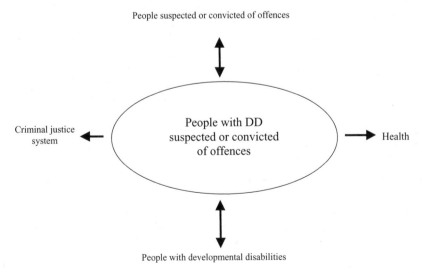

Figure 2.1   The context in which the category *people with developmental disability suspected or convicted of offences* is constructed.

DEVELOPMENTAL DISABILITIES

The term *developmental disability* is used here to refer to a highly heterogeneous group of people who have in common evidence of some delay in reaching, or a failure to reach, developmental milestones, a delay in or failure to acquire living, educational and social skills as expected for their age, and evidence, on standard psychological assessment, of a significant intellectual impairment. Some people with developmental disabilities will have an identifiable genetic or environmental explanation for their abnormality of brain development, and of their impaired cognitive and functional development. For others, the picture may be more complex and a combination of biological and psychosocial disadvantage may have given rise to learning disabilities (Fryers, 2000; Kaski, 2000). These two groups have been considered to be separate, although overlapping, and in the past the conditions were referred to as biological and subcultural "mental retardation", respectively (Lewis, 1933). Epidemiological studies have demonstrated that those in the former group are randomly distributed across socio-economic groups, whereas those in the latter, larger group are generally from families of poorer socio-economic status (Birch, Richardson, Baird, Horobin & Illsley, 1970; Rutter, Tizard & Whitmore, 1970). It is therefore possible that rather different patterns of biological and social influences may be present in the two groups, and it is likely that the processes and pathways that lead to offending, and the involvement or not of the criminal justice system or healthcare system, may be broadly different between the two groups.

As a group, people with developmental disabilities have high rates of physical (Beange, McElduff & Baker, 1995; Lennox & Kerr, 1997) and mental (see Deb, Thomas & Bright, 2001a, b; O'Brien, 2002 for reviews) health problems that may go unrecognised and untreated. These include, in those with more severe disabilities, epilepsy and complex problem behaviours, for those with mild disabilities, chronic depression (Richards *et al.*, 2001) and other major mental illnesses (Deb *et al.*, 2001a, b) and among those who offend, also substance abuse and problems associated with homelessness. (Winter, Holland & Collins, 1997). Thus, when the variables between individuals, such as the many different causes of developmental disabilities and the high rates of co-morbid disorders, combine with other variables, such as family and social care backgrounds, this leads to many different developmental, biological, psychological and socially determined factors, which, in combination, predispose, precipitate and maintain a particular pattern of maladaptive behaviour. This interaction of factors can be complex and may vary across the group of people with developmental disabilities considerably. Whether such behaviour in turn becomes 'an offence', because it results in contact with the criminal justice system and ultimately in conviction, adds yet other variables to an already complex situation. This is well illustrated by the Winter *et al.* (1997) police station study. She found that many factors such as substance abuse, a family history of offending, psychosocial disadvantage, homelessness, and mental health problems were all more common in people with a history of special schooling, who had been arrested and charged, compared to a comparison group. This group of people she assessed as part of the research had complex needs and were difficult to engage.

DEVELOPMENTAL DISABILITIES AND OFFENDING

There are extensive recent reviews of the relationship between offending and people with developmental disabilities (Murphy & Holland, 1993; Murphy & Mason, 1999; Holland *et al.*, 2002). This chapter will consider the methodology and key findings of relevant past studies and consider their implications in the light of some of the ethical dilemmas raised earlier.

Although there is evidence that people with developmental disabilities are over-represented within the criminal justice system (see below), it is far from clear whether they commit more crimes than those without a developmental disability. The relationship between the presence of a developmental disability and offending is a complex one. First, as illustrated above, what is meant exactly by the plethora of terms used to cover the group of people referred to in this chapter by the term developmental disability is problematic. In the borderline area, whether someone is or is not considered to have a developmental disability, will be influenced by the quality of the information available, and ultimately requires a judgement to be made as to whether the necessary criteria are present or not. There is no absolute measure or gold standard. While the component of the definition "a significant intellectual impairment" can be reliably measured, given the availability of well-constructed and standardised assessments, the cut-off of a full scale IQ score of 70 or 75 is statistically derived and does not distinguish between two groups who necessarily have very different levels of need. There may well be people with IQ scores above this point who are significantly functionally impaired (e.g. some people with Asperger's syndrome), and others with IQ scores below 70 who, in the right supportive environment, lead very successful lives. From a research perspective prevalence studies of offending cannot easily resolve these tensions concerning definitions. The definitions and assessment instruments used have to be pragmatic and should acknowledge that time constraints, difficulties engaging this group of people in research, and the lack of sound informant data are all potentially serious problems that cannot easily be resolved.

Similarly, the definition of *offending* is fraught with difficulties. At an epidemiological level the prevalence rates of offending will depend critically on where in the criminal justice process the measures are taken. Many more offences are committed than are reported to the police, or result in arrest and ultimately in conviction. Surveys to identify the characteristics of the alleged perpetrators of all crimes committed are not possible. Those surveys at the end of the process (i.e. at conviction) are but the tip of the iceberg, and represent a process that involves discretion and decisions at many different stages. For example, the *filter points* include whether a criminal offence is detected, the decision to report it, whether police action follows, whether the alleged perpetrator is arrested, and whether he/she is charged, brought to court, and found guilty. At each of these stages a decision has to be made by the relevant person as to whether to proceed to the next stage. For example, a victim may choose not to report an assault or the Crown Prosecution Service may decide that there is not a realistic chance of a successful prosecution or that such action is not in the public interest.

With respect to people with developmental disabilities there are additional issues that need to be considered and that may have a major influence on this process.

First, there is a legal issue. For an illegal act to result in conviction it is not sufficient for it to have been demonstrated that that act has been committed (*actus reus*), but that there has been a guilty state of mind (*mens rea*) or recklessness on the part of the alleged perpetrator. Often early decisions are taken not to proceed with criminal charges if the person has a developmental disability, since there is an assumption of lack of *mens rea*. Second, the decisions of carers whether to report an act by a person with a developmental disability that would normally be considered a crime appears arbitrary. Fear of what might happen to the person and the possible fear that carers will be blamed influence this process (Lyall, Holland & Collins, 1995a). Third, the alleged victims may be people with developmental disabilities themselves and a decision may be taken that they will not be able to give evidence and therefore, in the absence of forensic or other evidence, there is no real likelihood of a conviction. For people with learning disabilities this process whereby what might be considered *challenging behaviour* becomes an *offence* and, which in turn, leads to arrest, trial, and conviction, or not, may be even more arbitrary. Little is known about what might influence the decisions that have to be made along the way, although increasingly the attributions of others may be important (Crichton, 1995).

INCIDENCE AND PREVALENCE STUDIES

There are three research approaches that have been used when considering the relationship between the presence of a developmental disability and offending. In general these studies are investigating prevalence in that they are exploring the relationship between two variables—offending and intellectual disabilities. Incidence studies are concerned with the number of new "cases" over a defined period of time—e.g. how many people with intellectual disabilities offend in one month. All have methodological problems, many for the reasons given earlier. The first two of these research approaches are categorical in that they use the diagnosis of developmental disability. The third considers the influence of intellectual functioning as a continuous variable, IQ and offending controlling for other variables. The three broad methods are as follows. First, studies can be undertaken at different stages in the criminal justice process that seek to find out the numbers of people who have developmental disabilities (Gudjonsson, Clare, Rutter & Pearse, 1993; Lyall, Holland, Collins & Styles, 1995c). Besides the problems of definition and the filtering process that is intrinsic to the criminal justice system, the major difficulty with these studies is obtaining the necessary data that allows a reliable diagnostic judgement to be made. Second, the extent of offending among those known to a developmental disability service over a given period of time can be investigated. In these studies the use of an administrative sample has the severe drawback of only including those with developmental disabilities known to services (Lyall *et al.*, 1995c; McNulty, Kissi-Deborah & Newsom-Davies, 1995). It is less likely that this group will include those with mild levels of disability from socially disadvantaged backgrounds. The third approach follows predominately a criminological research strategy, and is concerned with the identification of individual and societal risk factors that might predispose to or protect against offending. Measures of intelligence, in the form of IQ scores, are used here as a continuous measure. Low IQ in childhood, independent of psychosocial status, has been found to be predictive of offending in later life (Farrington, 2000).

Prevalence of People with a Possible Developmental Disability in the Criminal Justice System

Police stations

These studies are inevitably limited in their methodology in that they invariably have to rely on the use of basic screening questionnaires that ask about special needs schooling and present ability in order to identify those with possible developmental disabilities. The Gudjonsson *et al.* (1993) study also used the short WAIS. The picture that emerges from these UK studies is that between 5% and 9% of people interviewed in police stations have a learning disability. In the Gudjonsson *et al.* study 8.9% of 156 people seen had an IQ of less than 70. The full information necessary to determine whether they met all criteria for developmental disability was not available and judgements about adaptive behaviour are not possible. Many may not meet the full criteria for having learning disabilities. This study also supports the findings of criminological studies that a greater proportion than would be expected have a below-average IQ. The mean IQ was 82 with a range from 61 to 131. In the Lyall *et al.* (1995c) study the screening methodology was based on the Gudjonsson study. No direct contact between the researchers and the suspects was allowed. The custody officers administered the screening questionnaire. It was therefore not possible to conclude how many would meet strict criteria for having a developmental disability. The offences may generally be of a minor kind such as public order offences.

Courts

Studies of court populations have been limited, with two studies by Hayes in Australia (Hayes, 1993, 1996). In the first study from mixed rural and urban settings 14% had IQs less than 70 points. In the rural setting there was a larger aboriginal group and 36% had IQs less than 70. Lyall *et al.* (1995a) did not systematically review the extent to which people with developmental disabilities appeared in court but did investigate the process. They found that those who had been to schools for children with emotional and behavioural disorders tended to have repeat court appearances before sentencing and longer periods between arrest and sentence, compared to other groups. The reasons for this were not specifically identified but there were indicators that this group of people came from disorganised and disadvantaged backgrounds and led chaotic lifestyles. This population of people who do not meet the full criteria for having developmental disabilities may also be particularly difficult to engage in services.

Prison

There have been many studies of the prevalence of people with developmental disabilities in prisons. As with police station studies, the methods used are limited and there is not any developmental or functional history that would allow a firm diagnosis of developmental disability to be made. The studies by and large rely on clinical interview and/or IQ data of varying quality. In the UK there are no studies that find greater than 2% of those in prison with IQs less than 70 (2% to 2.5% being the numbers in the general population with IQs ∘ 70). Coid (1988) noted that 5.1% of those on remand for psychiatric reports were known to developmental disability services. In the USA the picture is more varied and often dependent on the nature of the assessments used. MacEachron (1979) reported finding rates of between 1.5% and 5.6% of prisoners with developmental disabilities. While the exact rates of people with significant intellectual impairment (and by implication developmental disabilities) may vary for methodological reasons or due to geographical and cultural differences, by and large it would appear that few people with undoubted evidence of a developmental disability are imprisoned either on remand or as sentenced prisoners. Murphy, Harnett and Holland (1995) in an assessment of 157 men on remand in prison, found no one with an IQ less than 70. It was noted that those with below-average IQs also had evidence of mental ill-health, with high scores on the General Health Questionnaire. The authors argued that this group may well be at risk of mental ill-health or suicide in prison settings. What is not known is whether those who might have been imprisoned, if it was not for their developmental disability, are in fact having their liberty removed through the use of civil or hospital orders of the Mental Health Act and by diversion to secure hospital facilities. In the UK it would seem that the policy of keeping people with obvious developmental disabilities out of prison is effective, but whether not going to prison is necessarily a good thing requires research to look at what happens to those diverted in alternative provision (see Chapter 4). There is understandable concern about the vulnerability of this group of people when in prison, and the potential harm and long-term effects of, for example, assault in prison (Davison, Clare, Georgiades, Divall & Holland, 1994).

Retrospective studies

Another approach is to use case register data and match records of convictions with records of special educational need or use of developmental disability services. Hodgins (1992) examined the criminal convictions among a cohort of 15,000 children born in Stockholm, Sweden in 1953. Those men with a history of special education because of academic difficulties were three times more likely to have had a criminal conviction by 30 years of age compared to those with no such educational history. Women were four times more likely to have had a conviction. The findings, when concerned only with violent offences, were even more striking, with rates for men with developmental disabilities being four times higher, and for women 25 times higher. Studies such as these, however, cannot tease out possible underlying processes or cause and effect on what is likely to be a complex and confusing relationship, are entirely dependent on the quality of the records and can say nothing about individual characteristics.

Prevalence of Offending in Services for People with Developmental Disabilities

The prevalence of men and women known to developmental disability services in contact with the police over a defined period of time have been investigated by Lyall *et al.* (1995c) and McNulty *et al.* (1995). Both studies used a retrospective research design and asked social care managers if there had been contact between known service users and the police and other criminal justice agencies because of alleged offending. The Lyall *et al.* (1995c) study reported that 7 (2%) of 358 people (one suspected of two offences—i.e. eight offences were alleged altogether) using developmental disability services had had such contact in one specific year, compared to 9 people (5%) in the McNulty *et al.* study. Both studies were of adult services and therefore neither covered adolescent age group, the males of which in the general population are most at risk for offending; nor were the studies able to look in any systematic way at those adults who continued to live at home. In the former study, offences ranged from public order offences to offences against a person. In the latter study no information was given about the nature of offences. In the McNulty *et al.* study, two of the three arrested were convicted, but none was charged in the Lyall *et al.* (1995c) study. Both studies support the view that there is a remarkably low rate of offending defined either by some level of contact with the criminal justice system or by those actually convicted of offences among those accessing learning disability services. However, it would appear that there is a high level of tolerance of possible offences. Less serious crimes were rarely reported and the managers of some services were uncertain whether they would necessarily report allegations of offences such as rape (Lyall *et al.*, 1995b). A further factor may be the characteristics of the alleged victim. If the victim also has learning disabilities, the crime is less likely to be reported (Thompson, 1997).

The conclusion that can be drawn from these limited community studies is that rates of involvement of the criminal justice agencies are remarkably low. However, there is reluctance on the part of carers to involve these agencies, possibly even when a serious crime may have been committed. Further work needs to be done to explore what factors, whether relating to the alleged victim, perpetrator, or in the social care environment, influence the reporting of possible criminal action by those with learning disabilities.

Criminological and Population-Based Studies

West and Farrington (1973) and Farrington (2000) followed up 411 working class boys born in London in 1953 to examine the manner in which criminal behaviour may develop. Intellectual disadvantage, independent of social variables, was found to be predictive of *official* offending. One-third had been convicted of criminal offences by age 32 years. A small group of 6% were responsible for more than half the recorded crimes. Those men who committed crimes were more likely to have been impulsive and hyperactive in childhood, to have histories of limited academic achievement and to be both verbally and non-verbally intellectually disadvantaged, and to come from larger and more economically disadvantaged families. There was also greater parental conflict.

Conclusions from Prevalence Studies

Although these different studies have many drawbacks, it is possible to draw some general conclusions that create a picture that fits with clinical experience and with other research of direct prevalence studies. First, given the heterogeneity of people with developmental disabilities, when it comes to offending, two broad groups emerge. These include people who are often not known to services but who have mild levels of disability, but may come from severely disadvantaged backgrounds, often with family history of offending. This group may also coincide with those identified through cohort studies who in childhood engage in risk-taking behaviour, are impulsive, and present with a conduct disorder. For example, in Winter *et al.*'s (1997) study interviewing those with a history of special school attendance seen at a police station when suspected of offending, the main characteristics were problematic childhoods, homelessness, substance abuse and family dysfunction. The second group are in some respect a more complex group. They are likely to be known to developmental disability services, and, as a group, have less in common with each other compared to the other group and may engage in rarer but potentially more dangerous behaviours.

FUTURE RESEARCH CONSIDERATIONS

This chapter started by expressing concern as to how such prevalence data can be and is used, and how community and institutionally based services come under both direct and indirect political and social pressure. As fear of crime becomes heightened and as marginalized groups become associated with such behaviour, the pressure to protect society by the exclusion of this group to prisons, hospitals or camps becomes considerable. It cannot be overstressed that people with developmental disabilities are not committing large amounts crime—or at least if they are, it is not leading to arrest and conviction. In addition, there are certain crimes, such as fraud, motor offences and white-collar crime, which people with developmental disabilities do not commit.

If this statement is accepted, then several questions follow. First, it is important to identify what it is that is in fact protecting those who are intellectually disadvantaged, who may have limited social skills, and who may suffer from high levels of co-morbid disorders, from engaging in criminal activities to any greater extent than might be expected. Second, the extent and nature of services for people with developmental disabilities vary considerably across the UK. To what extent do different service models influence levels of offending and care pathways? Third, what influences the process of detection and reporting of an alleged crime by a person with developmental disabilities to arrest, conviction and sentencing. Finally, by better understanding these pathways, what legal framework should we have that facilitates arriving at the right balance between addressing issues of guilt, the rights of victims, and the legitimate right of the public to protection, on the one hand, and ensuring that people with developmental disabilities who are charged or convicted of an offence receive the help they need, and, given their vulnerability, are protected from abuse from within the criminal justice, health and social care systems, on the other.

ACKNOWLEDGEMENTS

My thanks to Robbie Patterson and Bonnie Kemske for their support in the preparation of this paper.

REFERENCES

Beange, H., McElduff, A. & Baker, W. (1995). Medical disorders of adults with mental retardation: a population study. *American Journal of Mental Retardation, 99,* 595–604.

Birch, H., Richardson, S.A., Baird, D., Horobin, G. & Illsley, R. (1970). *Mental subnormality in the Community: A Clinical and Epidemiological Study.* Cambridge, MA: Harvard University Press.

Coid, J.W. (1988). Mentally abnormal prisoners on remand: 1 – Rejected or accepted by the NHS? *British Medical Journal, 296,* 1779–82.

Crichton, J. (1995). *Psychiatric Patient Violence: Risk and Response.* London: Gerald Duckworth & Co.

Davison, F.M., Clare, I.C.H., Georgiades, S., Divall, J. & Holland, A. (1994). Treatment of a man with a mild learning disability who was sexually assaulted whilst in prison. *Medicine, Sciences and the Law, 34,* 346–53.

Deb, S., Thomas, M. & Bright, C. (2001a). Mental disorders in adults with intellectual disability. 1: Prevalence of functional psychiatric illness among community based population aged between 16 and 64 years. *Journal of Intellectual Disability Research, 45,* 495–505.

Deb, S., Thomas, M. & Bright, C. (2001b). Mental disorder in adults with intellectual disability. 2: The rate of behaviour disorders among a community-based population aged between 16 and 64 years. *Journal of Intellectual Disability Research, 45,* 506–14.

Department of Health (1999). *Reform of the Mental Health Act 1983.* London: Stationery Office.

Farrington, D.P. (2000). Psychosocial causes of offending. In M.G. Gelder, J.J. Lopez-Ibor & N. Andeasen (eds) *New Oxford Textbook of Psychiatry* (pp. 2029–36). Oxford: Oxford University Press.

Fennell, P. (1996). *Treatment without Consent. Law, Psychiatry and the Treatment of Mentally Disordered People since 1845.* London: Routledge.

Fryers, T. (2000). Epidemiology of mental retardation. In M.G. Gelder, J.J. Lopez-Ibor & N. Andeasen (eds) *New Oxford Textbook of Psychiatry* (pp. 1941–5). Oxford: Oxford University Press.

Goddard, H. (1913). *The Kallikak Family – A Study in the Heredity of Feeble-Mindedness.* New York: Macmillan.

Gudjonsson, G.H., Clare, I.C.H., Rutter, S. & Pearse, J. (1993). *Persons at Risk during Interviews in Police Custody: The Identification of Vulnerabilities.* London: HMSO.

Halstead, S. (2002). Service-user and professional issues. *Journal of Intellectual Disability Research, 46* (suppl. 1), 31–46.

Hayes, S. (1993). *People with an Intellectual Disability and the Criminal Justice System: Appearances before Local Courts.* Sydney, NSW: Law Reform Commission.

Hayes, S. (1996). *People with an Intellectual Disability and the Criminal Justice System: Two Rural Courts*. Sydney, NSW: Law Reform Commission.

Hodgins, S. (1992). Mental disorder, intellectual deficiency and crime: evidence from a birth cohort. *Archives of General Psychiatry*, **49**, 476–83.

Holland, T., Clare, I.C.H. & Mukhopadhyay, T. (2002). Prevalence of 'criminal offending' by men and women with intellectual disability and the characteristics of 'offenders': implications for research and service development. *Journal of Intellectual Disability Research*, **46** (suppl. 1), 6–20.

Kaski, M. (2000). Aetiology of mental retardation: general issues and prevention. In M.G. Gelder, J.J. Lopez-Ibor & N. Andeasen (eds) *New Oxford Textbook of Psychiatry* (pp. 1947–52). Oxford: Oxford University Press.

Lennox, N. & Kerr, M.P. (1997). Primary health care and people with intellectual disability. *Journal of Intellectual Disability Research*, **41**, 365–72.

Lewis, E.O. (1933). Types of mental deficiency and their social significance. *Journal of Mental Science*, **79**, 298–304.

Lyall, I., Holland, A. & Collins, S. (1995a). Offending by adults with learning disabilities: identifying need in one health district. *Mental Handicap Research*, **8**, 99–109.

Lyall, I., Holland, A. & Collins, S. (1995b). Offending by adults with learning disabilities and the attitudes of staff to offending behaviour: implications for service development. *Journal of Intellectual Disability Research*, **39**, 501–8.

Lyall, I., Holland, A., Collins, S. & Styles, P. (1995c). Incidence of persons with a learning disability detained in police custody: a needs assessment for service development. *Medicine, Sciences and the Law*, **35**, 61–71.

MacEachron, A.E. (1979). Mentally retarded offenders: prevalence and characteristics. *American Journal of Mental Deficiency*, **84**, 165–76.

McNulty, C., Kissi-Deborah, R. & Newsom-Davies, I. (1995). Police involvement with clients having intellectual disabilities: a pilot study in South London. *Mental Handicap Research*, **8**, 129–36.

Murphy, G.H., Harnett, H. & Holland, A. (1995). A survey of intellectual disabilities amongst men on remand in prison. *Mental Handicap Research*, **8**, 81–98.

Murphy, G.H. & Holland, A. (1993). Challenging behaviour, psychiatric disorders and the law. In R.S.P. Jones and C.B. Eayrs (eds) *Challenging Behaviour and Intellectual Disability: A Psychological Perspective* (pp. 195–223). Clevedon: BILD Publications.

Murphy, G.H. & Mason, J. (1999). People with developmental disabilities who offend. In N. Bouras (ed.) *Psychiatric and Behaviour Disorders in Development Disabilities and Mental Retardation* (pp. 226–45). Cambridge: Cambridge University Press.

O'Brien, G. (2002). Dual diagnosis in offenders with intellectual disability: setting research priorities: a review of research findings concerning psychiatric disorder (excluding personality disorder) among offenders with intellectual disability. *Journal of Intellectual Disability Research*, **46** (suppl. 1), 21–30.

Rabinow, P. (ed.) (1991). *The Foucault Reader: An Introduction to Foucault's Thought*. London: Penguin.

Richards, M., Maughan, B., Hardy, R., Hall, I., Strydom, A. & Wadsworth, M. (2001). Long-term affective disorder in people with mild learning disability. *British Journal of Psychiatry*, **179**, 523–7.

Rutter, M., Tizard, J. & Whitmore, K. (1970). *Education, Health and Behaviour*. London: Longman.

Thompson, D. (1997). Profiling the sexually abusive behaviour of men with intellectual disabilities. *Journal of Applied Research in Intellectual Disabilities*, **10**, 125–39.

Walker, N. & McCabe, S. (1968). Hospital orders. In A.V.S. de Reuck & R. Porter (eds) *The Mentally Abnormal Offender*. London: Churchill.

West, D.J. & Farrington, D.P. (1973). *Who Becomes Delinquent?* London: Heinemann.

Winter, N., Holland, A.J. & Collins, S. (1997). Factors predisposing to suspected offending by adults with self-reported learning disabilities. *Psychological Medicine*, **27**, 595–607.

PART II

LEGAL AND SERVICE CONTEXTS

Chapter 3

LEGAL ISSUES

GEORGE S. BAROFF,* MICHAEL GUNN[†] AND SUSAN HAYES[‡]

* University of North Carolina at Chapel Hill, North Carolina, USA
[†] Nottingham Law School, Nottingham Trent University, Nottingham, UK
[‡] University of Sydney, Sydney, Australia

In this chapter, issues are addressed that relate to the involvement of persons with developmental disabilities (DD) with the criminal justice systems in the US, England and Wales, and Australia. Essentially framed in terms of their disability-related vulnerabilities, topics include competency or fitness to plead to a charge and to stand trial, alternative dispositions for the incompetent or unfit defendant, competency to confess—especially important because of the cogency of confessions in establishing guilt and the vulnerability of the suspect to police interrogation—and intellectual disability (ID) as it pertains to the degree of personal responsibility/culpability and, if convicted, to appropriate sentencing.

As this is written, we in the US are celebrating the recent Supreme Court decision (*Atkins* v. *Virginia*, 2002) declaring as unconstitutional capital punishment for individuals with intellectual and developmental disabilities. Kyrgyzstan, a former Soviet republic, may now be the only country in the world in which persons with mental retardation can still be executed (Amici Brief, *McCarver* v. *North Carolina*, 2001).

The content of the chapter is germane to both juvenile and adult offenders but it is the latter who are our focus. This contributor's experience has been almost entirely with adults charged with serious crimes, e.g. first-degree or capital murder. It is in this context that I have come to recognize the vulnerabilities of this population to the criminal justice system.

To introduce the reader to the criminal justice system, and all three presented in this chapter derive from a common legal tradition, it seems useful to characterize its chief elements as these are experienced by the accused. The sequence begins with arrest and questioning. This is followed by a possible indictment, a trial and, if convicted, a sentence. Each phase presents special problems for the offender with limited intellect and, if the issue of intellectual disability and/or mental illness is raised, there may be preliminary hearings held to determine the defendant's mental

Offenders with Developmental Disabilities. Edited by W.L. Lindsay, J.L. Taylor and P. Sturmey.
© 2004 John Wiley & Sons, Ltd.

status. Given the now near universal protection of defendants with ID against the death penalty in capital cases, it is in their interest to try to establish such disability, a potentially adversarial procedure in which it is the judge and not the mental health practitioners who makes the ultimate legal determination.

THE LAW AND INTELLECTUAL DISABILITY

There is a body of law that specifically pertains to mental illness and intellectual disability (e.g. Parry & Drogin, 2000). Historically, our common English legal tradition recognized the relationship between intellectual status and criminal responsibility such that persons with extreme degrees of intellectual impairment, e.g. severe and profound ID, were regarded as incapable of forming the intent to commit a crime (*mens rea*) and were deemed "not responsible" for their acts (Fitch, 1992). By the seventeenth century, English courts were judging criminal responsibility in intellectually impaired persons in terms of their capacity to distinguish "right" from "wrong." Eventually, the courts abandoned an "all or none" view of moral understanding in favor of a more case-specific consideration.

In one study of defendants with ID (Petrella, 1992), 90% of those with "mild retardation" (IQs between 55 and 69) were considered "criminally responsible," and even in those with "moderate retardation" (IQs 40 to 54), two-thirds (67%) were judged "responsible." The proportion of criminal defendants with IQs below these two ranges would be miniscule.

The "right–wrong" test came to be amended with the acknowledgment that one might know that an act was wrong but be unable to control oneself. This is the so-called "irresistible impulse" defense, one that is highly controversial and more generally associated with the "insanity" defense.

More relevant to ID are mental health laws that recognize a decreased level of responsibility due to *either* a diminished appreciation of the wrongfulness of one's acts or an inability to conform one's behavior to the requirements of the law (Fitch, 1992; Parry & Drogin, 2000).

The standard of "diminished appreciation" in relation to the offender with mental retardation reflects an awareness that intellectual and moral understanding are "developmental" or age-related phenomena. Thus courts have viewed the pre-adolescent child as lacking criminal responsibility, a perception now challenged by violent acts, e.g. shootings by children under age 14. This has led to the trying of such children as "adults." Although courts have consistently rejected defense claims that laws protecting children are applicable to adults with "mental" or "developmental" ages comparable to children, this writer has commonly used these concepts to convey the meaning of intellectual disability to judge and jury. They help to characterize the defendant in terms understandable to everyone. In rendering their decisions in death penalty cases involving convicted defendants with ID (*Penry* v. *Lynaugh*, 1989; *Atkins* v. *Virginia*, 2002), the Supreme Court of the US has justified its view of diminished responsibility on the grounds of a lesser awareness of consequences, a heightened impulsiveness, and a decreased moral understanding. Two observations can be made here. Whatever their limitations in considering consequences, in my experience this becomes almost irrelevant because criminal acts are never undertaken with the expectation of failure! With respect to moral appreciation, even adults with mild ID may not be able to explain *why* acts of robbery or killing are "wrong" (Baroff, 1998). But some can!

As the reader may have surmised, and will be evident as the chapter unfolds, the interaction of offenders with ID with the criminal justice system raises many research questions. For example, how does "moral understanding" affect criminal responsibility? How does the degree of ID affect the various "competencies"? What are appropriate sentencing options for the convicted offender?

The following three sections now examine in some depth the vulnerabilities of defendants with ID in the criminal justice systems of the USA, England and Wales, and Australia. Of special interest are innovative legal protections in England and Wales and in Australia that relate to the conditions of police questioning.

1. CRIMINAL LAW AND MENTAL RETARDATION IN THE USA (GEORGE S. BAROFF)

Overview

In this section we review various "competencies" related to the criminal justice system—competencies (fitness) to stand trial, to confess, to plead guilty, and to be sentenced. In addition, the issues of "diminished culpability/responsibility" and sentencing are addressed.

Competency or Fitness to Stand Trial

Central to the criminal justice system is the determination of competency or fitness of the accused to stand trial. An incompetent defendant cannot be tried in a court of law, although the law provides other means of dealing with an accused who is considered dangerous. Current law, as expressed by the US Supreme Court in Dusky (1960) and in Drope (1975) recognizes the competent defendant as one who is both capable of consulting with his attorney and has a rational as well as factual understanding of the proceedings against him. The competency standard actually includes three elements: (1) an understanding of the crime with which one is charged and its seriousness in relation to possible penalties, (2) knowledge of the nature and purpose of a trial and the role of its principals, and (3) the ability to assist counsel in one's own defense—so-called "decisional competency."

"Competency" and the defendant with intellectual disability

A modest research literature (e.g. Petrella, 1992) suggests that most defendants with ID are deemed competent to proceed to trial, only about one-third being found otherwise. The latter were deficient in their understanding of the consequences of a conviction and also had much difficulty in providing a coherent description of the events surrounding the alleged offense. In this writer's experience, even competent defendants with mild ID tend to offer accounts that lack detail and are poorly recalled. Significantly affected by the degree of ID, 78% of those with mild ID were considered competent as against 68% of those with moderate ID. Clearly, the great majority of defendants were regarded as competent to stand trial. At greater degrees of severity, and as incompetence seems apparent, the prosecution may decline to press charges and seek non-judicial ways of dealing with the accused.

Psychological scales for the measurement of competency to stand trial and for other competencies, as well, e.g. competency to confess and "decisional competency," are described elsewhere in this volume and the reader is also referred to Parry and Drogin (2000) for a description of their clinical use.

Competency and "criminal responsibility"

A distinction is drawn between trial competency and "responsibility." The latter refers to "culpability" or "blameworthiness" with regard to the alleged act. This distinction is more likely to arise in the individual with both mental illness and ID and who has been found incompetent to stand trial. Virtually all competent defendants are viewed as "responsible," and even among those found incompetent, nearly one-half (45%) were still seen as responsible or blameworthy for the offense (Petrella, 1992). Obviously, the law sets a higher standard for fitness to be tried than it does for the appreciation of the wrongfulness of one's act. This issue of responsibility or blameworthiness in persons with ID is later addressed in the sections on "Diminished culpability" and "The death penalty."

Disposition of the incompetent defendant

Where the defendant has been judged incompetent, the state may choose to drop charges or to temporarily commit the individual to a mental health forensic facility. The intent is to either "restore" competency, as in the case of a psychotic defendant, or "create" it, as in the person with ID. In the former, the goal is "treatment" while in the latter, it is "education."

Prior to the 1970s, incompetent defendants with ID faced the prospect of indefinite commitment in a mental health facility if competency was not achieved. Their period of confinement could well exceed the time they would have served had they been tried and convicted! Recognizing this potential abuse, the US Supreme Court (*Jackson* v. *Indiana*, 1972) ruled that a defendant committed only on the basis of incompetence could not be held more than "a reasonable period of time" during which efforts to achieve competency would be pursued. This has commonly been construed as 18 months. At the end of this period, if competency has not been achieved and there is little expectation that additional efforts would be successful, the state (legal jurisdiction) must either release the individual or initiate a "civil" commitment, as in the case of the involuntary hospitalization of psychiatric patients. As implied, this ruling has much significance for incompetent defendants with ID. In the earlier-cited Petrella research, nearly two-thirds of incompetent defendants with ID were considered unlikely to ever achieve competence. They must either be civilly committed, if deemed dangerous, or released.

Competency to Confess

Not surprisingly, confessions to criminal acts are prized in criminal investigations; they are perhaps the most common means of solving murder cases. Police pressures to obtain confessions have led to physical and psychological abuse of suspects, an abuse to which the individual with ID is especially vulnerable. In such suspects, we often find an increased suggestibility, a need to please authority, and unawareness of the implications of confessing to a serious crime (Ellis & Luckasson, 1985).

False confessions are not unknown (Kassin, 1999) and the author has been involved in two capital murder cases involving confessions in which the accused were eventually acquitted because of their own retractions and a lack of physical evidence tying them to the crime. I have also seen cases where frightened defendants with ID, after confessing to murder, thought the police would let them go home!

Given natural investigative pressures and the potential for abuse, the US Supreme Court, in its Miranda decision (*Miranda* v. *Arizona*, 1966), provided a standard for determining the acceptability of a confession as evidence. That standard, the well-known "Miranda Warning" sets the conditions under which a suspect can be questioned following arrest. A confession is admissible as evidence only if it is (1) voluntary, (2) knowing, and (3) intelligent.

Voluntariness

The concern here is with coercion in the securing of a confession. The actual questioning is often neither recorded nor taped and all we have from the police is a written statement, prepared by the police and signed by the defendant, that purports to be his account of the events as told to his questioners. In evaluating "voluntariness," courts have recognized the vulnerability of the suspect with ID to promises of leniency and threats (Ellis & Luckasson, 1985) or when informed that an accomplice has implicated him (Toliver & Gathright, 1980). Parenthetically, if such a suspect has been involved with others, they will commonly implicate him in return for the promise of a lesser sentence.

Knowing

Relevant here is the accused's understanding of his right to silence and to an attorney. The defendant need not answer questions under his constitutionally protected Fifth Amendment right against self-incrimination. He is entitled to a lawyer at the time of questioning and a lawyer will be appointed for him if he does not have one. Moreover, he can choose to answer questions without a lawyer and then decide to stop and request the presence of a lawyer before questioning is resumed. After each of these rights is presented to him by the police, orally and in written form, he is asked if he understands what he has just heard and read. A simple "yes" is taken to mean understanding. There is almost never any effort to determine whether understanding really occurred and, in fact, subsequent examination commonly reveals little or no comprehension of what was presented. In my experience, and I have taken special interest in the Miranda warning as given to defendants with ID (Baroff, 1996), these individuals *invariably* respond affirmatively to the question of comprehension. The defendant is never asked by the police to explain, *in his own words*, the meaning of what was heard and that is why it is essential for psychological examiners to do this in checking Miranda comprehension. It is "human nature" for us to try to present ourselves in a favorable light to authority figures irrespective of our true understanding, the "sin of pride." At the end of each class, I would ask my students if there were any questions. There never were. If, in fact, this meant full comprehension, there would be no need to give examinations!

More specifically, the defendant with ID is likely to interpret the experience as one in which he is *expected* to respond to questions. He may have little or no understanding of the role of a lawyer and, if he does, it is likely to be connected with the courtroom and not the police station. He never understands that if he consents to answer questions, he has the right to discontinue and ask for legal representation at that time.

Intelligent

This aspect of a valid confession pertains to the understanding that, in waiving the right to silence and answering questions, the suspect is placing himself in jeopardy. The Miranda Warning is not subtle. It is commonly phrased as "Anything you say can be used against you in a court of law." The defendant, at that very moment, and in a setting that is likely to be frightening to all but the most experienced criminal, is asked to make a "reasoned choice." This process of "choice" is thought to require a greater level of understanding than that needed for competence/fitness to stand trial (Paull, 1993). It involves what has earlier been characterized as "decisional competency," a cognitive capacity that is also paramount in a defendant's decision to plead guilty. Except for the defendant with ID with a previous history of court and trial involvement, the accused is unlikely to fully grasp the implications of his response to questions. More than one such defendant, as indicated earlier in this section, was so naïve as to the effect of his confession to murder, as to think that, having given the police what they wanted, he would then be allowed to return home!

Some observations on the language of typical Miranda Warnings

In his forensic work, the author has made much of the complexity of the language within which the Miranda Warning is couched. Formal measures of the average length of its individual sentences and words place it commonly at a 7th grade level of reading difficulty (Fry, 1977), a level more appropriate to the mental abilities of the average 13-year-old than to those of the person with ID. This is to say nothing of the vocabulary within which the Warning is conveyed and the concepts it expresses, e.g. the abstract idea of "rights." Formal measures have been developed for assessing Miranda comprehension (Grisso, 1981, 1998), but before applying them one should first evaluate the defendant's understanding in terms of the actual language used by the police. A concern also noted by Parry and Drogin (2000), it is not only a question of understanding the vocabulary of a Miranda

Warning but also understanding it in the context of the specific language with which it was conveyed.

In fact, police are free to deviate from the specific language of their departmental Warning and not all Warnings are couched in exactly the same language. The Warning for juveniles, for example, is simpler, typically at a 6th grade level of complexity. The US Supreme Court spoke to this (*Hines* v. *State*, 1980) when it noted that the precise formulation of the warning is not a "talismanic incantation"!

Nor does mere repetition of the Miranda warning, a common practice, assure greater comprehension. On one occasion, while testifying, the author tried to illustrate the defendant's lack of comprehension by twice repeating a single line of Russian. In the absence of the hearer's understanding of that language, its mere repetition added nothing to his comprehension. The courts have also commented on this:

> The fact that the defendant was repeatedly read his rights and repeatedly responded that he understood (the pro forma "yes") is of little consequence, for the Defendant did not possess the intellectual or verbal skills to comprehend *mere rote reading of his rights* [our italics]. Clearly none of the interrogating police officers made an attempt to *clarify or explain* [our italics] the Miranda warnings apart from reading the Defendant his rights from a pre-printed card. (*People* v. *Redmon*, 1984)

Competency to Plead Guilty

The issue of "decisional competency" is central to a plea of guilty. This competency requires a "reasoned choice" with respect to a not-inconsequential and irrevocable decision. In pleading guilty, the accused waives his rights to defend himself against the crime with which he is charged. Nor can one raise the issue of competency to stand trial or to confess (Paull, 1993).

The question has been posed as to whether the standards for competency to plead guilty and competency to stand trial are equivalent. Although the Dusky competency standard has been held to be sufficient—that is, capacity to understand one's legal situation and to assist one's attorney—that standard has been challenged on the grounds that a plea of guilty requires a higher level of competency (*Seiling* v. *Eyman*, 1973). In 1993, the US Supreme Court (*Godinez* v. *Moran*, 1993) reaffirmed the Dusky standard as sufficient for a plea of guilty. In so doing, it qualified its opinion with the observation that Dusky met, at least, the *minimal* constitutional standard and that states were free to establish a higher one. In consequence, a number of jurisdictions now distinguish between the competencies to stand trial and to plead guilty.

Where separate tests exist for the two competencies, the defendant with ID may find himself in a potentially anomalous situation. Competent to stand trial but not to plead guilty, he is denied the opportunity to reduce a sentence via a plea bargain—an option available to other defendants. Under such circumstance, it has been proposed that the sentence reflect what would have been available had there been the opportunity to plea bargain (Ellis & Luckasson, 1985). Presumably, an infrequent occurrence, this situation could arise with defendants who function at the lower end of the range of mild ID or in the moderately ID range itself.

Diminished Culpability

This refers to mental states that reduce the level of responsibility for a criminal act. This category includes several forms of legal defense against "full" responsibility— *diminished capacity, not guilty by reason of insanity, automatism,* and one particularly relevant to the defendant with ID, *diminished responsibility*. The first three of these defenses are raised at trial, the fourth at sentencing.

With "diminished culpability" including the "insanity" defense, it behooves us to note that although this defense may evoke much media attention, in fact it is raised in only about 4% of felonies and is rarely successful in them (Gutheil, 1999). In relation to ID, "insanity" is most likely to be raised in the defendant with both mental retardation and major mental illness, e.g. psychosis.

Diminished capacity/"mens rea"

This mental state defense refers to the defendant's "state of awareness" during the alleged act and is concerned with "intent." A continuum of intent, from least to most purposeful, is offered in the Model Penal Code of the American Bar Association (Parry and Drogin, 2000). Four levels of "awareness" are proposed: negligence, recklessness, knowledge, and purposefulness. In *negligence*, there is conscious awareness that one's actions pose a risk. *Recklessness* is associated with not only the awareness of risk but its deliberate disregard. A seemingly hazier distinction, *knowledge* involves an awareness of risk and its disregard but falls short of the actual intent to commit a crime. *Purposefulness* entails the deliberate intent to act in a manner known to be criminal. In this author's experience, the issue of purposefulness has been most often raised in relation to unlawful sexual activity between youths with ID and younger children.

Not guilty by reason of insanity

Mentioned earlier, this defense is based on the presence of a mental disorder that affects either the capacity to appreciate the wrongfulness of one's actions or to conform them to the requirements of the law (irresistible impulse). If this defense is successful, the accused is relieved of all criminal responsibility. In contrast to "diminished responsibility," as in ID, the accused is held responsible for his behavior although the punishment may be reduced.

A less common variant of the "insanity" defense is "guilty but mentally ill." Here the accused is deemed fully responsible, that is, not "legally insane," but the acknowledged mental disorder may result in a treatment recommendation as a part of the sentence.

Automatisms

This refers to actions carried on out of consciousness. They are commonly associated with organic disorders—brain injury, metabolic diseases, and seizures, or following the accidental ingestion of alcohol or drugs. They are also found in two well-known psychiatric disorders—post-traumatic stress and multiple (dissociated) personality. The rationale for this legal defense lies in the loss of conscious control of one's behavior. Workers in ID are most likely to have encountered automatisms in persons with complex partial seizures (temporal lobe/psychomotor epilepsy).

Diminished responsibility

This is the legal issue with which the writer has had the most experience. As previously indicated, it is not a defense against the charge, *per se*, but rather pertains to the sentencing of a convicted defendant. The presumption is that the individual, by virtue of a cognitive impairment such as ID, is less responsible than a person without such a disability and should, therefore, be subject to a lesser punishment. In fact, such reasoning lies behind the recent US Supreme Court decision outlawing the death penalty for persons with ID. We can expect defendants with major intellectual impairment and charged with capital crimes to seek the protection now offered by a finding of "ID or mental retardation," a protection that can only be gained through a judicial agreement with that diagnosis.

Apart from now mooted death penalty considerations, in any criminal case with a convicted defendant with ID, there are several so-called "mitigating factors" that can be presented to a jury as a basis for a lesser sentence. These are: (1) acting under the influence of a mental or emotional disturbance; (2) playing a minor role in a crime involving other, and usually, brighter defendants; (3) acting under duress or the domination of others—the "suggestibility" and "need to please" of offenders with ID; (4) impaired capacity—as this may affect reasoning and moral judgment—also highly relevant to the offender with ID; and (5) the defendant's age, "mental" as well as chronological. All of these imply a cognitive-related "diminished responsibility."

Sentencing Considerations

The sentencing process is unique in that it is the first time in which the criminal justice system can consider the needs of the now-convicted defendant as well as of society at large. Sentencing involves considerations of control and supervision, punishment, and treatment or rehabilitation. A just sentencing system will allow for a range of options, from probation to incarceration. The significance of sentencing will be appreciated when it is recognized that the great majority of sentences follow a plea of guilty rather than a trial (Laski, 1992).

Competency to be sentenced

The issue of competency also obtains at sentencing. The now-convicted defendant must understand the sentence and its consequences. The Dusky trial competency standard applies here as well because it includes the analogous understanding of the crime for which one is charged and its possible penalties.

Disposition of the incompetent defendant

Addressed earlier in the section on trial competency, the abuses of "indeterminate" sentences were noted. These led to laws limiting the period during which an incompetent defendant could be confined. Confinement beyond the statutory limit, e.g. 18 months, where the offender is considered dangerous, would then require a "civil" commitment, as in the case of the mentally ill individual.

Sentencing of the defendant with ID

Access to a range of sanctions is especially relevant to the convicted defendant with ID (Laski, 1992). Given the assertion of a reduced degree of criminal responsibility attributed to a diminished capacity, consideration should be given to lesser sanctions. The presence of a mental disability warranting the diagnosis of ID should always be deemed a mitigating factor in sentencing. A range of such sentencing alternatives is described in Chapter 4.

The death penalty

Now prohibited for defendants with mental retardation in virtually every country in the world, it is the reasoning of the US Supreme Court in rendering this decision that is of interest. The Court has clearly seen the disability of intelligence as affecting culpability and, in its earlier consideration of the constitutionality of the death penalty in relation to persons with this disability, portrayed the individual with ID as *less able to control impulses* and *to consider the consequences of actions* (*Penry* v. *Lynaugh*, 1989). The earlier Court, not then ready to declare the death penalty unconstitutional for individuals with ID, did conclude that jurors considering a life or death sentence could decide that such defendants with ID were less "morally blameworthy" and impose the lesser sentence, "life" rather than "death."

In capital cases, this author has argued for a reduced level of culpability or criminal responsibility in persons with ID on the grounds of a lessened appreciation of the immorality of the act for which they were convicted. Specifically, while acknowledging that murder or killing is "wrong," there may be a diminished understanding of *why* it is wrong (Baroff, 1996, 1998). Simply by virtue of the legal actions against him, a defendant will understand that something he has done is "wrong." But to understand *why* it is wrong requires some *moral* appreciation and that appreciation is related to intellectual development, e.g. in the young child, distinguishing between accident and intent. Even offenders with mild ID may be unable to appreciate the wrongfulness of their act. In my own practice, of a dozen capital defendants with ID, only half could offer some reason for the wrongfulness of killing. Often lacking was such fundamental moral understanding as that conveyed by the reciprocity inherent in the Golden Rule. Moreover, even if such awareness applies to the morality of "robbery," an experience not necessarily alien to offenders with criminal histories, that principle of reciprocity may not generalize to "killing," an essentially one-time happening in their lives. Whether this moral lag is limited to the intellectually immature individual is unclear; what is certain is a lesser capacity to acquire this moral appreciation. A sentence should not only fit the crime, it should also be appropriate to the accused's understanding of *why* he is being punished. To do less is to truly inflict "cruel and unusual punishment."

2. LEGAL ISSUES: ENGLAND AND WALES (MICHAEL GUNN)

In essence a person with ID goes through the same criminal justice system as anyone else alleged to have committed a criminal offence, but there will be differences that apply, in particular should the accused wish to trigger them.

Crimes are tried at either the magistrates' court or the crown court. In the former, matters of both law and fact are determined by the magistrates (receiving advice on the law from the justices' clerk), and in the latter the judge determines questions of law with the jury making factual decisions, including determining whether or not the defendant is guilty of the crime charged. Some crimes can only be tried in a magistrates' court (summary offences), some can only be tried in the crown court (indictable-only offences) and some can be tried in either (either-way offences). The majority of cases are heard by magistrates. More often than not the defendant pleads guilty (whether in a magistrates court or the crown court) (Bailey, Ching, Gunn & Ormerod, 2002).

Magistrates' court trial is commenced by a summons sent to the defendant. Crown court trial is preceded by a charge and the period pre-trial involves a decision on whether to grant bail or to remand the defendant in custody. Before proceeding to a charge or a summons, it is possible that a person will have been arrested and questioned. The Police and Criminal Evidence Act 1984 and the accompanying Codes of Practice provide a system that is intended to enable the police to undertake the important task of questioning suspects while providing people detained with appropriate protection (Sanders & Young, 2000). One of the earliest and best known cases that led to the Act was the Maxwell Confait case, where a confession led to a sentence of imprisonment for murder, but it was not, as it turned out, possible for the person with ID to have committed the murder as he had an alibi for the time of the murder. This did not come out during questioning because of the inappropriateness of that questioning (Fisher, 1977). Therefore, in addition to the general protection afforded by sections 76 and 78, there is the additional provision in section 77 of the Police and Criminal Evidence Act 1984.

Section 76 endeavours to rule out confessions that were, or may have been, obtained by oppression or as a result of anything said or done that was likely, in the circumstances, to render a confession unreliable. Section 78 provides for a general power for the court to rule out any evidence that, if admitted and having regard to all the circumstances of the case, would have such an adverse effect on the fairness of the proceedings that it ought not to be admitted. Section 77 provides that a confession by a "mentally handicapped person" and not in the presence of an independent person should only be admitted after the judge has warned the jury that there is a special need for caution before convicting in reliance on it. While this is an important statutory provision, the reality is that it is not used often because of the relevance, in most cases, of sections 76 and 78. Most confessions (though a breach of a Code provision does not necessarily lead to exclusion) made in the absence of an independent person would be excluded by virtue of these provisions.

Therefore there would be no need for a warning as is required under section 77. It is quite clear that where a suspect has ID this is particularly relevant in determining the admissibility of any confession (see, e.g., *R. v. Everett*, 1988). In *R. v. Harvey* (1988) the confession of a woman with psychopathic disorder with low average intelligence was excluded under section 76 because she overheard her lover confess to a murder and that may have led her to make a false confession out of a child-like desire to protect her lover. In *R. v. Delaney* (1988) the failure to record an interview with D, who was likely to feel under pressure to escape from interrogation because of his psychology, meant that a subsequent confession should have been excluded at his trial. In *R. v. Moss* (1990) a confession should have been excluded where access to legal advice was improperly declined and no independent person was present, where the suspect was a person of low intelligence who was interviewed on nine occasions during a long period of detention. Where the breach of a Code is not sufficient to give rise to a problem under section 76, it may give rise to exclusion under section 78, so it is clear that the confession in *Moss* would have been excluded under section 78 had it not been excluded under section 76, and the provision of a warning under section 77 was not sufficient (see Murphy (2002) at paragraph F17.23).

Further, the Code of Practice C requires the presence of an appropriate adult before interviews with a person with ID or who appears to have such a disability commence. Where such a person is not present, it may well lead to the exclusion of any subsequent confession (as discussed above). It is important to note, however, that section 77 and the Code serve slightly different purposes. Under the statutory provision, an independent person may be present, and this would often be a solicitor (often available through the Criminal Defence Service, the new system for the provision of criminal legal aid, advice and assistance). However, a solicitor is unlikely to be an appropriate adult, as required by the Code. An appropriate adult is "(a) a relative, guardian or some other person responsible for his care or custody; (b) someone who has experience of dealing with mentally disordered or mentally handicapped people but is not a police officer or employed by the police; or (c) failing either of the above some other responsible adult aged 18 or over who is not a police officer or employed by the police" (PACE Code of Practice C, paragraph 1.7(b). See Annex E where there is a collation of all the relevant provisions of the Code).

Crown Court Trial

A trial commences by the defendant hearing the charge and being asked to plead guilty or not guilty. This is a significant point where a defendant's intellectual disabilities may have a specific role to play. It is possible for a defendant, in practice through his or her barrister, to claim that he or she is unfit to plead. The other means whereby this issue will be considered is where the defendant enters no plea or for other reasons the question of fitness to plead is raised by either the judge or the prosecution. The tests for whether a person is unfit to plead are not to be found in a statute but are the creation of the common law. The leading case is *R. v. Pritchard* (1836), where Baron Alderson said:

There are three points to be inquired into: First, whether the prisoner is mute of malice or not; secondly, whether he can plead to the indictment or not; thirdly, whether he is of sufficient intellect to comprehend the course of proceedings on the trial, so as to make a proper defence—to know that he might challenge [any jurors] to whom he may object—and to comprehend the details of the evidence. . . . [I]f you think that there is no certain mode of communicating the details of the trial to the prisoner, so that he can clearly understand them, and be able properly to make his defence to the charge, you ought to find that he is not of sane mind. It is not enough that he may have a general capacity of communicating on ordinary matters.

Although the words "not of sane mind" are used, it is not the case that a person need have a mental illness or other form of mental disorder. Clearly a person with ID may not be able sufficiently to comprehend the trial for it to take place. If that is likely to be the case, then there is real doubt as to whether it is appropriate to await the time of the trial for the matter to be raised. Where a person will not be able to understand the trial, diverting them from the criminal justice process may be entirely appropriate, and it can be done by way of the exercise of discretion by either the police or the Crown Prosecution Service, depending upon when the matter arises. However, there is a risk that the shadow of suspicion of criminal activity may fall over such a person, and so diversion is not always the right route to take.

If the matter is raised, the procedure for determining whether someone is fit to plead is laid down in the Criminal Procedure (Insanity) Act 1964, as amended. The matter should normally be determined as soon as it arises (section 4(4)), but it can be delayed until the opening of the defence case (section 4(2)). It will be so delayed where the trial judge is of the opinion that, having regard to "the nature of the supposed disability", postponement of the issue is "expedient" and "in the interests of the accused". When a jury, empanelled for the purpose, considers the matter, it must first hear medical evidence. If the jury considers that the defendant is not fit to plead, it must then determine whether he or she "did the act or made the omission charged against him as the offence" (section 4A(2), (3)). The jury acquits where it is not so satisfied. Thus there is a so-called "trial of the facts" whereby the case against the defendant is tested. However, it is not a trial and some defences cannot be raised (e.g. diminished responsibility according to the House of Lords in R. v. Antoine (2001). Nevertheless, the procedure does not fall foul of the European Convention on Human Rights, Article 6 because, according to the Court of Appeal in R. v. M (2001), the outcome cannot result in a criminal conviction, which must be a debatable reason as the effect is to regard the person as though they had committed the offence. Further, however, the court felt that the procedure was compliant with Article 6. But, as certain defences cannot be raised, this decision must also be open to challenge.

If a person is found unfit to plead, the court may make one of the following orders:

(1) an admission order to such hospital as the Secretary of State specifies;
(2) a guardianship order under the Mental Health Act 1983;
(3) a supervision and treatment order; or
(4) an order for the defendant's absolute discharge.

Until the changes introduced in 1991, the only consequence had been a transfer to a psychiatric hospital. There is some evidence that the wider range of disposal options is producing a slight increase in the usage of this procedure (Mackay & Kearns, 2000).

Before the trial commences, it is possible that certain specific provisions may apply to a person with ID in addition to the exercise of discretion to drop the case. Thus, the Mental Health Act 1983 allows for the remand of a person to hospital for either report (section 35) or treatment (section 36) at any stage prior to sentence (except in relation to offences after a finding of guilt where the charge is murder as there is then no option but to impose a sentence of life imprisonment).

At the trial, intellectual disability may be relevant in two ways: (a) as a denial that the defendant had the *mens rea* for the offence and/or (b) as an element in the defence of insanity. Most crimes do not involve any *mens rea*. However, serious crimes, such as murder, rape, violence against the person, theft, etc. do involve a *mens rea*. Usually, this involves the defendant either intending a consequence (meaning to produce the result or realising that the result is virtually certain (see *R. v. Woollin*, 1999) or recognising that there is a risk of the consequence and taking that risk. Where the *mens rea* is subjective in this sense, a defendant's ID may help to convince the court that they did not have the *mens rea* for the offence. However, even for some relatively serious crimes, there may be no requirement of *mens rea* at all (e.g. it is a crime of strict liability) or the *mens rea* is objective and little account is taken of the circumstances of the defendant. If, where the crime has a *mens rea* that is subjective, the defendant raises their intellectual disability as an explanation for the claim that they lacked *mens rea*, it is possible that this will, in effect, raise the defence of insanity. This defence still relies upon the principles created by the judges in the M'Naghten case (1843), where the law was stated as follows:

> the jurors ought to be told in all cases that every man is presumed to be sane, and to possess a sufficient degree of reason to be responsible for his crimes, until the contrary be proved to their satisfaction; and that to establish a defence on the ground of insanity, it must be clearly proved that, at the time of the committing of the act, the party accused was labouring under such a defect of reason, from disease of the mind, as not to know the nature and quality of the act he was doing, or, if he did know it, that he did not know he was doing what was wrong.

A disease of the mind simply refers to internal cause that may be regarded as a disease and affecting the mind. It need not be a recognised psychiatric disorder. There has been a view, expressed by Lord Denning, in *Bratty* v. *Attorney General for Northern Ireland* (1963), that "any mental disorder which has manifested itself in violence and is prone to recur is a disease of the mind". In *R. v. Sullivan* (1984) a disease of the mind was present where a person with epilepsy had attacked another. While this confirms that what is required is an internally caused disease (in a wide sense of that word) that has an effect on the mind/brain, it does not resolve the question of whether it has to have manifested itself in violence. Intellectual disability would fall within the definition of a disease of the mind subject to the possibility that it requires a manifestation of violence that is clearly not the case with all forms of intellectual disability nor their effect on all individuals. For there to be insanity, that disease of the mind must cause the defendant to have a defect of reason, which requires that a defendant's powers of reasoning must have been affected, not simply that they were not used (as was determined in *R. v. Clarke*, 1972). If a person has intellectual disability, it will be a matter for the expert evidence to assist the court in determining whether there was, in the individual case, a defect of reason. The consequence of the defect of reason must be that either the defendant did not know the nature and quality of the act (this means that the defendant was completely mistaken as to what they were doing, e.g. where someone believes that they are strangling a doll but are strangling a human being) or that the defendant did not know that what they did was legally wrong (the question is not whether the defendant understood that what they were doing was morally wrong, so knowledge that the act was legally wrong rules out the defence even if their condition produced a different perception of morality or they could not control their impulse to act; see *R. v. Windle*, 1952; *R. v. Kopsch*, 1925). The consequence of a defence of insanity is that the defendant is found not guilty by reason of insanity (Criminal Procedure (Insanity) Act 1964, s. 1). It used to be the case that the defendant then had to be sent to a psychiatric institution, but now the judge has a range of options open:

(1) an admission order to such hospital as the Secretary of State specifies;
(2) a guardianship order under the Mental Health Act 1983;
(3) a supervision and treatment order; or
(4) an order for the defendant's absolute discharge.

It is a defence to murder alone that a person has a diminished responsibility. This, if successful, reduces the conviction from murder to manslaughter, and so provides a range of sentencing options up to and including life imprisonment. Diminished responsibility is defined in the Homicide Act 1957, section 2 as existing where the defendant was "suffering from such abnormality of mind (whether arising from a condition of arrested or incomplete development of mind or any inherent causes of induced by disease or injury) as substantially impaired [their] mental responsibility for [their] acts and omissions in doing or being a party to the killing". Clearly, intellectual disability may be at the basis of a claim by the defendant that their killing was a product of a diminished responsibility. The other partial defence to murder is provocation. The Homicide Act 1957, section 3 provides that "Where on a charge of murder there is evidence on which the jury can find that the person charged was provoked (whether by things done or by things said or by both together) to lose his self-control, the question whether the provocation was enough to make a reasonable man do as he did shall be left to be determined by the jury; and in determining that question the jury shall take into account everything both done and said according to the effect which, in their opinion, it would have on a reasonable man". Thus there is a subjective question, i.e. did the defendant lose their self-control? And there is an objective question, i.e. would the reasonable person have lost their self-control and then have acted as did the defendant? For the latter, a crucially important question, where the defendant has ID, is the extent to which that disability may be taken into account. According to the most recent decision of the House of Lords, *R. v. Morgan Smith* (2000), any attribute of a defendant, and any of his history or circumstances, are relevant to determining the level of self-control that it was reasonable to expect of the defendant. This provides as generous an interpretation as possible of the law (see, e.g., Heaton, 2001).

It should be noted that the burden of proving the matter, for both insanity and diminished responsibility, is upon the defendant, but that the standard of proof is that it must be proved on a balance of probabilities and not beyond a reasonable doubt, which is the standard applying to the prosecution.

Magistrates' Court Trial

Some of the above issues will not arise at a magistrates' court trial. This is because the most serious offences, including murder, cannot be tried there. However, there is no equivalent procedure to unfitness to plead, so the approach, where a case has not already been diverted from the criminal justice system, is for the magistrates to adjourn *sine die* and, effectively, for the case to be dropped, often provided that the person is then admitted to a hospital or otherwise into the care of a psychiatrist. It used to be thought that the defence of insanity did not apply in a magistrates' court, but it is now clear that it does. However, it has less relevance, as the vast majority of crimes that may be tried are crimes of strict liability, to which the defendant's *mens rea* has no relevance.

Witnesses with intellectual disability

There has been concern about the difficulties that some witnesses with ID may face in court. These culminated in the Report of the Home Office Interdepartmental Working Group on the Treatment of Vulnerable or Intimidated Witnesses in the Criminal Justice System, *Speaking Up for Justice* (Home Office, 1998), which was followed by the Youth Justice and Criminal Evidence Act 1999. This legislation enables certain witnesses to have the benefit of special measures. A witness may be eligible because of their mental disorder or their significant impairment of intelligence and social functioning (Youth Justice and Criminal Evidence Act 1999, section 16). The court must then decide whether the person should have the benefit of special measures and, if so, which ones. The special measures available are:

(1) screening the witness from the accused (Youth Justice and Criminal Evidence Act 1999, section 23);
(2) the witness giving evidence by live link (Youth Justice and Criminal Evidence Act 1999, section 24);
(3) ordering the removal of wigs and gown while a witness gives evidence (Youth Justice and Criminal Evidence Act 1999, section 25);
(4) giving evidence in private, but only when it is either a sexual case or a case involving intimidation (Youth Justice and Criminal Evidence Act 1999, section 26);
(5) video-recording the witness's evidence in chief (Youth Justice and Criminal Evidence Act 1999, section 27);

(6) video-recording cross-examination of the witness and their re-examination, where the initial evidence is also recorded (Youth Justice and Criminal Evidence Act 1999, section 28);

(7) examining a witness through an intermediary, who might operate, e.g., as a form of interpreter (Youth Justice and Criminal Evidence Act 1999, section 29); and

(8) providing aids to communication, such as a letter board (Youth Justice and Criminal Evidence Act 1999, section 30).

The availability of such special measures should enable witnesses to be heard who previously would not be heard. All witnesses are presumed to be competent to give evidence, but they will not be competent if they cannot understand questions put to them as a witness and give answers to them which can be understood (Youth Justice and Criminal Evidence Act 1999, section 53). In deciding whether someone is competent, the special measures must be taken into account.

While the introduction of these measures during 2002 in the crown court and eventually in the magistrates' courts is to be applauded, the major drawback is that the special measures do not apply to the accused (Youth Justice and Criminal Evidence Act 1999, sections 16 and 17). This must be contrary to Article 6 of the European Convention on Human Rights and will have to be changed at some stage in the fairly near future (Birch & Leng, 2000, pp. 43–4).

Sentence

Where a person with ID is convicted, there is usually a sentencing discretion for the judge or magistrate. In crown court trials, there is no discretion where the offence is murder (mandatory penalty of life imprisonment: Murder (Abolition of Death Penalty) Act 1965, section 1(1)) or in certain repeat cases of sexual or violence offences (automatic penalty of life imprisonment: Crime (Sentences) Act 1997). Indeed, the simple existence of a mental disorder is not sufficient to prevent the imposition of an automatic life sentence under the 1997 Act, as was made clear in *R. v. Newman* (2000). However, where there is a discretion in the sentence that may be imposed, learning disability may be a relevant factor. For example, in *R. v. Barrass* (2002), the Court of Appeal accepted that B's "very severe intellectual limitations" and "having regard to the overwhelming material suggesting that he is capable of being led and was indeed led into these activities, and having regard to the material suggesting that the co-accused manipulated this manipulatable [person]" meant that his sentence should be reduced to less than that of the co-accused, both of whom had been convicted of manslaughter.

3. LEGAL ISSUES: AUSTRALIAN PERSPECTIVE (SUSAN HAYES)

Overview

This section reviews the Australian legislative frameworks relating to fitness to be tried, protections afforded the person with an intellectual disability in the various State, Territory and Federal jurisdictions, and some of the relevant defence issues.

Australian Law

Each state and territory in Australia has its own crime legislation and provisions for persons who are found unfit to be tried or have any other defence based on a mental condition. In addition, the Commonwealth of Australia enacts statutes pertaining to persons who commit crimes in breach of Commonwealth law, in practice these mainly being drug importation or illegal immigration matters. While there are some discrepancies between the various jurisdictions, similarity exists in the provisions for accused persons who may be unfit, or who may have another mental condition that affects their capacity to understand the nature and effect of the criminal act, or to participate fully in their own defence. A useful summary of all Australian legislation and case law may be found on the Australasian Legal Information Institute website (http://www.austlii.edu.au).

There is no requirement that a defendant in a criminal case be represented by counsel, although in practice, this is usually done. In local courts, especially in remote areas where legal aid services may not exist, a defendant may not be represented, however. In serious matters, a defendant might wish to defend himself or herself, but is likely to be advised against this by the judge. Since common-sense indicates that it is vital that a defendant with an intellectual disability be represented, whether at local, District or Supreme court level, recognition of the presence of intellectual disability becomes paramount. A magistrate in a local court, and the police prosecutor, may not realise that the accused has an intellectual disability. To mandate that an accused with an intellectual disability be represented by counsel would in effect require that all defendants be screened for the presence of intellectual disability, prior to the court hearing. A brief screening test has been developed that can identify those accused persons who may have an intellectual disability, and therefore need further diagnostic assessment, or special protections during police questioning or on reception to prison (Hayes, 2000).

Fitness to Stand Trial

Two basic "competence" issues need to be resolved for the defendant with an intellectual disability, arising directly out of the consequences of that disability. The first is whether the defendant can be tried at all—in other words, is the defendant "fit to be tried"? The second is whether the defendant, though fit to be tried, has a defence in or is not guilty of the offence owing to the effects of the intellectual impairment on his or her criminal responsibility (Hayes & Craddock, 1992).

The distinction between "fitness to plead" and "fitness to be tried" was analysed in the Supreme Court of the Northern Territory in a pre-trial ruling in R. v. *Bradley* (1986). Fitness to plead may be distinguished from refusal to enter a plea, with the former referring to the accused's ability to plead and to understand the plea. Nevertheless, the concept of the ability to enter a plea is incorporated in the issue of "fitness to be tried", and in some legislation the terms appear to be used interchangeably.

In each of the Australian jurisdictions, legislation sets out the procedure to be followed in District and Supreme Courts where it is thought that a defendant may not be fit to be tried (see, for example, the Mental Health (Criminal Procedure Act

1990 (NSW)). The legislation does not give a detailed definition of "fitness to be tried", and each has differing emphases. The Criminal Law Consolidation Act 1935 (SA), Section 269H is an example of a legislative provision that attempts to delineate the parameters for assessing fitness, and states:

> A person is mentally unfit to stand trial on a charge of an offence if the person's mental processes are so disordered or impaired that the person is–
>
> (a) unable to understand, or to respond rationally to, the charge or the allegations on which the charge is based; or
> (b) unable to exercise (or to give rational instructions about the exercise of) procedural rights (such as, for example, the right to challenge jurors); or
> (c) unable to understand the nature of the proceedings, or to follow the evidence or the course of the proceedings.

Where the legislation is unclear the common law definition tends to be accepted. In Australian jurisdictions, Smith J. in *R. v. Presser* (1958) made the most frequently quoted formulation of the fitness test. His Honour set out the following checklist of minimum standards which the accused (because of mental defect) needs to demonstrate before he or she can be tried without unfairness or injustice:

> He needs, I think, to be able to understand what it is that he is charged with. He needs to be able to plead to the charge and to exercise his right of challenge. He needs to understand generally the nature of the proceedings, namely, that it is an inquiry as to whether he did what he is charged with. He needs to be able to follow the course of the proceedings so as to understand what is going on in court in a general sense, though he need not, of course understand the purpose of all the various court formalities. He needs to be able to understand, I think, the substantial effect of any evidence that may be given against him, and he needs to be able to make his defence or answer to the charge. Where he has counsel he needs to be able to do this through his counsel by giving any necessary instructions and by letting his counsel know what his version of the facts is and, if necessary, telling the court what it is. He need not, of course, be conversant with court procedure and he need not have the mental capacity to make an able defence; but he must, I think, have sufficient capacity to be able to decide what defence he will rely upon and to make his defence and his version of the facts known to the court and to his counsel, if any.

The issue is not the accused's state of mind at the time of the alleged offence, as is the situation in a defence of insanity, but rather the ability of the accused at the time of the trial to take an active part in the proceedings. There is anecdotal evidence suggesting that some expert witnesses and lawyers misunderstand the crux of the issue of fitness to be tried, and erroneously apply the test of whether the accused understood the nature of the offence and understood that it was wrong. While the proceedings to determine fitness are meant to be non-adversarial, in practice an adversarial approach is often used, partly because of misunderstanding as to the outcomes for the accused who is found unfit. The Crown Prosecutor and police may believe that showing that the accused is fit is vital if he or she is to be tried and, if found guilty, punished accordingly. There may be the erroneous belief that an unfit accused is absolved from responsibility for his or her actions and "let off".

No evidence is available from Australian sources to indicate the frequency with which the issue of fitness to be tried is raised in matters concerning accused persons with intellectual disability, nor the frequency with which the accused is determined to be unfit.

Fitness to be tried may be an unresolved issue in some local (magistrates') court jurisdictions, as compared with District or Supreme Courts. In New South Wales local courts, for example, there is no legislative provision for determining a defendant's fitness to be tried in summary proceedings, that is, proceedings which are dealt with to finality in the local court. Sections 32 and 33 of the Mental Health (Criminal Procedure) Act 1990 (NSW) provide for the deferral or discontinuance of criminal proceedings where it is shown that the defendant is suffering from a mental condition for which treatment is available in a hospital, or a mental illness, or is mentally ill or developmentally disabled. The magistrate then has a discretionary power to dismiss the charge (except in the case of those mentally ill under the Mental Health Act where other legislation and provisions can apply), either conditionally or otherwise, or to adjourn the proceedings upon conditions including the requirement that the defendant be assessed as to the condition and/or treatment. There is no reference to the degree of disability necessary before the magistrate can use the sections, except in the case where it appears to the magistrate that the defendant is "mentally ill within the meaning of Chapter 3 of the Mental Health Act 1990" (s.33(1)). The provisions in the Crimes Act 1914 (Commonwealth) are similar. The conditions imposed are not, however, enforceable, which means that the accused cannot be brought back before the court for breaching the conditions, and no penalty applies. Consequently, magistrates are diffident about applying Section 32, especially for repeat offenders.

The discretions in Sections 32 and 33 of the New South Wales and Commonwealth Acts do not overcome the difficulty of the magistrate's power to deal with the unfit defendant because the magistrate may decline to exercise the discretion in favour of the defendant. The question of fitness is fundamental to the court's jurisdiction to hear charges and mete out punishments. Therefore, where there is no provision for a defendant facing a summary charge to be considered unfit to be tried, the court in essence has no option but to terminate the proceedings against the person. He or she cannot participate in the defence, and it is a cardinal principle of law that no person can be tried unless she or he is in a mental condition to do so. The result is that in a jurisdiction where there is no provision for dealing with unfitness in local courts, the magistrate faced with a potentially unfit defendant must first determine the question of whether the defendant is unfit before moving on to consider the discretions set out in the sections. If the magistrate finds that the defendant is unfit the only course is to dismiss the charge. After that, the defendant may only be detained and treated within the civil commitment provisions of the Mental Health Act 1990 (NSW), if those can be found to apply. Since people with an intellectual disability cannot be dealt with under mental health legislation in Australia unless they have a psychiatric illness (intellectual disability is not regarded as a psychiatric illness of itself), then there may be no course open to the magistrate.

No psychological scales for the specific assessment of unfitness to be tried exist in the Australian jurisdictions (Hayes, 1997). Expert witnesses (usually for both the prosecution and the defence) assess the defendant. While an objective, valid and reliable evaluation of the degree of intellectual disability can be arrived at, there may then be differences of opinion between expert witnesses as to the implications for the defendant's understanding of the charges and the court processes; hence, considerable argument about fitness may arise.

Disposition/Disposal of a Defendant Found Unfit to be Tried

In New South Wales, a person who is found unfit to be tried is then referred to the Mental Health Review Tribunal for a determination as to whether, on the balance of probabilities, the person will become fit during the following 12 months. A defendant whose intellectual disability renders him or her unfit is unlikely to alter and become fit during this time. If intellectual disability and a coexisting psychiatric illness or other mental condition are both present, the defendant may recover to some extent from the psychiatric condition during the period of time and therefore could become fit; hence this provision is relevant to defendants with an intellectual disability. If the person is likely to become fit, the Tribunal notifies the court of this determination and the court may then grant bail, or may order that the person be taken to and detained in a hospital or a place other than a hospital (usually a correctional centre, if the crime is serious), all of these orders not to exceed 12 months. When the person becomes fit, the matter is referred back to the court, which holds another inquiry into the person's fitness, and if found fit, the proceedings recommence. If the person remains unfit, then a special hearing must be held, to determine if the person performed the act of which they are accused.

If the Attorney General is notified by the Mental Health Review Tribunal of its determination that a person will not, on the balance of probabilities, become fit to be tried during the period of 12 months after the finding of unfitness, the Attorney General (after receiving and considering the advice of the Director of Public Prosecutions) may direct that a special hearing be conducted in respect of the offence with which the person is charged, or advise the relevant government minister and the court which referred the person to the Tribunal that the person will not be further proceeded against by the Attorney General or the Director of Public Prosecutions in respect of the offence (usually where the offence is not serious and the person has already spent time in prison).

A special hearing is conducted as nearly as possible as if it were a trial of criminal proceedings. The Crimes (Mental Impairment and Unfitness to be Tried) Act 1997 (Vic), Section 16, for example, sets down the procedure at special hearings, as follows:

(1) A special hearing is to be conducted as nearly as possible as if it were a criminal trial and, for that purpose, the Juries Act 1967 applies, subject to this section, as if a special hearing were a criminal inquest within the meaning of that Act.

(2) Without limiting sub-section (2), at a special hearing

(a) the defendant must be taken to have pleaded not guilty to the offence; and

(b) the defendant's legal representative (if any) may exercise the defendant's rights to challenge jurors (either for cause or peremptorily) or the jury;

(c) the defendant may raise any defence that could be raised if the special hearing were a criminal trial, including the defence of mental impairment;

(d) the rules of evidence apply;

(e) section 360A of the Crimes Act 1958 (adjournment or stay of trial) applies as if the special hearing were a criminal trial;

(f) any alternative verdict that would be available if the special hearing were a criminal trial is available to the jury.

(3) At the commencement of a special hearing, the judge must explain to the jury–

(a) that the defendant is unfit to be tried in accordance with the usual procedures of a criminal trial; and

(b) the meaning of being unfit to stand trial; and

(c) the purpose of the special hearing; and

(d) the findings that are available; and

(e) the standard of proof required for those findings.

There are a number of assumptions in this section, to take into account that the accused may not be able to take certain decisions about the conduct of their defence. These provisions have many advantages for an accused with an intellectual disability. The person cannot be incarcerated for an indefinite period of time, as could occur with "Governor's pleasure" provisions for defendants formerly regarded as unable to plead. The person does not have to prove that they are not dangerous or violent before being released from prison, as can be the case with a patient seeking to be discharged from a psychiatric hospital. A fixed and finite sentence is imposed if the person is found to have committed the offence. The hearing is conducted like a trial, and the offence must be proven beyond reasonable doubt. The explanation to the jury seeks to ensure that the jury will not believe that the accused will be "let off"; if a jury believes that an accused whom they think could be dangerous would be absolved from any responsibility for the crime because that person has a mental condition, they may be swayed in their verdict. On the other hand, these provisions ensure that a jury will not be swayed towards leniency by believing that an indefinite term of incarceration is so dreadful a prospect that they must find the accused not guilty.

While the legal provisions are a forward step, the disposition/disposal of the accused awaiting trial or special hearing, or of the defendant who is found guilty, is a major flaw in the criminal justice system. In Australia, the dearth of facilities for people with intellectual disabilities, which provide behaviour management programmes, secure or at least closely supervised accommodation, employment, living and adaptive behaviour skills training, and recreational and social activities, combined with the separation of mental health and intellectual disability services and systems, has significant results for such offenders. In the absence of appropriate options for disposition, over-representation of people with intellectual disability in the correctional system has increased over the past decade or more (Hayes, 1994, 1996, 2000; see also Chapter 4).

Diminished Responsibility

Apart from the issue of being unfit to be tried, other strategies and defences are available to a defendant with an intellectual disability in Australian jurisdictions. An example in a murder trial is the defence of diminished responsibility, under the Crimes Act 1900 (ACT), Section 14, which states:

> A person on trial for murder shall not be convicted of murder if, when the act or omission causing death occurred, the accused was suffering from an abnormality of mind (whether arising from a condition of arrested or retarded development of mind or any inherent cause or whether it was induced by disease or injury) that substantially impaired his or her mental responsibility for the act or omission.... A person who, but for [the above] subsection, would be liable (whether as principal or accessory) to be convicted of murder is liable to be convicted of manslaughter.

Similar provisions exist in other Australian states and territories (Hayes, 1991). The provision is similar to the diminished responsibility provisions in the USA, with the important difference that the sentencing outcome is not as significant, because no Australian states or territories impose the death penalty. The offender is sentenced under the provisions applying to manslaughter rather than murder, and may therefore receive a lesser sentence, but the sentence is a matter of degree rather than a matter of life and death.

Abnormality of Mind

Australian legislation has generally been amended to ensure that intellectual disability is not regarded as a form of mental or psychiatric illness, and that people with intellectual disabilities cannot be detained in psychiatric hospitals by reason alone of their intellectual disability. Nevertheless, people with an intellectual disability may be dually diagnosed with a concomitant psychiatric illness, and the defences of "insanity" or not guilty by reason of mental abnormality are open.

Furthermore, there is a provision in some Australian jurisdictions for a defence based in "substantial impairment by abnormality of mind" (e.g. Crimes Act 1900 (NSW), Section 23A). This section states that a person who would otherwise be guilty of murder is not to be convicted of murder, but rather of manslaughter, if:

(a) at the time of the acts or omissions causing the death concerned, the person's capacity to understand events, or to judge whether the person's actions were right or wrong, or to control himself or herself, was substantially impaired by an abnormality of mind arising from an underlying condition, and

(b) the impairment was so substantial as to warrant liability for murder being reduced to manslaughter.

If the intellectual disability fits the above criteria, the accused may have a defence. Self-induced intoxication is not accepted as a defence under this section. The term "underlying condition" means a pre-existing mental or physiological condition, other than a condition of a transitory kind, and the definition can include intellectual disability.

Competency to Confess and Voluntariness of the Confession

As in other jurisdictions, the pressure to confess and the lack of external constraints upon police interviews that lead to a confession can result in situations in which the accused with an intellectual disability is placed in a precarious situation (Hayes, 1997). Gudjonsson and colleagues have, through the course of many research projects, demonstrated that this group of accused persons tends to be vulnerable, suggestible, and unable to foresee the long-term consequences of their confessions (Gudjonsson, 1984; Gudjonsson, Clare, Rutter & Pearse, 1993; Clare & Gudjonsson, 1993; see also Hayes, 1997). Little legislative attention has been paid to the issue of confessional statements and their accuracy or otherwise in Australia. Recently, however, there have been some attempts to ensure that an accused with an intellectual disability receives some protections during police interviews. In New South Wales, police now have an obligation to provide special assistance to vulnerable suspects, during police interviewing and detention: Crimes Amendment (Detention after Arrest) Act 1997 (NSW) and Regulation (1998). Section 356N indicates that the person has a right to communicate with friend, relative, guardian or independent person and legal practitioner, and that the custody manager must inform the person of this right. Furthermore the custody manager must arrange for an interpreter to be present if the person appears not to communicate with reasonable fluency because of any disability. These are important new policing requirements, and failure to comply with the requirements may have serious implications for the police case against a suspect. These provisions are honoured more in the breach than in the observance, however, and many police appear not to be aware of the provisions. There are cases where police have arrested a person at a group home for people with intellectual disabilities, and have been informed by staff that the person has an intellectual disability, yet have not conformed with the provisions of the Act. Until training of police has improved, there is little hope that police will understand and recognise the presence of intellectual disability, despite the development of a brief screening to assist in identification of the condition (Hayes, 2000).

Tape recording or videotape recording of admissions by a suspect is an initiative which can assist in determining whether or not a suspect with an intellectual disability was treated fairly during police questioning, and all Australian jurisdictions provide for this. Legislation providing for this includes the Criminal Procedure Act 1986 (NSW), Section 108; Criminal Law (Detention and Interrogation) Act 1995 (Tas), Section 8; Summary Offences Act 1953 (SA), Section 74D; Crimes Act 1914 (Cth), Section 23V; and Crimes (Questioning of Suspects) Act 2000 (Vic), Section 6. Section 108 of the NSW Act states:

> (2) Evidence of an admission to which this section applies is not admissible unless:
>> (a) there is available to the court:
>>> (i) a tape recording made by an investigating official of the interview in the course of which the admission was made, or

(ii) if the prosecution establishes that there was a reasonable excuse as to why a tape recording referred to in subparagraph (i) could not be made, a tape recording of an interview with the person who made the admission, being an interview about the making and terms of the admission in the course of which the person states that he or she made an admission in those terms, or

(b) the prosecution establishes that there was a reasonable excuse as to why a tape recording referred to in paragraph (a) could not be made.

Videotapes are useful to an expert witness in attempting to determine whether the client understood the police questions or appeared intimidated or confused by police, because both facial expressions and body language are visible, and other important information is gained from the tone of voice of both parties, delays in answering questions, and non-verbal cues given by police as to the "correct" answer to a question. Videotapes are not always infallible, however, as sometimes "informal" questioning of suspects takes place in the police car on the way to the station, or before the videotape machine is started. On rare occasions, several videotaped confessions may be made, while only one is made available to the defence, the one in which the vulnerable suspect "gets it right". Defence lawyers must be alert to these possibilities, and request all videotapes.

After the interview is completed, an officer unconnected with the investigation enters the room and asks the suspect whether he or she has any complaints about the manner in which the interview was conducted, and whether they participated in the interview of their own free will, without the influence of any threats, promises or inducements. These innovations probably rule out some of the worst examples of police claiming to have obtained a confession when they have not, or agreeing between themselves to state that the suspect confessed, when he or she did not do so. Unacceptable police questioning practices such as bullying tactics and misleading or leading questions might also be minimised. Not all confessions are voluntary, however, despite these safeguards. The interviewee may not understand the police caution, and may not comprehend that they do not have to answer questions. Some suspects with an intellectual disability answer questions because they want to leave the police station and go home. Clare and Gudjonsson (1995) found that the subjects with intellectual disabilities were relatively unconcerned about the implications of making a false confession, and were more likely than non-disabled interviewees to believe that such a confession could be credibly retracted, and that it would not be considered as evidence of guilt even if produced in court. Further, they were more likely to believe that after confessing, they could return home, at least until the trial. The interviewees with intellectual disabilities placed less importance upon the need for legal representation during an interview with police. They indicated that they thought the suspect's guilt or innocence would be apparent to others, and if the suspect were innocent, he would be protected from the impact of a confession (the study used a male suspect in a short film). Thus, the researchers conclude, persons with an intellectual disability who are *innocent* of an offence may be most at risk during police interviews because they believe their innocence will be obvious, and they will not have to "fight for their rights".

Admissibility of Confessions

As the majority of crimes are resolved through confessions, the confession is a very important aspect of over-representation of people with intellectual disabilities in the criminal justice system. The suspect has the right to remain silent. The prosecution may have the burden to prove the voluntariness of an admission or confession, or that it was made in circumstances as to make it unlikely that the truth of the admission or confession was adversely affected. The judge may have, in a criminal proceeding, a discretion to reject a confession or admission made by the person charged if, having regard to the circumstances in which, or the means by which, the confession or admission was obtained, the judge is satisfied that it would be unfair to the person charged to admit the confession or admission in evidence, or if the evidence was obtained improperly. These or similar provisions are included in the Evidence Act 1995 (Cth), Part 3.4; Evidence Act 1971 (ACT), Part 10; Evidence Act 1958 (Vic), Section 149; Evidence Act 1977 (Qld), Section 130; Evidence Act (1996) (NT), Section 51(4); Evidence Act 1995 (NSW) Section 85; Summary Offences Act 1953 (SA), Section 74 D-E; Criminal Law (Detention and Interrogation) Act 1995 (Tas), Section 9; and Evidence Act 1906 (WA), Section 112.

In New South Wales, for example, the court may take into account "any relevant condition or characteristic of the person who made the admission, including age, personality and education and any mental, intellectual or physical disability to which the person is or appears to be subject, and ... if the admission was made in response to questioning, ... the nature of the questions and the manner in which they were put, and ... the nature of any threat, promise or other inducement made to the person questioned" (Section 85).

Sentencing Considerations

The presence of intellectual disability is a mitigating factor in sentencing, particularly as a recent NSW Court of Criminal Appeal decisions indicated that "whereas general deterrence is a relevant consideration in every sentencing exercise, it is a consideration to which less weight should be given in the case of an offender suffering from a mental disorder or severe intellectual handicap because such an offender is not an appropriate medium for making an example to others" (*R. v. Letteri*, 1992). A detailed discussion of sentencing issues regarding people with intellectual disability may be found in the NSW Law Reform Commission Discussion Paper (NSW Law Reform Commission, 1994). The presence of intellectual disability may be pertinent to the severity of sentence, and the structure of the sentence, that is, the balance between imprisonment and parole. The Commission recommended that pre-sentence reports be mandatory where the offender has an intellectual disability and is unrepresented, and that there be assessment and screening procedures in prisons. A fuller discussion of sentencing options may be found in Chapter 4.

Along with many other factors that courts take into account when imposing a sentence, it is appropriate for intellectual disability to be included in mitigating factors. The person with an intellectual disability may not comprehend the severity of their actions. By the time the matter goes to court, they may have very little recall of the events leading to the charges, and so there may not be a link in their mind between the action and the subsequent penalty. In extreme cases, the accused with an intellectual disability may not comprehend the concepts of injury or death, or consent (and lack thereof) to sexual intercourse. The court needs to weigh these and other considerations related to intellectual disability in sentencing the offender.

Discussion

In general, Australian States and Territories have introduced reforms to the criminal law which are designed to enhance the protection of the rights of people with intellectual disabilities who are in the criminal justice system. The legislative reforms have not, however, been accompanied by establishment of appropriate training programmes for police, lawyers, correctional staff, the judiciary and court staff. Alternative options for disposition of the unfit accused, or the offender with an intellectual disability are in a parlous state. Hence, the rights of people with intellectual disabilities are given lip-service, while the reality of their treatment within the criminal justice system is often unfair, unjust and harsh.

REFERENCES

References for Part 1

Atkins *v*. Virginia (2002) 260 Va 375,534 S. E. 2d 312, reversed and remanded.

Baroff, G.S. (1996). The mentally retarded offender. In J.W. Jacobson & J.A. Mulick (eds) *Manual of Diagnosis and Professional Practice in Mental Retardation* (pp. 311–21). Washington, DC: American Psychological Association.

Baroff, G.S. (1998). Why mental retardation is "mitigating." *The Champion,* **XXII**(7), 33–5.

Drope *v*. Missouri, 420 U.S. 162, 171 (1975).

Dusky *v*. United States, 362 U.S. 402 (1960).

Ellis, J.W. & Luckasson, R.A. (1985). Mentally retarded criminal defendants. *The George Washington Law Review,* **53**, 414–93.

Fitch, W.L. (1992). Mental retardation and criminal responsibility. In R.W. Conley, R. Luckasson & G.N. Bouthilet (eds) *The Criminal Justice System and Mental Retardation* (pp. 121–36). Baltimore, MD: Paul H. Brookes.

Fry, E.B. (1977). Fry's Readability Graph: clarification, validity and extension to level 17. *Journal of Reading,* **21**, 242–252.

Godinez *v*. Moran, 509 U.S. 389 (1993).

Grisso, T. (1981). *Juvenile's Waiver of Rights: Legal and Psychological Competence.* Sarasota, FL: Professional Resource Exchange.

Grisso, T. (1998). *Instruments for Asessing Understanding and Appreciation of Miranda Rights* Sarasota, FL: Professional Resource Exchange.

Gutheil, T.G. (1999). A confusion of tongues: competence, insanity, psychiatry, and the law. *Psychiatric Service,* **50**, 767–773.

Hines *v*. State, 384 S. 2d 1171,1181 (1980).

Jackson *v*. Indiana, 406 U.S. 715 (1972).

Kassin, S. (1999). The psychology of confession evidence. *American Psychologist,* **52**, 221–33.

Laski, F.J. (1992). Sentencing the offender with mental retardation: honoring the imperative for intermediate punishments and probation. In R.W. Conley, R. Luckasson & G.N. Bouthilet (eds) *The Criminal Justice System and Mental Retardation* (pp. 137–52). Baltimore, MD: Paul H. Brookes.

Miranda *v*. Arizona, 384 U.S. 436 (1966).

Parry, J. & Drogin, E.Y. (2000). *Criminal Law Handbook on Psychiatric and Psychological Evidence and Testimony*. Washington, DC: The American Bar Association, Commission on Mental and Physical Disability Law.

Paull, G. (1993). *Fitness to Stand Trial*. Springfield, IL: Charles C. Thomas.

Penry *v*. Lynaugh, 492 U.S. 302 (1989).

People *v*. Redmon, 127 Ill. App. 3d 342, 468 N.E.2d 1310, 1313, (1984).

Petrella, R.C. (1992). Defendants with mental retardation in the forensic services system. In R.W. Conley, R. Luckasson, & G.N. Bouthliet (eds) *The Criminal Justice System and Mental Retardation* (pp. 79–96). Baltimore, MD: Paul H. Brookes.

Seiling *v*. Eyeman, 478 F2d 211 (9th Cir. 1973).

Toliver *v*. Gathright, 501 F. Supp. 148, 150 (E.D. Va 1980).

References for Part 2

Bailey, S.H., Ching, J., Gunn, M.J. & Ormerod, D.C. (2002). *Smith, Bailey and Gunn on the Modern English Legal System*, 4th edn. London: Sweet & Maxwell.

Birch, D. & Leng, R. (2000). *Blackstone's Guide to the Youth Justice and Criminal Evidence Act 1999*. London: Blackstone.

Bratty *v*. Attorney General for Northern Ireland [1963] *The Law Reports: Appeal Cases* 386.

Fisher, H. (1977). *Report of the Inquiry in to the Death of Maxwell Confait*, House of Commons Papers No. 90.

Heaton, R. (2001). Anything goes. *Nottingham Law Journal*, no. 10, 50.

Home Office (1998). Report of the *Speaking Up for Justice*, Interdepartmental Working Group on the Treatment of Vulnerable or Intimidated Witnesses in the Criminal Justice System. London: Home Office.

Mackay, R.D. & Kearns, G. (2000). An upturn in unfitness to plead. *Criminal Law Review* 542.

M'Naghten case (1843) 10 Cl & Fin 200.

Murphy, P. (ed.) (2002). *Blackstone's Criminal Practice*. London: Blackstone.

R. *v*. Antoine [2001] 1 *The Law Reports: Appeal Cases* 340.

R. *v*. Barrass [2002] *England and Wales Court of Appeal Decisions: Criminal* 98.

R. *v*. Clarke [1972] 1 *All England Law Reports* 219.

R. *v*. Delaney (1988) 88 *Criminal Appeal Reports* 338.

R. *v*. Everett [1988] *Criminal Law Review* 826.

R. *v*. Harvey [1988] *Criminal Law Review* 241.

R. *v*. Kopsch (1925) 19 *Criminal Appeal Reports* 50.

R. *v*. M (2001) *The Times*, 1 November.

R. *v*. Morgan Smith [2000] 3 *Weekly Law Reports* 654.

R. *v*. Moss (1990) 91 *Criminal Appeal Reports* 371.

R. *v*. Newman (2000) *The Times*, 3 February.

R. *v*. Pritchard (1836) 7 C & P 303.

R. *v*. Sullivan [1984] *The Law Reports: Appeal Cases* 156.

R. *v*. Windle [1952] 1 *The Law Reports: Queens Bench* 826.

R. *v*. Woollin [1999] *The Law Reports: Appeal Cases* 82.

Sanders, A. & Young, R. (2000). *Criminal Justice*, 2nd edn. London: Butterworths.

References for Part 3

Clare, I. & Gudjonsson, G. (1993). Interrogative suggestibility, confabulation, and acquiescence in people with mild learning disabilities (mental handicap): implications for reliability during police interrogations. *British Journal of Clinical Psychology*, 32(3), 295–301.

Clare, I. & Gudjonsson, G. (1995). The vulnerability of suspects with intellectual disabilities during police interviews: a review and experimental study of decision-making. *Mental Handicap Research*, 8, 110–28.

Gudjonsson, G. (1984). Interrogative suggestibility: comparison between "False Confessors" and "Deniers" in criminal trials. *Medicine, Science and Law*, 24, 56.

Gudjonsson, G., Clare, I., Rutter, S. & Pearse, J. (1993). *Interviews in Police Custody: The Identification of Vulnerabilities*, Research Study report no. 12. London: Royal Commission on Criminal Justice.

Hayes, S.C. (1991). Diminished responsibility: the expert witness' viewpoint. In S. Yeo (ed.) *Partial Excuses to Murder* (pp. 145–57). Sydney: Federation Press.

Hayes, S.C. (1994). Intellectually disabled offenders – characteristics and psychological assessment. Paper presented at the First International Congress on Mental Retardation, Rome.

Hayes, S.C. (1996). People with an Intellectual Disability and the Criminal Justice System: Two Rural Courts (5). Sydney: New South Wales Law Reform Commission.

Hayes, S.C. (1997). Intellectual disability. In I. Freckelton & H. Selby (eds) *Expert Evidence* (pp. 6-1351–6-1477). Melbourne: Law Book Co.

Hayes, S.C. (2000). *Hayes Ability Screening Index (HASI) Manual*. Sydney: Behavioural Sciences in Medicine, University of Sydney.

Hayes, S.C. & Craddock, G. (1992). *Simply Criminal*, 2nd edn. Sydney: Federation Press.

NSW Law Reform Commission. (1994). *People with an Intellectual Disability and the Criminal Justice System: Courts and Sentencing Issues*, Discussion Paper 35. Sydney: NSW Law Reform Commission.

R. *v.* Bradley (1986) 21 A. Crim. R. 419.

R. *v.* Letteri (unreported) Supreme Court, NSW, Court of Criminal Appeal, 18 March 1992, CCA 60407/91, per Badgery-Parker J (with the concurrence of Gleeson, CJ and Sheller JA) at 14.

R. *v.* Presser [1958] VR 45.

Chapter 4

PATHWAYS FOR OFFENDERS WITH INTELLECTUAL DISABILITIES

SUSAN HAYES

University of Sydney, Sydney, Australia

INTRODUCTION

A tension exists concerning attitudes held by criminal justice personnel towards the offender with intellectual disability—some professionals interpret the concept of normalisation to mean that this offender group should be treated as any other offender, while others take the view that this group do not belong in the criminal justice system and should be diverted to other systems, including the mental health system. A feeling of frustration is often expressed because offenders with a intellectual disability are seen as vulnerable during police interviews and court proceedings, and unable to cope with the demands of parole, probation or community and custodial sentences. This offender group may not understand the nature of their offence and be capable of participating in their own defence. Their challenging behaviour can pose major management problems for correctional administrators. On the other hand, interviews with justice system personnel, people with disabilities and their carers and families in a Californian research study indicated consensus among all participants that "the person with a disability should not be relieved from legal obligations and responsibilities", and must be held accountable for their own good and that of the community (Petersilia, 2000). This apparent conflict of views between the "hold them accountable" and the "divert them from the criminal justice system" factions is not, however, a substantive conflict when the issue is pursued to the next step. The critical factor is not whether or not this offender group should be held accountable, but the way in which they are held accountable. Petersilia states that "holding them accountable should not mean they are denied due

Offenders with Developmental Disabilities. Edited by W.L. Lindsay, J.L. Taylor and P. Sturmey.
© 2004 John Wiley & Sons, Ltd.

process in the courts, housed in settings where they face high risks of victimisation, or denied access to work and treatment" (p. 41). Prison is an example of a setting where high risks of victimisation can occur, yet there is ample research evidence that in some jurisdictions the rate of imprisonment of this group far exceeds the population prevalence (Hayes, 2000; Petersilia, 2000). The offender with an intellectual disability can be held accountable, yet incarceration is not the only, and perhaps not the best, option. This chapter explores the range of alternative pathways for offenders with intellectual disability, discusses whether imprisonment is an overused or inappropriate option, and examines the extent to which alternative pathways serve the accountability goal while also achieving the best outcome for the person with intellectual disability and a society that seeks to support its less able members. A range of possible diversions, either from the criminal justice system itself or from prison, is explored, and the advantages and disadvantages, checks and balances, and relative effectiveness of each are investigated. Luckasson (1999) writes that for "people with developmental disabilities, the criminal justice system is the last frontier of integration". Appropriate and supported health care, education, welfare, housing and vocational resources, based on assessment of an individual's needs, tend to be taken for granted for people with intellectual disability who are not in the criminal justice system, yet, as the debate indicates, Western societies are still grappling with integration and support issues for offenders with intellectual disability.

Diversion from the criminal justice system for people with intellectual disability is not a new concept. As early as 1974, Menolascino proposed a system of prevention, advocacy and treatment options an array of residential, vocational and educational options (Menolascino, 1974). Community residential placements ranged from case-managed independent placements to structured group homes. Since the 1970s, efforts to provide appropriate and effective diversionary options for offenders with intellectual disability have been *ad hoc*, fragmented and uncoordinated; furthermore, these options are rarely evaluated in an objective and stringent manner. In 1992 McGee and Menolascino were still recommending that there be "diversion programs that focus on community-based and violence-free alternatives, that investigation [be conducted] of the long-term effect of such programs, as compared to the effects of incarceration or institution-based diversion programs ... [and there be] increased monitoring of ... programs to ensure habilitation and freedom from cruel and unusual punishment". During the intervening two decades, little had changed.

Diversionary schemes for offenders with intellectual disability are scarcer than the parallel system for offenders with a psychiatric diagnosis. For the latter group, a number of schemes have been established, designed to provide a quick assessment of the individual when they appear before a court, and to attempt diversion that may involve placement, medical intervention or welfare assistance (Chung, Cumella, Wensley & Easthope, 1999). The dearth of similar schemes for people with intellectual disability is possibly related to less awareness of the nature of intellectual disability, and ignorance of the fact that this condition affects a significant proportion of accused persons. Throughout this chapter, evaluations of diversionary options designed for offenders with psychiatric illnesses are used as examples where rigorous evaluations of similar schemes for those with intellectual disability have not been located.

IDENTIFYING THE OFFENDER WITH INTELLECTUAL DISABILITY

Opportunities for diversion from the criminal justice system exist, through legislation designed to protect accused persons who are unfit to be tried or who have a mental condition that impairs their ability to understand the nature and effect of the crime allegedly committed, or to understand that it was wrong. Diversion cannot occur, however, unless the presence of the relevant mental condition, in this instance, intellectual disability, is recognised at some point during the accused person's transit through the criminal justice system. Identification of the presence of intellectual disability has been poor, almost to the point of being accidental (Hayes & Craddock, 1992; Hayes, 1996; Shaw, Creed, Price, Huxley & Tomenson, 1999). The Americans with Disabilities Act (ADA), 1990, which bans discrimination based on disability, has affected the way in which United States' correctional agencies identify and treat intellectual disability, by providing a foundation for court intervention. As a result, states are no longer able indiscriminately to place offenders with intellectual disability in the mainstream of prisons; correctional facilities are required to establish screening and rehabilitation programmes specifically for this offender group, and to ensure that the programmes are evaluated and accessible (Petersilia, 1997). Many correctional systems are in breach of ADA, however, resulting in commencement of class actions on behalf of prisoners with intellectual disability. ADA was instrumental in the decision by the US state of Texas to administer group intelligence tests to all inmates entering the correctional system. The Texas Council on Offenders with Mental Impairments coordinates community-based interventions, special needs parole programmes, and continuity of care.

Screening for intellectual disability by non-psychologists, including police, lawyers, corrective services staff, probation and parole officers, and court personnel, is valuable in identifying those accused persons or offenders who need to be referred for a full-scale diagnostic assessment for intellectual disability, or who are vulnerable and in need of special protections during police interviews. A screening test designed for use in the criminal justice system has been developed, showing 87% accuracy in identifying those who need further full-scale diagnostic assessment (Hayes, 2000).

Establishing a diagnosis of intellectual disability may be problematical in the criminal justice system, owing to the difficulty in obtaining a complete and accurate health and development history, and the involvement of offenders in risk-taking behaviour and substance abuse from an early age. Therefore, determining whether limitations have been present during the developmental period can be difficult. The high rates of traumatic brain injury, other brain damage and substance abuse in prison populations contribute to deficits in verbal memory and learning, abstract thinking, general memory, and socialisation, the exact aetiology of which may never be determined (Barnfield & Leathem, 1998).

PREVENTATIVE PROGRAMMES

Preventative programmes are designed to address an individual's challenging behaviour and thus avoid involvement with the criminal justice system. Such programmes may overlap with options for diversion from the criminal justice system, which can be implemented once the person has entered the criminal justice system, and which are aimed at prevention of recidivism. There is evidence that early intervention for both individuals with and without intellectual disabilities is cost effective, and beneficial to the individual, potential victims, families and society in general (Everingham, 1998; New South Wales Parliament, 1999). This message about cost effectiveness has proved difficult to translate into political action, however, and the bulk of funding is poured into the other end of the correctional/rehabilitative spectrum, into corrective services, prisons in particular.

Risk factors contributing to offences on the part of individuals with intellectual disability can include features of the disability itself, difficult temperament, poor social skills, and poor problem solving (National Crime Prevention, 1996). Analyses by the Rand Corporation in the USA and other researchers demonstrate that early intervention programmes, including parent training, incentives to remain at and graduate from high school, delinquent supervision, and early home-visit and day-care programmes, are more cost effective than severely punitive legislation, such as mandatory sentencing to incarceration after three convictions (Everingham, 1998; Greenwood, Model, Rydell & Chiesa, 1998). Longitudinal research indicates that juvenile delinquents who are intellectually disabled have been identified as having challenging behaviour in pre-school years (White, Moffitt & Silva, 1989), yet the behaviour is rarely addressed during the intervening years by education, health or intellectual disability services.

Child abuse research has established that being the victim of abuse as a child is a risk factor for subsequent development of abusive behaviours (Martin, 1982). Both witnessing familial violence and experiencing it are important contributors to becoming an abuser, and can be exacerbated by discontinuity of care; boys who have been exposed to a climate of family violence and disruption have a greater need for support than girls (Skuse et al., 1998). Early intervention and preventative programmes can be highly significant in preventing individuals from becoming victims themselves, as well as short-circuiting the cycle where being a victim of violence may in turn cause the individual to become violent. Such programmes can improve the quality of life for people with intellectual disability who may become offenders, and be cost effective within a society (New South Wales Parliament, 1999).

CUSTODIAL OPTIONS

The term *custodial option* is employed here to describe situations where an individual has been or is at risk of being in contact with the criminal justice system, and as a result, has been sentenced or diverted to an institution where they are detained involuntarily, and segregated from society. Involuntary detention in a secure hospital or facility, remand centre or prison is included in this category.

Secure Hospitals

A major advantage of imprisonment is the imposition of a finite sentence, as opposed to the indeterminate incarceration that can result when mental health legislation is used to detain the accused in a psychiatric facility for their own good, or that of society. The individual may have been diverted from the criminal justice system before guilt or innocence was determined in the court, and in that sense, the individual therefore is an accused, and not an offender. Indeterminate incarceration under mental health legislation can place accused persons in the position of having to demonstrate that they are unlikely to reoffend; in contrast, when a term of imprisonment ends, the offender is released without having to convince boards and tribunals that they are rehabilitated, or no longer violent and dangerous. For people with intellectual disability who do not have a dual diagnosis of psychiatric illness, the use of psychiatric institutions as an alternative to prison is inappropriate, because the accused person is incarcerated in an environment segregated from the mainstream of society, with no possible mental health rehabilitation goal (since no psychiatric illness is present), designed for psychiatrically ill patients rather than for people with intellectual disabilities, and probably no programmes to address the challenging behaviour that led to incarceration. If the individual with intellectual disability is diverted from the criminal justice system into the mental health system prior to trial, the principles of natural justice must be applied, with appropriate reviews and testing of the evidence against the accused.

Maximum security hospitals in the United Kingdom admit about one-quarter of their patients from medium security units, most often owing to behavioural problems that could not be managed by the medium security facility (Exworthy, 2000). While some commentators argue that this demonstrates an enduring demand for maximum-security places, the issue of why the escalating behavioural difficulties were not adequately addressed has not been explored. Special hospital stays tend to be marked by incidents of self-harm, and violence from other residents (Exworthy, 2000). Medication, physical restraint and transfer to another clinical area are the most frequently employed management strategies (Gudjonsson, Rabe-Hesketh & Wilson, 2000). This picture does not describe the type of caring and rehabilitative environment that would be optimum for offenders with intellectual disability.

A 10-year study of admissions and discharges from secure hospitals in the United Kingdom revealed that most patients were discharged to another institution, such as another hospital or a prison, with only 24% returning to the community (Butwell, Jamieson, Leese & Taylor, 2000). The median length of stay was 6.3 years, whereas the small group of people detained under the category of "severe mental impairment" had the longest median stay (19.9 years), followed by those with "mental impairment" (8 years), "mental illness" (6.1 years) and "psychopathic disorder" (5.2 years). These data do not present an optimistic picture of secure hospitalisation as a soft alternative to prison for an offender with intellectual disability. Those patients who had received a criminal conviction remained in hospital for a shorter period of time than those who were there under a civil commitment order or a hospital order, suggesting that diversion out of the criminal justice system is not advantageous, in terms of the amount of time spent in some form of incarceration. The authors comment on the "greater length of stay for the minority group of patients who had not been convicted of a criminal offence prior to admission to special hospital and were detained only under Section 3 (of the Mental Health Act 1983, that is civil cases), without Home Office restrictions on discharge or transfer", and indicated that people with a intellectual disability are most likely to fall into this category. They concluded that "[a]lternative facilities are, if possible, even scarcer than for other patients". These data strongly indicate that the use of secure hospitalisation as a diversionary option, especially when the individual is hospitalised under mental health legislation rather than the criminal law, is an undesirable outcome for accused persons with intellectual disability irrespective of the severity of the offending behaviour.

While at the beginning of the study period in the 1980s, persons with mental impairment who were accepted to secure hospitals comprised 7.3% of admissions, this figure had dropped to 2.8% by 1995 (Jamieson, Butwell, Taylor & Leese, 2000), perhaps reflecting initiatives on the part of the Special Hospitals' Service Authority to reduce the numbers of people with intellectual disability residing in these hospitals. A survey over six months in 1993 found that 16% of patients in the secure hospitals of Ashworth, Broadmoor and Rampton had an intellectual disability, and only one in five of these had a dual diagnosis of psychiatric disorder (Taylor *et al.*, 1998). The majority of people with intellectual disability (68%) in the hospitals had first entered some form of treatment as a child, and only eight were new to treatment upon admission to a special hospital. These data suggest that early intervention programmes to address challenging behaviour had either not been available or were not effective for this group. The figure of 16% of patients in secure hospitals having a diagnosis of intellectual disability is consistent with data concerning the prevalence of intellectual disability in prison populations in many other Western jurisdictions (Hayes & Craddock, 1992; Hayes, 2000). In the United Kingdom, however, it appears that this group is diverted into the mental health system where they do not have a finite sentence. People with intellectual disability were three times more likely to be admitted to a high-security psychiatric setting than their non-disabled counterparts when not charged with any criminal offence, possibly owing to their inability to access advocacy services or legal representation (Woods & Mason, 1998). According to these authors, many of the offences allegedly committed by this group were not serious, and were either related to their communication deficits, or their inability to cope with frustration.

The use of secure hospitals and Mental Health Review Tribunals as diversionary options seems to be unnecessarily expensive, not only in terms of the time that an individual spends in custody, but also the mechanisms for considering release. Taylor, Goldberg, Leese, Butwell and Reed (1999) estimated that the process of a full tribunal hearing cost about £2000 sterling in 1992, yet in more than 90% of cases no change in the patient's status was ordered. When a change in status was ordered, not all of those who were supposed to leave the hospital and be placed elsewhere actually did so. Furthermore, the authors comment that unlike the Parole Board, the tribunal did not consistently or systematically use an actuarial approach to risk assessment, leaving the decisions possibly open to unknown sources of bias which may or may not work to the detriment of people with intellectual disability.

A period of time in a secure hospital appears not to cure offending behaviour, especially in the absence of appropriate adaptive skills and challenging behaviour programmes. Buchanan (1998) found that $10^{1}/_{2}$ years after discharge from a special, high security hospital in the United Kingdom, 32% of those with a classification of mental impairment and 11% of those classified as severely mentally impaired had been convicted of an offence, compared with 26% classified as having a mental illness, and 44% of those classified as having a psychopathic disorder. Patients discharged into the community were more likely to be convicted, compared with those discharged to another hospital, possibly owing to greater opportunity and less supervision in the community. The level of supervision accorded the severely mentally impaired group possibly accounts for their low level of recidivism, although the data may also reflect the fact that incarceration was unnecessary in the first place.

The use of secure hospitals as a means of diversion for people with intellectual disability is available only in those jurisdictions where this group can be committed to secure or psychiatric hospitals under mental health legislation, on the basis of intellectual disability alone. This option is not available in Australian states, for example, where a person with intellectual disability can be confined in a psychiatric hospital only if they have a diagnosable psychiatric illness. Intellectual disability is not a sufficient reason by itself for a person to be accepted into the mental health system, although an offender who is found not guilty on the ground of mental illness can be transferred from the criminal justice system into the mental health system. While the separation of intellectual disability and mental health systems, and the relevant criminal defences were measures designed to protect the interests of people with intellectual disability, and prevent indeterminate incarceration on the grounds of a condition from which they would never recover, there remain some disadvantages for this group—primarily because there is no real parallel diversionary system for intellectual disability. There are few secure units for people with intellectual disability who are accused of a crime or have been found guilty; the diversionary choices, therefore, are either corrective services, or mental health services (if the person's condition meets the provisions of mental health legislation). Neither of these is ideal for people with an intellectual disability, neither routinely offers the types of habilitation and rehabilitation programmes which are most suitable, and neither is staffed primarily with professionals expert in this field. By separating the mental health and intellectual disability systems, and not establishing a parallel system for people with intellectual disability, a serious gap in services has been created, which pushes people into the correctional system, or into a very overloaded, impecunious and inadequate welfare system.

Institutions and Facilities for People with Intellectual Disabilities

While most Western countries have attempted to de-institutionalise the population of people with intellectual disabilities, the process is by no means complete. A major difficulty in any large institution is that the environment itself may be a factor in the development of challenging or offending behaviours. Overcrowding, understaffing, lack of professionally trained staff, large ward or recreational areas, noise levels, boredom, inadequate recreational, social and pre-vocational activities, and a dearth of individual programme development, as well as the likelihood of abuse by staff or other residents, were some of the reasons why de-institutionalisation was deemed to be a good idea. Yet these conditions persist in the remaining institutions.

Research in an 810-bed intellectual disability facility in the north of England examined *inter alia* the use of emergency medication and seclusion as methods of dealing with challenging behaviour, and found that 80% of incidents involved emergency medication, 16% seclusion, and 4% used both (Rangecroft, Tyrer & Berney, 1997). More than half of the clients involved had a dual diagnosis. Agitation, followed by a negative interaction with a staff member (rarely with another resident) led to physical or verbal assault, which tended to be managed by seclusion, whereas self-harm was usually managed with medication. Physical illness contributed to some of the incidents, with boredom, physical proximity to others and lack of structured activity also being factors. The importance of the institutional environment for both staff and residents is indicated by the finding that the "[s]imple instruction to the nursing staff that treatment effects were going to be recorded dramatically reduced the use of restraint, increased the use of counselling, and promoted the use of oral (rather than intramuscular) medication". Put another way, staff altered their behaviour when they were being observed. The segregation from society that occurs in a large institution has long been a major reason for preferring community-based residential environments.

Despite the length of time over which institutional abuse has been documented in most Western nations, the process of de-institutionalisation is not yet complete, and the remaining institutions can be repositories for individuals who are accused of crimes or who have been found guilty. Again, the parallel with a prison sentence reveals that prison is the better option, because the sentence is finite, and also because of the more open environment in a prison. Incidents of abuse can be brought to the attention of prison visitors, and the integrated nature of a prison means that prisoners with an intellectual disability benefit from the general improvements to the prison environment that are achieved by more vocal non-disabled prisoner lobby and civil libertarian groups (Hayes & Craddock, 1992).

Special Units for Offenders with Intellectual Disability

Special units for offenders with intellectual disability (who have been found guilty and sentenced) can be found in the community, on the campuses of former intellectual disability institutions, and in prisons (in Australia, Victoria and New South Wales correctional services incorporate special units in prisons for small number of prisoners with intellectual disability). Few have been subjected to stringent evaluation of the outcomes for inmates, often because the main focus is management of difficult or vulnerable prisoners with intellectual disabilities, rather than rehabilitation. Development of plans to address challenging behaviour is a complex and specialised area, requiring carers and staff to be trained in consistent implementation of the plan. Where special units for offenders with an intellectual disability exist in the community, access to expert behaviour management teams is very limited, and long waiting lists can exist, limiting the court's options to recommend behavioural management as a condition of release or bail, or for diversion from the criminal justice system.

The Mental Impairment Evaluation and Treatment Service (MIETS) at the Bethlem Royal Hospital in Kent, UK, a 13-bed in-patient facility, offers a multidisciplinary assessment and treatment service for people with mild to moderate intellectual disability with challenging behaviours, who are mostly admitted under a section of the Mental Health Act 1983 (Xenitidis, Henry, Russell, Ward, & Murphy, 1999). Aggression, arson and sexually challenging behaviour are the most frequent reasons for admission, with most patients having been in prison, hospital or special hospital prior to placement at MIETS. The majority are discharged into community placements following intervention. Specific clinical questions are requested from the referrers, and the challenging behaviour is quantified before any intervention occurs. Hypotheses for the "origin and function of the behaviour are generated, and a single hypothesis is tested at a time" using behavioural, pharmacological, psychological and social interventions. Each patient receives an individualised treatment programme, the aim being to place people in the community. While the service is expensive, a cost-effectiveness study found the high cost to be a good investment, especially as regards quality of life outcomes for clients (Dockrell, Gaskell, Normand & Rehman, 1995). The development of other models is being undertaken, including a nurse-led outreach team to reduce the length of in-patient stay, through a pre-admission community intervention programme. Significant clinical improvement has been demonstrated in this client group, leading the authors to remark that "there is no room for therapeutic nihilism in this difficult-to-place group of patients". Behavioural methods also offer positive and cost-effective outcomes, although their successful implementation requires the ability to design programmes that address complex challenging behaviour (Lindsay & Walker, 1999).

Imprisonment

Imprisonment in institutions administered by correctional services, or in some cases, police services (holding cells) or sheriffs' departments, is a very different experience from incarceration in hospitals, specialist institutions or units. The major differences lie in the fact that the facility is administered by correctional services, rather than by health or disability services, and that the aim of incarceration is primarily punitive, with perhaps lip-service paid to a rehabilitation goal, whereas a specialist residential setting *should* emphasise the goals of habilitation or rehabilitation, and therefore eschew a punitive focus. Gunn (2000) eloquently sums up the differences between prisons and health service—hospitals are better resources in possessing the staff and general paraphernalia of therapeutics, and are intended to be benign, whereas prisons are intended to be sinister and punitive, to have a deterrence function, and be a place to which no one goes voluntarily. Whether the differences exist in practice depends on the cultures of the various organisations responsible for the prisons or other places of incarceration, the influence of policies and lobby groups, and the effectiveness of review mechanisms established to ensure that the institutions meet the requirements for which they were established. Sometimes residential institutions are more punitive, dangerous and violent than prisons (Community Services Commission and Intellectual Disability Rights Service, 2001). In one residential institution investigated by the Commission, 44% of injuries sustained by residents were a result of assaults by other residents and the true prevalence could have been higher, because a further 26% of injuries had unknown causes. Staff were also the perpetrators of violence towards residents, with reports of scalding, hitting, denial of food as a punishment, and verbal abuse.

Prison seems a preferred option by comparison. In a similar vein, anecdotal evidence indicates that individuals may commit crimes in order to be sent to prison, where they can receive adequate health care, accommodation and meals; this reason for seeking to be imprisoned allegedly occurs most frequently in the United States where there is a constitutional right to health treatment in prison (Petersilia, 1997). The accuracy of these anecdotes has not often been examined empirically, however, and in any event, the imposition of a custodial sentence should be based upon sentencing principles and principles of normalisation relating to intellectual disability, and not upon soft evidence about where and whether health and other programmes might be available. In an ideal world, prisons should offer inmates with intellectual disability the programmes and resources that they need in order to avoid reoffending, and which will enhance their skills and abilities. In the USA, the ADA is creating an opportunity for intellectual disability lobby groups to ensure that appropriate programmes are available to offenders with intellectual disability. According to Petersilia (1997), public interest law firms have filed class action civil rights lawsuits against correctional facilities for their failure to apply ADA to the population of inmates with intellectual disability within those facilities.

In a comprehensive research project examining resources in prison, over 1,200 female arrestees in Cook County, Illinois, participated in a study that attempted to determine whether mentally ill women received needed services (Teplin, Abram & McClelland, 1997). While nearly one-quarter of those who were evaluated on intake as needing psychiatric service actually received them, so also did 10% of those assessed as not needing service. Particular types of psychiatric symptoms led to a greater likelihood of receiving treatment. Previous history of psychiatric treatment increased the odds of receiving treatment, as did being white and a high school graduate, whereas having two or more prior arrests reduced the chance. Compared with men, significantly fewer women received needed mental health services, possibly because women have higher rates of depression, four times that of men, and depression appeared to be under-diagnosed and under-resourced. The researchers concluded that gaols may need better intake assessment instruments, more training for correctional officers to identify serious psychiatric disorder, especially depression, better mental health and substance abuse services in the community post-release, and facilitated access to such programmes. No similar study has been located that examines the health and rehabilitation needs of prisoners with intellectual disability, although it is likely that lack of identification on admission to gaol, the need for further training for correctional officers, and greater liaison between gaol and community service provision systems would probably be the recommendations to emerge from a similar study of arrestees with intellectual disabilities.

NON-CUSTODIAL OPTIONS

Non-custodial options range from dismissal of charges without conditions, through to intermediate sanction programmes (ISPs) used in the USA (Petersilia, 1997), which are community-based programmes that are tougher than traditional parole but less stringent and expensive than prison. ISPs can include "intensive supervision, day reporting centers, house arrest, electronic monitoring, substance abuse treatment, and boot camps" (Petersilia, 1997). Petersilia maintains that these programmes have not made significant savings in public expenditure, primarily because they have been used for offenders who would have been in low-cost programmes in any case (parole or probation violators). True cost savings, she argues, can be made only when a segment of the prison population who would otherwise spend a significant length of time in prison is identified as being non-dangerous and diverted to an ISP. An ideal target group is offenders with intellectual disability. Furthermore, there is likely to be widespread public support for such alternatives.

Court Diversion

Many jurisdictions have schemes that identify accused persons with psychiatric illness at the time of the court appearance, and attempt to divert them from the criminal justice system into options that can address their illness and concomitant factors such as homelessness, lack of support, unemployment, and non-compliance with medication. Even when the defendant is not diverted (possibly owing to the nature and seriousness of the crime), identification of psychiatric illness at the court enables this information to be passed on to custodial facilities, so the defendant can obtain appropriate treatment as soon as is feasible. Few court diversion schemes for accused persons with intellectual disability exist, however.

Experience with the psychiatric court diversion schemes indicates that features of court assessment and diversionary schemes, and the category of personnel staffing of such schemes, have significant implications for defendants. A comparison of outcomes when defendants were evaluated by either a medical practitioner or a nurse found that irrespective of the personnel assessing the defendant, remands in custody were reduced, and bail was granted more often for people suffering from mental disorder, although referrals to out-patient treatment were not often followed up by the defendants. Differences between the outcomes of evaluation by the two professions were found, however. Medical practitioners were more likely than nurses to identify medical problems that needed to be brought to the attention of correctional health care services; those prisoners assessed by nurses were less likely to attend substance abuse treatment services to which they were referred, and more likely to spend longer on remand before being admitted to hospital (Chambers & Rix, 1999). Follow-up of offenders with a psychiatric diagnosis after one year shows that they tended to have unstable residential patterns, and seldom had their own home to which they could return after diversion. Employment or educational opportunities were similarly parlous, they tended to have a poor quality of life, could not look after themselves, and had few social or recreational outlets (Chung et al., 1999). Thus, diversion alone is not the only requirement; individuals who are diverted from the criminal justice system need to be followed up, and supported by a wide, flexible and responsive network of professionals, including medical practitioners, lawyers and social services (Chung et al., 1999).

The forensic diversion service established at the Birmingham (UK) court complex provides an example of the network of facilities required for such a scheme to work effectively (Chung, Cumella, Wensley & Easthope, 1998). While the focus is upon identifying and diverting offenders with psychiatric symptoms, the model could readily be adapted for offenders with intellectual disability. The aims are to identify the individual with psychiatric symptoms before the court appearance, help to decide on an appropriate response to the proceedings, and reduce unnecessary time spent in custody. Diversion can occur at point of arrest, utilising input from a community psychiatric nurse at the police station who interviews the offender, gathers information about the alleged offence and the accused's history, identifies whether the person is mentally ill, and recommends hospital or out-patient treatment. A remand prison liaison scheme forms another part of the diversion network. The community psychiatric nurse attends the prison to interview all new receptions, and identify those with psychiatric illness. The latter are then housed in the Health Care Centre in the prison, and referred for full mental health assessment with a visiting forensic psychiatrist. A bail hostel specifically for mentally ill prisoners is an alternative to remanding accused persons in custody. Residents are regularly reviewed, and alternative placements are arranged where possible and feasible. Two rooms in a 20-place hostel are available for residents with physical disabilities. Residents with unmanageable drug or alcohol problems, or who are violent, are excluded. Difficulties with the bail hostel include high staff turnover, leading to problems with establishing good relationships and adequate communication with residents, and the length of time needed to obtain reports from health professionals who have previously treated the resident. Furthermore, when a psychotic episode occurs, difficulties can be experienced in finding a hospital bed for the resident. Accused persons who are bailed can also be referred to a "landlady scheme", in which boarding houses provide a range of facilities and resources, and maintain contact with psychiatric hospitals and mental health teams. A key aspect of the scheme is the networking of the components, with the aims of improving the quality of life of the clients, increasing their independent living skills, providing better mental health care, and lowering recidivism rates.

Programmes and facilities for diversion from the criminal justice system for offenders with intellectual disabilities have been established also in various states and towns in the USA (Petersilia, 1997). These include residential programmes staffed on a 24-hour basis, living skills programmes, vocational preparation, halfway houses, and personalised justice plans that are monitored until the individual completes their sentence. Petersilia indicates that while few formal programme evaluations exist, those who operate and fund the programmes believe that they protect the public, teach offenders with intellectual disabilities to obey the law, and are cost effective.

Probation and Parole

The Lancaster County, Pennsylvania, USA, Office of Special Offender Services (SOS) was the first of its kind in the United States to address the special needs of offenders with intellectual disability (SOS also services mentally ill offenders), and has become a model for other similar projects. A ten-year evaluation has shown a consistently low recidivism rate of 5% (Wood & White, 1992). The SOS programme utilises a cooperative approach between the criminal justice and human services systems. Individual probation/parole clients are intensively supervised.

In addition SOS provides an education resource to members of the legal, educational and intellectual disability communities regarding the issues and concerns specific to these offenders. This is accomplished through conference, seminar and classroom presentations. After being placed on probation or parole supervision by a judge of the Lancaster County Court of Common Pleas, each client is accepted into the programme based on established diagnostic criteria and can be placed in one of the three units available—for juveniles or adults with intellectual disability, or for adults having mental health problems. Inter-agency cooperation is vital to the success of the programme, which incorporates aspects such as intensive supervision, medication monitoring, personal and family counselling, substance abuse programmes, psychometric assessments, and vocational training and placement assistance.

SPECIALIST REHABILITATION PROGRAMMES

Substance Abuse

While use of tobacco and alcohol may be lower among the population of people with intellectual disabilities, compared with non-disabled people in the general population, substance abuse is prevalent among offenders with an intellectual disability; within the population of people with an intellectual disability the likelihood of offending is increased if the individual is dependent upon substances or uses illicit drugs (Winter, Holland & Collins, 1997). In one study of a group of defendants with intellectual disability, more than half reported a problem with alcohol, usually over about 10 years (Hayes, 1994). Various research studies indicate that between two-thirds and three-quarters of defendants with intellectual disability indicate that they had consumed alcohol at the time of the offence (Hayes, 1994, 1996). Substance abuse is not confined to offenders with intellectual disability, of course. Research in Florida found that 74% of inmates consecutively admitted to a prison reception centre had a history of substance abuse or dependence disorders at some time during their life, and more than half were diagnosed as such in the 30 days prior to incarceration (Peters, Greenbaum, Edens, Carter & Ortiz, 1998). People with intellectual disabilities are consuming as much alcohol as non-disabled people, prior to engaging in behaviour which brings them to the attention of the police (Hayes, 1994, 1996). Up until the early 1990s, alcohol appeared to be the most frequent substance abused by this group, with outcome behaviours typically including aggression, binge drinking, memory loss and blackouts. Clinical experience since then points to an increase in illicit drug use generally by offenders with an intellectual disability, with marijuana, heroin, cocaine and amphetamines now being used; users state that they want to feel confident and forget their worries. Substance abuse is linked to violence in both people with mental conditions and those without any mental health diagnosis (Gunn, 1998), and therefore cannot be overlooked as an important area for therapeutic intervention for crime and recidivism prevention among defendants with intellectual disability.

A survey of staff in alcohol and drug treatment programmes in Canada found a need for specialist services and extra training for staff, in order to assist people with intellectual disability and substance abuse problems (Tyas & Rush, 1993). A major difficulty for a client with intellectual disability is lack of insight and executive functioning enabling comprehension of the importance of engaging in a programme; staff find it almost impossible to achieve gains when clients are uncooperative or unwilling, or fail to present to the programme (Clarke & Wilson, 1999). In some cases, the court may make attendance at a substance abuse programme a condition of parole, to ensure compliance. On the other hand, if the client then fails to attend, he or she may be regarded as having breached the conditions of their parole, with serious outcomes. Community-based sentences with conditions must take care not to set the clients up to fail.

Therapeutic Interventions

Multi-systemic therapy (MST) has been used with success with violent and chronic juvenile offenders (Bourdin, 1999), although evaluation of its use with juveniles with intellectual disability has not been located. MST interventions target child and family problems related to the multiple systems in which family members are embedded, including home, school, neighbourhood and peer group. Interventions occur at the levels of family, peer, school and individual child, using treatment strategies derived from strategic family therapy, structural family therapy, behavioural parent training and cognitive-behavioural therapy. MST is claimed to be comprehensive and flexible in addressing the multiple determinants of delinquent behaviour. As is the case with other effective and early interventions, MST is costly in terms of expertise (masters level therapists are utilised) and caseloads (four to eight families per therapist), in order to demonstrate long-term reductions in criminal activity, violent offences, drug-related arrests and incarceration.

Along similar lines, although targeting youths who have been removed from the family home rather than attempting to preserve residence at home, the effectiveness of multi-dimensional therapeutic foster care (MTFC) has been compared with group care (GC) for chronic juvenile offenders (Chamberlain & Reid, 1998). MTFC integrates multiple intervention modes, including individual and family therapy, and social skills training, in multiple domains such as family, school and peer group. The community families in the MTFC intervention were trained in the use of behaviour management techniques (see Chamberlain & Reid, 1998, for details). The MTFC intervention produced more favourable results, with boys truanting from the programme less often, completing the requirements more often, and returning to detention or training schools less frequently. They had fewer criminal referrals and self-reported delinquent acts, including serious or violent crime. The authors state firmly that the lynchpins in the programme (which has been conducted for over 15 years) are the foster parents, who are carefully selected, trained and supported.

Sex Offenders

Sex offenders with intellectual disability typically have confused self-concepts, poor peer relations, a lack of sexual and socio-sexual knowledge, and a lack of personal power (Hudson, Nankervis, Smith & Phillips, 1999). Furthermore, they are likely to have been sexually abused, including being raped in institutions or by family members. An important diagnostic issue in assessing and treating this group is whether the behaviour can be diagnosed as paraphilia, or is instead a reflection of the individual's functional age (Hayes, 1991). Research indicates a higher preva- lence of sex offences as a proportion of all offences committed by people with an intellectual disability, compared with the rate of sex offending among non-disabled offenders; furthermore, recidivism rates are high (Law, Lindsay, Quinn & Smith, 2000). These authors followed up clients of a service for sex offenders with an in- tellectual disability, finding that reoffending was more likely when treatment was unexpectedly terminated for some reason (including lack of cooperation by the client), and shorter periods of intervention were significantly less effective than treatment for two or more years. Lindsay, Olley, Baillie and Smith (1999) reported the outcome of a cognitive behavioural psychotherapy group for four adolescent males with intellectual disability who had offended against children. A primary issue was the lack of motivation for change, so that effort needed to be put into building up the cohesion of the group and encouraging insight into the offend- ing behaviour. Compulsory attendance and accurate feedback were crucial, and with all these features, any impact on issues related to denial of intent or denial of responsibility took 6–9 months of treatment.

Group treatments for non-disabled sex offenders based on a broad cognitive- behavioural model have led to effective treatment programmes. The technique has been applied with success to sex offenders with intellectual disability (Sinclair & Murphy, 2000), over one year, during 50 sessions. Using baseline measures that in- clude both mainstream sex-offender and specific intellectual disability measures, the results indicate that treatment was effective in impacting on cognitive and social skills measures. Cognitive-behaviour therapy as a treatment option for of- fenders with intellectual disability was also used in the Brooklands Sex Offender Treatment Programme, which evolved from a collaboration between HM Prison Service, UK, and a team of health professionals who specialise in working with this type of offender (Hordell et al., 2000). The treatment programme consists of 12 modules aimed at understanding the offence cycle and challenging cognitive dis- tortions as well as addressing relapse prevention strategies. The results emphasise the continuing support needs of the men.

Taylor (2000) reported on the Northgate Sex Offender Project, a multi-faceted treatment programme administered to five men with intellectual disabilities and convictions for sexual aggression detained in low-security facilities within a spe- cialist forensic service in the North East of England. Following successful comple- tion of a *Pre-Treatment* phase of intervention (12 sessions) aimed at desensitising participants to work in a group setting, and then a second 18-session *Intermediate* phase of group therapy that encouraged them to discuss more personal issues and emotional difficulties, including stress, anger and sadness, patients moved into the *Offence-Specific* phase of treatment (approximately 50 sessions). Before and imme- diately following this phase of work, participants were assessed by independent raters in relation to six specific treatment targets: (a) acceptance of guilt; (b) ac- knowledgement of personal responsibility for their offences; (c) understanding of victim issues; (d) victim empathy; (e) understanding of high-risk elements in their offence cycles; and (f) acceptance of risk of future offending. In all six target areas the group's mean scores improved markedly following treatment. In five of the six target areas the group's mean scores were at either a "satisfactory" or "better than expected" level post-treatment. Only for acceptance of risk of future offending did the group's mean score fall just below a satisfactory level following treatment.

Innovative research (Brown & Stein, 1997) compared cases of sexual abuse of adults with intellectual disabilities perpetrated by men with intellectual disabilities, with those committed by other male perpetrators. Consistent with other research, this study indicated that men with intellectual disabilities offend against more male victims than non-disabled sex offenders and that their offences are somewhat less serious. The authors comment that "peer abuse" is a widespread problem, which service agencies have failed to address; repeated offences are frequent and lack of appropriate intervention is the norm. Therefore, in any programme for sex offenders with intellectual disability, one of the major aims must be to protect participants against abuse from other participants.

Research about the most effective strategies for programmes aimed at sex offenders with intellectual disabilities is inconclusive, possibly owing in part to the diverse aetiology. It is clear that brief interventions are unlikely to be effective, that cognitive-behavioural techniques are useful, and that a multi-disciplinary approach, and long-term support and follow-up are essential.

Challenging Behaviour

Challenging behaviour encompasses many aspects of problematical behaviour in people with intellectual disability, but in this context, the focus is upon behaviour that leads to contact with the criminal justice system, and threatens the individual's ability to continue to reside in the community and access community resources. It has been estimated that 19% of people with intellectual disability have challenging behaviour, and a third of these have hard-to-manage behaviour (Joyce, Ditchfield & Harris, 2001). The same authors found an apparent over-representation of people with intellectual disability and challenging behaviour among Black minority groups in the UK. Families, staff and co-residents bear the brunt of challenging behaviour, which can result in significant stress. Interpersonal aggression is clearly a major cause of charges of assault, manslaughter or murder. Programmes to manage aggressive behaviour in people with intellectual disability can encounter difficulties owing to the disparate nature of the causes of the aggression, ranging from effects of organic brain damage, to substance abuse, to modelling on familial violence and abuse, through to poor socialisation. Research exploring the differences between aggressive and non-aggressive people with intellectual disability has found that a vulnerable sense of self contributes to aggression (Jahoda, Pert, Squire & Trower, 1998). Those individuals who perceived that they were being treated as if they were stupid or intellectually disabled were more likely to respond aggressively in interpersonal situations. Understanding the nature of the individual's self-perceptions may provide valuable insight into what may otherwise be regarded as unpredictable outbursts.

Medication, frequently used in mental hospitals and prisons to control behaviour, appears to be of little use for offenders with intellectual disability. A review of research on the effectiveness of anti-psychotic medication for people with intellectual disability and challenging behaviour provided no evidence as to whether anti-psychotic medication does or does not help these individuals (Brylewski & Duggan, 1999). Only eight randomised controlled trials could be included in the review, and the authors concluded that good quality research is urgently needed.

This is not an appropriate forum for a detailed discussion and analysis of the design of programmes to address challenging behaviour in offenders with intellectual disability (see, for example, Xenitidis *et al.*, 1999). It is important to note, however, that these programmes must be designed, implemented and monitored by specialist staff experienced in the area. Programmes need to be designed for each individual, after collection of appropriate baseline data, and to continue for as long as is necessary to address the behaviours, rather than be time limited according to waiting lists and cost. The programme must be reinforced periodically, on a long-term basis, and an important key is coordination of all of the systems and services which assist the individual.

Psychiatric Illness and Treatment

The presence of psychiatric illness can create extra problems for a client by exerting an effect upon behaviour, reasoning, memory, social and adaptive skills, and motivation. Studies on prevalence of psychiatric illness in this group have found rates between 13% and 37%. Most epidemiological studies find that the rate of psychiatric diagnosis among people with intellectual disability is higher than in the general population, however (Deb & Weston, 2000). A higher rate of dual diagnosis of intellectual disability and psychiatric illness has been found among offending populations (Hayes, 1994). Making an accurate diagnosis of psychiatric illness in a person with an intellectual disability is complex, partly owing to their communication impairments, and lack of ability to recognise and articulate the nature of their symptoms. Very few professionals are expert in the combined fields of psychiatric illness and intellectual disability, and therefore one aspect of the diagnosis may often be overlooked. The difficulty can be further confounded by drug or alcohol abuse. Specialist diagnostic instruments have been developed to assist in recognising psychiatric symptoms in people with intellectual disabilities (Deb & Weston, 2000). While the full spectrum of psychiatric diagnoses occurs in this population, the most frequent are schizophrenia, organic brain disorders, adjustment disorders (including conduct disorders), affective disorders, psychosexual disorders, personality disorders and anxiety disorders. Males and females are affected in almost equal proportions. In the prison population, however, females have been found to have a higher rate of dual diagnosis (Hayes & McIlwain, 1988), possibly because of the fact that when a woman receives a custodial sentence there are often extra factors present that the court takes into account, such as violent and unpredictable behaviour related to psychiatric symptoms.

An advantage of de-institutionalisation was touted to be reduction in levels of challenging behaviour, but research findings appear to be equivocal. While almost all studies show significant improvements in adaptive behaviour, not all report significant improvements in challenging behaviour (Kim, Larson & Lakin, 2001). De-institutionalisation and improved living conditions for people with intellectual disability may not solve problems connected with their mental health. Instead an increase in behavioural problems has been noted, and this group receives less qualified help from psychiatric and psychological specialist services once they reside in the community (Nottestad & Linaker, 1999). These researchers concluded that the institutional environment itself does not necessarily cause challenging behaviour and mental health problems, and de-institutionalisation should not be regarded as a substitute for psychiatric and psychological services. No research has been located about whether a similar situation exists for those who are released after imprisonment. Gunn (1998) comments on the apparent lack of major therapeutic activity for mentally ill offenders in the criminal justice system, a situation that is likely to be even more parlous for those with a dual diagnosis.

RELEASE INTO THE COMMUNITY

Release into the community after imprisonment or as diversion from a custodial sentence needs to be managed carefully, if the individuals are to avoid reoffending. Training in community living skills appears to be optimum when carried out in a community situation rather than in a classroom setting. Adequate time must be spent developing independent living skills, with the optimum time frame being two years (Lindsay, Smith & Michie, 2000). Mentally disordered offenders who are released into the community or diverted from the criminal justice system tend to have transient living patterns, poor quality of life, no employment or educational programmes, and turbulent life experiences (Chung et al., 1999). They usually keep in touch with a general practitioner, but not with specialist medical practitioners, despite high prevalence of psychiatric symptoms. Few receive support from social services. The implications of these data are that integration of correctional and community services and resources is vital. The mission statement of the Texas Council on Offenders with Mental Impairments (TCOMI) provides a good summary:

> [TCOMI aims to] provide a formal structure for criminal justice, health and human service, and other affected organizations to communicate and coordinate on policy, legislative, and programmatic issues affecting offenders with special needs [including those with] mental retardation (Kifowit, 2002).

SUMMARY AND CONCLUSIONS

Expressing opinions about psychiatrically ill offenders that can equally be applied in the realm of intellectual disability, an increasing number of commentators are concerned that "quietly but steadily, jails and prisons are replacing public mental hospitals as the primary purveyors of public psychiatric services for individuals with serious mental illnesses" (Torrey, 1995). Furthermore, Torrey stated, "the most sobering side of gaol diversion . . . is the assumption that there are public psychiatric services to which the mentally ill individual can be diverted. This, as many law enforcement officials have learnt, frequently is not the case". Gunn (2000) speculates upon the style of political administration that allows prisons rather than mental hospitals to be the preferred placement for people with mental disorders. Gunn (2000) suggests that the following four factors influence administrative style (pp. 334–5) (the emphasis on intellectual disability rather than mental disorder has been added here):

1. Public panic about the dangerousness of people with intellectual disabilities is part of the age-old stigmatisation of those who are different. The fear of unpredictable behaviour can be readily manipulated by the media.
2. Prison may be perceived by politicians and civil servants as a cheaper option than other forms of management for offenders with intellectual disability.
3. The "death of liberalism" that has occurred since the 1960s and 1970s reflects a socio-political attitudinal change towards caring less and condemning more (in the words of the former British Prime Minister, John Major, cited by Gunn). Inadequate funding for intellectual disability is a basic form of discrimination, and a potent example of society caring less for its vulnerable members.
4. The attitudes of caring professionals have changed in a similar direction, so that some clients are regarded as untreatable, or too difficult, or difficult to like. As Gunn emphasises, the clients who are "untreatable" do not disappear, and have to be looked after by other agencies, including corrective services.

While prison may not be consciously selected as the cheaper option to adequate preventative and community services, the decision is made by default when inadequate funding is devoted to the latter two alternatives. Corrective services claim that they cannot turn away those who arrive at their gates, unlike other systems, where there is some choice and voluntariness on the part of participants. If, however, corrective services placed a cap on the numbers in gaols, and insisted that governments find alternative options for all but the most violent and dangerous offenders, the community would probably not tolerate the apparent lawlessness that would result, as increased numbers of homeless and substance abusing people with mental illnesses and intellectual disabilities appeared on the streets. Compassion as well as distaste would dictate that other options be designed and funded. Loading up the prisons with these difficult members of society is a conscious choice that is made at some level in government and political circles, and yet, as the data cited above demonstrate, this is not the cheap option that politicians and civil servants believe it to be.

The issue of provision of alternatives to prison has been addressed judicially. In *R. v. Roadley* (in Victoria, Australia) a critical requirement for diversion out of the criminal justice system into a community-based option was supported accommodation. Such accommodation could not be provided to this offender with an intellectual disability, however, owing to a lack of any vacant accommodation and a dearth of funds to acquire any additional accommodation. The judge commented:

> It was made plain to the court that budgetary restraints operate to defeat substantially the declared worthy aims and aspirations of the legislation ... Disappointingly the Justice Plan concludes with these words of despair: "The Department [of Community Services, Victoria] is unable to propose a viable plan for Terry Roadley ... It is not the curial system but the community which must be held answerable".

His Honour quoted from the judgement in *R. v. Clarke*:

> Her Majesty's Courts are not dustbins into which the social services can sweep difficult members of the public. Still less should Her Majesty's judges use their sentencing powers to dispose of those who are socially inconvenient. If the Courts became disposers of those who are socially inconvenient the road ahead would lead to the destruction of liberty. It should be clearly understood that Her Majesty's judges stand on that road barring the way.

The quality of the care and services, both in the prison and the community, that are available to offenders with intellectual disability is variable and idiosyncratic, differing greatly between localities even within the same nation. A Canadian study comments on the parlous state of prison health services in that nation (Ford & Wobeser, 2000), concluding that "the broad issue of health care in prisons is too important to be left to prison administrators". The authors call for "rigorous national standards for accreditation of health care facilities in prisons, adequate funding to allow those standards to be met and supervisory bodies (independent of prison authorities) . . . to ensure compliance". Especially in prisons, programmes for inmates with intellectual disability can be *ad hoc*, dependent upon the skill, expertise and interest of possibly one staff member, inadequately evaluated and documented, lacking in professional and scientific rigour, and of little use to the participants except as a time-filler. The scarcity of scientific evaluation of the effectiveness of programmes for offenders with intellectual disability is apparent from reviews of the literature. Accreditation of programmes for offenders with intellectual disability is essential, whether the programmes be in prisons, special hospitals or institutions, residential settings, or day attendance centres. Only in this way will standards be set and adhered to, outcomes evaluated, and progress determined. The President's Committee on Mental Retardation recommends that alternative pathways should promote choices that are very flexible and highly individualised. The diversion programmes must be able to be accessed by judges, probation officials and law enforcement personnel, rather than hidden away and known to only a few specialist agencies. Service brokerage and flexible funds to pay for essential supports should be available, administered in a genuinely cooperative manner through all of the relevant government agencies. A system of court-appointed special advocates should be established to ensure that the individual with intellectual disability understands their rights and is aware of the available supports, while others in the criminal justice system are educated concerning the issues relating to people with intellectual disability in the criminal justice system (President's Committee on Mental Retardation, 1999).

Despair saps the hope of offenders with intellectual disability, their families and carers, and the professionals who attempt to improve their plight. Thirty years have passed since a comprehensive outline of the requirements for a system of diversion from the criminal justice system was first proposed (Menolascino, 1974) and yet little change has been effected that can substantially improve the lot of this group. A cynical community and its politicians have moved away from a caring perspective. Those who care passionately about the fate of people with intellectual disability in the criminal justice system continue to try to turn around the juggernaut of inequitable funding.

What we call despair is often only the painful eagerness of unfed hope.

George Eliot

REFERENCES

Barnfield, T.V. & Leathem, J.M. (1998). Neuropsychological outcomes of traumatic brain injury and substance abuse in a New Zealand prison population. *Brain Injury*, **12**, 951–62.

Bourdin, C.M. (1999). Multisystemic treatment of criminality and violence in adolescents. *Journal of the American Academy of Child and Adolescent Psychiatry*, **38**, 242–9.

Brown, H. & Stein, J. (1997). Sexual abuse perpetrated by men with intellectual disabilities: a comparative study. *Journal of Intellectual Disability Research*, **4**, 215–24.

Brylewski, J. & Duggan, L. (1999). Antipsychotic medication for challenging behaviour in people with intellectual disability: a systematic review of randomized controlled trials. *Journal of Intellectual Disability Research*, **43**, 360–71.

Buchanan, A. (1998). Criminal conviction after discharge from special (high security) hospital. Incidence in the first 10 years. *British Journal of Psychiatry*, **172**, 472–6.

Butwell, M., Jamieson, E., Leese, M. & Taylor, P. (2000). Trends in special (high-security) hospitals: 2: Residency and discharge episodes, 1986–1995. *British Journal of Psychiatry*, **176**, 260–5.

Chamberlain, P. & Reid, J.B. (1998). Comparison of two community alternatives to incarceration for chronic juvenile offenders. *Journal of Consulting and Clinical Psychology*, **66**, 624–33.

Chambers, C. & Rix, K.J. (1999). A controlled evaluation of assessments by doctors and nurses in a magistrates' court mental health assessment and diversion scheme. *Medicine, Science, and the Law*, **39**, 38–48.

Chung, M.C., Cumella, S., Wensley, J. & Easthope, Y. (1998). A description of a forensic diversion service in one city in the United Kingdom. *Medicine, Science, and the Law*, **38**, 242–50.

Chung, M.C., Cumella, S., Wensley, J. & Easthope, Y. (1999). A follow-up study of mentally disordered offenders after a court diversion scheme: six-month and one-year comparison. *Medicine, Science, and the Law*, **39**, 31–7.

Clarke, J.J. & Wilson, D.N. (1999). Alcohol problems and intellectual disability. *Journal of Intellectual Disability Research*, **4**, 135–9.

Community Services Commission and Intellectual Disability Rights Service (2001). *Crime Prevention in Residential Services for People with Disabilities. A Discussion Paper*. Sydney: Community Services Commission.

Deb, S. & Weston, S.N. (2000). Psychiatric illness and mental retardation. *Current Opinion in Psychiatry*, **13**, 497–505.

Dockrell, J.E., Gaskell, G. Normand, C. & Rehman, H. (1995). An economic evaluation of hospital-based specialised housing for people with learning disabilities and challenging behaviour. *Social Science and Medicine*, **7**, 895–901.

Everingham, S. (1998). Crime prevention: the costs and benefits. Paper presented at the Crime Prevention through Social Support Conference, Sydney.

Exworthy, T. (2000). Secure psychiatric services. *Current Opinion in Psychiatry*, **13**, 581–5.

Ford, P.M. & Wobeser, W.L. (2000). Health care problems in prisons. *Canadian Medical Association Journal*, **162**(5), 664–5.

Greenwood, P.W., Model, K.E., Rydell, C.P. & Chiesa, J. (1998). *Diverting Children from a Life of Crime. Measuring Costs and Benefits*. Santa Monica, CA: RAND.

Gudjonsson, G., Rabe-Hesketh, S. & Wilson, C. (2000). Violent incidents on a medium secure unit: the target of assault and the management of incidents. *Journal of Forensic Psychiatry*, **11**, 105–18.

Gunn, J. (1998). Forensic psychiatry at a crossroads. *Current Opinion in Psychiatry*, **11**, 661–2.

Gunn, J. (2000). Future directions for treatment in forensic psychiatry. *British Journal of Psychiatry*, **176**, 332–8.

Hayes, S. (1991). Sex offenders. *Australian and New Zealand Journal of Developmental Disabilities*, **17**, 221–7.

Hayes, S.C. (1994). *Intellectually disabled offenders – characteristics and psychological assessment*. Paper presented at the First International Congress on Mental Retardation, Rome.

Hayes, S.C. (1996). *People with an Intellectual Disability and the Criminal Justice System: Two Rural Courts* (5). Sydney: New South Wales Law Reform Commission.

Hayes, S.C. (2000). *Hayes Ability Screening Index (HASI) Manual*. Sydney: Behavioural Sciences in Medicine, University of Sydney.

Hayes, S.C. & Craddock, G. (1992). *Simply Criminal*, 2nd edn. Sydney: Federation Press.

Hayes, S.C. & McIlwain, D. (1988). *The Prevalence of Intellectual Disability in the New South Wales Prison Population: An Empirical Study*. Canberra: Criminology Research Council.

Hordell, A., Hill, J., Forshaw, N., Bendall, S., Hipkins, R. & Robinson, D. (2000). Cognitive behavioural treatment of male sex offenders with intellectual disability [abstract]. *Journal of Intellectual Disability Research*, **44**, 324.

Hudson, A., Nankervis, K., Smith, D. & Phillips, A. (1999). *Identifying the Risks. Prevention of Sexual Offending Amongst Adolescents with an Intellectual Disability*. Melbourne: Research Unit, DisAbility Services Division, Victorian Department of Human Services.

Jahoda, A., Pert, C., Squire, J. & Trower, P. (1998). Facing stress and conflict: a comparison of the predicted responses and self-concepts of aggressive and non-aggressive people with intellectual disability. *Journal of Intellectual Disability Research*, **42**, 360–9.

Jamieson, E., Butwell, M., Taylor, P. & Leese, M. (2000). Trends in special (high-security) hospitals: 1: Referrals and admissions. *British Journal of Psychiatry*, **176**, 253–9.

Joyce, T., Ditchfield, H. & Harris, P. (2001). Challenging behaviour in community services. *Journal of Intellectual Disability Research*, **45**, 130–8.

Kifowit, D. (2002). *Mission*. Retrieved 1 May 2002 from Texas Council on offenders with Mental Impairments website: http://www.tdcj.state.tx.us/tcomi/tcomi-home.htm.

Kim, S., Larson, S. & Lakin, K.C. (2001). Behavioural outcomes of deinstitutionalisation for people with intellectual disability: a review of US studies conducted between 1980 and 1999. *Journal of Intellectual and Developmental Disability*, **26**, 35–50.

Law, J., Lindsay, W.R., Quinn, K. & Smith, A.H.W. (2000). Outcome evaluation of 161 people with mild intellectual disabilities who have offending or challenging behaviour [abstract]. *Journal of Intellectual Disability Research*, **44**, 360–1.

Lindsay, W., Olley, S., Baillie, N. & Smith, A. (1999). Treatment of adolescent sex offenders with intellectual disabilities. *Mental Retardation*, **37**, 201–11.

Lindsay, W.R., Smith, A.H.W. & Michie, A. (2000). Successful community integration following community living skills training: a controlled study [abstract]. *Journal of Intellectual Disability Research*, **44**, 368.

Lindsay, W.R. & Walker, B. (1999). Advances in behavioural methods in intellectual disability. *Current Opinion in Psychiatry*, **12**, 561–5.

Luckasson, R. (1999). *Crimes Against People with Developmental Disabilities*. Washington, DC: National Research Council.

Martin, H.P. (1982). Abused children – what happens eventually. In R.K. Oates (ed.) *Child Abuse. A Community Concern* (pp. 154–75). Sydney: Butterworth.

McGee, J.J. & Menolascino, F.J. (1992). The evaluation of defendants with mental retardation in the criminal justice system. In R.W. Conley, R. Luckasson & G.N. Bouthilet (eds) *The Criminal Justice System and Mental Retardation. Defendants and Victims* (pp. 55–77). Baltimore, MD: Paul Brookes.

Menolascino, F.J. (1974). The mentally retarded offender. *Mental Retardation*, **12**, 7–11.

National Crime Prevention (1996). *Pathways to Prevention: Developmental and Early Intervention Approaches to Crime in Australia*. Canberra: National Crime Prevention, Attorney-General's Department, Commonwealth of Australia.

New South Wales Parliament (1999). *First Report of the Inquiry into Crime Prevention through Social Support*. Sydney: NSW Parliamentary Standing Committee on Law and Justice.

Nottestad, J.A. & Linaker, O.M. (1999). Psychiatric health needs and services before and after complete deinstitutionalization of people with intellectual disability. *Journal of Intellectual Disability Research*, **43**, 523–30.

Peters, R.H., Greenbaum, P.E., Edens, J.F., Carter, C.R. & Ortiz, M.M. (1998). Prevalence of DSM-IV substance abuse and dependence disorders among prison inmates. *American Journal of Drug and Alcohol Abuse*, **24**, 573–87.

Petersilia, J. (1997). Unequal justice? Offenders with mental retardation in prison. *Corrections Management Quarterly*, **1**, 36–44.

Petersilia, J. (2000). *Doing Justice? The Criminal Justice System and Offenders with Developmental Disabilities*. University of California, Irvine.

President's Committee on Mental Retardation (1999). *The Forgotten Generation*. Washington, DC: President's Committee on Mental Retardation.

R. *v*. Clarke (1975). 61 Cr App R 320 at 323, per Lawton LJ.

R. *v*. Roadley (1990). 51 A Crim R 336, Victorian Court of Criminal Appeal.

Rangecroft, M.E.H., Tyrer, S.P. & Berney, T.P. (1997). The use of seclusion and emergency medication in a hospital for people with learning disability. *British Journal of Psychiatry*, **170**, 273–7.

Shaw, J., Creed, F., Price, J., Huxley, P. & Tomenson, B. (1999). Prevalence and detection of serious psychiatric disorder in defendants attending court. *Lancet*, **353**, 1053–6.

Sinclair, N. & Murphy, G. (2000). Preliminary results from a treatment group for men with intellectual disability who sexually offend [abstract]. *Journal of Intellectual Disability Research*, **44**, 466.

Skuse, D., Bentovim, A., Hodges, J., Stevenson, J., Andreou, C., Lanyado, M., New, M., Williams, B. & McMillan, D. (1998). Risk factors for development of sexually abusive behaviour in sexually victimised adolescent boys: cross sectional study. *British Medical Journal*, **317**, 175–9.

Taylor, J.L. (2000). Northgate sex offender project [abstract]. *Journal of Intellectual Disability Research*, **44**, 483–4.

Taylor, P., Goldberg, E., Leese, M., Butwell, M. & Reed, A. (1999). Limits to the value of mental health review tribunals for offender patients: suggestions for reform. *British Journal of Psychiatry*, **174**, 164–9.

Taylor, P.J., Leese, M., Williams, D., Butwell, M., Daly, R. & Larkin, E. (1998). Mental disorder and violence. A special (high security) hospital study. *British Journal of Psychiatry*, **172**, 218–26.

Teplin, L.A., Abram, K.M. & McClelland, G.M. (1997). Mentally disordered women in jail: who receives services? *American Journal of Public Health*, **87**, 604–9.

Torrey, E.F. (1995). Jails and prisons – America's new mental hospitals. *American Journal of Public Health*, **85**, 1611–13.

Tyas, S. & Rush, B. (1993). The treatment of disabled persons with alcohol and drug problems: results of a survey of addiction services. *Journal of Studies on Alcohol*, **54**, 275–82.

White, J., Moffitt, T.E. & Silva, P.A. (1989). A prospective replication of the protective effects of IQ in subjects at high risk for juvenile delinquency. *Journal of Clinical and Consulting Psychology*, **57**, 719–24.

Winter, N., Holland, A.J. & Collins, S. (1997). Factors predisposing to suspected offending by adults with self-reported learning disabilities. *Psychological Medicine*, **27**, 595–607.

Wood, H.R. & White, D.L. (1992). A model for habilitation and prevention for offenders with mental retardation. The Lancaster County (PA) Office of Special Offenders Services. In R.W. Conley, R. Luckasson & G.N. Bouthilet (eds) *The Criminal Justice System and Mental Retardation. Defendants and Victims* (pp. 153–65). Baltimore, MD: Paul H. Brookes.

Woods, P. & Mason, T. (1998). Mental impairment and admission to a special hospital. *British Journal of Developmental Disabilities*, **44**, 119–31.

Xenitidis, K.I., Henry, J., Russell, A.J., Ward, A. & Murphy, D.G.M. (1999). An inpatient treatment model for adults with mild intellectual disability and challenging behaviour. *Journal of Intellectual Disability Research*, **43**, 128–34.

Chapter 5

HOW CAN SERVICES BECOME MORE ETHICAL?

JENNIFER CLEGG

University of Nottingham and Nottinghamshire Healthcare NHS Trust, Nottingham, UK

INTRODUCTION

Sean Walton was committed to Moss Side High Security Hospital in England aged 15½ years following an allegation of indecent assault on a four-year-old girl which he admitted. He said he knew it was wrong, but did not know why he had done it. No trial took place. Prior to the index offence Sean had been a minor delinquent with only one suggestion of sexual disinhibition. An inquiry concluded that the severity of his mental impairment had been overestimated while the presence of a treatable psychotic illness had been missed, because there was no evidence of further psychosis once he became settled on medication following his admission to hospital. However, by that time he had developed antisocial sexual behaviour and coprophagia, which made him difficult to manage. Three requests for multi-disciplinary assessment of these behaviours were made during case conferences, but no assessment was carried out nor was a therapeutic care plan developed.

The evening before he died Sean was found in the toilets attempting to sexually assault a fellow resident. Although staff argued the decision to make him mop the toilet floor was not a punishment, that they had merely deleted the explanation that this was to "cool his ardour" from the record in case it was misconstrued, the Inquiry did consider this inappropriate punishment of a vulnerable man. Sean then hit the supervising nursing assistant with the mop. A number of different accounts were obtained about precursors of that event. Nurses had either not seen it or described the assault as unprovoked. A number of residents said that Sean's attack occurred after the supervising nurse had kicked over his bucket a number of times, on each occasion making Sean re-mop the floor. That nurse was said to often act in this way. One resident also stated that the nurse had assaulted Sean with a snooker cue first, although that account was considered unreliable. Whatever the events, Sean was secluded at 20:00 hours. He was found dead at 13:00 hours

Offenders with Developmental Disabilities. Edited by W.L. Lindsay, J.L. Taylor and P. Sturmey.
© 2004 John Wiley & Sons, Ltd.

the following day. Doubts were cast on how regularly staff had checked his well-being when records were found to have been made in advance of behaviour. The seclusion book had "remains disturbed and unpredictable" recorded against most entries including for the three hours after he was found dead. The Committee of Inquiry (HMSO, 1992) concluded:

> Sean Walton's miserable existence was, at best, unrelieved by his inappropriate placement and by his stay for $4\frac{1}{2}$ years at Moss Side Hospital; at worst, it was made more wretched by the inferior service of care and treatment supplied by management and staff.

Some may argue this occurred a decade ago and that services have been reviewed and reorganised to prevent recurrence. I find it very recent, and it gives me cause to reflect. Indeed, the Committee recommended all staff should read its four detailed case histories and they certainly lay bare ethical issues for scrutiny. There is committal without trial, in a system both offenders and professionals consider arbitrary, although there is not space to consider that here. There is the problem of how to ensure staff in closed environments provide minimum control and maximum care. Managers must strike a balance between assuming staff to be trustworthy, and being able to identify those who are not. There is also the problem of confused responsibility when no individual or profession can hold all the answers.

Yet the dreadful stories of demeaning practices go beyond mere problems of management and leadership; they make the reader wonder how a "therapeutic" service could sink to this. Dismissing, striking off and/or taking the offending staff to court cannot of itself ensure that the desired therapeutic service will follow. Perhaps the answer to how staff can sink so low lies in understanding how people survive working in such environments at all. After all, these settings have repeatedly demonstrated their capacity to blunt if not brutalise residents and staff alike. What help do care staff get to develop and hold onto the beliefs in human goodness and resourcefulness that are the hallmarks of effective change agents?

So this chapter does not address the dramatic and casuistic dilemmas that have come to be understood as the province of ethicists. There are to be none of the flow diagrams, nor rules of thumb for decision making, familiar from bioethics; nor heartfelt pleas about the autonomy or empowerment of people with intellectual disability. I have started with Sean Walton's story even though many services for offenders occur in the community, because it illustrates not only the depths of malpractice but the problems encountered when trying to change them. The breach lay in all of the everyday relationships that created the context of Sean Walton's life; yet changing the moral context of such practices is self-endangering. I will argue that ethics are as relevant to our relationships with colleagues as they are to clients, and that being willing to wade repeatedly into such dangerous waters is what ethical integrity requires.

THEORETICAL STANDPOINTS

Ethical codes published by professional bodies generally imply there is one perspective that provides certainty on matters of behaviour. This position has been criticised by philosophers. O'Donohue and Mangold (1996) characterised the APA code of conduct as "A series of bald, undefended, un-argued, authoritarian fiats" (p. 377). Ethics imposed by rule in such codes protect the public by specifying minimum standards, but fail to support the debate and reflectiveness needed to develop ethical responses to complex clinical situations. That requires a move to a greater level of sophistication, by understanding the range of different types of theories and positions described by ethicists.

Honderich (1995) distinguishes three major groups or schools of ethical theorising: (1) deontological, (2) teleological and (3) virtue ethics. Deontological theories prescribe the ethical act by drawing on different frameworks such as religious creeds or rationalist positions. They are often described as theories of duty. By contrast, teleological theories are future-oriented, and might (somewhat simplistically) be described as theories of rights. They too focus on actions but, unlike deontological theories, which identify right actions irrespective of consequences, teleological theories identify right actions as those that bring a theoretically ideal state closer. Theories of justice comprise a significant proportion of teleological approaches to ethics, because most laws and rights are intended to create a more just society. Utilitarianism is the other main branch of teleological theorising, because "the greatest good to the greatest number" (and of course what is construed to be "good" is itself the focus of considerable theorising) also intends to improve society.

Virtue ethics takes a different position from both deonotological and teleological theories. It focuses on the way people are with each other, in networks of relationships that endure through time to comprise ethical communities. It is an Aristotelian position interpreted for the twentieth century by MacIntyre (1985, 1999), and applied to learning disability by Reinders (2000). There is concern for practical action but the right thing to do is secondary to, and dependent upon, the ethical relationships that contextualise the particular situation. From this perspective it is an error to conceptualise ethics from a solely individual perspective in the way that deontological theories do, for example, when theorising duty. It is also an error to imagine that adherence to the bioethical principles of autonomy, beneficence, justice, and non-maleficence can identify the right action for a particular situation. These medical ethics principles (Beauchamp & Childress, 2001) derive from fragments of different ethical theories, and are considered by many ethicists to be conceptually incoherent and thus of questionable utility (see, for example, Reinders, 2000). Medical ethics' advocacy of autonomy is a key assumption of liberal individualism, questioned by virtue theorists. I will develop that point after the substance of virtue ethics has been outlined.

MacIntyre (1985) regards human events as so complex and uncertain that it is impossible to prescribe the ethical act. He argued that in "real life . . . moving one's knight to QB3 may always be replied to with a lob across the net" (p. 98). Instead, virtue ethics provides a conceptual basis for understanding how to develop and support ethical persons and create an ethical society. These persons will know how to reflect upon or negotiate situations appropriately, whatever occurs. Honderich (1995) separated virtue ethics from teleological theories, and indeed it can be distinguished from utilitarian and justice theories on many points. However, virtue ethics is concerned with ends as well as means; in people working out what they need to do, and how they need to be, in order to ensure that humankind flourishes. It has three elements:

1. *Practices*. Learning to express a range of virtues by experiencing and observing the way an ethical person behaves with you and others, as they perform a specific practice. Such *apprenticeships* allow people to observe and internalise ways to express virtues such as courage, compassion or honesty, despite circumstances that may be disheartening. Practices encompass both actions and motivation for actions. The ethical practitioner seeks to express goods internal to a practice (not breaking a confidence because to do so corrodes trust) rather than external to it (not breaking a confidence because the listener might judge you a gossip).

2. *Narrative unity*. Integrity of action across time and persons. One cannot be ethical occasionally, nor only in selected settings. Narrative unity is the quest to understand what it is to live a good life, by repeatedly asking oneself how that can be reflected in word and deed. A moral life has unity when reflective attention to ethical practices is sustained. Hoshmand's (1998) analysis of narratives of identity among psychologists regarded to be moral persons found their life-narratives had been significantly influenced by either religious or political ideals.

3. *Moral traditions*. Build the ethical society by establishing "how we do things here". What aspects of the community enable people to attain narrative unity or integrity, what tells them what local expectations are, and how does the community determine who is the narrator or culture carrier? How does this community enable the men and women in it to seek for the good together? This argues against the liberal idea that we can choose how to be. Rather, virtue ethics states that we inherit a moral starting point from family, tribe (perhaps service or professional culture) and other influences. We are embedded within tradition because practices always have histories. This is not an argument for stasis. MacIntyre (1985, p. 222) asserted: "When a tradition is in good order it is always partially constituted by argument", and some of Hoshmand's (1998) participants were shaped by early influences because they rebelled against them. Considering the type of personhood a service sets out to support within its clients is an example of reflecting on moral tradition, be it implicit or explicit. Contemporary focus on recidivism reduction appears to be an agenda solely concerned to make people safer for society. If services also address the development of individuals themselves, how should they make this apparent to users, new staff and the external agents with whom they interact?

Virtue theorists consider ethical behaviour to be expressed and embedded in long-term relationships. It starts in, and inevitably involves, critical scrutiny of one's own behaviour and the way it is negotiated with others. It is much less interested in identifying the unethical behaviour of others, and for that reason has been criticised as unable to address malpractice such as the treatment offered to Sean Walton. Yet MacIntyre (1994) argues such behaviour is rarely the result of individuals alone. An environment that treats patients as human ashtrays, that allows them to be taunted by staff as "half brain", has lost meaningful contact with any ethical practice. Virtues such as courage, honesty or justice are not in evidence and the environment is corrupt. The problem is whether to raze the corrupt institution completely, or to import enough people who do know what virtue and ethical practices mean, in order to start the difficult task of spreading them.

Let me return to a key difference between virtue ethics on the one hand, and deontology and teleological theories on the other; the value placed on autonomy. This is such a central component of ethical thinking in contemporary health services that it is difficult for many people to see it as an assumption, and therefore an idea that is open to question. Yet Reinders (2000) argues that liberal focus on autonomy provides people who have intellectual disability with no meaningful protection. Valuing the self-determination of people who are capable of choosing and acting provides relatively little guidance about how to respond to people whose choices damage others (until they encounter the justice system) or whose actions are self-harming (until they justify compulsory detention in a psychiatric hospital). Of course, this confusion between care and control is exactly the territory that offender services occupy, territory that Reinders argues gets no guidance from liberal culture. Rose (1999) also warns against an ethic of authentic self-hood, questioning injunctions about autonomy, self-mastery and self-realisation. He argues that we are impoverished when ideas of dependency, mutuality, self-sacrifice and commitment to others are dismissed.

If services for adults with intellectual disability who offend were to acknowledge and incorporate relationships of dependency, they would offer a different service to that offered to non-disabled offenders. Some would complain that the families were the offender's problem: but that was a view taken by staff in youth offender services, to nobody's advantage. Others would fear patronising the adult, treating them as if a child—a major transgression from a normalisation perspective. These concerns are in part grounded within the final concern about liberal autonomy identified by Reinders (2000), that since all people are independent moral agents, they should be treated the same. This anti-discriminatory stance is vociferously defended by members of the disability rights movement, although most authors (e.g. Oliver, 1992) primarily describe the rights of people with physical or sensory rather than intellectual disabilities. Anti-discrimination is an argument used by some specialist professionals in offender services, when they advise against special measures for offenders with intellectual disability provided by the mental health or guardianship systems. Instead, they argue the better approach is to support people through the criminal justice system. I return at the end of this chapter to the origins of a range of perspectives held on this point by different parties involved with offender services. This issue has been raised at this juncture in order to focus attention on what virtue theory has to say about treating everybody the same.

There has been no meaningful debate about the appropriateness of including all persons with intellectual disability in the rights debate. Reinders (2000) argues this is partly because liberal morality treats people without autonomy as either potential persons (babies) or as non-persons (foetuses). This dichotomy raises entirely justifiable fears about people with intellectual disability being rendered disposable. In order to ensure they are treated as persons, liberal convention counters with the unsustainable fiction that all people with intellectual disability are autonomous, or if not could be if everybody around them tried hard enough. When this clearly fails to apply to individuals with the greatest disabilities, proponents insist that they should be treated *as if* they are autonomous despite clear evidence to the contrary. The position is not argued but asserted. It appears to ward off the feared implications of becoming a non-person in a liberal culture.

Things become rather less emotive if we can successfully theorise dependence, and drop the person/non-person dichotomy imposed by liberal convention. In showing how common it is for philosophers to avoid theorising states of vulnerability or dependency, MacIntyre (1999) argued the illusion of self-sufficiency is common. It obscured the significance of dependency to past philosophers and also influences us. Our habits of mind refuse to acknowledge bodily dimensions of existence, and the benefits conferred on us by others. Occasions when we find our cognitive capacity insufficient to look after our interests may be temporary because we are young, old or ill. Nevertheless, depending on others to think and speak for us on those occasions clearly does not render us less than human. The fear of being rendered a non-person is not justified.

The task is not theorising independence but human interdependence. Hermeneutic philosophers from Heidegger to Ricoeur have addressed this over the past century, informing virtue theorists. MacIntyre (1999) argues that truthfully acknowledging our dependence on others, and developing virtues of graceful giving and graceful receiving, are prerequisites for all ethical relationships. The importance of relationships for offenders is exemplified by the following case summary:

> Jimmy had been married, with a son who had died and a wife who had left him some years previously. He developed relationships of trust with two six-year old girls in his neighbourhood, who visited his house unaccompanied until he was convicted for sexual offences against them and placed on probation for three years. His house was subsequently petrol bombed and his windows smashed, and people in the community verbally and physically attacked him. He became extremely self-neglectful. Things changed markedly when his wife returned to him. He told anyone who would listen how happy and fulfilled he was. Most people, including Jimmy himself at times, believed his generous invalidity benefits were a significant factor in her return, but this did not affect his pleasure in the companionship and status he enjoyed as a married man. Most important, Jimmy revelled in the restrictions his marriage brought, which conferred safety on him as well as neighbourhood children; "No I can't do that, you see the wife wouldn't be pleased if I did that".

If offenders consent, working with key people in their social network may support far more change, and change that is sustained, than attempting to promote their autonomy. Yet we continue to prioritise the idea of empowerment. This not only makes the fallacious assumption that all people could be autonomous, but the value of the idea itself also requires critique. Baistow (2000) identified the paradox of professionals "empowering" people with disabilities who either cannot or will not manage themselves. Bugental and Lewis (1999) summarised a decade of research demonstrating that when people who feel powerless acquire power, they are likely to misuse it because hypervigilance to power makes some people ignore other possible dimensions of relationships. Given positions of power, such as child-care, any sign of their authority being ignored or challenged evokes control-oriented thoughts. Aroused and defensive, they are more likely to engage in coercive interactions. None of this would have surprised Bateson (1972), who argued that "The *idea of power* corrupts. Power corrupts most rapidly those who believe in it, and it is they who will want it the most . . . the *myth* of power is of course a very powerful myth" (p. 494, his italics). So although empowerment has prompted professionals to consider to what degree people can take their own decisions given adequate support, as a contemporary "ethical" discourse it may fail offenders whose thinking is already saturated by the idea of individual power. The ethical task is to broaden their understanding of relationships beyond it, not to entrench their one-dimensional thinking further.

Many people find the systemic perspective of virtue ethics difficult to grasp. Its realm of influence differs from the individualism of deontological and teleological positions. It can also be contrasted against standpoint ethics (e.g. Addelson, 1993), which advocates taking a particular perspective, abandoning the notion that any "ethical" position can be taken or agreed. Thus a feminist ethicist might investigate the effects of using the gender-neutral term "offender" when three times as many men as women fall within this category (a gender imbalance recorded, for example, in Xenitidis, Henry, Russell, Ward & Murphy, 1999), without imagining they had addressed all possible ethical considerations. Let me conclude this section by re-stating that virtue ethics is not a theory to tell clinicians what are good actions or decisions, frustrating as that will be for some. It is a theory of how to develop and sustain ethical practices between members of an ethical community, expressing identifiable traditions that intend to increase human flourishing. At its core is a deceptively simple statement; the good life is one spent finding our own answers to the question "what is the good for humanity?". Therein lies the rub, since liberal philosophies actively avoid determining what is a good life. It requires commitment: taking a stand. MacIntyre has complained about the "privatization of the good", that discussion of it has been removed from public life. When liberal philosophies fail, pre-existing moral convictions and attitudes that people bring to debate are essential to achieving a resolution. Reinders (2000) argues against attempts to purge considerations of the good from ethical discussion. He prefers to allow liberal assumptions their central position, but when they fail "to remind our society that its moral fabric is much richer than liberal morality allows us to acknowledge" (p. 35).

"BEING ETHICAL": PROFESSIONAL NARRATIVES

So far I have questioned ethics from a conceptual position: is the pursuit of autonomy and empowerment for people with learning disabilities automatically an ethical act? I have argued that virtue ethics is at least a viable position for clinicians in this field. Before proceeding further it may be useful to explore cultural narratives that tell professionals what it is to act ethically.

A familiar construction of the ethical person, derived from the Enlightenment, is that of the lone thinker who makes a stand against injustice. There are many examples of people who helped to change the world but lost their lives for taking such a stand; Bonhoeffer against Nazism, Romero against the corruption that maintained mass poverty in South America. Closer to home the *Ashworth Five* (three clinical psychologists, a psychiatrist and a social worker) demanded and gave evidence to a committee of inquiry that explored Sean Walton's case, at considerable personal cost (HMSO, 1992). In its conclusions, that inquiry fully endorsed their concerns about "a hospital environment which has given rise to numerous incidents arising from an uncaring and demeaning attitude towards patients" (p. 252).

Yet however important it is to identify and root out abuse, and however power-fully such accounts shape our understanding of the ethical duties of professionals, stands against malpractice are far from being the only possible expression of ethical behaviour. Why? Partly because inquiries and disciplinary actions are relatively ineffective ways to create change. Ashworth High Security Hospital (Moss Side was renamed) was subject to another committee of inquiry only seven years later (HMSO, 1999). As one way to "do" ethics, complaining about others fits with popu-lar culture, which encourages people to cast themselves as victims of a melodrama in which everyone else is wrong. Yet it is clear that identifying evil makes little contribution towards engendering the good.

Thus while reporting malpractice is ethical behaviour, and it does take courage, it is not necessarily the most ethical or relevant action for every situation. "Conduct-ing our lives responsibly starts with the fabric of actual relationships—personal and institutional—that constitutes our moral world" (Reinders, 2000, p. 153). The challenge is at least to match time spent investigating malpractice with time spent promoting ethical practice.

ETHICAL PRACTICES

The country that was best able to defend its Jews from the Nazis was Denmark. Hitler thought it would be difficult to implement the *Final Solution* there, because the Jews were so well integrated: when he did attempt to round up and deport Jewish people, he was able to locate less than 10%. Over 7,000 were hidden; their flight to neutral Sweden was supported by ordinary Danes in "the most remarkable rescue operation of the war" (Kershaw, 2000, p. 604). It was not the heroism of a single individual, but thousands upon thousands of ethical relationships that made Denmark such a strong protector of the Jews. In similar vein, professionals express their ethics most effectively by supporting development of an ethical community throughout the workplace. It is not the heroic whistle-blower who will create the most change, vital though they are to stopping abuse. What institutional services for offenders need are sufficient staff with an understanding of ethics, who have sufficient support to engage with difficult people in stressful circumstances without losing sight of what they should do.

Competent and ethical care-giving in intellectual disability services requires per-sonal characteristics such as receptivity, judging the level of closeness a client can tolerate, and creating circumstances that invite moments of psychological meeting (Meininger, 1998). Perhaps most challenging within offender services is Meininger's requirement to imaginatively anticipate positive aspects of the per-son's character, so they can be evoked more easily. Staff working with some clients may find it difficult to imagine positive characteristics when they are hidden behind behaviour originating in rejection, abuse or neglect. Other clients require effort in the opposite direction; keeping the gravity of the offence in focus when the person wants staff to collude with them in denial. Striking the balance is im-portant in both cases; holding in mind different and contradictory aspects of the person. Meininger regards the attitudes and discourses that people employ to be fundamental to an ethical relationship, yet life-stories filled by disadvantage or disaster are easy neither to tell nor to hear. As Flaskas (1996, pp. 43–4) comments:

> Being on the receiving end of feelings that someone else cannot bear is generally not much fun, and an unreflective stance on the part of the therapist in this situation very often means that her or his capacity for empathy is diminished, which in turn compounds engagement difficulties.

Open receptiveness could overwhelm staff in extended contact with offenders. Staff need ways to defuse hostile or ambiguous feelings if they are to avoid returning them to the person with interest. They also need both high personal standards and effective support to avoid projecting their own needs and ideals onto the person.

Most descriptions of treatments and interventions focus on specific therapies, carried out for an hour or so a week. What help do direct care staff receive in developing and maintaining ethical relationships with offenders? The therapeutic culture of clinical supervision is starting to influence most autonomous professionals, and those who work with sex offenders often go beyond supervisory discussion to debrief where necessary. Yet despite many policy initiatives, direct care staff and qualified nurses in institutional and community settings rarely find the time for clinical supervision, nor can many access skilled supervisors. Moreover, intellectual disability service cultures commonly bar discussion of the difficulties and intrusions direct care staff experience, because people often conceal discomfort at speaking personally behind criticism of clients.

This culture contrasts with support for staff who work outside intellectual disability, such as with challenging youth. Canonical books such as *The Other 23 Hours* (Trieschman, 1969, cited by Richardson, 2001) have long existed to guide staff in this work, and Richardson (2001) provides a contemporary, evidence-based description of the interpersonal skills staff need to survive. He starts by summarising the problems experienced by young people who challenge services:

1. they experience a wide range of emotions which they struggle to express or manage constructively;
2. they rarely manage to meet their needs to belong, to feel competent and worthwhile;
3. they tend to elicit from others the opposite of what they need; and
4. they seldom seek help voluntarily.

Staff who succeed in helping such people generally do so through effective relationships, which require self-awareness. Such staff aim to understand before being understood or, more prosaically, to learn about the car before tinkering with the engine. They recognise that the urge to rush in and try to resolve stories of pain is based on our inability to witness it. They communicate concern, but also the expectation that the person can change. In discussing how staff can avoid having to choose between "drill sergeant and doormat", Richardson (2001) details ways that effective helpers balance support and challenge.

Dual responsibility is emphasised by Richardson (2001). Staff need to acknowledge the way upbringing and disadvantage combine to facilitate offending and ruin lives, but also to hold high expectations of the people they work with despite their history. Richardson focuses on language, helping staff to resist the temptation to use counter-productive terms, and teaching the creative art of reframing to open new possibilities for action. He introduces *solution-focused therapy* techniques such as looking out for, and amplifying, exceptions to failure. He recommends asking clients questions that invite positive descriptions they can live up to, repeating them when they have no good answer to start with; simple questions such as "what are you good at?". Finally, he moves beyond the individual relationship to consider systemic aspects of the service—exploring how collaborative and preventative approaches can supersede isolated, reactive ones.

Richardson (2001) synthesises many useful narratives and discourses described by social science research for an audience of care staff. Similar books in the intellectual disability field tend to focus on action rather than attitudes or ideas. Generating an ethical dimension in the relationship between carers and offenders with intellectual disabilities requires we do more than blame staff or family members for their shortcomings; relationships between them and the wider professional community need to change too.

ETHICAL ENVIRONMENTS

Meininger (2002) describes how a hospital ethics committee that drew on bioethical principles could provide little support to staff. The four principles informed their recommendations, but these failed to remove the feeling of moral uncertainty that made staff approach the ethics committee in the first place. This committee realised that professional care practices in intellectual disability cannot be reduced to a set of procedures, or actions, for two reasons. It was often far from self-evident what a meaningful life is or could be for that person; and the relationship between any care giver and care receiver was not exchangeable but particular, idiosyncratic. The committee changed from advice-giving and alibi-providing to acting as partners in dialogue and reflection. They ceased to regard ethics as the realm of decision making about dilemmas, which were developed by ethicists to illustrate theories, not to replace them. Instead, the ethics committee started supporting staff to develop and enact their own moral responsibility.

Hoshmand (1998, p. 4) argues that "the resolution of moral conflicts and existential questions in a person's articulation of professional identity [is] a creative process in itself". Anderson and Swim (1993) outline ideal conversations as those that help each person to identify their unique competencies, creativity and imagination, enabling them to translate personal and professional growth from any areas of life into the clinical setting. Yet staff in many British intellectual disability services can be reluctant to blend the personal and professional. Opportunities for shared reflectiveness seem to be feared as another opportunity to be criticised; or another reason for professional jealousies to dominate over skills exchange. Elizur (1994) observed that parents of offenders commonly have to tolerate breaches in their family boundaries. They experience those breaches as intrusive and enmeshed with social control. Having had many experiences of failure and blame, they quickly close ranks against any perceived intrusion into their personal space. This description is reminiscent of the responses of some staff when clinicians attempt to broaden out and consider the therapeutic environment. The pace needs to be measured, and as much control as possible left in the hands of those who feel exposed.

Difficult it may be, but it needs to be attempted. Research into the way people develop their ethical thinking shows it is not a matter that can be left on the shelf until a "dilemma" jumps out. Ethics necessarily involves regular attention if people are to increase the integrity between self and moral goals (MacIntyre, 1985) and between self-description and experience of self that others reflect (Hoshmand 1998). Reflection may be aided by introducing new structures to open new conversations.

The Ashworth Hospital Inquiry (HMSO, 1992) identified widespread use of dehumanising language as a significant factor in appalling treatment of residents. Perhaps knowing too much about the brutalities people inflict on one another eroded the integrity staff had when they started work. Yet too much criticism of negative language risks driving both it and the emotions it reflects underground, preventing people from processing their feelings. It also invites care staff to believe that visiting professionals have no care for them as persons who can be hurt, frightened or overwhelmed. Clearly, meeting "he can be a real bugger sometimes" with prissy responses such as, "I don't like to think about people that way" achieves little more than alienation. Yet if the thoughts, feelings and discourses staff use in talking with and about offenders with intellectual disablities lie at the heart of ethical practice, how can those thoughts and discourses change?

A move beyond clinical literature provides one vantage point. Weingarten (2000) describes the impact of a visit to South Africa by discussing the central paradox of voice in a violent country. In the subtle negotiations about whether and what to say, speakers also need to work out what audiences can bear to hear. Listening to atrocities done to or by others involves risk; witnessing changes us. At worst, listening makes experience endure, and provokes the stigma that attaches to victims. At best, it generates a silence many experience as spiritual, a silence in which change occurs for the victim. Weingarten reports how a journalist who covered the Truth and Reconciliation hearings for South African radio decided that capturing the experience in the right words controlled it. Losing the power to haunt, the right words allow witnesses to move more than one layer away from the chaos they fear.

So words matter; but words often fail people. When staff can find no good words to describe what they know or experience, harsh ones get used that entrench a way of thinking. One way to create change is to intervene at the place where words are used most. In residential settings that is the handover. Mason (1989) argued that traditional handovers cause many difficulties in human services. Tired, outgoing staff warn oncoming colleagues of problems they may encounter, even though these are already recorded in the notes. Events are generally described unreflectively, as a series of facts about the client and not as an interaction between them and the care system. Without problems people find little to discuss; animation accompanies the subtle message "wait until you hear this one!". A tired rush to hand over information and go home discourages exploration of meanings or careful word selection. Some listeners feel sullied by hearing vulnerable clients described in negative terms; others feel demoralised before they even start their shift.

The *systemic handover* is Mason's (1989) alternative. This reverses the dynamic, ensuring that the person responsible for the oncoming shift arrives soon enough to read the running record written by those leaving. This frees the handover to become a different sort of conversation, one that constructs alternative views of people and events. The fresh, oncoming team interviews outgoing staff, leading the discussion from a systemic family therapy perspective. This uses questions to construct a different account, one that opens new possibilities for change. The systemic handover prompts a move from analysis to synthesis by inviting staff to hypothesise about what might be going on.

- Now you can think coolly about when Jeff threw the chair at Joe, replay an imaginary videotape of yourself and the situation. What went well, and would you have done anything differently?
- You obviously tried a number of different ways to manage a difficult situation this morning. Which ones worked best for you? And for Sara?
- If you decided it wasn't just luck that Clyde got up in such a good mood this morning, but that somebody had done something right, who and what might it be?
- It sounds as if there is a connection between Pervez' behaviour and staff disagreeing with each other about how to respond. Let's put aside discussion of whether anybody is right or wrong for the moment, and wonder what the connection might be.

I have recently explored the systemic handover with a team of nurses and psychiatric colleagues. Providing staff with a new discursive script seems to have changed conversations in other places too. It provides staff with a way to talk about the difficulties of direct care without demeaning residents. Practices like this, focused not on the extraordinary but the mundane, can engender talk that is both authentic and ethical. These ideas may also assist conversation between different professionals trying to have useful dialogue in community settings. Systemic family therapists have long argued against an individual understanding of human distress and change. Elizur (1993, 1994) applied systemic ideas to change the oppositional triangle that commonly develops between youth offenders, therapeutic services and families. To do so he worked first with the staff to address tensions between members of the professional system in both institutional and community settings. Establishing the common goal of learning how to work with offenders and their families required staff to overcome the "acrid" relationships between them which created such barriers to change in the offenders. This was far from straightforward. It required the author to create alliances with all staff groups while favouring none; to understand their culture, including aspects that were hostile to families; and to identify naturally occurring meeting points where change could occur. Elizur reported many staff–family–offender triangles related to unresolved and submerged conflicts between staff, usually stemming from fear of losing position. These required active attention before it became possible for the service to look outside itself and work constructively with clients and their families.

A number of authors and clinicians have recommended holistic approaches to the treatment of offenders. These take into account poverty of opportunity and being under-supported because they display basic self-help skills (e.g. Murphy, 1997). Others urge intervention to counter reluctance between professionals to refer on (Mental Health Foundation, 1997). However, most published treatments for offenders remain at the individual level; developing self-control, lowering arousal, desensitisation to the excitements of fire raising, learning social skills, and so on. By contrast, virtue ethics regards individual action as insufficient—environmental interventions are also required. In addition to professionals managing their own responses to and practices with the person, and negotiating with others in the professional community, difficulties created by the community context also need to be considered. In the UK, increasing hostility towards offenders in general, and sex offenders in particular, has recently been amplified by campaigns led by tabloid newspapers.

Thus the final environmental requirement of an ethical service is that it should at least attempt to influence attitudes within the community. Sophisticated approaches to community intervention concerning people who present other problems, such as problem drinking, have been developed by community clinical psychologists (Orford, 1992). Such interventions combine individual intervention with community prevention, with the aim of minimising irrelevant anxieties while ensuring members of the public can assess risks realistically and act to minimise them. They involve information sharing, and sometimes working proactively with local people to identify and act on matters of concern. Wertsch (1995) recognises that cultures which dichotomise individual and society prefer individual treatments, and find such thinking difficult. Nevertheless, he advocates conceptualising clinical intervention as social action. This is indeed a tall order in a hostile social environment that shows little interest in developing a balanced view; but it is probably only the clinical and research communities that are in a position to effect it.

ETHICS AND TRADITIONS

Virtue ethics invites reflection on the moral traditions that shape the way we work, but traditions are often difficult to see. Rose (1999, p. xii) argues that history is a vital tool that enables us to reflect:

> [History] sensitises us to the kinds of connections and relations amongst diverse elements that have brought our contemporary ways of thinking, judging, acting into being ... opening the possibility that things could have been different, they try to make it easier to assess that present in order to make judgements about how to act upon it. If the history of our present is more accidental than we may like to believe, the future of our present is also more open than it sometimes appears.

Thomson's (1998) history tracks how people with mental deficiency in Britain became the focus for a range of anxieties in the first quarter of the twentieth century. Doctors first identified the problem of the "weak-minded prisoner" in the 1870s, when they requested separate care for them because they were disruptive and not reformed by prison. From their inception mental deficiency services were expected both to protect users from the community, and the community from them. The 1913 Mental Deficiency Act confirmed mental deficiency as a medico-legal phenomenon, making provision for permanent care of the weak-minded habitual criminal even though a similar experiment for habitual inebriates had failed. This soon received press criticism for "restricting individual rights rather than providing a therapeutic service". In Thomson's (1998) view the 1959 Mental Health Act involved much linguistic sleight of hand to liberalise services, but it extended "medical control to reach that 'borderline' area, lying between mental illness and deficiency, which had always been of greatest moral, social, and eugenic concern" (p. 294). The problem of balancing control and care was built into the service.

By 1931 the cost of a mental deficiency bed was 63% of that spent on a mental illness bed. Members of new professions were expected to provide high quality care and therapy on the one hand, and to satisfy demands for greater economy on the other. Thomson (1998, p. 148) concluded there was:

> constant competition for resources between and within professional groups, professional alliances were frequently shattered by divisions which ran along lines of class and gender, and there was constant threat of care being shifted to more efficient and cheaper lay management.... If professionals were to secure positions within the welfare system they often had to compromise on the "professional ideal".

The (im)moral traditions relevant to service provision documented in Thompson's history are confused purpose, uncertainty about who will deliver the service, and intermittent cost reductions that put professionals into conflict with each other. What history helps us to see is that while problems seem individual in origin, the heavy influence of historical relationships makes it unlikely they will go away. We may have to live with them, take their presence into account, use the knowledge to cool what appear to be interpersonal conflicts, and act to minimise their deleterious effects on clients.

If history gives us one kind of story, experience provides another. When intervention creates relatively limited change in multiply stressed people; is intermittently resisted or rejected by many of them; and when this involvement disrupts more effective types of work, it must be very tempting to believe somebody else would do it better. The communication problems documented by Thompson (1998) are often writ large in services for offenders with intellectual disabilities. They develop between staff providing mainstream intellectual disability services, staff who provide specialist services to intellectually disabled offenders, and the criminal justice system. These problems can appear to be petty boundary disputes between professionals. One NHS minister of health famously declared he would "knock their heads together" if people failed to cooperate. Nevertheless, this underestimates the problem of people feeling ill-equipped to help and anxious to make others who could manage it better take on additional responsibilities. Although it looks like buck-passing to outsiders, those engaged in it often feel they are on an ethical crusade to get the right help for their clients.

Service boundaries do represent a major problem for staff in mainstream intellectual disability services. Many health staff attempt to defend an intelligence level boundary around 70; acknowledging its arbitrary nature, they nevertheless fear that extending services to people in the borderline range (up to IQ 80) will overwhelm their small service. If generic services were to include people in the borderline range, cursory inspection of population data such as that given in WAIS-III (1998) demonstrate that a service designed for 2% of the population would be attempting to support 9%. This is clearly an impossible task. Nevertheless, professionals outside intellectual disability express impatience over such boundary disputes. Palmer and Hart (1996) cite a court of appeal as having no interest which side of IQ 70 a person falls, preferring to use more qualitative judgements to identify people who have "significant impairment of intelligence and social functioning". Xenitidis *et al.* (1999) are not unusual in describing a specialist service for people with "mild intellectual disability and challenging behaviour" which includes people within the borderline and low average ranges of intelligence (IQ 70–84). Thus, while the inclusion or otherwise of people outwith the classification is a major issue for mainstream intellectual disability staff, it causes no problem for tertiary national services that attract external funding.

Another boundary is with the criminal justice system. Staff in mainstream community intellectual disability services are often concerned that regular offenders get too many discretionary warnings at police stations. They believe some offenders with intellectual disablities must experience real consequences of their actions before they will engage with therapy. Perhaps the main concern expressed by mainstream staff, however, is that offenders with intellectual disability engage with treatments intermittently if at all. Supporting them in the community requires patience over missed appointments, only to be faced with demands for immediate support made in dramatic ways. The negative impact of such behaviour on the care of other clients means many staff breathe easier when the person's behaviour warrants admission under a section of the Mental Health Act (in the UK).

By contrast staff in the criminal justice system believe it is care in the community that has failed. Offences are generally considered secondary to limited ability and social disadvantage, but inadequate resource and services mean that many court diversion schemes work poorly.

> At no stage in our research did we encounter anything other than the gravest concern for the plight of those suffering from mental disorder or mental handicap who find themselves involved with the Criminal Justice System. (Palmer & Hart, 1996, p. 91)

Palmer and Hart (1996) studied what were then new British safeguards for vulnerable adults. The main problem for police was identifying people with intellectual disability, because they present in similar ways to people under the influence of alcohol or drugs. Alcohol can usually be detected with a breathalyser but a doctor is required to detect drugs. Even then the authors concluded police surgeons were neither accurate nor consistent in their judgements. Concerns expressed by many criminal justice staff were that suggestibility makes people with intellectual disability more likely to confess and be wrongfully convicted; once imprisoned, they are more likely to be physically or sexually assaulted by other prisoners.

Clearly, many different and incommensurate views operate at service interfaces. Connecting these different perspectives within a *seamless service* is problematic when numbers are small and cultures so different. Buck-passing sometimes appears to be the dominant tradition. Palmer and Hart (1996) concluded that a strategic group should be established in each area to maintain an overview of mentally disordered offenders living in the community, to ensure effective liaison between police, probation, social services and psychiatry. They argue this would make identification more robust. It would ensure appropriate accommodation was available for people who needed to be detained overnight, since there is a serious risk of assault from other prisoners in police cells. It would also ensure that Appropriate Adults obtained effective training and support. Yet now such panels are being established, it seems that the offences committed by people with intellectual disability are often considered too mild to warrant such a coordinated approach.

CONCLUSIONS

Intellectually disabled offenders have been the subject of social and moral concern for a century. Despite much contemporary discussion of ethics, MacIntyre (1991) debunked ambiguous exchanges in 'How to seem virtuous without actually being so'. He argued that deploying indeterminate concepts in public rhetoric allows people to disguise the fundamental moral disagreements that divide contemporary political culture. Concepts such as autonomy, anti-discrimination and empowerment may appear to be self-evidently ethical goods for people with intellectual disability, but they merely express the dominant assumptions of liberal culture and are open to critical evaluation. A positive ethical vision should go beyond the exchange of stale ideas, and beyond goals of zero recidivism and reduction of harm, to state how the service sets out to influence positively the narrative wreckage that comprises the subjectivity of many offenders, and what good it might do.

Perhaps Sean Walton's life will be honoured by acting on the issues his case raised. Everyday interaction had gone awry for him. Attending to such practices weaves ethics into the fabric of ordinary relationships. Since relationships are difficult to create with clients who are chaotic and unused to being helped, mistakes and malpractice are likely. We should stop perceiving malpractice as something done by hidden enemies who must be smoked out and metaphorically killed. From a virtue ethics position, ethical environments can be created by ordinary staff who are encouraged to imagine, and keep in mind, positive aspects of the offender's character. As Brecht (1939) said, "Unhappy the land that needs heroes". Staff who offer such relationships without naïvety or burn-out usually work in physical or intellectual communities that respect their unique competencies and creativity. Such staff may find it easier to anticipate the best the person could become within systemic handovers, or through careful attention to the language deployed in meetings that coordinate community management. The task is to ensure that discourse remains therapeutic, by acknowledging and addressing discouragements rather than denying that frustration is a central component of this work.

The other issue that Sean's life highlighted was that of confused responsibility. Nobody organised or wrote a therapeutic care plan, nobody asked what unsupervised nursing assistants were doing, nor did anybody take responsibility for helping them to develop a more therapeutic approach to interaction. These problems have dogged intellectual disability services throughout their history; numerous inquiries suggest that working with offenders amplifies this confusion. There is an outside chance that central government will ensure that responsible ministers negotiate differences between their ministries. However, individual professionals are more likely to remain the people who shoulder responsibility for making the service work. Those who are most confident of their own ethical standpoint will be able to maintain an ethical relationship with both offenders and people employed by partner agencies, despite different perspectives and priorities. That requires regular time to reflect on issues and positions, both individually and as a member of a local ethical community, wherever it is housed. In my view, the ethical priority for professionals who work with offenders who have intellectual disability is engaging with and changing the moral traditions that dictate "how we do things here".

REFERENCES

Addelson, K.P. (1993). Knowers/doers and their moral problems. In L. Alcoff & E. Potter (eds) *Feminist Epistemologies* (pp. 265–94). London: Routledge.

Anderson, H. & Swim, S. (1993). Learning as collaborative conversation: combining the student's and the teacher's expertise. *Human Systems*, **4**, 145–53.

Baistow, K. (2000). Problems of powerlessness. *History of Human Sciences*, **13**, 95–116.

Bateson, G. (1972). *Steps to an Ecology of Mind*. London: University of Chicago Press.

Beauchamp, T. & Childress, J. (2001). *Principles of Biomedical Ethics*, (5th edn). Oxford: Oxford University Press.

Brecht, B. (1939). *Galileo*, 13, cited in *Bloomsbury Biographical Dictionary of Quotations* (1997). London: Bloomsbury.

Bugental, D. & Lewis, J. (1999). The paradoxical misuse of power by people who see themselves as powerless: how does it happen? *Journal of Social Issues*, **55**, 51–64.

Elizur, Y. (1993). Ecosystemic training: conjoining supervision and organizational development. *Family Process*, **32**, 185–201.

Elizur, Y. (1994). Working with families in institutions for juvenile offenders: an ecosystemic model for the development of family involvement. *Human Systems*, **5**, 253–66.

Flaskas, C. (1996). Understanding the therapeutic relationship. In C. Flaskas & A. Perlesz (eds) *The Therapeutic Relationship in Systemic Therapy* (pp. 34–52). London: Karnac.

HMSO (1992). *Report of the Committee of Inquiry into Complaints about Ashworth Hospital*, vols. I & II. London: HMSO.

HMSO (1999). *Report of the Committee of Inquiry into the Personality Disorder Unit, Ashworth Special Hospital*. London: HMSO.

Honderich, T. (ed.) (1995). *The Oxford Companion to Philosophy*. Oxford: Oxford University Press.

Hoshmand, L.T. (1998). *Creativity and Moral Vision in Psychology*. London: Sage.

Kershaw, I. (2000). *Hitler 1936–45: Nemesis*. London: Allen Lane.

MacIntyre, A. (1985). *After Virtue*, 2nd edn. London: Duckworth.

MacIntyre, A. (1991). How to seem virtuous without actually being so. Occasional paper no. 1, Centre for the Study of Cultural Values, Lancaster University.

MacIntyre, A. (1994). A partial response to my critics. In J. Horton & S. Mendus (eds) *After MacIntyre* (pp. 282–304). Cambridge: Polity Press.

MacIntyre, A. (1999). *Dependent Rational Animals: Why Human Beings Need the Virtues*. London: Duckworth.

Mason, B. (1989). *Handing Over*. London: Karnac.

Meininger, H. (1998). "... as yourself". Care for persons with mental disabilities from the perspective of moral theology, unpublished PhD thesis, university of Utrecht [English chapter summary available from the author].

Meininger, H. (2002). *Ethics committees in human service organisations for people with learning disabilities in the Netherlands*. *Tizard Learning Disabilities Review*, **7**, 35–9.

Mental Health Foundation (1997). Working with men with learning disability who sexually abuse others: basic structures not in place. Briefing paper no. 12, London: Mental Health Foundation.

Murphy, G. (1997). Treatment and risk management. In J. Churchill, H. Brown, A. Craft & C. Horrocks (eds) *There Are No Easy Answers* (pp. 109–24). ARC & Napsac with SSI & DoH.

O'Donohue, W. & Mangold, R. (1996). A critical examination of the ethical principles of psychologists and code of conduct. In W. O'Donohue & R. Kitchener (eds) *The Philosophy of Psychology* (pp. 371–80). London: Sage.

Oliver, M. (1992). Changing the social relations of research production. *Disability, Handicap and Society*, **7**, 101–14.

Orford, J. (1992). *Community Psychology: Theory and Practice*. Chichester: John Wiley & Sons.

Palmer, C. & Hart, M. (1996). A PACE in the right direction. University of Sheffield & Mental Health Foundation.

Reinders, H. (2000). *The Future of the Disabled in Liberal Society: An Ethical Analysis*. Notre Dame, IN: University of Notre Dame Press.

Richardson, B. (2001). *Working with Challenging Youth: Lessons Learned Along the Way*. Hove: Brunner-Routledge.

Rose, N. (1999). *Governing the Soul: The Shaping of the Private Self*, 2nd edn. London: Free Association Books.

Thomson, M. (1998). *The Problem of Mental Deficiency: Eugenics, Democracy and Social Policy in Britain c1870–1959*. Oxford: Clarendon Press.

Wechsler Adult Intelligence Scale-III (UK) (1998). London: The Psychological Corporation.

Weingarten, K. (2000). Witnessing, wonder and hope. *Family Process*, **39**, 389–402.

Wertsch, J.V. (1995). Sociocultural research in the copyright age. *Culture and Psychology*, **1**, 81–102.

Xenitidis, K., Henry, J., Russell, A., Ward, A. & Murphy, D. (1999). An inpatient treatment model for adults with mild intellectual disability and challenging behaviour. *Journal of Intellectual Disability Research*, **43**, 128–34.

PART III

ASSESSMENT AND EVALUATION

Chapter 6

THE ASSESSMENT OF INDIVIDUALS WITH DEVELOPMENTAL DISABILITIES WHO COMMIT CRIMINAL OFFENSES*

EDWIN J. MIKKELSEN

Associate Professor of Psychiatry, Harvard Medical School, Medical Director for The MENTOR Network, and Consultant to the Massachusetts Department of Mental Retardation, Boston, USA

The aim of the assessment of individuals with developmental disabilities who also commit criminal offenses is to provide as comprehensive an understanding of the individual as possible. A thorough assessment can then provide the necessary information to make determinations with regard to the programmatic requirements needed to provide future safety and guide the development of treatment strategies that have the potential to produce meaningful change. Thus, throughout the assessment phase of treatment planning, there is a dual focus on the broad issues of community safety and the clinical needs of the individual who has committed the offense.

The actual clinical assessment process involves careful consideration of a number of different factors. These factors include accountability, destabilizing factors, history of prior offences, treatabilty, community safety, and future risk. Accountability refers to whether or not the individual will be held accountable for those actions by the legal system. Destabilizing factors include the degree to which the crime was a volitional act related to an underlying personality disorder, or was affected by destabilizing factors, such as major mental illness and/or concomitant substance abuse. History of prior offenses, including the likelihood that the individual will commit another criminal act, is, in part, related to the frequency and severity of past criminal acts. Treatability refers to the degree to which the individual's behavior can be expected to ameliorate with appropriate treatment. Assessment of community safety involves evaluating the type of residential programming that

---

* Address for correspondence: 67 Yarmouth Road, Wellesley Hills, MA 02481, USA. Telephone number: +1 617 790 4248; email address: mikk@attbi.com.

Offenders with Developmental Disabilities. Edited by W.L. Lindsay, J.L. Taylor and P. Sturmey.
© 2004 John Wiley & Sons, Ltd.

will be necessary to provide a safe environment while treatment proceeds. Finally, an assessment of future risk involves an evaluation of the risk of future occurrence of another criminal act, which takes into account all of the above factors.

ACCOUNTABILITY

The evaluation of the individual with developmental disabilities who has committed a criminal offense usually begins with an assessment as to whether or not the individual is subject to criminal prosecution. This question will usually not even be raised for those individuals who are functioning in the severe–profound range of developmental disabilities, no matter how serious the offense has been. In general, acts that could be considered criminal that are committed by this group are in the form of severe aggression. Even though this aggression can appear to be volitional and the effects can be significant, such as fractured bones, impairment of vision, etc, the severe degree of intellectual impairment will usually mean that the question of criminal culpability will not even be considered. The major exception to this is homicide. In these cases, the legal system will often become involved, even though it is fairly obvious that the assailant does not possess sufficient intellectual ability to be deemed competent or responsible. As intelligence increases into the high moderate, mild, and borderline levels of intellectual functioning, the assessment of accountability becomes more of an issue, and can be quite subjective.

The first of the accountability questions relates to the cognitive ability of the individual to stand trial for his offenses. In the United States, this is referred to as "competency to stand trial," and in the United Kingdom the concept is referred to as "fit (or unfit) to plead." Both concepts have their roots in English law and the concept that an individual cannot be tried for an offense if he does not possess the cognitive ability to participate in his own defense. The generally accepted common law criteria for competence to stand trial include the ability to understand the nature and potential consequences of the charges levied against oneself, a general understanding of the workings of the court, and an ability to work cooperatively with one's attorney.

If the individual is found to be competent to stand trial or fit to plead, then another question that arises may be whether or not they were criminally responsible for the act. This question usually depends on whether or not the individual is felt to have possessed sufficient capacity *at the time of the crime* to know the wrongfulness of the act. Although in practice these evaluations are often quite subjective, there have been sound empirical studies that address these issues.

The assessment of competency to stand trial varies substantially in different jurisdictions. The common law criteria as set forth above are relatively subjective in nature, which leaves a great deal of room for the individual bias of the evaluator. The bias problem is compounded by the fact that in many areas, only one or a few professionals perform these evaluations, so that one person's bias can have far-reaching implications in that locale. In some jurisdictions within the United States, virtually all individuals with developmental disabilities may be found not competent to stand trial. Presumably, this is due to a bias on the part of the evaluator to protect the individual from the criminal justice system. In the United States, this usually translates into the charges being completely dropped. In some cases this is appropriate, but in others it only perpetuates a pattern of lack of accountability that contributes to the occurrence of future criminal behavior. In other jurisdictions, one can observe the opposite effect of bias in that most individuals with developmental disabilities will be found competent to stand trial, even though they seem to have a tenuous grasp of the basic concepts. The rater bias that can lead to this pattern is a belief in the power of natural consequences, such as imprisonment, to change future behavior. Occasionally, one will also find situations where an individual has been found incompetent in the past for significant offenses, which have persisted and then the individual is found competent, presumably because the authorities can find no other method to exert some control over the individual's behavior.

Despite the subjective nature of the concept of competency, there have been some detailed systematic studies regarding the application of the concept to individuals with developmental disabilities. Smith and Broughton (1994) reviewed the records of 160 alleged offenders with developmental disabilities who were referred for evaluation of competency to stand trial and/or criminal responsibility over a five-year period in the state of South Carolina. The sample was predominantly male (93%), with a mean age of 28 years. The mean IQ for the entire group was 62 (s.d. = 8.46). Those who were found competent to stand trial had higher intelligence (mean = 64.39, s.d. = 7.99) than those who were found not competent to stand trial (mean = 58.02, s.d. = 8.18). Similar results were found with regard to the assessment of criminal responsibility. The mean IQ of those judged to be criminally responsible was 63.83 (s.d. = 7.99), as compared to 57.18 (s.d. = 8.82) for those found not criminally responsible. Related to this is a study by Grubin (1991), who reviewed the records of all 295 defendants who were found unfit to plead in England and Wales over a 12-year period. Again, the population was predominantly male (88%), with a mean age of 35.7 years. The majority of these individuals did not have intellectual disability, but rather were diagnosed with mental illness, usually schizophrenia. Within the group that had developmental disabilities there were also some individuals who had both mental illness and developmental disabilities; 32% had an IQ in the range 60–70, whereas 38% were in the range 50–60. Thus, most individuals with developmental disabilities who are charged function in the mild or moderate range of development disabilities, and those who are found to be incompetent to stand trial tend to have greater degrees of cognitive impairment.

Research has also focused on the procedural difficulties in assessing the competency of individuals with intellectual disabilities. For example, Clare and Gudjonsson (1993) identified and investigated related problems of suggestibility, acquiescence and confabulation. Suggestibility refers to the tendency to respond to subtle clues and messages in a way that the interviewer wants. Acquiescence refers to a tendency to give affirmative answers, regardless of the question or the interviewee's true opinion. Confabulation is defined by the authors as "the distortion or fabrication of story elements, which occurs when people replace gaps in their memory with imaginary experiences that they believe to be true." This research suggests that these factors are more apt to be operative in the examinations of those with intellectual deficiencies than in those with average intelligence. Related studies by other investigators have identified difficulty understanding seven critical terms as important in the assessment of competency to stand trial in individuals with developmental disabilities. The specific terms identified were guilty, testify, strategy, plead, prosecutor, jury, and trial (Smith, 1993; Smith & Hudson, 1995).

The Smith and Hudson (1995) study involved 55 defendants (mean age 27.4 years; mean Wechsler Full-Scale IQ 60.9) who were charged with felonies that carried potentially severe sentences. With regard to the seven terms identified above, the authors found that "while 96% and 92% of those judged Competent had knowledge of 'testify' and 'plead,' 70% and 84% of those judged Not Competent lacked knowledge of these terms." There was also a significant difference between the competent and not competent groups with regard to their understanding of the concept of "strategy."

DESTABILIZING FACTORS

A central aspect of the clinical assessment of the criminal offender with developmental disabilities relates to the degree to which a major mental illness and/or substance abuse contribute to the offence. These factors have been found to significantly contribute to criminal activity by individuals with mental illness (Arseneault, Moffitt, Caspi, Taylor & Silva, 2000; Borum, 1996; Monahan & Steadman, 1996; Steadman et al., 1998). Thus, by extrapolation, they would also be expected to decrease the impulse control of individuals with developmental disabilities. The assessment process for these destabilizing factors would include a thorough analysis of the current offense, as well as past offenses (Link & Stueve, 1998). It will usually become obvious if all or most of the offenses have been committed while the individual was in a manic, psychotic, and/or intoxicated state. To a certain extent, the presence of destabilizing factors as a causative factor can be a positive prognostic sign. For example, if the psychotic symptoms are related to medication non-compliance, the treatment team may well be able to substantially reduce the risk of future occurrences by utilizing strategies that ensure or increase compliance with the medication regimen. Alternately, if the illness has been refractory to previous pharmacological treatment, one can proceed to more aggressive pharmacological interventions, which may be more effective (Mikkelsen & McKenna, 1999; Reiss & Aman, 1998). In a similar fashion, if substance abuse is a major contributing factor to the offensive behavior, then renewed efforts at treatment are worthwhile. In cases where the individual has been resistant to substance abuse treatment, the ability to document this pattern may predispose the courts to legally mandate treatment.

In individuals who are functioning at the higher levels of developmental disabilities, it is usually not that difficult to make a valid psychiatric diagnosis (Mikkelsen, 1997), unless there are special circumstances that specifically decrease the individual's ability to communicate out of proportion to his/her level of developmental disability. However, the psychiatric assessment process will often need to be more comprehensive, and usually involves more collateral sources of information than the routine assessment of mental disorders in the general population (Silka & Hauser, 1997; Hauser, 1997). The process of psychological assessment in individuals with developmental disabilities can also be facilitated by the utilization of one or more of the behavioral rating scales specifically developed for individuals with developmental disabilities. These include the Aberrant Behavior Checklist (Aman & Singh, 1986, 1994), the AAMR Adaptive Behavior Scale (Nihira, Leland & Lambert, 1993), the Diagnostic Assessment of the Severely Handicapped (DASH) (Matson, Coe, Gardner & Sovner, 1991), the Developmental Behavior Checklist (Einfield & Tonge, 1995), the Emotional Problem Scales (Strohmer & Prout, 1991), the Psychopathology Inventory for Mentally Retarded Adults (PIMRA) (Matson, 1997), and the Reiss Screen for Maladaptive Behavior (Reiss, 1988). In general, these scales are more useful for individuals in whom it is difficult to make a valid psychiatric diagnosis, due to their level of disability. There are also efforts to modify existing scales that have proven to be quite useful in the general population. For example, Lindsay and Michie (1988) adapted the Zung Self-Rating Anxiety Scale to make it applicable to individuals with developmental disabilities. A similar modification of the Beck Anxiety and Depression Inventories has also been developed (Lindsay, Law & MacLeod, 2004). The adaptation of existing well-proven rating instruments for use in this population would appear to be a productive area for future endeavors.

HISTORY OF PRIOR OFFENCES

Destabilizing factors are, of course, an important contribution to the risk of future reoccurrence of criminal offenses. Another significant component of risk assessment is a thorough review of the individual's prior offenses and the context in which they occurred. This process takes into account the prior severity of the offenses, as well as their frequency. The logical assumptions underlying this analysis are that past behavior is the best predictor of future behavior, that the likelihood of a behavior being repeated in the future is positively correlated with the frequency with which that behavior has occurred in the past, and that patterns of behavior are apt to remain relatively constant over time. The above assumptions are predicated on a naturally evolving system. Destabilizing factors can greatly alter the evolution of behavior in a negative manner, while interventions that tend to stabilize the individual can ameliorate the risk. Thus, the historical frequency–severity assessment must be viewed as one part of the overall risk-assessment process. It is also unlikely that an individual will be allowed by society to continue to perpetrate criminal acts on a repetitive basis without the introduction of some sort of intervention to control the behavior and lessen the likelihood of reoccurrence. These environmental controls then become another artifact to be factored into the risk-assessment equation. For example, one might ask if an offender has not reoffended in the last three years because he has internalized more self-control, or simply because he has been in a semi-secure community program with one-to-one supervision.

It is difficult to numerically account for all of these factors in one mathematical formula. However, we have made an attempt to provide a rudimentary framework for quantifying, and then visualizing the frequency–severity of past offenses (Mikkelsen & Stelk, 1999). This process begins with three 10-point continua to quantify the severity of physical and sexual aggression (Table 6.1) The number of occurrences of each behavior would, of course, determine frequency. In order to capture frequency within a 10-point scale, which provides symmetry with the

Table 6.1   Aggression rating scales

Physical	Sexual
1. Verbal aggression and threats	1. Sexually inappropriate or suggestive statements
2. Verbal behavior accompanied by tantrum behavior (e.g. slamming doors, hitting walls, etc.)	2. Sexually aggressive—threatening behavior and comments.
3. Throwing objects without producing physical injury to others or property destruction	3. Exposing genitals to others, or voyeurism
4. Minor property destruction (e.g. breaks own possessions or inexpensive property of others) and/or minor theft, shoplifting	4. Exposing genitals to others, accompanied by masturbation and/or sexually inappropriate aggressive statements
5. Major property destruction (completely destroys interior of residence, vandalizes autos) and/or major theft (breaking and entering, car theft)	5. Surreptitious or minor sexually inappropriate touching of others (e.g. rubbing up against women)
6. Physical aggression (hitting or kicking, but does not cause tissue damage) or armed theft without using a weapon	6. Overt physically forceful, inappropriate touching/fondling
7. Physical aggression that produces tissue damage	7. Consensual but inappropriate sexual activity, usually due to age differential (e.g. statutory rape)
8. Physical aggression with severe but reversible injury (broken bone, lacerations)	8. Coerced oral sex (no penetration)
9. Physical aggression which produces severe irreversible injury (loss of vision, paralysis)	9. Rape (penetration) 9.5. Rape (penetration with physical beating)
10. Death	10. Death

Source: Reproduced with permission from Mikkelson and Stelk (1999).

severity scale, one can use a combination of absolute numbers to capture the high-severity behaviors and ranges for the higher frequencies that are usually seen for the less severe behaviors. Mikkelsen and Stelk's (1999) assessment used the following scale: 1 (1), 2 (2), 3 (3), 4 (4), 5 (5), 6 (6–9), 7 (10–15), 8 (16–20), 9 (21–30), 10 (over 30). Thus, the numbers 1 through 5 each correspond to a single act, so that if an individual had a history of two completed rapes, the marker would register 2 on the vertical frequency scale and 9 on the horizontal severity scale. The numbers 6 through 10 are used to denote ranges as indicated above. These are useful for less severe behaviors, which may have occurred several times. For example, for an individual who had a history of 18 incidents of minor property destruction, the marker would be placed over the 4 on the horizontal severity axis, and by the 8 (15–20) on the vertical frequency axis. An individual's team could also modify the ranges to represent averages per month for the behaviors at the lower end of the severity continuum, which might be expected to occur on a frequent, ongoing

Table 6.2   Overt behavior matrix grid

1. *Low Severity, Low Frequency, Distant Past*
   Lowest risk category, especially if the individual has had unrestricted community access in recent past.
2. *Low Severity, Low Frequency, Recent Past*
   Relatively low risk category. Look for destabilizing factors which could increase incident probability.
3. *Low Severity, High Frequency, Distant Past*
   Relatively low risk, especially if recent past included unrestricted community access.
4. *Low Severity, High Frequency, Recent Past*
   Will need supervision, not necessarily because of dangerousness, but to prevent incidents which may result in a social or legal consequence that far exceeds the severity of the offense.
5. *High Severity, Low Frequency, Distant Past*
   If the severe behavior was inflicted upon someone significant to the offender and was only repeated within the context of that relationship or associated relationships (i.e. family members), and has recently had unrestricted community access, risk may be low as long as individual avoids the high-risk relationships.
6. *High Severity, Low Frequency, Recent Past*
   In this category, probability of future offense is highly dependent on status of destabilizing factors and response to supervision.
7. *High Severity, High Frequency, Distant Past*
   Potentially high risk, but depends on level of supervision in recent past. If unrestricted supervision and no incidents, then may have developed internal controls. If there have been no incidents due to restrictive supervision, then probability of future incidents could be high if supervision is relaxed.
8. *High Severity, High Frequency, Recent Past*
   Highest risk category. Needs continual supervision or physical security.

Source: Reproduced with permission from Mikkelson and Stelk (1999).

basis, i.e. verbal aggression and threats or sexually inappropriate or suggestive statements. These two continua then form the two axes of a graph with severity on the horizontal axis and frequency on the vertical axis.

Another important historical factor is the time since the most recent offensive behavior. Presumably, an offense that occurred six months ago would be more worrisome than an event that occurred eight years ago. This factor is, of course, affected by the degree of supervision that has been in place since the last offense. Mikkelsen and Stelk's (1999) 10-point scale for latency was: 1 (less than 1 year), 2 (1 up to 2 years ago), 3 (2 up to 3 years ago), 4 (4 up to 5 years ago), 5 (5 up to 6 years ago), 6 (6 up to 7 years ago), 7 (7 up to 8 years ago), 8 (8 up to 9 years ago), 9 (9 up to 10 years ago), 10 (10 years or greater). If one were to visualize latency as a third axis going back in time you would create a three-dimensional cube, which can then be dissected into eight categories that combine the elements of severity, frequency, and latency (see Table 6.2).

TREATABILITY

Closely related to the concept of destabilizing factors is the issue of treatability. As noted above, the presence of the major destabilizing factors, such as major mental illness and/or substance abuse, may actually be a positive prognostic factor, as these conditions are often treatable if problems with non-compliance can be overcome. Clinical traits, such as impulsivity, also factor into the assessment of treatability. Primarily, these are factors that appear to be manifestations of an individual's basic temperament and personality and, thus, may be less amenable to treatment. Included in this grouping would also be individual characteristics, such as a fascination with fire, an innate sexual attraction toward children, and a propensity to express oneself through physical action and aggression, rather than words.

These can be difficult concepts to quantify and capture in a clinically meaningful way. However, there are instruments that can aid in this process. An example is Novaco's cognitive analysis of anger (Novaco 1986, 1994), which is meant to provide information on an individual's potential to develop anger in situations that would be expected to provoke that emotion, such as frustration, jealousy, disappointment, embarrassment, and provocation. Another instrument that can be useful in assessing attitudinal contributions to sexually offensive behavior in individuals with developmental disabilities was being developed by Lindsay, Carson and Whitefield (2000). This instrument was designed to assess attitudes that may contribute to incidents of pedophilia, stalking, rape, voyeurism, exhibitionism, homosexual assault, and dating abuse. The Novaco and Lindsay instruments are of particular interest, as they are designed to be applicable to individuals with developmental disabilities.

Hurley and Sovner (1995) have pointed out that some individuals with developmental disabilities can also have an antisocial personality disorder. Diagnostic criteria for this disorder from the 4th edn of the *Diagnostic and Statistical Manual of Mental Disorders* (DSM-IV; American Psychiatric Association, 1994) list the following signs and symptoms: repeatedly performing acts that are grounds for arrest, deceitfulness, irritability, aggressiveness, impulsivity, reckless disregard for safety of self or others, consistent irresponsibility, and lack of remorse for one's actions. The importance of this diagnosis is, of course, that individuals whose criminal acts are an outgrowth of an antisocial personality disorder may be less amenable to treatment than those whose criminal acts are an outgrowth of a destabilizing factor, such as major mental illness that may be more amenable to treatment.

A significant number of criminal offenses by individuals with developmental disabilities are of a sexual nature. Recent analytic studies involving recidivism and follow-up outcome in adults with histories of sexual aggression towards others provide some insight into the treatability of paraphilia and related disorders of sexual aggression (Grossman, Martis & Fichtner, 1999; Hall, 1995). Although the individuals involved in the original studies were usually of average intelligence, the data is still of interest to those who work with sexual offenders who have developmental disabilities. The most striking findings of this meta-analysis were that the baseline untreated recidivism rate for sexual offenders was much less than generally recognized at 27%. Also of interest was the finding that hormonal treatment and cognitive behavioral therapy were equally effective, as both lowered the recidivism rate by approximately 30%. A natural criticism of these studies is that they are primarily based on police arrest records and, thus, most likely under-represent the true rate of recidivism. Nevertheless, this methodology provides the best current data available. Unfortunately, comparable data for sexual offenders with developmental disabilities is not available. There are a number of thorough studies that describe the characteristics of offenders with developmental disabilities (Day, 1994; Gilby, Wolf & Goldberg, 1989; Kearns & O'Connor, 1988; Murrey, Briggs & Davis, 1992), but they do not provide the type of follow-up data that would be needed to determine recidivism rates.

Day (1988) has reported his follow-up data on 26 individuals who were treated in a hospital-based residential treatment program in England between 1974 and 1982. The average age was 21.4 years, with an average IQ of 64.6 (range 58–81). The mean age of the subjects was 30 years, with an age range from late teens to early 50s. The frequency of prior offenses ranged from 1 to "over 100." The range of severity was equally broad, extending from phone calls and stealing of fetish material, up to rape of men and women with disabilities, and child molestation. The follow-up period ranged from 6 months to 5 years, with 8 individuals followed for 5 years and 16 for at least 2 years. In 15 cases, the discharge was planned, while the remainder left the unit for a variety of reasons, including escape and legally mandated discharges.

With regard to discharge dispositions, half went to live with family, five went on to less restrictive but supervised settings, four went to their own apartment, and one went to a specialized program for people with hearing impairments. The outcome data indicated that "during the follow-up period 11 re-offended—8 between 2–4 times, and 6 within the first year." The author also noted that the risk of reoffending is "greatest in the immediate post-discharge period, emphasizing the need for high quality support during this particularly vulnerable time." Day made a natural distinction between offenders against the person (physical and sexual aggression) as opposed to property offenders (destruction of property and/or arson). There was a statistically significant difference (at the 0.05 level) in the outcome data in these two groups in that only 42% of the offenders against the person reoffended, as compared to 88% of the property offenders. Of interest in this regard is the observation that "seven of the twelve offenders against the person received regular tranquilizing or sex-suppressant medication throughout the follow-up period, as compared with only one of the eight property offenders ($p < 0.05$)." This appears to have been an important variable as "there were no significant differences in duration of inpatient treatment, quality of after-care, or length of follow-up between the two groups."

There is also some follow-up data in a manuscript, which is primarily devoted to the description of a treatment program that primarily utilizes group therapy (Swanson & Garwick, 1990). The primary focus of the program was "to replace the sexual offenses with private, relatively safe and non-prosecutable sexuality." As indicated above, the primary focus of this article is not on the follow-up data, therefore, it is not presented in great detail. However, it is noted that if recidivism is defined as the occurrence of any new offense, then "6 (40%) of the clients have recidified," while "by the looser standard of re-arrest only 2 (13%) have been reinvolved with the police for sex offenses."

It is quite possible that individuals with developmental disabilities who commit sexual offenses may be more prone to detection and apprehension than those who are of average or greater intelligence. They may also be more likely to be under some sort of ongoing observation, even if their incompetence to stand trial meant that there could be no formal legal hold on them. The meta-analysis cited earlier would suggest that sexual-suppressant medications and cognitive-behavioral therapy would be considerations for sexual offenders with developmental disabilities. There is published literature concerning the use of the sexual-suppressant medications cypototerone acetate (CPA), flutamide, and medroxyprogesterone acetate (MPA or Depro Provera), all of which serve to decrease functional testosterone levels although they have different mechanisms of action (Clarke, 1989; Cooper, 1995; Myers, 1991). In general, these reviews describe positive results comparable to those seen in populations of sexual offenders with average or greater intelligence quotients. Compliance can be a factor (Cooper, 1995), as in one study only 18 of 48 offenders agreed to take MPA and "it is interesting that individuals who declined MPA were significantly less intelligent than those who agreed to take it."

There have also been successful attempts to apply cognitive behavioral interventions to individuals with developmental disabilities who also commit sexual offenses. Lindsay, Olley, Jack, Morrison and Smith (1998) have reported on the treatment of two men with intellectual disabilities who engaged in stalking behavior. Both men were treated with a cognitive-behavioral approach, one in a group format and the other in individual sessions. The authors report that the individual seen in the group format had a successful outcome, while the individual who was treated individually reoffended after nine months. A similar case controlled methodology was also applied to a follow-up study of the cognitive treatment of four men with developmental disabilities who had been convicted of exhibitionism (Lindsay, Marshall, Neilson, Quinn & Smith, 1998). Careful attention was given to the beliefs of the men regarding the sexually inappropriate behavior, and this was a primary focus of treatment. The length of follow-up was greater than six years, and during that time there were no incidents of indecent exposure for any of the four subjects. A somewhat larger study utilized a similar cognitive-behavioral approach for 14 men with developmental disabilities who collectively had prior charges of sexual offenses ranging from indecent exposure to attempted rape and sexual assault. Many of the incidents involved children. One group of seven men in this study had been given a one-year probationary term, while the other seven had been sentenced to two years probation. This allowed the authors to investigate the issue of attitudinal change against length of treatment. The authors note that there was significant treatment effect in both groups, which was greater in those who received two years probation. The authors note that the group who had received a one-year probation had a greater incidence of reoffending, and the positive attitudinal changes were not sustained as well as they were in the two-year group, who had no incidence of reoffending in the two-year period (Lindsay & Smith, 1998). This cognitive-behavioral approach has also been employed with adolescents with developmental disabilities who have committed sexual offenses, with similar success, both in terms of changes in beliefs and cessation of offending behavior at follow-up (Lindsay, Olley, Baillie & Smith, 1999).

COMMUNITY SAFETY

The purpose of a thorough assessment of risk is to provide the offender with a therapeutic environment that is sufficient to provide safety to themselves and the community at large, while also providing them with as normal a life as possible. There exists a multiplicity of program models that have been developed to serve individuals with developmental disabilities who are also criminal offenders. In order to simplify the discussion, a six-point continuum has been developed, which extends from least restrictive to most restrictive (Mikkelsen, Stelk, Martel & Van Almkerk, 1997). While this continuum does not capture the universe of residential programs that are available, it does elucidate the principal components of security and supervision in a hierarchical manner (see Table 6.3) The brief description of the program model in Table 6.3 is followed by an overview of the characteristics of an individual who would be appropriate for each programmatic subtype.

In practice, one encounters a surprisingly large number of individuals who can be served by program model 4, despite having a history of fairly significant offenses. For the most part, these are individuals whose criminal acts have been impulsive and opportunistic rather than calculated, premeditated, and/or predatory. These offenders can be viewed as individuals who require an "auxiliary ego" with them at all times to prevent them from acting on their impulses when the opportunity arises. For example:

> A Clinical Coordinator indicated in a case conference that whenever she took John (a developmentally impaired individual with a history of pedophilia) to a fast food restaurant in the community, she had to instruct him to go to the bathroom before they left the residence. In response to a comment that this seemed somewhat intrusive, she responded that in the past, before she had implemented this procedure, John would wait until he saw a young boy enter the restroom and then (with a large smile on his face) would say that he had to use the restroom. As she could not follow him into the restroom, she would either have to take the risk that he would not sexually approach the child (which seemed doubtful given his history), or leave the restaurant. Thus, the "using the bathroom before going out" intervention allowed her to take him into the community without putting anyone at risk.

An interesting observation about John and those with similar opportunistic profiles is that they will not physically confront or overpower the staff to offend. All they appear to need is an "auxiliary ego" at their side to provide the external control to compensate for their lack of internal control. Some programs refer to this as "external relapse prevention," as opposed to "internal relapse prevention," which would come from the internalization of treatment goals.

FUTURE RISK

Quinsey, Harris, Rice and Cormier (1998) have developed a rigorous, statistically-based methodology for the assessment of an individual's risk of reoffending, which is referred to as the Violence Risk Appraisal Guide (VRAG). This methodology

Table 6.3 The continuum of community-based treatment programs for criminal offenders with mental retardation

Program type	Individual profile
1. *Case management services only*	The individual presents virtually no risk to the community, danger of offending is extremely low, and/or behaviors are of very low severity.
2. *Supported living—several hours per day unsupervised*	The individual presents virtually no risk to the community or past experience indicates that a minimal amount of staff supervision/support is sufficient to keep the behavior from occurring.
3. *Specialized home care or concrete living environment that provides substantial daily support and supervision, but the individual does have some unsupervised time, which would provide opportunity for continued offenses*	The individual's history and presentation suggest that when living in a structured-supported setting, they do not engage in the dangerous maladaptive behavior, thus indicating that they are not at risk of reoffending during the unsupervised periods of time.
4. *Living environment that provides continuous eyes-on supervision during all waking hours, but does not require awake, overnight staffing*	The individual's behavior pattern indicates that they will potentially utilize any unsupervised time to reoffend, but will respond to verbal redirection and/or can exert self-control, if accompanied by staff. They will not elope from the program during the night to offend.
5. *Program provides continuous eyes-on supervision with awake, overnight staff, and the capacity to physically restrain the individual, if necessary*	The individual displays ongoing frequent aggressive behavior and has demonstrated little ability to exert self-control. When physical restraint is required, it is of relatively brief duration and does not usually result in physical injury to staff.
6. *Program provides locked-door security, the capacity to physically restrain if necessary, and the capability to seclude the individual from others for brief periods of time*	The behavior profile is characterized by high levels of physically and/or sexually aggressive behavior. The individual is able to exert almost no self-control. Prolonged physical restraint may be required, and there is a history of physical injury to staff.

Source: Reproduced with permission from Mikkelson and Stelk (1999).

considers the history of past criminal offenses, as well as other historical and psychosocial risk factors. While the research that this instrument is based on primarily relates to offenders with mental illness, it is also applicable in many ways to the issues presented by offenders with developmental disabilities (see also Chapter 7).

The outline contained in Figure 6.1 provides a format for integrating the relevant elements of risk assessment discussed in this manuscript into a coherent report. It can also be used as an outline for guiding the discussion in case conferences. Figures 6.2–6.4 provide completed examples of this form, which are derived

---

RISK ASSESSMENT PROFILE FORM

Demographics:

Age/sex:
Level of mental retardation:
Living environment:
Level of supervision: (Use Continuum of Services Scale)

Actual incidents: (Use Aggression Rating Scales)

Physical:

Sexual:

Risk probability rank: (Use Probability Ranking Scale)

Legal history:

Destabilizing factors:

Stabilizing factors:

Systems issues:

Overall risk assessment:

Figure 6.1   Risk assessment profile form.
Source: Reproduced with permission from Mikkelsen and Stelk (1999).

from composite cases and do not reflect actual individuals due to concerns about confidentiality. There are a few entries on the risk assessment outline (see Figure 6.1) that are not discussed above. The sub-heading "Legal history" refers to the historical response of the legal system to the individual's criminal acts in the past. For example, "arson 1996 severity level 4—not competent to stand trial". The sub-heading "Stabilizing factors" is meant to provide a place for discussion of those factors that militate against destabilizing influences in the individual's life and provide a buffer to life's stressors. This can also be used as a place to note the absence of significant destabilizing factors. Active alcohol and/or substance abuse are such powerful destabilizing factors that it can be worthwhile to note their absence here as a stabilizing factor. The subheading "Systems issues" is meant to provide the opportunity to discuss specific factors, which complicate management, but are not accounted for in the more general headings above. An example would be an individual who presents a significant risk, has been found not competent to stand trial, and is under guardianship of a parent who refuses

RISK ASSESSMENT PROFILE

Demographics:

Age/Sex: 28-year-old male.
Level of mental retardation: Low, mild-high, moderate.
Living environment: Apartment, frequent contact with dysfunctional
                                 family.
Level of supervision: 1

Actual Incidents:

Physical:

(1)   Arson, unoccupied building (2 years ago) = Severity Level 6.
(2)   Arson, unoccupied building (5 years ago) = Severity Level 6.
(3)   Intermittent theft (socialized with family), not involving physical
      aggression = Level 4.

Sexual: None

Overt Behavior Matrix Rating: 6

Legal history:

(1)   Arrested for arson (5 years ago)—found Not Competent—released after
      brief period of evaluation.
(2)   Arrested for arson (2 years ago)—hospitalization in forensic psychiatry
      unit (18 months) for competency evaluation—Not Competent final
      assessment—released.

Destabilizing factors:

Refuses environmental supports or treatment; also resistant to case
management, ongoing involvement with dysfunctional, antisocial family.

Stabilizing factors: No substance abuse.

Systems issues: Adjudication of Not Competent, plus resistance to services.

Overall risk assessment: Likelihood of future theft and low-level arson is high.

Figure 6.2   Risk assessment profile 1.
Source: Reproduced with permission from Mikkelsen and Stelk (1999).

RISK ASSESSMENT PROFILE

Demographics:

Age/sex: 29-year-old male.
Level of mental retardation: Mild.
Living environment: Group home.
Level of supervision: 24-hour awake staff—Option 5.

Actual Incidents:

Physical: Frequent, ongoing non-violent theft = Severity Level 4.

Sexual: Sexual involvement with lower functioning peer (4 years ago),
                thought to be consensual = Security Level 7.

Risk probability rank:

Physical: Level 4—Low Severity, High Frequency, Recent Past.
Sexual: Level 5—High Severity, Low Frequency, Distant Past.

Legal history:

Has had extended psychiatric-forensic evaluations—never found competent.

Destabilizing Factors:

Mixed personality disorder with antisocial properties; resistant to treatment
and environmental supports/supervision; frequent runaway behavior.

Stabilizing factors: No substance abuse.

Systems issues: Legal findings of Not Competent.

Overall Risk Assessment:

Very high for continued level of behavior with regard to theft. No indication of
recent sexual victimization of others.

Figure 6.3   Risk assessment profile 2.
Source: Reproduced with permission from Mikkelsen and Stelk (1999).

appropriate services for the offender. This can occur due to the parent's denial of the
severity of the risk the individual presents to the community, the parent's own psychopathology, and/or their reluctance to see any restrictions placed on their child's
activities.

RISK ASSESSMENT PROFILE

Demographics:

Age/sex:	38-year-old male
Level of mental retardation:	Moderate
Living environment:	Group home
Level of supervision:	Awake overnight staff—Option 5

Actual incidents:

Physical:

(1) Attacked staff person with knife causing laceration which required suturing, but no internal injuries (within the last year)—Severity Level 7;
(2) Set fire to residence. No loss of life, but substantial property destruction. Subject knew no one was in residence so no risk to life (over 10 years ago)—Severity Level 6.

Sexual: None

Risk probability rank: Level 6—High Severity, Low Frequency, Recent Past

Legal history:

(1) Arrested after fire, but charges dismissed.
(2) Police called after assault, but no charges filed.

Destabilizing factors: Borderline personality disorder.

Stabilizing factors: No substance abuse.

Systems issues:

Treatment team is conflicted over how to respond to aggressive acts in regard to responsibility.

Overall risk assessment:

Supervision is adequate to prevent frequent incidents—short-term risk is low, but possibility of another high profile event at some time in future is high.

Figure 6.4 Risk assessment profile 3.
Source: Reproduced with permission from Mikkelsen and Stelk (1999).

CONCLUSION

The comprehensive clinical assessment of individuals with developmental disabilities who commit criminal offenses should include consideration of the related domains of accountability, destabilizing factors, history of prior offenses, treatabilty, community safety, and future risk. The goal of this process is to guide in the development of individualized community-based residential programs that greatly diminish the risk of another offense, while providing the individual with as normal a life as possible. Ideally, a continuum of programs would exist so that a given individual could gradually progress to less restrictive environments as their behavior showed positive responses to treatment. The lack of such a graduated continuum can lead to either the individual being stuck in a more restrictive program than is necessary, or alternately being released to relatively unrestricted settings which do not provide enough supervision to prevent relapse.

ACKNOWLEDGMENTS

Tables 6.1–6.3 and Figures 6.1–6.4 are reprinted with permission of NADD and are from E.J. Mikkelsen and W.J. Stelk (1999). *Criminal Offenders with Mental Retardation: Risk Assessment and the Continuum of Community-Based Treatment Programs*. Kingston, NY: NADD Press.

The author would like to acknowledge the assistance of Ms Patsy Kuropatkin in the preparation of this manuscript.

REFERENCES

Aman, M.G. & Singh, N.N. (1986). *Aberrant Behavior Checklist Manual*. East Aurora, NY: Slosson Educational Publications.

Aman, M.G. & Singh, N.N. (1994). *Aberrant Behavior Checklist Community Supplementary Manual*. East Aurora, NY: Slosson Educational Publications.

American Psychiatric Association. (1994). *Diagnostic and Statistical Manual of Mental Disorders*, 4th edn. Washington, DC: American Psychiatric Association.

Arseneault, L., Moffitt, T.E., Caspi, A., Taylor, P.J. & Silva, P.A. (2000). Mental disorders and violence in a total birth cohort. Results from the Dunedin Study. *Archives of General Psychiatry*, **57**, 979–86.

Borum, R. (1996). Improving the clinical practice of violence risk assessment: technology, guidelines, and training. *American Psychologist*, **51**, 945–56.

Clare, I.C.H. & Gudjonsson, G.H. (1993). Interrogative suggestibility, confabulation, and acquiescence in people with mild learning disabilities (mental handicap): implications for reliability during police interrogations. *British Journal of Clinical Psychology*, **32**, 295–301.

Clarke, D.J. (1989). Anti-libidinal drugs and mental retardation: a review. *Medicine, Science, and the Law*, **29**, 136–46.

Cooper, A.J. (1995). Review of the role of two antilibidinal drugs in the treatment of sex offenders with mental retardation. *Mental Retardation*, **33**, 42–8.

Day, K. (1988). A hospital-based treatment programme for male mentally handicapped offenders. *British Journal of Psychiatry*, **153**, 635–44.

Day, K. (1994). Male mentally handicapped sex offenders. *British Journal of Psychiatry*, **165**, 630–9.

Einfeld, S.L. & Tonge, B.J. (1995). The Developmental Behaviour Checklist: the development and validation of an instrument for the assessment of behavioral and emotional disturbance in children and adolescents with mental retardation. *Journal of Autism and Developmental Disorders*, **25**, 81–104.

Gilby, R., Wolf, L. & Goldberg, B. (1989). Mentally retarded adolescent sex offenders: a survey and pilot study. *Canadian Journal of Psychiatry*, **34**, 542–8.

Grossman, L.S., Martis, B. & Fichtner, C.G. (1999). Are sex offenders treatable? A research overview. *Psychiatric Services*, **50**, 349–61.

Grubin, D.H. (1991). Unfit to plead in England and Wales, 1976–88: a survey. *British Journal of Psychiatry*, **158**, 540–8.

Hall, G.C.N. (1995). Sexual offender recidivism revisited: a meta-analysis of recent treatment studies. *Journal of Consulting and Clinical Psychology*, **63**, 802–9.

Hauser, M.J. (1997). The role of the psychiatrist in mental retardation. *Psychiatric Annals*, **27**, 170–4.

Hurley, A. & Sovner, R. (1995). Six cases of patients with mental retardation who have antisocial personality disorder. *Psychiatric Services*, **46**, 828–31.

Kearns, A. & O'Connor, A. (1988). The mentally handicapped criminal offender. A 10-year study of two hospitals. *British Journal of Psychiatry*, **152**, 848–51.

Lindsay, W.R., Carson, D. & Whitefield, E. (2000). Development of a questionnaire on attitudes consistent with sex offending for men with intellectual disabilities. *Journal of Intellectual Disability Research*, **44**, 368.

Lindsay, W.R. , Law, J. & MacLeod, F. (2004). Intellectual disabilities and crime: issues in assessment, intervention and management. In: A. Needs & G. Towl (eds) *Applying Psychology to Forensic Practice*. London: Blackwell.

Lindsay, W.R. , Marshall, I., Neilson, C., Quinn, K. & Smith, A.H.W. (1998). The treatment of men with a learning disability convicted of exhibitionism. *Research in Developmental Disabilities*, **19**, 295–315.

Lindsay, W.R. & Michie, A.M. (1988). Adaptation of the Zung Self-rating Scale for Anxiety for people with a mental handicap. *Journal of Mental Deficiency Research*, **32**, 485–90.

Lindsay, W.R., Olley, S., Baillie, N. & Smith, H.W. (1999). Treatment of adolescent sex offenders with intellectual disabilities. *Mental Retardation*, **37**, 201–11.

Lindsay, W.R., Olley, S., Jack, C., Morrison, F. & Smith, A.H.W. (1998). The treatment of two stalkers with intellectual disabilities using a cognitive approach. *Journal of Applied Research in Intellectual Disabilities*, **11**, 333–44.

Lindsay, W.R. & Smith, A.H.W. (1998). Responses to treatment for sex offenders with intellectual disability: a comparison of men with 1- and 2-year probation sentences. *Journal of Intellectual Disability Research*, **42**, 346–53.

Link, B.G. & Stueve, A. (1998). New evidence on the violence risk posed by people with mental illness. On the importance of specifying the timing and the targets of violence. *Archives of General Psychiatry*, **55**, 403–4.

Matson, J.L. (1997). *The PIMRA Manual*, 2nd edn. Worthington, OH: IDS Publishing.

Matson, J.L., Coe, A., Gardner, W.I. & Sovner, R. (1991). A factor analytic study of the diagnostic assessment for the severely handicapped scale. *Journal of Nervous and Mental Disorders*, **179**, 553–7.

Mikkelsen, E.J. (1997). Risk–benefit analysis in the use of psychopharmacologic interventions for difficult-to-diagnose behavioral disorders in individuals with mental retardation. *Psychiatric Annals*, **27**, 207–12.

Mikkelsen, E.J. & McKenna, L. (1999). Psychopharmacologic algorithms for adults with developmental disabilities and difficult-to-diagnose behavioral disorders. *Psychiatric Annals*, **29**, 302–14.

Mikkelsen, E.J. & Stelk, W.J. (1999). *Criminal Offenders with Mental Retardation: Risk Assessment and the Continuum of Community-Based Treatment Programs*. Kingston, NY: NADD Press.

Mikkelsen, E.J., Stelk, W.J., Martel, D. & Van Almkerk, P. (1997). The continuum of community-based treatment programs for criminal offenders with mental retardation. In D.N. McNelis and T.M. McNelis (eds) *Proceedings of the 14th Annual Conference of the*

National Association for the Dually Diagnosed (Mental Retardation/Mental Illness), National Association for the Dually Diagnosed (pp. 77–181) Kingston, NY: NADD Press.

Monahan, J. & Steadman, J.H. (1996). Violent storms and violent people: how meteorology can inform risk communication in mental health law. *American Psychologist*, **51**, 931–8.

Murrey, G.J., Briggs, D. & Davis, C. (1992). Psychopathic disordered, mentally ill, and mentally handicapped sex offenders: a comparative study. *Medical Science Law*, **32**, 331–6.

Myers, B.A. (1991). Treatment of sexual offenses by persons with developmental disabilities. *American Journal on Mental Retardation*, **95**, 563–9.

Nihira, K., Leland, H. & Lambert, N. (1993). *Adaptive Behavior Scale: Residential and Community*. Washington, DC: American Association of Mental Retardation.

Novaco, R.W. (1986). Anger as a clinical and social problem. In R. Blanchard & C. Blanchard (eds) *Advances in the Study of Aggression*, vol. 2. New York: Academic Press.

Novaco, R.W. (1994). Anger as a risk factor for violence among the mentally disordered. In: J. Monahan and H.J. Steadman (eds) *Violence in Mental Disorder: Developments in Risk Assessment*. Chicago, IL: University of Chicago Press.

Quinsey, V.L., Harris, G.T., Rice, M.E. & Cormier. C.A. (1998). *Violent Offenders: Appraising and Managing Risk*. Washington, DC: American Psychological Association.

Reiss, S. (1988). *Test Manual for the Reiss Screen for Maladaptive Behavior*. Worthington, OH: IDS.

Reiss, S. & Aman, M.G. (eds) (1998). *Psychotropic Medications and Developmental Disabilities: The International Consensus Handbook*. Columbus, OH: Ohio State University.

Silka, V.R. & Hauser, M.J. (1997). Psychiatric assessment of the person with mental retardation. *Psychiatric Annals*, **27**, 162–9.

Smith, S.A. (1993). Confusing the terms "guilty" and "not guilty": implications for alleged offenders with mental retardation. *Psychological Reports*, **73**, 675–8.

Smith, S.A. & Broughton, S.F. (1994). Competency to stand trial and criminal responsibility: an analysis in South Carolina. *Mental Retardation*, **32**, 281–7.

Smith, S.A. & Hudson, R.L. (1995). A quick screening test of competency to stand trial for defendants with mental retardation. *Psychological Reports*, **76**, 91–7.

Steadman, H.J., Mulvey, E.P., Monahan, J., Robbins, P.C., Appelbaum, P.S., Grisso, T., Roth, L.H. & Silver, E. (1998). Violence by people discharged from acute psychiatric inpatient facilities and by others in the same neighborhoods. *Archives of General Psychiatry*, **55**, 393–401.

Strohmer, D.C. & Prout. H.T. (1991). *The Emotional Problems Scales*. Odessa, FL: Psychological Assessment Resources.

Swanson, C.K. & Garwick, G.B. (1990). Treatment for low-functioning sex offenders: group therapy and interagency coordination. *Mental Retardation*, **28**, 155–61.

Chapter 7

RISK ASSESSMENT AND MANAGEMENT IN COMMUNITY SETTINGS

VERNON L. QUINSEY
Queen's University at Kingston, Ontario, Canada

This chapter reviews assessment and management approaches with individuals who have intellectual disabilities and are at risk for the commission of violent and sexual offences in community settings. Particular attention is given to the distinction between static and dynamic risk because of its importance in decision making and the management of offenders.

Before beginning, it is worth noting that there is a substantial literature bearing on risk management in institutional contexts. This literature, although primarily dealing with physical assaults on staff and institutional residents, is relevant to risk assessment and management in community contexts. This is partly because we may expect many of the same proximal causes to be operative and partly because individuals who have intellectual disabilities often live in supervised community settings, not unlike tiny institutions. Harder outcome data are often also obtainable in institutional settings, where frequencies of assaults and their antecedents can be directly observed. Matson and his colleagues (Applegate, Matson & Cherry, 1999; Duncan, Matson, Bamburg, Cherry & Buckley, 1999; Matson, Bamburg, Cherry & Paclawskyj, 1999) present extensive functional assessment, behavioral treatment, and outcome data on institutionalized individuals who have intellectual disabilities.

Studies on institutional violence among individuals with intellectual handicaps and mental illnesses demonstrate that: (1) actuarial methods can estimate the long-term likelihood with which individuals will be assaultive, (2) dynamic variables signal the imminence of very serious assaults, (3) certain medications can reduce assaults among patients with particular diagnoses, (4) behavioral methods can markedly reduce or eliminate assaults, and (5) training staff in interview, security, and physical management can reduce assaults and staff injury. For reviews of this material see Quinsey (2000) and Rice, Harris, Varney & Quinsey (1989).

Offenders with Developmental Disabilities. Edited by W.L. Lindsay, J.L. Taylor and P. Sturmey.
© 2004 John Wiley & Sons, Ltd.

APPRAISING RISK IN COMMUNITY SETTINGS

Although a minority of individuals who have intellectual disabilities exhibit problems of aggression, their absolute number is not inconsiderable. In a study of all individuals who were involved with educational, health, or social services for individuals with intellectual disabilities in two regions in England, Emerson *et al.* (2001) found that 10–15% exhibited some form of challenging behavior. Aggression was shown by 7%, destructive behavior by 4%, and self-injury by 4% of the sample. The majority of individuals who showed one form of challenging behavior also showed others. These challenging individuals were disproportionately young, male, and more severely handicapped.

The risk of violent or sexual offending the client presents to the community or open setting (Quinsey & Walker, 1992; Zamble & Quinsey, 1997) consists of two separable components: (1) the long-term likelihood with which a person might commit a new sexual or violent misbehavior determined by static or historical information, including treatment outcome, and (2) short-term changes that are related to the imminence of aggressive behavior. Short-term predictors indicating when an individual is more or less likely to engage in antisocial behaviors are termed fluctuating or acute dynamic risk factors because they change continuously over time. Acute dynamic risk factors, such as current mood, although unsuitable for estimating long-term propensities to engage in antisocial behavior, can indicate when supervision or management should be changed to reduce a client's risk.

Considerable progress has been made in the actuarial assessment of long-term risk in forensic psychiatric and correctional populations but little of this actuarial work has been specifically applied to clients who have intellectual disabilities. Moreover, little research has been done to identify dynamic indicators of changing risk in any at-risk population. A decision to close institutions that housed men with intellectual disabilities and serious histories of antisocial and aggressive behaviors provided an opportunity to determine how well static predictors could forecast the likelihood of their committing similar behaviors while living in community settings (Quinsey, Book & Skilling, submitted). In addition, these closures provided an opportunity to investigate the extent to which monthly staff ratings of client characteristics and behaviors were related to the imminence of antisocial and aggressive behaviors.

In the study, 58 men were followed up for an average of 16 months. Their average age at the start of the follow-up was 40 years (s.d. = 10.59). All clients had a chart diagnosis of mental retardation. In addition, 80% of the participants had at least one additional diagnosis, and 29% of the sample had at least two additional diagnoses: 56% had a diagnosis of some type of personality disorder, 36% had been diagnosed with some type of paraphilia, 11% had a diagnosis of psychosis, 9% were diagnosed with affective disorder, and 2% had been diagnosed with a substance abuse disorder.

The histories of the antisocial behaviors in which clients had engaged varied widely in seriousness and chronicity. The most serious offense with which a client had been charged was manslaughter. About 70% of the clients had documented incidents and/or arrests for sex offenses of various kinds. Almost all of these were offenses in which physical contact was made with the victim. It was common for clients to have had sexual offenses against children in the community and against adult peers in the institution. Clients were sometimes charged for their misbehaviors, particularly if they occurred in a community setting, but often these charges were dropped upon their institutionalization or transfer to a more secure institution. More than half of the clients presented chronic management problems involving sexual and/or physical aggressiveness within the institution.

There were over 500 incidents reported by the staff during the follow-up period. Most of these were minor and two subjects contributed more than half of them; 39 of the 58 clients had at least one incident. In terms of the most serious incident per subject, there were 7 incidents of being absent without leave, 1 incident of fire setting, 4 incidents involving hands-on sexual misbehaviors, and 27 violent incidents involving physical contact between the client and another person. None of the violent or sexual incidents involved community members; all were against staff or other clients. Only two of the victims of violent incidents required medical attention, although minor physical injuries, involving scratches, bite marks, and bruising were common. Many of the incidents required staff to intervene physically to restrain the client.

The Violence Risk Appraisal Guide (VRAG; Harris, Rice & Quinsey, 1993) was used to estimate long-term risk because it is currently among the most accurate predictors of which men in forensic psychiatric and correctional populations will commit a new violent or sexual offense. It yields a specific probability estimate of violent or sexual recidivism. The VRAG has been cross-validated on a variety of forensic psychiatric and correctional samples (Quinsey, Harris, Rice & Cormier, 1998; see http://www.mhcva.on.ca/Research). More importantly, in the original construction sample, the VRAG was as accurate with offenders who had intellectual disabilities as with offenders who did not (Quinsey, Harris, Rice & Cormier, 1998). The version of the VRAG used in this research substituted a measure of childhood and adolescent antisocial behavior (the Childhood and Adolescent Taxon Scale) for the Revised Psychopathy Checklist (Hare, 1991). This was done because of the difficulties in scoring one of the VRAG items, the psychopathy measure, with intellectually handicapped clients, particularly from file data.

In addition to the VRAG, two other measures of risk were used in this project. The Problem Identification Checklist (Rice, Harris, Quinsey & Cyr, 1990) was used because it can be completed quickly by treatment staff and can also be scored from institutional files. Previous research has demonstrated that the Inappropriate Social Behaviors and Procriminal Attitude Subscale of the Problem Identification Checklist is related to elopement and violent reoffending of mentally disordered offenders (Quinsey, Coleman, Jones & Altrows, 1997). The Dynamic Antisociality Subscale of the Proximal Risk Factor Scale was chosen as a third measure because it is strongly related to elopement and violent reoffending among supervised mentally disordered offenders and, like the Problem Identification Checklist, can be scored from file or staff interview (Quinsey et al., 1997).

There is evidence that both the Problem Identification Checklist and the Proximal Risk Factor Scale can also be used as measures of dynamic risk from a study that used within-offender changes in scores on these instruments to forecast imminence of violent reoffending (Quinsey et al., 1997). In the first part of the research reported below these measures were taken from pre-release file data and changes in them were not examined. They thus functioned as static predictors suitable for making long-term estimates of risk.

Static Prediction

The VRAG was the only statistically significant predictor of new violent or sexual misbehaviors. The VRAG results confirm the enduring nature of the risk for reoffending, suggesting that programs for high-risk clients must be available for the indefinite future. The need for long-term support is, of course, not restricted to clients who are at risk to reoffend but also applies to persons with intellectual disabilities who have other behavioral or psychiatric problems (Reid & Ballinger, 1995) and chronic mental patients.

Dynamic Prediction

In the field trial, monthly staff ratings of client characteristics from months in which clients exhibited no antisocial behaviors differentiated clients who subsequently had antisocial incidents from those who did not, suggesting that these changes may be useful for establishing treatment targets and titrating supervision. These differences remained significant even when the best measure of static risk, the VRAG, was controlled for statistically. There was suggestive evidence from within-client analyses of variance that changes in staff ratings foreshadowed new antisocial behaviors, but these results were inconclusive. The scales that were most closely related to incidents were those that have been found to predict eloping, aggression, and criminal conduct in our previous research (Quinsey et al., 1997).

Of course, some of the items of the various subscales performed better as predictors than others. The best items were therefore chosen for inclusion in a new scale that might be of use to clinicians in research with developmentally handicapped men who have histories of serious aggressive incidents. Below is a description of how the items for this new, briefer, scale were selected and how well the instrument performed as a dynamic indicator of risk.

Items from the Problem Identification Checklist and the Proximal Risk Factor Scale were selected if they exhibited a significant linear trend across previous, prior, and index months for those clients who had incidents. Previous months were the average of up to six months data prior to the month before the incident (the prior month) that did not contain an incident. The index month was the month containing the incident. Because ratings were obtained at the end of the month, index month ratings could be contaminated by retrospective bias. The analyses identified eight items by their statistical significance. The average alpha of these eight items, designated as the Short Dynamic Risk Scale (see Figure 7.1), was 0.82 based on an average N of 32.27.

There were 22 clients included in the analyses predicting any incident. The means for the previous, prior, and index months were 8.32 (5.60), 12.01 (7.42), and 14.51 (6.07), respectively. The linear trend was significant ($F(1,21) = 30.70, p < 0.001$). All contrasts among the three means were significant ($p < 0.05$).

Short Dynamic Risk Scale

For each of the eight items, circle the *one* number that best describes the client's presentation *over the past MONTH*. If the problem area does not apply to this client because the client has not had the opportunity to show the behaviors concerned or if insufficient information is available to make a judgement, circle "999" for N/A or Unknown. If you are able to say that the client has *not* had the particular problem at *any* time during the past month, record 0 for No Problem. If the problem has existed *at any time in the past month*, circle 1, 2, 3, or 4 as appropriate.

****

1. In the past month, takes no responsibility for behavior: Tries to blame others or circumstances for his/her acts or problems. Sees him/herself, inappropriately, as a victim.

0	1	2	3	4	999
No problem		Moderate problem		Severe problem	N/A or Unknown

2. In the past month, exhibits few positive coping skills: Deals inappropriately with anger, i.e. reacts aggressively rather than assertively. Does not deal with stressful or upsetting events in a constructive way, i.e. aggressive or self-defeating.

0	1	2	3	4	999
No problem		Moderate problem		Severe problem	N/A or Unknown

3. Anxiety or anger or frustration in the last month.

0	1	2	3	4	999
No problem		Moderate problem		Severe problem	N/A or Unknown

4. Anger in the past month: Inappropriate displays of losing temper. If the anger expressed is minor, then an isolated instance can be ignored.

0	1	2	3	4	999
No problem		Moderate problem		Severe problem	N/A or Unknown

5. Insulting, teasing, and obnoxious verbal behavior: This must be beyond good-natured play and is not just an isolated incident.

0	1	2	3	4	999
No problem		Moderate problem		Severe problem	N/A or Unknown

6. Lack of consideration for others: Callousness, little empathy—anything that shows an attitude of thinking only about their own concerns and never of the thoughts, feelings of, or consequences for, other clients or staff.

0	1	2	3	4	999
No problem		Moderate problem		Severe problem	N/A or Unknown

7. Poor housekeeping or cooking: Sleeping area is a mess. Leaves a mess in kitchen or common areas. Does not pick up after himself.

0	1	2	3	4	999
No problem		Moderate problem		Severe problem	N/A or Unknown

8. Poor self-care and personal hygiene: Does not wash or washes infrequently.

0	1	2	3	4	999
No problem		Moderate problem		Severe problem	N/A or Unknown

Figure 7.1   Short dynamic risk scale

There were eight clients included in the analyses predicting violent incidents. The means for the previous, prior, and index months were 8.98 (6.82), 14.28 (6.66), and 17.25 (5.60), respectively. The linear trend was significant (F (1,7) = 21.58, p = 0.002). The only contrast that was not significant ($p < 0.05$) was index versus prior month.

The finding that the Short Dynamic Risk Scale differentiated previous from prior months for both incidents of any type and violent incidents is particularly encouraging because the effect is large and not influenced by retrospective bias. This optimistic conclusion must be tempered by the small number of clients in these analyses and the capitalization of these findings on chance caused by the way the items were identified. Nevertheless, although we expect shrinkage in the effect sizes in cross-validation, the Short Dynamic Risk Scale deserves testing in a new prospective study.

MANAGING RISK IN COMMUNITY SETTINGS

A reasonably accurate estimate of long-term risk is required to determine the appropriate level of supervision required for individual clients. Actuarial instruments such as the VRAG appear capable of providing such an estimate for clients with intellectual disabilities. Ongoing management of risk and changes in level of supervision, however, require monitoring of changes in dynamic risk so as to proactively adjust supervision. The dynamic variables rated in the field trial described above appear promising for this task because changes in them differentiated clients who subsequently exhibited antisocial behaviors from those who did not, most clearly in the case of incidents of any kind. The changes in staff ratings were prospectively related to risk and some of these changes occurred over a period of months. Therefore, staff could use them to increase or decrease supervision level or to adjust programs designed to reduce the likelihood with which clients become involved in aggressive or antisocial behaviors.

Further research will be required to demonstrate the degree to which temporal changes in dynamic variables, such as those sampled by the Short Dynamic Risk Scale, are related to the imminence of violent and sexual misbehaviors within individual clients. It is likely that predictive accuracy will be maximized from staff ratings that occur more frequently than once a month. Our previous research (Quinsey et al., 1997) documented dynamic risk factors by comparing measures documented during the month leading up to an incident of antisocial behavior in comparison to measures taken in a month period a year earlier. Even ratings made weekly would be more likely to reflect changes in client characteristics that are temporally more closely linked to the occurrence of antisocial events.

We have described specific treatment methods for clusters of forensic clients who present different patterns of risk and need in detail elsewhere (Quinsey et al., 1998; Rice, Harris, Quinsey & Cyr, 1990). Interventions for clients who have intellectual disabilities that have the potential to reduce long-term risk have been reviewed by Cipani (1989). Additionally, work on Assertive Community Treatment (e.g. Burns & Santos, 1995; Lafave, de Souza & Gerber, 1996) also appears to be an appropriate model for the provision of services because of its implementation with high-risk individuals in community settings. However, two further elements of programming require careful attention: supervision and crisis intervention.

The degree of risk that an agency is able to assume depends on the amount and quality of supervision available in the community and the characteristics of the environment, such as access to young or vulnerable persons, in which the client is placed. Supervision for very high risk clients requires that a particular person be responsible for authorizing a particular level of supervision for an individual client and for coordinating its implementation. It is also necessary that that person has the legal authority to compel compliance (Wiederanders, 1992; Wiederanders, Bromley & Choate, 1997).

One of the components of Assertive Community Treatment is 24-hour availability of staff. In the Rochester model, Davidson *et al.* (1995) have documented the importance of the availability of a crisis team in the management of persons with intellectual disabilities together with behavioral and psychiatric problems. Part of the crisis team's resources were in-patient beds where clients could be stabilized before re-entering the community. This is a particularly important capability in the management of high-risk clients.

An illustration of these recommendations is provided by Bird, Sperry and Carreiro (1998), who describe a successful program for 10 individuals with intellectual disabilities and psychiatric disorders who had failed in a previous community placement because of aggressive, antisocial, and suicidal behaviors. The program involved a network of mental health and developmental disabilities services. It focused on applying psychiatric rehabilitation principles and environmental behavior support strategies through "goal-setting, comprehensive case management, social skills training, positive reinforcement, crisis intervention, competency-based skills teaching, medication monitoring, data-based outcome measurement, and community-living arrangements" (p. 331). Compared to their pre-intervention status, all participants showed "significant reductions in targeted behaviors, maintained extended placement within the community without emergency hospitalizations, developed effective and adaptive social skills, secured job placement, and reported satisfaction with their quality of life" (p. 331).

APPRAISING THE RISK OF SEXUAL OFFENDING

A large literature, including studies of siblings from within the same family, documents an inverse relationship between intelligence and criminal activity (for a review see Jensen, 1998). The inverse relationship is found in both self-report and officially recorded data (White, Moffitt & Silva, 1989). More importantly, men with intellectual disabilities are more likely than others to have pedophilic sexual preferences (Blanchard *et al.*, 1999). The reason for this association is unknown. Although intellectual disability is a risk factor for antisocial behavior in general and for pedophilia in particular, it is a poor predictor of recidivism in and of itself.

Because there has been little predictive or evaluative research conducted specifically with sex offenders who are intellectually handicapped (Nezu, Nezu & Dudek, 1998), recommendations rely primarily on studies on non-intellectually disabled sex offenders or on studies that include intellectually disabled sex offenders with others. Quinsey and Lalumière (2001) have summarized actuarial instruments for the assessment of violent or sexual recidivism among sexual offenders against children. These include the VRAG, the Sex Offender Risk Appraisal Guide (SORAG), and the Static-99 (Hanson & Thornton, 2000). The Risk Appraisal Guides yield an actuarial estimate of violent or sexual recidivism and the Static-99 estimates sexual recidivism alone. Phallometric measures of sexual deviance employing suitable stimuli and testing protocols have excellent discriminant validity among both rapists (Lalumière & Quinsey, 1994) and sexual offenders against children (Harris, Rice, Quinsey, Chaplin & Earls, 1992). Phallometrically measured sexual preferences are also related to recidivism and are incorporated into the SORAG. Although not yet part of an actuarial instrument, the interaction of sexual deviance as determined by phallometric assessment and psychopathy as measured by the revised Psychopathy Checklist (PCL-R; Hare, 1991) is a potent predictor of recidivism among both juvenile and adult sex offenders: sex offenders who are both psychopathic and sexually deviant are uniquely likely to reoffend (Gretton, McBride, Hare, O'Shaughnessy & Kumka, 2001; Rice & Harris, 1997).

MANAGING THE RISK OF SEXUAL OFFENDING

Interventions are designed to reduce the risk of sexual offending in the long term through psychological treatments or managed in the short-term through supervision. Treatment interventions for reducing the likelihood of sexual offending have produced variable effect sizes and the literature is bedeviled with methodological difficulties. The principal problems in the literature pertain to pre-treatment differences in risk between treated and untreated groups and the effects of attrition since clients most likely to reoffend are most likely to fail to complete treatment programs. The most comprehensive meta-analysis to date (Hanson et al., 2002) concludes that there is likely a positive, but rather small, beneficial effect of psychological treatment on sexual recidivism. For clients who are at moderate to high risk for sexual reoffending based on an actuarial assessment or who have multiple sexual offenses, bona fide paraphilic interests as determined by elements of their offense history (Seto & Lalumière, 2001), self-report, or phallometric assessment, the variable and modest effects of treatment mean that some form of supervision is usually required.

Treatment programs for sex offenders who have intellectual disabilities differ from those designed for non-intellectually disabled sex offenders in important respects. The time needed for cognitive assessments and interventions is greater and simplified materials and methods tailored to the cognitive abilities of the clients are required (e.g. Haaven, Little & Petre-Miller, 1990; Kolton, Boer & Boer, 2001). Issues of informed consent are more difficult and often require the use of client advocates. Inappropriate attitudes toward sexual behavior acquired in institutions often need to be changed, and acceptable feasible sexual outlets may need to be identified and encouraged (Griffiths, Quinsey & Hingsburger, 1989; Hingsburger et al., 1999; Johnston & Halstead, 1995). Regrettably, there are as yet no random assignment evaluations of treatment efficacy with intellectually disabled sex offenders.

Supervision involves curtailing opportunity to reoffend. A combination of supervision and treatment in a community-based specialized clinic has been associated with low sexual recidivism among intellectually handicapped clients (Griffiths, Quinsey & Hingsburger, 1989; Hingsburger *et al.*, 1999). Clients who have intellectual disabilities are easier to supervise than their non-intellectually disabled counterparts. This is because there is often a system of supervision already in place to deal with difficulties in living due to their intellectual disability that can profitably be incorporated into supervision designed to prevent sexual recidivism (Hingsburger *et al.*, 1999). Follow-up studies of intellectually disabled men who had committed sexual offenses involving children or indecent exposure suggest that longer periods of treatment and supervision (two years) provided by probation orders are more effective in reducing recidivism than a one-year period (Lindsay, Neilson & Morrison, 1998; Lindsay & Smith, 1998).

CONCLUSIONS AND FUTURE RESEARCH

The important risk factors for sexual recidivism among sex offenders with intellectual disability resemble those of sex offenders more generally. This appears to be true for static risk factors, thus encouraging the use of actuarial instruments in estimating long-term risk, as well as dynamic risk factors that can be used in treatment planning and risk management. While further research is required to refine risk appraisal for this population, the most pressing need is for rigorous evaluations of interventions designed to manage and reduce risk.

AUTHOR'S NOTE

This research was supported by an Ontario Mental Health Foundation Senior Research Fellowship and research contracts from the Ontario Ministry of Community and Social Services and the Kingston Psychiatric Hospital. Small parts of the paper have been adapted from Quinsey, Book and Skilling (submitted).

REFERENCES

Applegate, H., Matson, J.L. & Cherry, K.E. (1999). An evaluation of functional variables affecting severe problem behaviors in adults with mental retardation by using the questions about behavioral function scale (QABF). *Research in Developmental Disabilities*, **20**, 229–37.
Bird, F.L., Sperry, J.M. & Carreiro, H.L. (1998). Community habilitation and integration of adults with psychiatric disorders and mental retardation: development of a clinically responsive environment. *Journal of Developmental and Physical Disabilities*, **10**, 331–48.
Blanchard, R., Watson, M.S., Choy, A., Dickey, R., Klassen, P., Kuban, M. & Ferren, D.J. (1999). Pedophiles: mental retardation, maternal age, and sexual orientation. *Archives of Sexual Behavior*, **28**, 111–27.
Burns, B.J. & Santos, A.B. (1995). Assertive community treatment: an update of randomized trials. *Psychiatric Services*, **46**, 669–75.
Cipani, E. (ed.) (1989). *The Treatment of Severe Behavior Disorders: Behavior Analysis Approaches*. Washington, DC: American Association on Mental Retardation.

Davidson, P.W., Cain, N.N., Sloane-Reeves, J.E., Giesow, V.E. & Quijano, L.E. (1995). Crisis intervention for community-based individuals with developmental disabilities and behavioral and psychiatric disorders. *Mental Retardation*, **33**, 21–30.

Duncan, D., Matson, J.L., Bamburg, J.W., Cherry, K.E. & Buckley, T. (1999). The relationship of self-injurious behavior and aggression to social skills in persons with severe and profound learning disability. *Research in Developmental Disabilities*, **20**, 441–8.

Emerson, E., Kiernan, C., Alborz, A., Reeves, D., Mason, H., Swarbrick, R., Mason, L. & Hatton, C. (2001). The prevalence of challenging behaviors: a total population study. *Research in Developmental Disabilities*, **22**, 77–93.

Gretton, H.M., McBride, M., Hare, R.D., O'Shaughnessy, R. & Kumka, G. (2001). Psychopathy and recidivism in adolescent sex offenders. *Criminal Justice and Behavior*, **28**, 427–49.

Griffiths, D., Quinsey, V.L. & Hingsburger, D. (1989). *Changing Inappropriate Sexual Behaviors: A Community Based Approach for Persons with Developmental Disabilities*. Toronto: Brookes.

Haaven, J., Little, R. & Petre-Miller, D. (1990). *Treating Intellectually Disabled Sex Offenders: A Model Residential Program*. Orwell, VT: The Safer Society Press.

Hanson, R.K., Gordon, A., Harris, A.J.R., Marques, J.K., Murphy, W., Quinsey, V.L. & Seto, M.C. (2002). First report of the Collaborative Outcome Data Project on the Effectiveness of Psychological Treatment for Sex Offenders. *Sexual Abuse*, **14**, 155–68.

Hanson, R.K. & Thornton, D. (2000). Improving risk assessments for sex offenders: a comparison of three actuarial scales. *Law and Human Behavior*, **24**, 119–36.

Hare, R.D. (1991). *The Hare Psychopathy Checklist—Revised*. Toronto: Multi-Health Systems.

Harris, G.T., Rice, M.E. & Quinsey, V.L. (1993). Violent recidivism of mentally disordered offender: the development of a statistical prediction instrument. *Criminal Justice and Behavior*, **20**, 315–35.

Harris, G.T., Rice, M.E., Quinsey, V.L., Chaplin, T.C. & Earls, C. (1992). Maximizing the discriminant validity of phallometric data. *Psychological Assessment*, **4**, 502–11.

Hingsburger, D., Chaplin, T., Hirstwood, K., Tough, S., Nethercott, A. & Roberts-Spence, D. (1999). Intervening with sexually problematic behavior in community environments. In L. Meyer & J. Scotti (eds). *New Directions for Behavioral Interventions: Principles, Models, and Practices* (pp. 213–36). New York: Brooks.

Jensen, A.R. (1998). *The g Factor: The Science of Mental Ability*. London: Praeger.

Johnston, S.J. & Halstead, S. (1995). Forensic issues in intellectual disability. *Current Opinion in Psychiatry*, **13**, 475–80.

Kolton, D.J.C., Boer, A. & Boer, D.P. (2001). A revision of the Abel and Becker Cognition Scale for intellectually disabled offenders. *Sexual Abuse*, **13**, 217–20.

Lafave, H.G., de Souza, H.R. & Gerber, G.J. (1996). Assertive community treatment of severe mental illness: a Canadian experience. *Psychiatric Services*, **47**, 757–9.

Lalumière, M.L. & Quinsey, V.L. (1994). The discriminability of rapists from non-sex offenders using phallometric measures: a meta-analysis. *Criminal Justice and Behavior*, **21**, 150–75.

Lindsay, W.R., Neilson, C.Q. & Morrison, F. (1998). The treatment of six men with a learning disability convicted of sex offences with children. *British Journal of Clinical Psychology*, **37**, 83–98.

Lindsay, W.R. & Smith, A.H.W. (1998). Responses to treatment for sex offenders with intellectual disability: a comparison of men with 1- and 2-year probation sentences. *Journal of Intellectual Disability Research*, **42**, 346–53.

Matson, J.L., Bamburg, J.W., Cherry, K.E. & Paclawskyj, T.R. (1999). A validity study on the Questions About Behavioral Function (QABF) scale: predicting treatment success for self-injury, aggression, and stereotypies. *Research in Developmental Disabilities*, **20**, 163–75.

Nezu, C.M., Nezu, A.M. & Dudek, J.A. (1998). A cognitive behavioral model of assessment and treatment for intellectually disabled sexual offenders. *Cognitive and Behavioral Practice*, **5**, 25–64.

Quinsey, V.L. (2000). Institutional violence among the mentally ill. In S. Hodgins (ed.) *Violence Among the Mentally Ill: Effective Treatments and Management Strategies* (pp. 213–35). NATO Science Series. Dordrecht: Kluwer.

Quinsey, V.L., Book, A. & Skilling, T.A. (submitted). A follow-up of deinstitutionalized men with intellectual disabilities and histories of antisocial behavior.

Quinsey, V.L., Coleman, G., Jones, B. & Altrows, I. (1997). Proximal antecedents of eloping and reoffending among mentally disordered offenders. *Journal of Interpersonal Violence*, **12**, 794–813.

Quinsey, V.L., Harris, G.T., Rice, M.E. & Cormier, C. (1998). *Violent Offenders: Appraising and Managing Risk*. Washington, DC: American Psychological Association.

Quinsey, V.L. & Lalumière, M. (2001). *Assessment of Sexual Offenders Against Children*, rev. edn. Thousand Oaks, CA: Sage.

Quinsey, V.L. & Walker, W.D. (1992). Dealing with dangerousness: community risk management strategies with violent offenders. In R. DeV. Peters, R.J. McMahon & V.L. Quinsey (eds) *Aggression and Violence throughout the Lifespan* (pp. 244–60). Newbury Park, CA: Sage.

Reid, A.H. & Ballinger, B.R. (1995). Behaviour symptoms among severely and profoundly mentally retarded patients: a 16–18 year follow-up study. *British Journal of Psychiatry*, **167**, 452–5.

Rice, M.E. & Harris, G.T. (1997). Cross validation and extension of the Violence Risk Appraisal Guide for child molesters and rapists. *Law and Human Behavior*, **21**, 231–41.

Rice, M.E., Harris, G.T., Quinsey, V.L. & Cyr, M. (1990). Planning treatment programs in secure psychiatric facilities. In D. Weisstub (ed.) *Law and Mental Health: International Perspectives*, vol. 5, (pp. 162–230). New York: Pergamon Press.

Rice, M.E., Harris, G.T., Varney, G.W. & Quinsey, V.L. (1989). *Violence in Institutions: Understanding, Prevention and Control*. Toronto: Hogrefe and Huber.

Seto, M.C. & Lalumière, M.L. (2001). A brief screening scale to identify pedophilic interests among child molesters. *Sexual Abuse*, **13**, 15–25.

White, J., Moffitt, T.E. & Silva, P.A. (1989). A prospective replication of the protective effects of IQ in subjects at high risk for juvenile delinquency. *Journal of Clinical and Consulting Psychology*, **57**, 719–24.

Wiederanders, M. (1992). Recidivism of disordered offenders who were conditionally vs. unconditionally released. *Behavioral Sciences and the Law*, **10**, 141–8.

Wiederanders, M., Bromley, D.L. & Choate, P.A. (1997). Forensic conditional release programs and outcomes in three states. *International Journal of Law and Psychiatry*, **20**, 249–57.

Zamble, E. & Quinsey, V.L. (1997). *The Process of Criminal Recidivism*. University of Cambridge Press.

Chapter 8

APPROACHES TO THE EVALUATION OF OUTCOMES[*]

Nigel Beail

Barnsley Learning Disability Service and University of Sheffield, UK

Reports on treatment approaches and their effectiveness with people with developmental disabilities in general are sparse (Butz, Bowling & Bliss, 2000; Nezu & Nezu, 1994; Prout & Nowak-Drabik, 2003). There has been a long "history of therapeutic disdain" (Bender, 1993) and enduring professional negative biases against the use of verbal psychotherapies with people with intellectual disabilities (Hurley, Pfadt, Tomasulo & Gardner, 1996; Nezu & Nezu, 1994). Since about 1980 case reports concerning a wider range of treatments, including cognitive and psychodynamic therapies, with people with developmental disabilities began being published with increasing regularity (Beail, 1995; Nezu & Nezu, 1994). At the same time several papers were published drawing attention to the lack of provision and calling for research (Hurley, 1989; Nezu & Nezu, 1994). At the same time, work on developing treatment approaches for offenders with developmental disabilities was progressing. The outcome of some of that work is presented in the chapters in Part IV. These chapters describe treatment approaches for a range of offending behaviours and for those with additional problems such as a dual diagnosis. Some of these treatments are provided in secure settings and some in community settings. Of concern to the courts, the wider criminal justice system and the public is that the treatment provided is effective and serves to protect the public. Thus, the most significant factor will be the extent to which treatments impact upon reoffending. The aim of this chapter is to provide an overview of research designs and methods that may be employed to evaluate outcomes at clinical, programme and service levels.

[*]Address for correspondence: Barnsley Psychological Health Care, The Keresforth Centre, Off Broadway, Barnsley S70 6RS, UK. Tel.: + 44 (0) 1226 777865; Fax.: + 44 (0) 1226 287604.

Offenders with Developmental Disabilities. Edited by W.L. Lindsay, J.L. Taylor and P. Sturmey.
© 2004 John Wiley & Sons, Ltd.

EVALUATING OUTCOMES

In order to evaluate treatments decisions need to be made concerning what questions need to be answered. The nature and extent of the evaluation will be a function of for whom, or for what purpose, the questions are being asked. This chapter considers four main areas of evaluation: (a) service audit, (b) quality assurance, (c) effectiveness, and (d) cost benefits, cost-efficiency and cost effectiveness. The methods described can be used to evaluate any intervention. However, there are particular issues that place limitations on the designs that can be employed, and these will be explored. However, prior to considerations of design and method we need to consider what outcomes are relevant: what should we measure?

WHAT SHOULD WE MEASURE?

There are three areas in the field of treatment outcome research that measures should be drawn from. These include different symptom domains (such as frequency of offending, feelings, thoughts and behaviour), different domains of functioning (such as social, interpersonal and adaptive), and different perspectives (such as those of the recipient, a close relative, carer or independent observer). There is little consensus on the precise measures to be employed. For a discussion of these issues in psychotherapy research in general see Lambert and Hill (1994) and Roth and Fonagy (1996). In the field of developmental disability outcome research there are no well-established methods or measures of treatment outcome. Reviews by Aman (1994) and Sturmey, Reed and Corbett (1991) showed that most measures developed are concerned with diagnosis rather than outcome (Kellett, Beail, Newman & Frankish, 2003).

DIFFERING SYMPTOM DOMAINS

The Index Offence

When treatment is being considered as an alternative to penal sentences or as part of secure provision or a probation or community order, those administering justice and the public will be primarily concerned with the extent to which the treatment will impact on reoffending. Thus recidivism is the main outcome variable in the majority of studies of offender treatment programmes. Most of the offences committed by people with developmental disabilities can be defined in behavioural terms. Hayes (1996) found that people with developmental disabilities were more likely to engage in offences against the person such as physical and sexual assault rather than fraud, drug offences, breaking and entering, and driving offences. Some studies, but not all, have found a higher incidence of arson offences in this client group (Puri, Baxter & Cordess, 1995; Raesaenen, Hirvenoja, Hakko & Vaeisaenen, 1994).

There is a large literature on behavioural interventions and their evaluation with people with developmental disabilities (Didden, Duker & Korzilius, 1997; Scotti,

Evans, Meyer, & Walker, 1991). These outcome studies have largely consisted of single case experimental designs in which individualised outcome measures were developed. They have not been concerned with offending behaviour *per se* but high-frequency behaviours occurring in staffed environments. One of the main issues in consideration of these studies is the extent to which the findings of this large body of research are generalisable to working with offenders. In contrast to high-frequency behaviours in staffed environments, offending behaviour tends to be low frequency and occurs in community settings. However, meta-analyses of these studies suggest that a functional analysis of the behaviour contributes significantly to treatment outcome. This would suggest that researchers employing behavioural interventions should conduct a careful functional analysis of the offending behaviour. Such an analysis may also be appropriate for other interventions, as it would enable the development of individualised measures including frequency, intensity, number, duration and severity. These can then be monitored over time and at outcome and follow-up.

There are significant problems ensuring the reliability and validity of data on reoffending. The pre-treatment data could be based on police records of the offence together with an interview with the participant. However, the police records will only contain information on what has been reported or observed leading to the arrest of the offender and any later confession. The offender may have conducted many more offences but not been detected. Further information may be obtained concerning the index offence through an interview with the client. However, we are dependent on their willingness to self-report. They may be unwilling to tell us more than we already know from the trial and police records for fear of further incriminating themselves. Furthermore, self-reports of behaviour are strongly influenced by the interviewee's learning history and understanding of the consequences of being honest or dishonest. If treatment takes place in a secure setting then opportunities for reoffending are significantly reduced. Thus, outcome can only be properly evaluated after the client has been discharged back to the community. Also, incarcerated clients may learn to conceal the truth about their offending behaviour. On the other hand some clients may be susceptible to interrogative pressure and be coerced into making false confessions (see Beail, 2002 for a discussion on this issue). For clients living in the community during treatment, and for those discharged back to the community, the researcher is dependent on them either disclosing that they have reoffended or on them being caught. Thus while the index offence and reoffending are highly significant variables to monitor they are fraught with measurement difficulties.

Studies of recidivism rates for non-disabled and developmentally disabled offenders report that reoffending rates increase with the period of follow-up (Bailey & MacCulloch, 1992; Lindsay, Law & Macleod, 2002; Marshall & Barbaree, 1988). Thus, follow-up needs to continue for several years. The accuracy of such reports will depend on the willingness of the participant to self-disclose their offending behaviour or on them being arrested. Also, if at any stage the participant does disclose that they have reoffended then there is a requirement on the researcher to report this to the police. Thus, there is little incentive for the client to cooperate with your research project.

Other Behavioural Problems

Clients may present with a broader range of problem behaviours than the index offence. In order to assess and evaluate these, measures such as the Aberrant Behaviour Checklist (Aman, Singh, Stewart & Field, 1985) could be used. This was developed as a measure of drug treatment outcome in institutional settings. However, some questions have been modified for its use with community populations (Aman, Burrow & Wolford, 1994). Both versions have been found to be highly reliable measures of behavioural problems. Part II of the Adaptive Behaviour Scales could also be used (Lambert, Nihira & Leland, 1993).

Offence-Specific Inventories

A range of offence-specific inventories have been developed for use in forensic work. These include the Fire Interest Rating Scale, the Fire Assessment Schedule (see Clare & Murphy, 1998) and Wilson's Sexual Fantasy Questionnaire (Salter, 1988). However, these would need to be modified for use with offenders with developmental disabilities. Such assessments are often too linguistically complex or have rating scales that have a large number of options, requiring sophisticated self-perception of increasing levels of emotion. It would also be necessary to establish their reliability and validity with this population.

Anger

In crimes involving assault on the person it has been argued that anger plays an important determining role. Novaco (1994) asserts that anger is a subjective emotional state involving physiological arousal and cognitions of hostility, and is a causal determinant of aggressive behaviour. Thus, a measure of anger will be essential to evaluating treatments for some offenders (see Chapter 11). Several measures are available to assess anger. The Provocation Inventory (Novaco, 1988) has been modified for use with people with developmental disabilities to evaluate treatment outcomes in secure (Black & Novaco, 1993) and community (Walker & Cheseldine, 1997) settings. Novaco and Taylor (2002) have evaluated the reliability and concurrent validity of the State-Trait Anger Expression Inventory (STAXI; Spielberger, 1996), the Novaco Anger Scale (Novaco, 1994) and the Provocation Inventory. They found high levels of internal reliability and concurrent validity. Taylor has subsequently employed these measures to evaluate treatment outcome (see Chapter 11).

Mental Health Problems

Some offenders have additional mental health problems (see Chapter 13) and therefore this should be monitored as part of any treatment programme. Treatment outcome studies concerning mental health difficulties have traditionally employed a range of checklists. Most of these are in a self-report format requiring at least average reading ability. Despite this, researchers evaluating treatments with people with developmental disabilities have been employing self-report measures for evaluating change in presenting problems (Beail, 2000; Beail & Warden, 1996; Nezu, Nezu & Arien, 1991).

A number of single-trait measures such as the Zung Anxiety Scale and the Beck Depression Inventory have been modified for people with developmental disabilities and are administered in an interview format. Several multi-trait measures have been developed specifically for use with people with developmental disabilities. For example, the Reiss Screen (Reiss, 1988) has 36 items administered to an informant regarding the recipient. The Psychopathology Instrument for Mentally Retarded Adults (PIMRA; Matson, Kazdin & Senatore, 1984) has 56 items divided into seven subscales. It has both self-report and informant versions which yield information on DSM psychiatric diagnoses. Beail and Warden (1996) and Beail (2000) used the Symptom Checklist 90-Revised (SCL-90-R) (Derogatis, 1983), and Nezu, Nezu and Arien (1991) have used the Brief Symptom Inventory (Derogatis, 1993), which is a shorter version of the SCL-90-R. Both checklists are widely used in outcome studies to monitor changes in symptomatology. Kellett, Beail, Newman and Mosley (1999) and Kellett *et al.* (2003) have evaluated their utility in indexing psychological distress with people with developmental disabilities when administered in an assisted completion format. They found the global indices and nine symptom scales to have good internal consistency, split half reliability and discriminative validity. Many of these measures have been investigated in only a few studies. Hence, uncertainty remains over their robustness, validity, and sometimes even their reliability.

DIFFERING DOMAINS OF FUNCTIONING

Interpersonal and Social Skills

Clare (1993) has emphasised the need to assess interpersonal skills. Measures of interpersonal relationships and functioning have recently been introduced into treatment outcome studies. The most widely used has been the Inventory of Interpersonal Problems (IIP) (Horowitz, Rosenberg, Baer, Ureno & Villasenor, 1988). The original inventory has 127 items, but short forms are available. Beail and Warden (1996) and Beail (2000) used a 32-item version of the IIP (Barkham, Hardy & Startup, 1996) in their study with adults with developmental disabilities who have mental health problems. However, work concerning its reliability and validity when used with people with developmental disabilities remains to be carried out. Nezu and Nezu (1994) argue that generalisation effects, especially with regard to changes in adaptive functioning, should be assessed, whereas Cullen (1993) suggested that programmes of intervention should aim to develop adaptive sociable coping skills that might replace offending behaviour. Thus, measures of adaptive and coping behaviour could also be used.

Knowledge and Attitudes

Several authors have suggested the need to evaluate and monitor sex offender's socio-sexual knowledge and attitudes (Caparulo, 1991; Clare, 1993). Caparulo (1991) recommends the Socio-Sexual Knowledge and Attitudes Test (SSKAT), but it is not clear how this relates to outcome. Lindsay, Neilson, Morrison and Smith (1998) have developed an assessment of attitudes and beliefs consistent with sexually offending, which they have employed in evaluations of treatments and have demonstrated positive change. This approach could also be developed with other offences.

Empathy

Empathy refers to sharing the mental state of another (Eisenberg & Strayer, 1987). In offender treatment programmes the offender's capacity for empathy for his or her victims is a significant issue. Little is known about empathy and its measurement with people with developmental disabilities. Rose, Jenkins, O'Connor, Jones and Felce (2002) used the Victim Empathy Scale (Beckett & Fisher, 2002) in their evaluation of group therapy for sex offenders. However, the psychometric properties of this and other empathy measures have not been established with adults with developmental disabilities.

DIFFERING PERSPECTIVES

Some of the data collection methods described involve direct assessment with the participant; others involve gaining the perspective or observations of a relative, carer or independent observer. There are, however, problems inherent with both methods. Information provided by care staff has at times been found to be of questionable reliability and validity (Nadarajah, Roy, Harris & Corbett, 1995). Also Kroese (1997) has noted common problems associated with obtaining self-reports from adults with developmental disabilities. These include social desirability, memory and recency effects as well as anxiety and incomprehension. However, Aman (1994) states that obtaining self-ratings has considerable merit as symptoms are, by definition, experienced by the individual and are not always or consistently observable. For example, a sex offender can self-report that he is fantasising about offending or tell you what he feels about his offending behaviour. Without his self-report we have no way of knowing. Kroese (1997) suggests that self-report can be enhanced by the use of pictorial materials, open-ended questions and the use of probes to establish comprehension. However, there will always be significant problems gaining self-report of reoffending and we will be, by and large, dependent on individuals being rearrested. Despite the difficulties in measuring recidivism, it is important to ensure that the evaluation of the reliability and validity of other measurement tools remains firmly on the research agenda.

Service Audit

A service audit aims to find out who uses a service and how resources are allocated, and comprises systematic data collection and analysis. An audit would involve the collection of socio-demographic information such as age, gender, geographic location and occupation. Information on referring agent and range of current and previous offending and other presenting problems would be particularly relevant. Everyone referred to the service could also be assessed on appropriate measures, which could be offence related, or on psychological well-being. These measures could be repeated routinely to audit service outcomes. Such a database enables services to have basic information on their service users. This facilitates the production of reports for service managers and purchasers as well as service evaluation projects. An example of an audit and evaluation system for a service for sex offenders and abusers with developmental disabilities is described in Lindsay *et al.* (2002). These authors reported on the kinds of information mentioned above, including reoffending.

Quality Assurance

Quality assurance focuses on the process by which treatments are delivered, and involves the setting and monitoring of standards of performance. In quality assurance practitioners evaluate the quality of their service and devise and implement strategies for improving it. What can be achieved depends on the resources available. Maxwell (1984) has put forward six dimensions by which the quality and success of a service can be achieved: relevance, equity, accessibility, acceptability, effectiveness and efficiency.

Service providers should ask whether the interventions they are providing meet the needs of the offenders referred to them. At the same time they need to consider whether their service is equitable. Services can be made inequitable by unwarranted exclusion criteria. In the past treatments such as cognitive-behavioural and psychodynamic psychotherapy have not been made available to people with developmental disabilities. Having "at least average intelligence" has been used as an exclusion criterion. This has subsequently been challenged as it is without empirical foundation. Service providers need to ensure that their service is accessible. People with developmental disabilities who live in the community are often dependent on someone else to take them to out-patient appointments or teach them how to get there.

Service providers need to monitor whether or not their service is acceptable to their recipients. Would offenders with intellectual disabilities find some form of treatment acceptable? We would also need to ask whether or not they have the capacity to make informed decisions about the treatment on offer. The public and expert opinion also need to be taken into consideration when issues of acceptability are being addressed.

The empirical data generally available on which to evaluate the effectiveness of treatments such as cognitive therapy and psychodynamic psychotherapy with people with developmental disabilities is weak and sparse compared to behavioural interventions and medication. Hence the need for more research on effectiveness and efficacy.

Evaluating Effectiveness and Efficacy

The provision of treatments for offenders with developmental disabilities is a fairly recent phenomenon. This type of provision would also appear to be on the increase and is being embraced by some sections of the criminal justice system. Often the courts can see little point in incarcerating offenders with developmental disabilities in ordinary prisons and seek alternative disposal. However, in all societies questions are being asked about the efficacy (the results the treatment achieves in the setting of a research trial) and effectiveness (the outcome of the treatment in routine clinical practice) of the treatments on offer. Also, the treatments provided for offenders are often more expensive as they may involve secure accommodation in addition. If a community option is considered then treatment may be very lengthy and may need long-term follow-up and monitoring. Thus, those funding such services may also have legitimate questions about anticipated outcomes. These are more paramount in forensic contexts as it is the protection of the public that is of most concern.

Salkovskis (1995) describes a process of development he called the "hourglass" model. In practice what usually happens first is the reporting of case studies concerning theory and practice. These can be narrative case reports at first, followed by single-case experimental designs or studies of a series of recipients in which technical standards of design and implementation are relatively relaxed. This kind of exploratory analysis then allows a narrowed focus on key effects. Here there is a requirement for research that conforms to the most rigorous standards of enquiry—equivalent to the pinch in the hourglass. In some areas of treatment evaluation, the single-case experimental design, often involving multiple baselines, is the most viable approach. Over time, series of such $N = 1$ designs can be evaluated through meta-analyses (Didden *et al.*, 1997). The alternative is a group design involving a fuller range of control groups, more stringent measures and statistical techniques, and careful specification of recipients to ensure replicability. Paradoxically the designs of these studies can limit the clinical applicability of the research as internal validity takes priority. However, issues concerning generalisability can be answered in a subsequent phase of research, which returns to an externally valid form of enquiry.

SINGLE-CASE EVALUATION OF TREATMENT OUTCOME

Case reports of interventions with offenders with developmental disabilities have been published in considerable numbers. However, the applications of single-case experimental designs are notably absent. This limits the conclusions that can be drawn over time, as it is not possible to apply meta-analytic techniques. This contrasts with the behavioural treatment literature concerning people with developmental disabilities, which is dominated by single-case experimental designs, which have been evaluated through meta-analyses (Didden *et al.*, 1997; Scotti *et al.*, 1991). A single-case experimental design involves at least two conditions: a baseline phase (A) and an intervention phase (B). The baseline may consist of no intervention, although in some cases a control condition is used. For example, if the intervention is a reinforcement procedure then a control condition in a baseline might include non-contingent reinforcement. Target behaviours are identified that reflect the nature and degree of the recipient's current problems (offending behaviour) and these are coupled with positive alternative behaviours that are expected as a consequence of therapy. Following intervention there is a follow-up period. If experimental control is to be shown, then a reversal phase is introduced. This is called a reversal or ABA design. Behavioural interventions assume that once the intervention is terminated then the previous contingencies will reapply and the old behaviour patterns will re-emerge. Other psychotherapeutic interventions assume that the treatment causes internal change and that at the end of treatment the client should not return to pre-treatment behaviours. Reversal designs have limited applicability with offenders, where it would be unethical to withdraw treatment and evaluate the number of new offences during the return to baseline phase. Other small *n* designs, such as multiple baseline designs across subjects, circumvent this objection.

Single case studies usually present their data graphically to illustrate any change. Indeed visual inspection is the primary basis for evaluating change in these designs. Statistical tests can also be applied to the data to see if differences between baseline, treatment and follow-up or reversal are significant. These data can then be grouped with other studies by applying a common metric to enable a meta-analysis. Didden *et al.* (1997) and Scotti *et al.* (1991) employed the percentage of non-overlapping data as an index of treatment effectiveness in their meta-analyses.

Roth and Fonagy (1996) point out that single case studies have a number of attractive features. They can be carried out in routine clinical practice, do not require the facilities associated with larger scale research and can be conducted fairly quickly. They also have a number of limitations. It seems unlikely that single-case experimental designs will be viable in outcome studies with offenders despite their popularity in behavioural research. The main problem is the requirement for a baseline period. It would be unethical to include a no-treatment baseline period where the researcher is monitoring further offences. Thus in order to evaluate a single case ethically we need to employ less robust but more ethical procedures.

The simplest way to evaluate the outcome of treatment for a single case is to measure the symptoms, behaviour or well-being of the recipient before they undergo the treatment and again when treatment is complete. In longer term treatments measurements may also be taken at intervals. An extensive follow-up period would also need to be built into the design. Over time cases could be grouped and subjected to statistical analysis. The problem with these designs is that the results may be open to competing explanations, which reduces their value and informativeness. A client may improve anyway. This is referred to as spontaneous remission. Other independent variables may be at work, which were not controlled in the design, and contribute to the change. On the other hand symptoms or behaviour may remain the same. This could be interpreted as meaning that the treatment was ineffective whereas it could also indicate that a deteriorating course has been stemmed. Issues such as these have led to the use of no-treatment controls, a procedure that would be unethical in offender treatment research, as mentioned above.

GROUP DESIGNS

Open Trials

Open trials usually involve the evaluation of a series of recipients of treatment using pre and post measures. Entry to treatment may be governed by some criteria but there is no control group. Such designs reflect a more naturalistic treatment protocol. Salkovskis (1995) states that at this stage of the hourglass model resources are often limited (often small groups or solitary clinicians engaged in routine service provision), recipient sizes are small and measures unsubtle. To date research reports concerning the outcome of interventions for offenders with developmental disabilities have been open trial designs.

Lindsay *et al.* (1998) describes a cognitive therapy for six men with developmental disabilities convicted of sexual offences against children. They were treated in two therapy groups. The outcome measure employed was the QACSO (Questionnaire on Attitudes Consistent with Sex Offences) and offending behaviour was followed up for four years. A baseline was established as the participants were assessed prior to court proceedings and following conviction during assessment prior to treatment starting. All six cases were reported to have changed their attitudes towards offending against children. Also none of the participants was charged with any further offences at four years follow-up.

Beail (2001) reports a study of recidivism rates following psychodynamic psychotherapy among male offenders with intellectual disabilities. The recipients were 18 men who had been diverted from the criminal justice system. Thirteen participated in treatment and five refused. Of the thirteen who completed treatment two reoffended. The rest remained offence-free at four years follow-up. The five who refused treatment all reoffended within two years.

These pre–post group designs suffer from the same difficulties as pre–post single case reports. They also examine the truth of the null hypothesis—that is, that treatment has no effect. When quantitative measures are employed the convention is to report statistical significance in terms of a confidence level of $p < 0.05$. However, demonstration of statistical effects may not be equivalent to clinically significant change. One alternative is to compare recipient's pre- and post-treatment scores with clinical and non-clinical population norms on outcome measures. Unfortunately very little normative data has been collected to enable such analyses.

These pre–post uncontrolled exploratory analyses allow a narrowed focus on key effects, progressively moving towards more rarefied research. In the area of outcome research with developmentally disabled offenders, that progress to date has been very slow.

Randomised Control Trials

The blind, randomised control trial (RCT) gives the clearest indication of the efficacy of treatment. RCTs ask questions about the comparative benefit of two or more treatments. The design permits active treatments to be compared with no treatment, waiting list or placebo. Some commentators argue that when possible group designs with random assignment and adequate control groups should be standard (Nezu & Nezu, 1994; Whittaker, 2001). However, they have not considered the special difficulties posed to evaluations involving offenders with developmental disabilities. It is therefore important that these issues be explored and discussed.

In RCTs participants are randomly allocated to the different conditions. A high degree of control is exercised over factors such as demographic variables, symptomatology and its severity, and level of functioning. The length of treatment is controlled, therapist experience is standardised, the treatments are manualised and therapist adherence monitored. There are three basic research designs employed to evaluate treatments. For information on a wider range of approaches, see Kazdin (1994).

Treatment versus no-treatment or waiting list control

In these studies recipients are randomly assigned to treatment or no-treatment groups. Thus spontaneous remission and impact of the passage of time are controlled for. Any change in the control group provides an estimate of what would have happened to the treatment group if they had not undergone treatment. It is assumed that the groups comprise individuals who are comparable in their personal characteristics and circumstances. Lindsay (2002) points out that it is noticeable in the area of treatment for sex offenders with developmental disabilities that there is no controlled study of any kind on any treatment approach. Lindsay states that the most difficult issue would be ethical approval. Ethical committees are not going to sanction no-treatment control groups of offenders. Similarly the criminal justice system would expect that an offender with developmental disabilities would be taken into treatment after the trial, not some time in the future. The courts' concern is the protection of the public and courts would want to know how soon the offender would be seen for treatment. If there were any delay they would want to know what safeguards would be in place to protect the public. The courts would have little interest in services that deferred treatments for research purposes.

Treatment versus placebo controls

It may be that people improve when they undergo treatment due to the expectation that they will do so rather then due to the treatment. In drug research participants are given placebos. However, in other treatment outcome research this design is beset by the difficulty of finding an activity which could be guaranteed to have no therapeutic element, which controls for the effect of attention and which is viewed by recipients as being as credible as the active intervention (Roth & Fonagy, 1996).

Although ideal designs would involve contrasting treatment with no treatment and/or a placebo treatment, it is unlikely that this would be possible, either ethically or practically. In the field of outcome research with non-disabled recipients researchers have restricted themselves to the comparison of active treatments.

Comparative outcome designs

In this design recipients are randomly assigned to one of several active treatments. As all treatments share the non-specific benefit arising from participants' belief in their value, this design reduces the need for a placebo condition. This also improves the ethical status of the design as everyone is given active treatment. However, there is a distinct lack of studies employing this design. Taylor reports a study comparing cognitive treatment for anger with routine treatment with men with developmental disabilities detained in a secure unit (see Chapter 11).

RCTs and Offenders with Developmental Disabilities

Nezu and Nezu (1994) argue that "samples should be homogeneous". In research designs with offenders with developmental disabilities this would mean that participant groups would need to be similar in terms of the offence committed, level of intellectual disability, sex and age. Additional factors would also need to be included, depending on the outcome measures employed. If there were an issue of dual diagnosis then the groups would need to be matched on a measure of mental health. In mental health outcome studies all participants would have the same diagnosis and score above a diagnostic cut-off point on a measure of, say, depression or anxiety. If anger is being evaluated then all participants would need to be assessed on an anger scale and the comparison groups would need to have similar levels of anger.

RCTs are usually restricted to the evaluation of treatment of one problem. The requirement for one RCT to evaluate a treatment or treatments for sexual offending would require strict specification of recipient inclusion criteria. Such criteria would include level of intellectual disability (e.g. IQ between 55 and 70), meeting the research definition of sexual offence, and not experiencing any other mental health problems or behaviour disorders. Homogeneity is usually achieved through randomisation when participant numbers are sufficiently large. In group designs where numbers are small some direct matching is typically carried out. Researchers would also have to specify treatment length and therapist experience, and manualise the treatment. A system of therapist adherence to the treatment manual would also need to be established. A set of outcome measures would be needed and frequency of administration set. The researcher would also need to establish the frequency and length of treatment. This could be based on research designs in work with non-disabled offenders as there is insufficient outcome research with developmentally disabled offenders on which to base time estimates.

A major issue in outcome research is the extent to which a study can detect differences between groups when differences exist in the population. This notion is referred to as statistical power and reflects the probability that the test will lead to the rejection of the null hypothesis. Power is a function of the criteria for statistical significance; sample size and the effect size (the difference that exists between groups). Thus researchers need to determine whether the design of the evaluation is sufficiently powerful to detect meaningful differences.

In outcome research, issues of power might emerge as a function of the different types of comparison that are made and the different effect sizes the comparisons are likely to yield. To compare an active treatment with no treatment it is reasonable to expect a large effect around one standard deviation unit (i.e. the mean of the treated group one standard deviation better than the mean of the untreated group). To detect such an effect a sample size of approximately 20 to 30 recipients in each condition is needed (Kraemer, 1981). When comparing two treatments, however, considerably larger groups are required because the average effect sizes obtained in such studies are only one-half of a standard deviation (Kazdin & Bass, 1989). Thus around 60 to 70 recipients completing each treatment would be required. All recipients would also have to meet the study's selection criteria. These are minimum figures as several times as many participants are usually needed in studies of non-disabled recipients due to attrition. Further high levels of attrition will invalidate any group design.

Participants, or in the case of minors, their legal guardians, have to give their consent to involvement in the research. In studies of treatment outcome consent has to be obtained to treatment and to being a research participant. Consent involves an ability to list the benefits, risks and alternatives and understand the consequences of having and not having treatment. The participant needs to be able to retain the information, weigh it in the balance and arrive at a choice. After consent to treatment is obtained the researcher needs to obtain the participant's consent to being a research participant. Arscott, Dagnan and Kroese (1998) found that adults with mild intellectual disabilities appeared to understand the nature of an interview-only research study but had a limited understanding of the risks and benefits of being involved or their right to refuse to participate or drop out of the study. Thus some participants that are accepted by services for treatment from the courts may not be able to consent to being a research participant. The decision concerning consent to an RCT is more complex than the issues investigated by Arscott *et al.* (1998). In addition to being interviewed, the prospective participant would need to make a decision regarding randomisation and its implications for them. This may be difficult to comprehend. However, being allocated to one of two treatments, which may potentially benefit the person, would be a sounder option. The capacity of people with intellectual disabilities to weigh in the balance the risks and benefits of alternative treatments in order to arrive at a choice, as well as their understanding of their right to refuse or opt out, makes obtaining informed consent difficult (for a discussion of the issues see Dinerstein, Herr & O'Sullivan, 1999)

These issues make it very difficult to meet the highest standards of outcome research design. Roth and Fonagy (1996) identify the problem for all outcome researchers in the tension between satisfying the demands of internal and external validity when developing research strategies. RCTs rarely monitor the outcome of interventions in routine practice. In order to satisfy the demands of internal validity the generalisation of the results to normal practice is poor. Thus we need to compromise between the scientific rigour of the RCT on the one hand and generalisability on the other. There is clearly a lot of scope for further research on interventions with offenders with developmental disabilities. However, it seems unlikely that studies meeting the "gold standard" of the RCT will be carried out. The no-treatment option would be unethical and therefore comparison of treatments is the best option. However, the requirements for large numbers of participants in order to detect differences is a major obstacle. Studies would also need extensive follow-up periods to appropriately evaluate levels of recidivism. Thus, studies would need to be carried out over many research sites over extended periods of time. Taking on board all the difficulties with RCTs, researchers may conclude that we may learn a lot more from more compromised designs or open trials carried out in normal clinical practice. The main compromise will be around participant numbers and the extent to which the groups are comparable. However, Taylor (see Chapter 11) provides an excellent example of a compromised design which provides valuable information on the treatment of anger in offenders with developmental disabilities. We also have to consider that some offenders are represented in very small numbers and therefore better single-case designs with clear documentation or studies of case series need to be conducted.

PROCESS RESEARCH

The process of change can be evaluated more intensely by the use of interval and process measures. An example of interval evaluation can be found in Lindsay *et al.* (1998). They measured beliefs consistent with offending on a monthly basis. This could also be carried out after every session. This would then be termed a process measure as it evaluates the impact of the treatment session by session. Detailed evaluations of the sessions can also be made. An example of this approach to evaluation of treatment, with people with intellectual disabilities, is that of Beail and Newman (2002) and Newman and Beail (2002). They used the Assimilation of Problematic Experiences Scale (APES) (Stiles *et al.*, 1990) to see if adults with intellectual disabilities could assimilate their problematic experience during the course of treatment. This design involved tape recordings of sessions being made. These were transcribed and one problematic experience was identified. The transcript was edited to contain only episodes of dialogue concerning the problematic experience. Evaluators trained in the use of the APES then rated each episode on the scale. Newman and Beail (2002) found increases in the recipients' level of assimilation of their problematic experience during treatment sessions and across sessions. Beail and Newman (2002) have also reported the application of this design to evaluate work with a sex offender with developmental disabilities.

COST BENEFIT, COST EFFICIENCY AND COST EFFECTIVENESS

A cost–benefit analysis aims to evaluate the costs and benefits of a treatment in solely monetary terms. A cost-efficiency study involves a comparison between two or more treatments in terms of the cost of achieving a specified outcome. A cost-effectiveness study defines outcomes in more substantive or unspecified terms (for example, recidivism) and aims to find out which treatment obtains the best result for the cost input. Here only the cost of treatment implementation is expressed in monetary terms. An example might involve the comparison between providing individual versus group treatments for offenders with developmental disabilities. The outcome on measures such as the QASCO, reoffending behaviour or interpersonal functioning may show individual treatment to have better outcomes. However, the difference between the treatments might not warrant the additional cost in terms of therapist time or clients' waiting time. Such studies have not yet been conducted with offenders with developmental disabilities.

CONCLUSION

This chapter provides an overview of research designs and methods for use in the evaluation of treatment programmes for offenders with developmental disabilities. In terms of the hourglass model we are still in the very early stages. Consideration of research issues concerning the more rigorous research at the pinch of the hourglass reveals major issues which need thought, examination and debate. It should also be recognised that research on outcomes with offenders with intellectual disabilities is taking place in services and has not been given attention by the research centres. Judging by the contributions in this book this state of affairs is set to continue. Thus research has to be designed to meet the limitations imposed upon it and should not be compared unfavourably with the gold standard of the RCT. Indeed the problems identified in RCT research design when applied to work with offenders with intellectual disabilities suggest that only limited progress can be made in that direction. Considerable effort also needs to be focused on methods of outcome measurement, especially reliability and validity.

The principal aim of this chapter has been to inform practitioners providing treatment services to offenders with developmental disabilities about evaluation. The methods described will enable them to incorporate evaluation techniques into their routine clinical practice. Increased attention to evaluation will enable practitioners and researchers to find a way forward on the issues that more rarefied research would entail.

REFERENCES

Aman, M.G. (1994). Instruments for assessing treatment effects in developmentally disabled populations. *Assessment in Rehabilitation and Exceptionality*, **1**, 1–20.

Aman, M.G., Burrow, W.H. & Wolford, P.L. (1994). The Aberrant Behaviour Checklist—Community: factor validity and effect of subject variables for adults in group homes. *American Journal of Mental Retardation*, **100**, 283–92.

Aman, M.G., Singh, N.N., Stewart, A.W. & Field, C.J. (1985). The Aberrant Behaviour Checklist: a behaviour rating scale for assessment of treatment effects. *American Journal of Mental Deficiency*, **89**, 485–91.

Arscott, K., Dagnan, D. & Kroese, B.S. (1998). Consent to psychological research by people with an intellectual disability. *Journal of Applied Research in Intellectual Disabilities*, **11**, 77–83.

Bailey, J. & MacCulloch, M. (1992). Patterns of reconviction in in-patients discharged directly to the community from a Special Hospital: implication for aftercare. *Journal of Forensic Psychiatry*, **3**, 445–61.

Barkham, M., Hardy, G. & Startup, M. (1996). The IIP32: a short version of the Inventory of Interpersonal Problems. *British Journal of Clinical Psychology*, **35**, 21–36.

Beail, N. (1995). Outcome of psychoanalysis, psychoanalytic and psychodynamic psychotherapy with people with intellectual disabilities. *Changes*, **13**, 186–91.

Beail, N. (2000). *An evaluation of out-patient psychodynamic psychotherapy for adults with intellectual disabilities*. Paper presented at the 11th World Congress of the International Association for the Scientific Study of Intellectual Disabilities. Seattle. *Journal of Intellectual Disability Research*, **44**, 204.

Beail, N. (2001). Recidivism following psychodynamic psychotherapy amongst offenders with intellectual disabilities. *British Journal of Forensic Practice*, **3**, 33–7.

Beail, N. (2002). Interrogative suggestibility, memory and intellectual disability. *Journal of Applied Research in Intellectual Disabilities*, **15**, 129–37.

Beail, N. & Newman, D. (2002). *Defence mechanisms and assimilation of problematic experience in a male sex offender with intellectual disabilities*. Paper presented at the European Congress of the International Association for the Scientific Study of Intellectual Disabilities, Dublin.

Beail, N. & Warden, S. (1996). Evaluation of a psychodynamic psychotherapy service for adults with intellectual disabilities: rationale, design and preliminary outcome data. *Journal of Applied Research in Intellectual Disabilities*, **9**, 223–8.

Beckett, R. & Fisher, D. (2002). Victim empathy scale. Oxford Regional Forensic Service (unpublished).

Bender, M. (1993). The unoffered chair: the history of therapeutic disdain towards people with a learning difficulty. *Clinical Psychology Forum*, **54**, 7–12.

Black, L. & Novaco, R.W. (1993). Treatment of anger with a developmentally disabled man. In R.A. Wells & V.J. Giannetti (eds) *Casebook of the Brief Psychotherapies* (pp. 143–58). New York: Plenum Press.

Butz, M.R., Bowling, J.B. & Bliss, C.A. (2000). Psychotherapy with the mentally retarded: a review of the literature and the implications. *Professional Psychology: Research and Practice*, **31**, 42–7.

Caparulo, F. (1991). Identifying the developmentally disabled sex offender. *Sexuality and Disability*, **9**, 311–22.

Clare, I.C.H. (1993). Issues in the assessment and treatment of male sex offenders with mild disabilities. *Sexual and Marital Therapy*, **8**, 167–80.

Clare, I.C.H. & Murphy, G.H. (1998). Working with offenders or alleged offenders with intellectual disabilities. In E. Emerson, C. Hatton, J. Bromley & A. Caine. (eds) *Clinical Psychology and People with Intellectual Disabilities* (pp. 154–76). Chichester: John Wiley & Sons.

Cullen, C. (1993). The treatment of people with learning disabilities who offend. In K. Howells & C.R. Hollin (eds) *Clinical Approaches to the Mentally Disordered Offender*. Chichester: John Wiley & Sons.

Derogatis, L.R. (1983). *SCL-90-R; Administration, Scoring and Procedures: Manual II*. Towson, MD: Clinical Psychometric Research.

Derogatis, L.R. (1993). *Brief Symptom Inventory: Administration, Scoring and Procedures Manual*, 3rd edn. Minneapolis, MN: National Computer Systems.

Didden, R., Duker, P.C. & Korzilius, H. (1997). Meta-analytic study on treatment effectiveness for problem behaviors with individuals who have mental retardation. *American Journal of Mental Deficiency*, **101**, 387–99.

Dinerstein, R.D., Herr, S.S. & O'Sullivan, J.L. (1999). *A Guide to Consent*. Washington, DC: American Association on Mental Retardation.

Eisenberg, N. & Strayer, J. (1987). *Empathy and its Development*. Cambridge: Cambridge University Press.

Hayes, S. (1996). Recent research on offenders with developmental disabilities. *Tizard Learning Disability Review*, **1**, 7–15.

Horowitz, L.M., Rosenberg, S.E., Baer, B.A., Ureno, G. & Villasenor, V.S. (1988). Inventory of Interpersonal Problems: psychometric properties and clinical applications. *Journal of Consulting and Clinical Psychology*, **56**, 885–92.

Hurley, A.D. (1989). Individual psychotherapy with mentally retarded individuals: a review and call for research. *Research in Developmental Disabilities*, **10**, 261–75.

Hurley, A.D., Pfadt, A., Tomasulo, D. & Gardner, W.I. (1996). Counselling and psychotherapy. In J.W. Jacobson & J.A. Mulick (eds) *Manual of Diagnosis and Professional Practice in Mental Retardation* (pp. 371–8). Washingtron, DC: American Psychological Association.

Kazdin, A.E. (1994). Methodology, design, and evaluation in psychotherapy research. In A.E. Bergin & S.L. Garfield (eds) *Handbook of Psychotherapy and Behaviour Change*, 4th edn (pp. 19–71). New York: John Wiley & Sons.

Kazdin, A.E. & Bass, D. (1989). Power to detect differences between alternative treatments in comparative psychotherapy outcome research. *Journal of Consulting and Clinical Psychology*, **57**, 138–47.

Kellett, S., Beail, N., Newman, D.W. & Frankish, P. (2003). Utility of the Brief Symptom Inventory in the assessment of psychological distress. *Journal of Applied Research in Intellectual Disabilities*, **16**, 127–34.

Kellett, S., Beail, N., Newman, D.W. & Mosley, E (1999). Indexing psychological distress in people with intellectual disabilities: use of the Symptom Checklist-90-R. *Journal of Applied Research in Intellectual Disabilities*, **12**, 323–34.

Kraemer, H.C. (1981). Coping strategies in psychiatric clinical research. *Journal of Consulting and Clinical Psychology*, **49**, 309–19.

Kroese, B.S. (1997). Cognitive-behaviour therapy for people with learning disabilities: conceptual and contextual issues. In B.S. Kroese, D. Dagnan & K. Loumidis (eds) *Cognitive-Behaviour Therapy for People with Learning Disabilities*. London: Routledge.

Lambert, M.J. & Hill, C.E. (1994). Assessing psychotherapy outcomes and processes. In A.E. Bergin & S.L. Garfield (eds) *Handbook of Psychotherapy and Behaviour Change*, 4th edn (pp. 72–113). New York: John Wiley & Sons.

Lambert, N., Nihira, K. & Leland, H. (1993). *AAMR Adaptive Behaviour Scale*. Austin, TX: Pro-Ed.

Lindsay, W.R. (2002). Research and literature on sex offenders with intellectual and developmental disabilities. *Journal of Intellectual Disability Research*, **46**, (Suppl. 1), 74–85.

Lindsay, W.R., Law, J. & Macleod, F. (2002). Intellectual disabilities and crime; issues in assessment, intervention and management. In A. Needs & G. Towl (eds) *Applying Psychology to Forensic Practice*. Oxford: British Psychological Society Books/Blackwell.

Lindsay, W.R., Neilson, C.Q., Morrison, F. & Smith, A.H.W. (1998). The treatment of six men with learning disability convicted of sex offences against children. *British Journal of Clinical Psychology*, **37**, 83–98.

Lindsay, W.R., Smith, A.W.H., Law, J., Quinn, K., Anderson, A., Smith, A., Overend, T. & Allan, R. (2002). A treatment service for sex offenders and abusers with intellectual disability: characteristics of referrals and evaluation. *Journal of Applied Research in Intellectual Disabilities*, **15**, 166–74.

Marshall, W.L. & Barbaree, H.E. (1988). Long term evaluation of a behaviour treatment programme for child molesters. *Behaviour, Research and Therapy*, **26**, 499–511.

Matson, J.L., Kazdin, A.E. & Senatore, V. (1984). Psychometric properties of the Psychopathology Instrument for mentally retarded adults. *Applied Research in Mental Retardation*, **5**, 881–9.

Maxwell, R.J. (1984). Quality assessment in health. *British Medical Journal*, **288**, 1470–2.

Nadarajah, J., Roy, A., Harris, T.O. & Corbett, J.A. (1995). Methodological aspects of life events research in people with learning disabilities: a review and initial findings. *Journal of Intellectual Disability Research*, **39**, 47–56.

Newman, D.W. & Beail, N. (2002). Monitoring change in psychotherapy with people with intellectual disabilities: the application of the Assimilation of Problematic Experiences Scale. *Journal of Applied Research in Intellectual Disabilities*, **15**, 48–60.

Nezu, C.M. & Nezu, A.M. (1994). Outpatient psychotherapy for adults with mental retardation and concomitant psychopathology: research and clinical imperatives. *Journal of Consulting and Clinical Psychology*, **62**, 34–42.

Nezu, C.M., Nezu, A.M. & Arien, P. (1991). Assertiveness and problem-solving therapy for mild mentally retarded persons with dual diagnosis. *Research in Developmental Disabilities*, **12**, 371–86.

Novaco, R.W. (1988). Novaco Provocation Inventory. In M. Herson & A.S. Bellack (eds) *Dictionary of Behavioural Assessment Techniques*. Oxford: Pergamon Press.

Novaco, R.W. (1994). Anger as a risk factor for violence among the mentally disordered. In J. Monahan & H.J. Steadman (eds) *Violence and Mental Disorder: Developments in Risk Assessment*. Chicago, IL: University of Chicago Press.

Novaco, R.W & Taylor, J.W. (2002). Assessment of anger and aggression in offenders with developmental disabilities (unpublished manuscript).

Prout, H.T. & Nowak-Drabik, K.M. (2003). Psychotherapy with persons who have mental retardation: an evaluation of effectiveness. *American Journal of Mental Retardation*, **108**, 82–93.

Puri, B.K., Baxter, R. & Cordess, C.C. (1995). Characteristics of fire setters: a study and proposed multi-axial psychiatric classification. *British Journal of Psychiatry*, **166**, 393–6.

Raesaenen, P., Hirvenoja, R., Hakko, H. & Vaeisaenen, E. (1994). Cognitive functioning ability of arsonists. *Journal of Forensic Psychiatry*, **5**, 615–20.

Reiss, S. (1988). *Reiss Screen for Maladaptive Behaviour*. Worthington, OH: IDS.

Rose, J., Jenkins, R., O'Connor, C., Jones, C. & Felce, D. (2002). A group treatment for men with intellectual disabilities who sexually offend or abuse. *Journal of Applied Research in Intellectual Disabilities*, **15**, 138–50.

Roth, A. & Fonagy, P. (1996). *What Works for Whom: A Critical Review of Psychotherapy Research*. New York: Guildford Press.

Salkovskis, P.M. (1995). Demonstrating specific effects in cognitive and behavioural therapy. In M. Aveline and D.A. Shapiro (eds) *Research Foundations for Psychotherapy* (pp. 191–228). Chichester: John Wiley & Sons.

Salter, A. (1988). *Treating Child Sex Offenders and Victims*. Newbury Park, CA: Sage.

Scotti, J.R., Evans, I.M., Meyer, L.H. & Walker, P. (1991). A meta-analysis of intervention research with problem behaviour: treatment validity and standards of practice. *American Journal of Mental Retardation*, **96**, 233–56.

Spielberger, C.D. (1996). *State-Trait Anger Expression Inventory Professional Manual*. Odessa, FL: Psychological Assessment Resources Inc.

Stiles, W.B., Elliot, R., Llewelyn, S.P., Firth-Cozens, J.A., Margison, F.R. Shapiro, D.A. & Hardy, G.E. (1990). Assimilation of problematic experiences by clients in psychotherapy. *Psychotherapy*, **27**, 411–20.

Sturmey, P., Reed, J. & Corbett, J. (1991). Psychometric assessment of psychiatric disorders in people with learning difficulties (mental handicap): a review of measures. *Psychological Medicine*, **21**, 143–55.

Walker, T. & Cheseldine, S. (1997). Towards outcome measurement: monitoring effectiveness of anger management and assertiveness training in a group setting. *British Journal of Learning Disabilities*, **25**, 134–7.

Whittaker, S. (2001). Anger control for people with learning disabilities: a critical review. *Behavioural and Cognitive Psychotherapy*, **29**, 277–93.

PART IV

TREATMENT AND PROGRAMME ISSUES

Chapter 9

SEX OFFENDERS: CONCEPTUALISATION OF THE ISSUES, SERVICES, TREATMENT AND MANAGEMENT

WILLIAM R. LINDSAY

The State Hospital, Carstairs; NHS Tayside & University of Abertay Dundee, Dundee, UK

Prurient interest in sex offending has increased considerably over the past decade. In his opening address to the biennial conference of the International Association for the Treatment of Sex Offenders, Pfaefflin (2002) memorably called this "lust without guilt". Many of us have experienced the local outcry when a group home for people with intellectual disabilities is proposed in a middle class area. The implicit fear is that the new residents may be both sexually disinhibited and predatory and their visible presence will reduce house values. While these distorted perceptions continue, several researchers and clinicians are developing a body of knowledge to evaluate the realistic extent of the problem, ways of assessing, treating and managing individuals and outcomes. In addition to reviewing these areas of work, this chapter will begin by summarising some of the aetiological mechanisms which have been proposed or suggested by workers in the field.

At the outset, it should be stated that the material is exclusively related to men. While some authors have recorded that women with developmental disabilities have committed sexual offences (Allan, Lindsay, Macleod & Smith, 2001; McKerracher, Street & Segal, 1976), these are all related to prostitution or procurement and are therefore non-coercive on the one hand and not primarily sexual on the other. Material related to women and offending is reviewed in Chapter 14.

WHY SOME MEN WITH INTELLECTUAL DISABILITY COMMIT SEX OFFENCES: HYPOTHESES ON CAUSES

A number of authors have reported on common characteristics of sex offenders in clinical samples with which they have contact. By implication these are

Offenders with Developmental Disabilities. Edited by W.L. Lindsay, J.L. Taylor and P. Sturmey.
© 2004 John Wiley & Sons, Ltd.

hypotheses about the factors which may influence or cause sex offending. For example, Caparulo (1991), Day (1993) and Langevin and Pope (1993) have mentioned behavioural disturbance at school, poor ability to form relationships, poor impulse control, a history of family psychopathology and a low specificity for age and sex in offending. However, clinical samples must be treated with caution since the characteristics may simply reflect the nature of the referral pattern in that area or to that researcher. Hayes (1991) notes that sex offenders with intellectual disability typically have confused self-concepts, poor peer relations, a lack of social sexual knowledge, negative early sexual experiences (including sexual abuse) and lack of personal power. Day (1993) reports that in a significant percentage of cases, childhood development is characterised by multiple family pathology, gross marital disharmony, parental separation, violence, neglect and poor control. He observes that many clients have a history of school adjustment and relationship problems, behavioural problems, psychiatric illness and other delinquent behaviours. All these authors are highly experienced in assessment and treatment of sex offenders with intellectual disability but one cannot help but notice that their identification of characteristics is comprehensive and inclusive. All of these authors review single samples of sex offenders with intellectual disability without any comparison with control subjects. It may be that an appropriate controlled comparison would find several or all of these features in men with intellectual disability who have offended in other ways or have not offended at all.

Counterfeit Deviance

Perhaps the first hypothesis to conceptualise sex offending in this population as a result of variables other than sexual deviance was that of "counterfeit deviance". Hingsburger, Griffiths and Quinsey (1991) and Luiselli (2000) note that the term refers to behaviour which is undoubtedly deviant but may be precipitated by factors such as lack of sexual knowledge, poor social and hetero-social skills, limited opportunities to establish sexual relationships and sexual naivety rather than sexual deviance. Therefore remediation should focus on educational issues and developmental maturation rather than deviant sexuality. Clinically, this author has found that sex offenders who are referred have a much greater sexual knowledge than other clients. However, there are cases where this hypothesis is clearly relevant.

Case example

Mr D was referred for an incident of indecent exposure to an adult female in a local park. On initial assessment, his sexual knowledge seemed reasonable. However, on further investigation, it was clear that his sexual knowledge was all rote learning from sex education classes. He knew that in order to have sex a man put his penis in the woman's vagina. However when asked if the man's penis had to be hard or soft, he deduced that it would have to be soft so that the man did not harm the woman. Although he was able to talk about masturbation and the production of semen, after a few sessions it became clear that, at 21 years old, he had never masturbated. He said he exposed himself in order to interest the woman in him but realised immediately on her reaction that he had made a mistake.

In the author's experience Mr D is an unusual case, but counterfeit deviance is a reasonably well established hypothesis. Furthermore, we should consider that this hypothesis may be partially supported. Even if sex offenders are more knowledgeable than non-sex offenders, it does not necessarily follow that they have a comprehensive sexual knowledge.

Mental Illness

Here, the hypothesis is not necessarily that mental illness causes sexual offending but rather that it influences the rate of offending in this client group by loosening inhibitions or promoting aberrant behaviour through, for example, mania or psychotic delusions.

The rate of mental illness in cohorts of offenders with intellectual disability has been investigated more frequently. Day (1994) reported that 32% of the sample of sex offenders with intellectual disability had suffered psychiatric illness in adulthood, while Lindsay et al. (2002), in a study of 62 sex offenders and abusers with intellectual disability, also reported that 32% were found to have significant mental illness, including psychotic disorders, bipolar disorder and major depression.

Lund (1990), in a comprehensive study of offenders in Denmark, reported on 274 offenders with intellectual disability, most of whom were under care orders or restriction orders imposed by the legal system. This was a longitudinal study which was not confined to individuals admitted to hospital and Lund reported a surprising 91.7% of this cohort had a diagnosed mental illness of which 87.5% were categorised as behaviour disorder. This gives rise to further questions about the inclusion criteria for mental illness across various studies. The most obvious methodological issue would be whether or not challenging behaviour/behaviour disorder is included as a mental illness or is classified separately in these studies. In the Day (1994) study and the Lindsay et al. (2002) study behaviour disorders were classified separately. Notwithstanding these methodological issues, there is little doubt that mental illness is an important characteristic when considering this client group.

Smith and O'Brien (Chapter 13) make two important caveats in this regard. First, since mental illness does not directly cause sexual offending, the treatment of mental illness will not necessarily stop the propensity towards sexual offending. There may be residual problems related to offence-specific tendencies themselves which have to be addressed. The second important observation is that in some cases mental illness may cause a state of extreme disorganisation. Once the mental illness is treated these individuals may become more organised and therefore able to commit sex offences in a more structured and planned manner.

Sexual Abuse

Another frequently investigated variable is sexual abuse in childhood, which has often been associated with sexual offences in adulthood. Several authors have found a high incidence of childhood sexual abuse among samples of abusers (Thompson & Brown, 1997). However, Langevin and Pope (1993) and, with non-handicapped offenders, Briggs and Hawkins (1996) note that not all sexual abusers will have themselves been abused and it is not the case that all individuals who have been sexually abused will become sexual abusers or offenders. Lindsay, Law, Quinn, Smart and Smith (2001) compared 48 sex offenders and 50 non-sexual offenders, all with intellectual disability, and found that the rate of sexual abuse in the sex offending cohort was significantly higher than in the cohort of other offenders (38% versus 12.7%) and, correspondingly, the rate of physical abuse was significantly higher in the cohort of other offenders (14% versus 36%). Therefore, while there were significantly higher rates of sexual abuse in the sex offending cohort and physical abuse in the other offending cohort, it was still true that those reporting physical and sexual abuse accounted for less than 50% in both cases. This finding, on offenders with intellectual disabilities, is consistent with the major review of sexual abuse conducted by the House of Representatives (General Accounting Office, 1996) which concluded that "The experience of childhood sexual victimisation is quite likely neither a necessary nor a sufficient cause of adult sexual offending" (p. 14). Sequeira and Hollins (2003) note that the few existing studies on sexual abuse in people with intellectual disabilities such as Beail and Warden (1995) suggest that behavioural problems such as sexual disinhibition may be a consequence of sexual abuse in childhood. However, lack of standardised assessments, lack of appropriate control and an absence of agreed criteria used to report sexual abuse make such conclusions speculative.

Persistent Tendencies Towards Sex Offending and Lack of Discrimination

This hypothesis is more conventional in terms of the general literature on sex offending. The hypotheses are elucidated in detail in general texts on non-disabled offenders (e.g. Marshall, Laws & Barbaree, 1990) but basically take the position that persistent deviant sexual behaviour is a result of deviant sexual preferences, which are in turn mediated by distorted cognitions towards victims, selective attention, inappropriate sexual arousal and so on. One variant of this hypothesis with sex offenders with intellectual disability is that these individuals are less discriminating in their victims.

Lindsay *et al.* (2002) reported that for 62% of referrals there was either a previous conviction for a sexual offence or clear documented evidence of sexual abuse having been perpetrated by the subject. This is consistent with previous offending rates for referrals suggested by Scorzelli and Reinke-Scorzelli (1979) where they found that 68% of a mixed group of offenders with intellectual disability had previous offences. In terms of index offence frequency they found that offences against adults totalled 33% of the cohort (sexual assault 11%, sexual harassment 8%, attempted rape 8%, rape 6%), offences against children totalled 28% and indecent exposure accounted for 18% of the main offences committed. The authors note that several subjects had a number of similar offences while others had a number of different offences but the figures reported the most serious index offence.

There does seem to be some consensus that sex offenders with intellectual disability may be more likely to commit sex offences across categories and be less discriminating in their victims. In a well-controlled study of 950 sexual offenders, Blanchard *et al.* (1999) found that sex offenders with intellectual disability were more likely to offend against younger children, male children and across victim categories than non-disabled sex offenders. Several authors (Day, 1993, Walker & McCabe, 1973) have written that sex offenders with intellectual disability are less likely to commit offences involving serious bodily harm, violence or death.

Impulsivity

Impulsivity is generally considered to be behaviour which is not planned and is committed without any consideration of the consequences on self and others. There is an extensive literature relating impulsivity to violent and non-violent offending (Nussbaum *et al.*, 2002). Glaser and Deane (1999) invoked the concept of impulsivity in a comparison of two cohorts of sex offenders and non-sexual offenders with intellectual disability. They found no differences between these two groups on age, educational history, family disturbance in childhood/adolescence or history of contact with the psychiatric services. Of particular note was that there was no difference between the two groups in the number of sex crimes with which they had been previously charged. These authors presented the hypothesis that sex crimes in this population could be seen as a pattern of impulsivity and poorly controlled behaviour rather than any inherent propensity for sexual deviation. Such a hypothesis might account for an increased prevalence of both sex offending and fire raising. The only differences found by Glaser and Deane (1999) between the two groups were that fewer sex offenders had abused alcohol and/or drugs and fewer sex offenders had served prior terms in prison.

Parry and Lindsay (2003), on the other hand, compared 22 sex offenders with comparison groups of non-sexual offenders and non-offenders, all with intellectual disability, using the Barratt Impulsiveness Scale. They found that sexual offenders reported significantly lower impulsiveness traits in all areas when compared to both comparison groups. These authors noted that the high frequency of grooming behaviour, albeit simple grooming behaviour, by such offenders suggested that they were aware of the importance of gaining the victim's trust and friendship and also suggested ability to delay gratification, which is exactly the opposite to the features of impulsiveness. However, it may also be the case that different categories of sexual offender may differ on impulsiveness. For example, offenders against children may have a greater ability to plan and delay gratification than offenders against adults, who may have a greater tendency to act on the spur of the moment. Parry and Lindsay also made the important distinction between trait and state impulsiveness and agitation. They assessed trait impulsiveness whereas more transitory states of agitation and impulsiveness may have different effects.

Conclusions

Several authors have considered reasons alternative to sexual deviance for sexual offending in this client group. Looking across these various studies, mental illness and sexual abuse in childhood would appear to be significant characteristics when considering sex offenders with intellectual disability. The obvious caveat is that for both of these variables, despite the fact that they were significantly prevalent in various cohorts, the majority of individuals showed evidence of neither. Following the writings of several authors, we should consider the hypothesis that sexual deviancy may be less salient in the commission of sex offences for this population than certain other variables such as impulsivity and lack of appropriate sexual partners. We should, however, be cautious in considering the reports of characteristics which are based on clinical samples with no appropriate control condition. It may be that sex offenders with intellectual disability are more likely to commit sex offences across categories and be less discriminating in their victims. It would also appear that a high proportion of referrals have previous convictions for sexual offences or well-documented incidents of perpetrating sexual abuse.

EPIDEMIOLOGY

As with other services, the major influence affecting provision of assessment, treatment and management services for sex offenders with intellectual disability has been that of de-institutionalisation. Institutions would have locked wards to accommodate clients with aberrant sexual behaviour, aggression and so on. This amounted to a considerable number of individuals. It is certain that since there are far fewer individuals placed in large institutions, there are more people with intellectual disabilities who have forensic problems living in some sort of community arrangement. Lund (1990) identified a significant increase in offenders with mild intellectual disability receiving a first sentence in 1984 compared to 1973. Day (1993) felt that this may be an early result of the influence of care in the community policies. Since these policies have advanced considerably since this study was conducted, this will clearly have an effect on incidence, appropriate treatments, management and services. In this regard, Lund (1990) found a doubling of the incidence of sex offending among people with intellectual disabilities when comparing sentencing in 1984 with 1973.

Several researchers have noticed relatively high prevalence of sex offending in this population. Gross (1985) found that between 21% and 50% of intellectually disabled offenders had committed a sexual crime. Walker and McCabe (1973) in their study of patients committed under a hospital order, found that of 331 men with an intellectual disability, 28% had committed a sexual offence. Hodgins (1992) in a study of all offenders in Copenhagen, Denmark, reported that offenders with intellectual disability were five times more likely to commit a violent offence. Unfortunately, violent offences were undifferentiated and included robbery and assault in addition to rape and molestation. Sundram (1989) also reports a high rate of serious crimes including sexual offences, with 38% of inmates with an IQ below 70 in

New York state prisons, committing or attempting to commit murder, manslaughter, assault and sexual offences (again undifferentiated). As a result of evidence such as this, Day (1994) has little doubt that sex offences are over-represented among this client group. However, one has to recognise that these studies have been conducted in highly specific settings. It could well be that the high-security hospitals and prisons in which these studies have been conducted distort the prevalence rates of sex offenders with intellectual disability.

There is some evidence that prevalence rates may not be as high as those found in these previous studies. Hayes (1991) reports that 3.7% of offenders with intellectual disability had been convicted of a sexual offence and that this figure was similar to the 4% of non-disabled offenders similarly convicted. Hayes (1991) concludes that "There seems no clear evidence for either over-representation or under-representation of intellectual disability clients in the sex offender population". Perhaps the most pragmatic conclusion is to focus on the provision and nature of services bearing in mind the conclusion of Noble and Conley (1992), that "There is little point in trying to nail down to the nearest decimal point the percentage of people with mental retardation and other mental disabilities who reside in the nation's prisons. We know that the number is significant and that many inmates with mental retardation are not receiving appropriate services". Translated to be relevant for sex offenders with intellectual disability—it is pointless trying to determine the percentage of sex offenders with intellectual disability. We know the number is significant and we should focus on the most effective way to provide assessment, treatment and management services.

ASSESSMENTS SPECIFIC TO SEX OFFENDERS

Several authors have outlined a range of areas in which assessment is important. These are based implicitly on the hypotheses for the development of sex offences outlined earlier. So it has been considered that sex offenders may have deficits in heterosexual social skills and sexual knowledge, dysfunctional attitudes towards sexuality, cognitions consistent with sex offences and deviant sexual preferences. Assessment is directed towards evaluation of ability, knowledge, thoughts, behaviour and physiological response in these areas.

Caparulo (1991), Clare (1993) and Seghorn and Ball (2000) have each outlined areas which require assessment with sex offenders with intellectual disabilities. Caparulo described the use of the Socio-Sexual Knowledge and Attitudes Test (SSKAT; Wish, McCooms & Edmonson, 1980) for establishing the level of sexual knowledge and attitudes in referrals. As with other authors, he noted that sexual offending may arise from a variety of variables, including lack of sexual knowledge, lack of appropriate sexual attitudes, developmental delay in relation to social situations and so on. Therefore it is important to assess that the individual has an appropriate level of sexual knowledge in relation to conventions of society, taboos and rules, in addition to acceptable sexuality. The SSKAT assesses knowledge and attitudes in the areas of parts of the body, adolescent development, appropriate social behaviour, appropriate sexual behaviour, birth control, venereal disease, long-term relationships and parenting.

Several authors have shown that, in general, people with intellectual disabilities have poor sexual knowledge especially in the areas of sexually transmitted disease and birth control (Bender, Aitman, Biggs & Haug, 1983; Lindsay, Bellshaw, Culross, Staines & Michie, 1992). There are no studies comparing the sexual knowledge of sex offenders with control subjects to establish whether or not sex offenders have a greater sexual knowledge than control subjects. Seghorn and Ball (2000) noted that the assessment should specify the nature of the problem as well as identify and focus on goals of treatment. Assessment should also establish a baseline against which change can be evaluated. Specifically, in relation to the offence, they recommended assessment of deviant sexual arousal, deviant sexual development, cognitive distortions which may mitigate responsibility for the offence and degree of empathy. Caparulo (1991) gave a detailed outline of the requirements for a comprehensive assessment of sex offenders with developmental disabilities. This includes everything from pre-sentencing investigation, through laboratory reports to psychiatric assessment. He recommended taking a sexual history, assessing sexual knowledge, determining level of moral development, social deviance and risk of reoffending, and developing clear recommendations for treatment.

While several authors have been comprehensive in recommending important areas, it has to be recognised that there are few assessments which have been developed to be appropriate for individuals with intellectual disabilities. Clare (1993) noted that understanding the complex language and concepts which may be inherent in assessments with sex offenders may be very difficult for people with intellectual disabilities. The discriminations involved in self-report questionnaires may prove difficult for clients to complete. She recommended that it is particularly important to supplement any self-report information or interview information with other methods of assessment such as reports from carers and significant others. However, many existing assessments are too linguistically complicated to ensure that the offender with intellectual disability has understood the requirements and items of the test. Therefore, it will be necessary in future to develop new assessments or alter existing assessments so that the presentation and concepts are appropriately understood by clients with intellectual disabilities. Essential to the development or modification of assessments is that the psychometric properties have to be established for the client group.

This is particularly important since any new assessment or checklist developed by a particular researcher for a particular client group will have unknown psychometric properties. This is true in all the main areas of psychometrics, including reliability, validity and standardisation. Therefore it is very difficult to determine the extent to which a given score from a particular client is different from clients without that problem, is representative of clients with that problem or is entirely idiosyncratic (standardisation). It is also important to know the extent to which this particular client is likely to give similar responses to the same question on a subsequent testing (reliability). If these psychometric properties are not established there is the serious possibility of introducing random error into both the assessment of treatment programmes and research methodologies. Because of the problems peculiar to developmental disabilities, such psychometric data should be gathered in relevant populations with developmental disabilities.

There is recent evidence that people with intellectual disabilities can and do report in a reliable and valid way on personal experiences, emotions and other self-perceptions. Kazdin, Matson and Senatore (1983) and Helsel and Matson (1989) have suggested ways in which graded self-report information can be organised so that it is more reliable. Employing these developments in assessment procedures, Lindsay, Michie, Baty, Smith and Miller (1994) demonstrated a significant degree of consistency and convergent validity in the assessment of mood in 58 individuals with mild intellectual disabilities. They found significant correlations between a variety of assessments of anxiety and depression. These assessments also correlated positively with measures of introversion but showed no relationship with measures of extraversion. Dagnan and Sandhu (1999) modified the Rosenberg Self-Esteem Questionnaire and the Social Comparison Scale so that they were understandable to people with intellectual disabilities. They found good internal and test/retest reliability for both scales and found that for the Rosenberg Self-Esteem Question-naire the factor structure was consistent with the original scales. This latter finding is important since self-esteem is often considered a fundamental assessment and treatment issue for sex offenders with intellectual disabilities.

Ward, Hudson, Johnston and Marshall (1997) and Ward, Keenan and Hudson (2000) have argued that cognitive distortions and attitudes which might be con-sidered to support sex offending are important in the development of any inci-dent of sexual abuse. As a result, a number of assessments of cognitive distortions and thinking errors have been developed for use with sex offending populations. Bumby (1996) and Vanhouche and Vertommen (1999) have described assessments, with excellent psychometric properties, which are designed to assess attitudes that might be considered consistent with sex offending. These assessments include items such as "I think women who wear short skirts and tight clothes are asking to be raped"; "some children enjoy having sex with men"; "if a woman knows a man is looking through curtains at her it would turn her on"; "if a man exposes himself to a woman it is a good way of showing her he wants to have sex". Clearly such attitudes present the individual with a cognitive framework which is permissive of sexually offending behaviour. These cognitive misconceptions may prompt the individual to commit offences, and alteration of these misconceptions through cognitive re-structuring may be a crucial aspect of treatment (Marshall & Barbaree, 1990).

Abel, Becker and Cunningham-Rathner (1984) and Abel *et al.* (1989) developed an assessment which assesses the extent to which sex offenders hold cognitive distor-tions that might justify or mitigate their sexual offending against children. Kolton, Boer and Boer (2001) recently employed the Abel and Becker Cognition Scale with 89 sex offenders with intellectual disabilities. They found that the response op-tions of the test needed to be changed from the four-choice system (1 = agree, 4 = strongly disagree) to a dichotomous system (agree/disagree) to reduce extremity bias in the sample. The revised assessment provided "adequate" total score, and item correlations and test/retest reliability and internal consistency were "accept-able" and preserved the psychometric integrity of the assessment. It is unfortunate that the degree of cognitive ability of the participants was not mentioned in this paper. Neither were values reported for item/total correlations, test/retest reliabil-ity or internal consistency. However, this study provides some evidence that cognitive distortions and attitudes in sex offenders with intellectual disability can be assessed with some reliability and validity.

Lindsay and Smith (1998) outlined cognitive assessments which might be used for exhibitionists and offenders against children, both with intellectual disabilities.

Carson, Whitefield and Lindsay (2002) describe the development of a series of questionnaires dealing with attitudes consistent with rape, voyeurism, exhibitionism, dating abuse, homosexual assault, offences against children and stalking. Preliminary results indicate that the questionnaires may prove reliable, internally consistent and valid, and will discriminate between sex offenders, other offenders and non-offenders. Therefore, in the area of cognitive distortions related to offending, there are some current developments.

Caparulo (1991) and Seghorn and Ball (2000) outline variables which are important in risk assessment of sex offenders. These include cooperation with the evaluation, sex offence history, criminal history, violence, management of anger, willingness to discuss the offence, acceptance of responsibility, expression of remorse, deviant sexual interest, perversions, victims, substance abuse, empathy for the victim, adjustment, mental illness, history of abuse and motivation for treatment. Clearly, this is an extensive list and includes crucial variables and issues to which the assessor would wish to attend. However, there is little empirical research on the importance of these various risk factors in the genesis of sex offences, their importance in the process of treatment and their predictive value in relation to outcome.

In summary, the work on assessment is at an early stage. While we have some rudimentary measures to assess sexual knowledge, attitudes permissive of sexual offending, emotion, self-esteem and the like, there is a paucity of information on the way sex offenders may differ from other individuals with intellectual disability on all of these measures. There is also little information beyond hypotheses on how these assessed variables might affect or relate to sexual offending. For example, as has been described, there is an assumption that cognitive distortions may be important in the development of a sexual offence. However, there is no empirical evidence suggesting that this may be the case or, if it is, the processes by which cognitions might influence sex offending. Other cognitive processes, such as selective attention towards women or children, the ability to solve problems in risky situations, or the way in which such attitudes interact with aspects of the situation to affect decision making, may be more important, or less important, than attitudes.

TREATMENT

The three most commonly reported treatments for sex offenders with intellectual disabilities are behavioural treatment, increasingly cognitive interventions and pharmacological treatments.

Behavioural Management and Comprehensive In-Patient Treatment

Behavioural management approaches have been reported in two major texts in the area. Haaven, Little and Petre-Miller (1990) described a wide-ranging series of treatments, including the promotion of self-control of aberrant sexual behaviour, social skills training and sex education all combined in a comprehensive residential programme. Griffiths, Quinsey and Hingsbuger (1989) described a similarly integrative behavioural management regime for sex offenders. Their programme included addressing the deviant sexual behaviour through education, training social competence and improving relationship skills, reviewing relapse prevention through alerting support staff and training on issues related to responsibility. In a review of over 30 cases, they reported no reoffending and they described a number of successful case studies to illustrate their methods.

Plaud, Plaud, Colstoe and Orvedal (2000) have written that behavioural management approaches remain the most common psychological treatments for the management of sexual offending. They note that the purpose of a behavioural treatment programme is to advance behavioural competency in daily living skills, general interpersonal and educational skills and specialised behaviour skills related to sexuality and offending. Plaud *et al.* (2000) review aversion therapy techniques and masturbatory retraining techniques in some detail. With reference to deviant sexual arousal, aversion therapy essentially links thoughts and behaviour associated with the deviant sexual arousal with an aversive image or event. This then results in a negative reaction to the deviant sexual stimulus. The aversive stimulus/event may be tactile, olfactory, behavioural or imagined. For example, this author has used imagined aversive events in relation to deviant sexual arousal.

Case example

Mr P had been reasonably successful in treatment over a period of one year. His original offence had been a non-penetrative sexual offence against a girl of eight years old. He had also downloaded a number of child images (non-subscription) from the internet. During one session about a year into treatment, he reported having arousing images of watching a prepubescent girl in a park. He reported that this image was not any girl with whom he was familiar but was simply an image which had come to him spontaneously one night and had returned on several occasions. We began by encouraging him to imagine the scene as it would normally come to him and then began inserting aversive stimuli into the sequence. The first aversive stimulus was being tapped on the shoulder by a policeman while he was watching the girl, having to report his name and, since he was a known sex offender, being taken to the police station. A second aversive event in the sequence was the presence of two large young men who noticed that he was a single man watching a girl in a park and came over to him in an accusing and aggressive manner. Both of these sequences were rehearsed frequently over four consecutive treatment sessions and Mr P reported that they were successful in reducing his sexual arousal to this particular deviant sexual stimulus. At the same time he reported that it was not replaced with any other deviant sexual stimulus but rather he began masturbating to thoughts of having consenting, ordinary sex with adult women.

Masturbatory retraining techniques follow similar principles through decreasing the sexual stimulatory value of deviant stimuli while attempting to increase the sexual arousal associated with acceptable stimuli. While there is a reasonable literature on these procedures in the general sex offender literature (Marquis, 1970; Marshall, 1969), Plaud *et al.* (2000) note that there is a paucity of studies employing these techniques with individuals who have intellectual disability.

Grubb-Blubaugh, Shire and Balser (1994) employed a behavioural management and peer review approach in a closed unit to promote appropriate socialised skills in a group of offenders and abusers. The jury system consisted of peer review which recommended positive or negative consequences for individuals' behaviour. Twelve adult men participated in the study and they recommended consequences such as group socialisation for the day, elimination of shopping or telephone privileges, community service hours, removal of a personal television and a simple warning. This peer review system and the consequences for behaviour which were derived from it resulted in significant reductions in a range of non-compliant, aggressive and sexually inappropriate behaviours. This system was implemented in a closed unit and while the authors noted improvements in a range of behavioural skills, there was little opportunity for individuals to demonstrate these skills or indeed any self-control outside the unit.

Charman and Clare (1992) reported the success of an educational group model when they demonstrated gains in sexual knowledge and more appropriate sexual attitudes in a group of offenders and abusers with intellectual disability. However, there was no follow-up of clients to note the effect of these improvements on subsequent offending behaviour and tendencies. Sex education and the acquisition of social and personal skills are emphasised in the group treatment described by Swanson and Garwick (1990). In their report they assessed and treated 15 individuals who had committed a variety of incidents of sexual abuse and sexual offending. Much of their treatment was directed at responsibility training in addition to the acquisition of skills and knowledge. The mean length of treatment for participants was 14 months and they reported that 6 of the 15 participants (40%) reoffended.

Comprehensive in-patient treatments have also been developed to cater for the needs of people with intellectual disabilities who have severe challenging and offending behaviour, including sexual offending. In reports of the MIETS Unit, Murphy and Clare (1991) and Murphy, Holland, Fowler and Reep (1991) have described treatments for individuals with mental illness, assaultive behaviour, firesetting tendencies and sexually aberrant behaviour with a series of successful case descriptions. Xenitidis, Henry, Russell, Ward and Murphy (1999) reported on 64 patients admitted to the MIETS Unit. While only 17% had been admitted from community facilities, 84.2% were discharged back to community placements. There was also a significant reduction in the frequency and severity of challenging and abusing behaviour.

Cognitive Techniques and Problem Solving

A major recent development in the use of psychological treatment for sex offenders with intellectual disability has been the employment of cognitive and problem solving techniques within therapy. These methods have been developed to a sophisticated degree with the general population of sex offenders (Marshall, Anderson &

Fernandez, 1999). Treatment methods are based on the analysis that cognitive distortions set a personal framework which may be permissive of, or consistent with, sexual offending. Ward, Hudson, Johnston and Marshall (1997) have elucidated an integrative theory designed to promote understanding of the way in which a range of cognitive structures might underpin the initiation, commission and personal mitigation of sexual offences. These authors recommend that assessment and treatment should focus on information processing in addition to addressing "pre-existing attitudes, initial planning and misinterpretation of a victim's interaction with the offender, as well as post-offence evaluations and expectations" (p. 498).

There have been several reports which have considered these cognitive processes during treatment. O'Conner (1996) developed a problem-solving intervention for 13 adult male sex offenders. This involved consideration of a range of risky situations in which offenders had to develop safe solutions for both themselves and potential victims. She reports positive results from the intervention with most subjects achieving increased community access. Lindsay and colleagues (Lindsay, Marshall, Neilson, Quinn & Smith, 1998a; Lindsay, Neilson, Morrison & Smith, 1998b; Lindsay, Olley, Jack, Morrison & Smith, 1998c; Lindsay, Olley, Baillie & Smith, 1999) report a series of case studies on offenders against children, exhibitionists, stalkers and adolescent sexual offenders using a cognitive intervention in which various forms of denial and mitigation of the offence are challenged over treatment periods of up to three years. Consistently, across the studies they report changes in cognitions during treatment and low reoffending rates 4–7 years following initial conviction.

Rose, Jenkins, O'Connor, Jones and Felce (2002) report a 16-week group treatment for five sex offenders with intellectual disabilities. The group treatment employed self-control procedures, consideration of the effects on victims, identifying emotions within oneself, in addition to sex education, appropriate assertiveness and avoiding risky situations. Individuals were assessed using an attitudes scale, a measure of locus of control, the sexual behaviour and the law scale, and a victim empathy scale. The only significant differences from baseline to post-treatment were found on the locus of control scale. This indicated a more external locus of control after the intervention. The authors also reported that the participants did not reoffend for one year. They felt that the changes in locus of control scores might have been due to a significant part of the sessions emphasising the possible external consequences of any future offending behaviour.

Case example

Mr M, 45 years old, WAIS IQ 64. Mr M was referred following an aggressive rape on a woman with whom he was sharing a flat. Forensic and medical evidence indicated that considerable violence had been employed during the sexual assault and Mr M made an immediate frank admission. Mr M had no previous sexual offences and, after careful assessment, since this author was willing to accept him for treatment, he was given three years probation. As a condition of probation there was a requirement to attend for treatment. Treatment was conducted by repeated review of the cognitive processes involved in Mr M's own offence and other, hypothetical, similar offences. Therefore a range of problem solving, risky situations were reviewed with Mr M; for example:

Jane is in a bar waiting for her friend. She is sitting at the bar and looks over towards the door. John is sitting on his own at the bar between Jane and the door. John notices Jane looking and thinks she is looking at him. Jane keeps looking over at the door for her friend. John still notices that Jane keeps looking in his direction and smiles at her. Jane smiles back and says that she is waiting for her friend and that it is a lovely bar. John thinks Jane is interested in him and begins to feel sexy. Jane decides that her friend is not coming and leaves the bar, saying goodbye to John. John follows Jane out and says that it is a cold night tonight. Jane agrees that it is a cold night and walks down the road in the same direction as John. John pushes Jane into a dark corner and sexually assaults her.

The client was then asked a series of questions about the scenario.

What was Jane thinking as she looked over in John's direction?

What was John thinking when he saw Jane look over in his direction?

Did Jane notice John and fancy him?

Did John fancy Jane?

What were Jane's thoughts when she smiled at John?

What were John's thoughts when he saw Jane smiling at him?

What was Jane thinking she was going to do when she went to the door?

What was John thinking Jane wanted to do when she left?

What did Jane think when John talked to her at the door of the bar?

What was John thinking when he talked to her at the door of the bar?

What did Jane think as they were walking up the road?

What was John thinking when they were walking up the road?

Who was to blame for the rape taking place? Jane or John?

This kind of situation was presented in a group setting and group members were asked who was to blame for the sexual assault taking place. At first Mr M would indicate that Jane was to blame for the sexual assault because she took an interest in John and kept looking in John's direction so that it was easy for him to make the mistake that she was interested in him. There would then follow a discussion about what Jane was thinking, what John was thinking and the way in which cognitive distortions were developing in John's frame of reference for the incident. The problem-solving ideas would be directed towards the solution that as they left the bar John and Jane would have completely different ideas about the nature of the interaction which had taken place. Therefore John's cognitive processes had distorted the reality of the situation with regard to Jane.

Another method was to show one of the slides from the Kempton (1988) series in a small group setting. In the transcript to follow, the slide selected shows a man and a woman meeting in a park with the woman smiling to the man. The therapist then asks the question "What is happening here?" and with a series of questions allows group members to establish appropriate circumstances for the meeting between the two. On this occasion it was established that they had just met in the park and perhaps they both had dogs. The following is a short transcript from the treatment session:

THERAPIST (T)	What is this woman thinking?
MR M	She is looking at him and smiling. She must like him.
T	So, what would she be thinking?
M	I don't know. She might want to have sex with him.
A	No, I don't think she would want to have sex with him. She had just met him.
T	I am interested in what M thinks is happening here and we all have different opinions.
M	Well, she might be interested in him, but I don't know if she would want to have sex.
A	Why would she want to have sex with him?
T	M, you thought she might want to have sex with him. Why do you think she would want to have sex with him?
M	Well, she is smiling at him and she quite likes him, so she might want to have sex.
T	So, you think she wants to have sex with this man who she had just met?
M	Well, she might. Yes, she could want to have sex with him.

In this way, a cognitive distortion has been elicited. In this case it is that a woman who meets a strange man in a park and discusses a mutual interest in dogs, might want immediately to have sex with the man. The next section of the session went on to review the extent to which Mr M thought the woman was to blame if the man forced her to have sex with him. Once again, beliefs permissive of sexual offending and cognitive distortions were being elicited. The therapist would ask Mr M to repeat these cognitive distortions a number of times so that there was no possibility of him, in future, denying that he had generated these beliefs. The therapeutic session would then go on to review the woman's thoughts and the man's thoughts from their individual points of view. In this way it would be established that the woman had arrived at the park with her dog, not thinking about sex, would be thinking about walking the dog and then going home, might be thinking about what she was going to make for her evening meal and so on. At no time would she be thinking about having sex. We would also review whether or not a woman would want to have sex with any man she met under these circumstances and at that time.

All of this process would be conducted through socratic questioning and inductive reasoning. The therapist tries not to provide any of the socially acceptable answers but rather uses a series of questions to help the client think about the issues, to generate answers which will give evidence that he is considering the relevant issues, and in turn will induce him to consider more socialised possibilities in his responses. Therefore all of the socially acceptable beliefs were being generated by Mr M himself. At the end of this process, Mr M himself would conclude that the woman was not wanting to have sex with the man and did not have any particular personal interest in him. Following this process, the contradiction between Mr M's original cognitive distortions and the socialised beliefs which he had himself generated were emphasised. The cognitive dissonance within Mr M's thought processes evidenced by the difference between the two beliefs which he himself had generated was highlighted and promoted for consideration. At all times the new socialised belief was supported by the therapist.

During this process, the hypothetical situation and the offence which Mr M had committed were compared in very direct ways. Therefore the therapist would say "OK—so now you think that the woman is not wanting to have sex with this man. But he thinks that she is interested so he is going to force her to have sex. And you tell me that it is wrong for him to do this. And you are correct—it is wrong. But that is exactly what you did, isn't it M? So why if you think that it is wrong for this man did you think it was OK for you to go ahead and do it?" Again, this forces the cognitive dissonance between the socialised beliefs which Mr M has recently generated and his own offending behaviour. Once again the socialised cognitive framework for thinking about women is supported and reinforced.

It has to be said that this process is not always straightforward. Occasionally clients will accept that the attitude consistent with offending which they expressed at the start of the process was wrong and that the new belief is correct. Occasionally they will accept their socialised belief but say something like "But that woman in the picture wants to have sex". Occasionally they will accept both beliefs and accuse the therapist of deliberately confusing them. However, the important aspect of the process is that any cognitive distortions are beginning to be challenged in the client. These problem-solving and cognitive-challenging processes are continued repeatedly throughout treatment.

Mr M was assessed on a Questionnaire on Attitudes Consistent with Sex Offending (QACSO) (Lindsay, Carson & Whitefield, 2000; Carson, Whitefield & Lindsay, 2002). His scores on the rape scale indicate that his progress through treatment was reasonably orderly over the first year. Thereafter he maintained low levels of attitudes consistent with sexually offending until discharge at three years. He has been followed-up at six-monthly intervals since then and there have been no reports of reoffending seven years following the index offence. The author has a wide range of social work, criminal justice, police and health service contacts within a defined geographical area and if Mr M had engaged in any other incident, even if it had not been prosecuted, it would be highly likely to come to his attention.

Pharmacological Treatment

Pharmacological treatment for sex offenders has a fairly longstanding history. Broadly, intervention can be divided into two categories—the first is direct hormonal intervention which attempts to reduce the effect of sex hormones on parts of the brain associated with creation and maintenance of sexual urges. The second consists of indirect intervention with pharmacological regimes directed at co-morbid conditions such as aggression, impulsivity and a range of psychiatric disorders such as major depression or bipolar disorder which might influence sexual disin-hibition.

The two most commonly used hormonal treatments are medroxyprogesterone acetate (MPA) and cyproterone acetate (CPA). In a review of studies of male of-fenders with intellectual disability who were treated with CPA, Clarke (1989) noted improvement in the index behaviours (sexual assault or public masturbation) in approximately one half of the subjects being studied. Cooper (1995), in a review of both anti-libidinal medications, estimated that around 10% of individuals in controlled trials had an intellectual disability. He noted that the medication would be likely to reduce the intensity of sexual drive but not its direction, which might be particularly problematic in the case of sex offenders with intellectual disability since if medication was discontinued, it may be associated with quick relapse. He also felt that there was a pressing need for double-blind placebo-controlled studies with well-defined inclusion criteria, including cognitive abilities. In general, work in this area is typified by case studies (Myers, 1991; Sherak, 2000).

It should always be noted that there are contraindications and cautions with drugs used to reduce male sexual drive. For example, CPA should not be prescribed for men who are aged less than 18 or whose bone or testicular development is not complete. It should also be noted that intellectually disabled men may not be as capable of reporting side-effects and bodily changes. Given that, there may be additional ethical and consent considerations when using such pharmacological agents with these clients.

The importance of further case investigations and controlled studies to estab-lish the range of effectiveness of these medications is emphasised by some of the experiences of the author and his colleagues.

Case example

A, a 20-year-old man who offended against children, tolerated MPA but refused to engage in any psychological treatment to re-orientate his sexual interest or induce self-control. B, again 20 years old and convicted of offences against teenagers, was unable to tolerate MPA. C was 28 years old on being referred for offences against boys. He was diagnosed with bipolar disorder and appropriate medication enabled him to be accessible for extended psychological treatment.

The variation in outcome of all these cases simply emphasises that all of this work is at an early stage and further process and outcome studies are required. It is particularly noticeable that in the area of treatment for sex offenders with intel-lectual disability there is no controlled study of any kind on any of the treatment approaches mentioned. One particularly difficult issue in relation to this is that of ethical approval for research. Given that most sex offenders with intellectual disability will remain in the community and could therefore reoffend, it is partic-ularly difficult for an ethical committee to approve a no-treatment condition in a randomly assigned controlled study for sex offenders. This is true even when all treatments are at an early stage of development, as they obviously are in this field.

OUTCOME

Because of the lack of controlled studies in this area, if one is to gauge the effectiveness of interventions, it is important to consider studies which have simply reported reoffending rates in offenders with an intellectual disability. Walker and McCabe (1973), in a study on hospital order patients, reported 39% reconviction rates in 370 patients with intellectual disability. Gibbens and Robertson (1983) in a study of 250 male patients with intellectual disability, all on hospital orders, reported a reconviction rate of 68%. Lund (1990), in a study of 93 patients with intellectual disabilities on statutory care orders, reported reoffending rates of 72% over 10 years. Therefore these reoffending rates are extremely significant. Scorzelli and Reinki-Scorzelli (1979) reported reoffending rates of 68% in a mixed group of untreated offenders with intellectual disability. Klimecki, Jenkinson and Wilson (1994) found an overall reoffending rate of 41.3% in previous prison inmates with intellectual disability, two years after release. They reported that the reoffending rate for sex-related offences was 30.8%. However, they noted that several individuals who had received prison sentences for sex offences were still incarcerated and were therefore unable to reoffend. Therefore they felt that this figure may be artificially depressed.

After their group treatment involving some cognitive and educational aspects, Swanson and Garwick (1990) found 40% reoffending in their group of 15 participants. Griffiths et al. (1989) reported excellent outcomes and no reoffending in 30 subjects. Both Xenitidis et al. (1999) and O'Conner (1996) have reported substantial increases in community access following treatment for sex offending problems. However, it has to be recognised that these positive outcomes are collateral and could easily reflect a number of changes in service systems rather than the individuals themselves. For example, it may be that following treatment, the care agencies are simply more willing to allow these individuals more community access and the treatment has served to reassure the carers rather than change the behaviour or cognitions of the offender. Lindsay and colleagues (Lindsay et al., 1998a, b, c, 1999) report low rates of reoffending with relatively long follow-up periods (4–7 years) but again the problem of lack of adequate experimental controls is clearly evident. Lindsay et al. (2002) reported that of 48 sex offenders who had completed one-year follow-up, 4% had reoffended; 39 followed up for two years had a reoffending rate of 12.5%, 29 followed up for three years had a reoffending rate of 13% and for 19 clients at four years follow-up the reoffending rate was 21%. These reoffending rates are eminently reasonable in relation to other treatment and follow-up studies. In this study, these authors also found that those subjects who had a planned discharge had a significantly better outcome than those subjects for whom discharge was not planned (normally these subjects simply discharge themselves after the cessation of probation). They felt that although this finding made intuitive sense, there was no particular reason from a review of outcome studies to conclude that this might be the case. Studies of untreated offenders (Klimecki et al., 1994) have found reoffending rates of 34% following release from prison. On the other hand, studies in which clients had previously undergone hospital treatment (Walker & McCabe, 1973; Gibbens & Robertson, 1983; Lund, 1990) report reoffending rates of 39–72%. While these studies cannot be directly compared, they certainly give no indication that reoffending rates following organised treatment will be any lower than reoffending rates following a non-therapeutic prison sentence. However, Lindsay *et al.* (2002) do acknowledge that because of the comprehensive nature of the treatment, it was difficult to know which particular aspect of the service had contributed to specific outcomes.

One interesting finding in relation to outcome and length of treatment has been reported by a number of authors. Day (1988) found a positive correlation between length of stay of over two years and better outcomes. Walker and McCabe (1973) found that a shorter duration in institutional care was associated with a greater likelihood of reconviction or imprisonment. Lindsay and Smith (1998) found that sex offenders treated for less than one year showed significantly poorer progress and were more likely to reoffend than those treated for at least two years. Therefore, it would seem that shorter periods of treatment may be of limited value for this client group. As Lindsay *et al.* (2002) conclude, "The data have altered our own practice so that we are reluctant to accept a case where there is little prospect of conducting treatment for at least two years with subsequent planned discharge".

CONCLUSION

This chapter has considered hypotheses on why some men with ID commit sexual offences and has reviewed studies on prevalence, assessment, treatment and outcome in relation to sex offenders and intervention. It is clear that a robust start has been made to the development of our knowledge in this area. We are much clearer regarding deficits in knowledge and, as a result, are clearer on the (considerable) amount of work that is required in this field. We can, however, draw some tentative conclusions. Mental illness and sexual abuse in childhood may be important variables, to consider in assessment. Sexual deviancy is likely to be an important variable, with studies finding that around two-thirds of sex offenders have committed a previous sexual offence and clients are more likely to commit sexual offences across categories and be less discriminating in their victims. Any assessment should attend to those variables in addition to sexual knowledge and attitudes, although work in this area is at a very rudimentary stage. While some treatment and management approaches seem promising, some authors have reported that treatment of less than one year is of little value.

ACKNOWLEDGEMENT

Case studies were compiled with the help of my colleague, Dr Anne Smith, consultant psychiatrist.

REFERENCES

Abel, G.G., Becker, J.V. & Cunningham-Rathner, J. (1984). Complications, consent and cognitions in sex between children and adults. *International Journal of Law and Psychiatry*, **7**, 89–103.

Abel, G.G., Gore, D.K., Holland, C.L., Camp, N., Becker, J.V. & Rathner, J. (1989). The measurement of the cognitive distortions of child molesters. *Annals of Sex Research*, **3**, 135–53.

Allan, R., Lindsay, W.R., Macleod, F. & Smith, A.H.W. (2001). Treatment of women with intellectual disabilities who have been involved with the criminal justice system for reasons of aggression. *Journal of Applied Research and Intellectual Disabilities*, **14**, 340–7.

Beail, N. & Warden, S. (1995). Sexual abuse of adults with learning disabilities. *Journal of Intellectual Disability Research*, **39**, 382–7.

Bender, M., Aitman, J., Biggs, F. & Haug, U. (1983). Initial findings concerning a sexual knowledge questionnaire. *Mental Handicap*, **11**, 168–9.

Blanchard, R., Watson, M., Choy, A., Dickey, R., Klassen, P., Kuban, N. & Feren, D.J. (1999). Paedophiles: mental retardation, maternal age and sexual orientation. *Archives of Sexual Behaviour*, **28**, 111–27.

Briggs, F. & Hawkins, R.M.F. (1996). A comparison of the childhood experiences of convicted male child molesters and men who were sexually abused in childhood and claimed to be non-offenders. *Child Abuse and Neglect*, **20**, 221–33.

Bumby, K.M. (1996). Assessing the cognitive distortions of child molesters and rapists: development and validation of the MOLEST AND RAPE scales. *Sexual Abuse: A Journal of Research and Treatment*, **8**, 37–54.

Caparulo, F. (1991). Identifying the developmentally disabled sex offender. *Sexuality and Disability*, **9**, 311–22.

Carson, D.R., Whitefield, E. & Lindsay, W.R. (2002). The uses and abuses of assessments of cognitions and attitudes. *Book of Abstracts, British Psychological Society Annual Conference 2002*, p. 10.

Charman, T. & Clare, I. (1992). Education about the laws and social rules relating to sexual behaviour. *Mental Handicap*, **20**, 74–80.

Clare, I.C.H. (1993). Issues in the assessment and treatment of male sex offenders with mild learning disabilities. *Sexual and Marital Therapy*, **8**, 167–80.

Clarke, D.J. (1989). Anti-libidinal drugs and mental retardation: a review. *Medicine, Science, and the Law*, **29**, 136–48.

Cooper, A.J. (1995). Review of the role of two antilibidinal drugs in the treatment of sex offenders with mental retardation. *Mental Retardation*, **33**, 42–8.

Dagnan, D. & Sandhu, S. (1999). Social comparison, self-esteem and depression in people with learning disabilities. *Journal of Intellectual Disability Research*, **43**, 372–9.

Day, K. (1988). A hospital-based treatment programme for male mentally handicapped offenders. *British Journal of Psychiatry*, **153**, 635–44.

Day, K. (1993). Crime and mental retardation: a review. In K. Howells & C.R. Hollin (eds) *Clinical Approaches to the Mentally Disordered Offender*. Chichester: John Wiley & Sons.

Day, K. (1994). Male mentally handicapped sex offenders. *British Journal of Psychiatry*, **165**, 630–9.

General Accounting Office (1996). *Cycle of Sexual Abuse: Research Inconclusive about whether Child Victims become Adult Abusers.* Report to the Chairman, Subcommittee on Crime, Committee on the Judiciary, House of Representatives. Washington DC: United States General Accounting Office.

Gibbens, T.C. & Robertson, G. (1983). A survey of the criminal careers of restriction order patients. *British Journal of Psychiatry*, **143**, 370–5.

Glaser, W. & Deane, K. (1999). Normalisation in an abnormal world: a study of prisoners with intellectual disability. *Journal of Offender Therapy and Comparative Criminology*, **43**, 338–50.

Griffiths, D.M., Quinsey, V.L. & Hingsburger, D. (1989). *Changing Inappropriate Sexual Behavior: A Community-Based Approach for Persons with Developmental Disabilities*. Baltimore, MD: Paul Brookes.

Gross, G. (1985). *Activities of a Development Disabilities Adult Offender Project*. Olympia, WA: Washington State Developmental Disabilities Planning Council.

Grubb-Blubaugh, V., Shire, B.J. & Balser, M.L. (1994). Behaviour management and offenders with mental retardation: the jury system. *Mental Retardation*, **32**, 213–17.

Haaven, J., Little, R. & Petre-Miller, D. (1990). *Treating Intellectually Disabled Sex Offenders: A Model Residential Programme*. Orwell, VT: Safer Society Press.

Hayes, S. (1991). Sex offenders. *Australia and New Zealand Journal of Developmental Disabilities (Journal of Intellectual and Developmental Disabilities)*, **17**, 220–7.

Helsel, W.J. & Matson, J.L. (1989). The relationship of depression to social skills and intellectual functioning in mentally retarded adults. *Journal of Mental Deficiency Research*, **32**, 411–18.

Hingsburger, D., Griffiths, D. & Quinsey, V. (1991). Detecting counterfeit deviance: differentiating sexual deviance from sexual inappropriateness. *Habilitation Mental Health Care Newsletter*, **10**, 51–4.

Hodgins, S. (1992). Mental disorder, intellectual deficiency and crime: evidence from a birth cohort. *Archives of General Psychiatry*, **49**, 476–83.

Kazdin, A.E., Matson, J.L. & Senatore, V. (1983). Assessment of depression in mentally retarded adults. *American Journal of Psychiatry*, **140**, 1040–3.

Kempton, W. (1988). *Life Horizons I and Life Horizons II*. Santa Monica, CA: James Stanfield & Company.

Klimecki, M.R. Jenkinson, J. & Wilson, L. (1994). A study of recidivism among offenders with intellectual disability. *Australia and New Zealand Journal of Developmental Disabilities (Journal of Intellectual and Developmental Disabilities)*, **19**, 209–19.

Kolton, D.J., Boer, A. & Boer, D.P. (2001). A revision of the Abel and Becker Cognitions Scale for intellectually disabled sex offenders. *Sexual Abuse: A Journal of Research and Treatment*, **13**, 217–19.

Langevin, R. & Pope, S. (1993). Working with learning disabled sex offenders. *Annals of Sex Research*, **6**, 149–60.

Lindsay, W.R., Bellshaw, E., Culross, G., Staines, C. & Michie, A.M. (1992). Increases in knowledge following a course of sex education for people with learning difficulties. *Journal of Intellectual Disability Research*, **36**, 531–9.

Lindsay, W.R., Carson, D. & Whitefield, E. (2000). Development of a questionnaire on attitudes consistent with sex offending for men with intellectual disabilities. *Journal of Intellectual Disability Research*, **44**, 368.

Lindsay, W.R., Law, J., Quinn, K., Smart, N. & Smith, A.H.W. (2001). A comparison of physical and sexual abuse histories: sexual and non-sexual offenders with intellectual disability. *Child Abuse and Neglect*, **25**, 989–95.

Lindsay, W.R., Marshall, I., Neilson, C.Q., Quinn, K. & Smith, A.H.W. (1998a). The treatment of men with a learning disability convicted of exhibitionism. *Research on Developmental Disabilities*, **19**, 295–316.

Lindsay, W.R., Michie, A.M., Baty, F.J., Smith, A.H.W. & Miller, S. (1994). The consistency of reports about feelings and emotions from people with intellectual disability. *Journal of Intellectual Disability Research*, **38**, 61–6.

Lindsay, W.R., Neilson, C.Q., Morrison, F. & Smith, A.H.W. (1998b). The treatment of six men with a learning disability convicted of sex offences with children. *British Journal of Clinical Psychology*, **37**, 83–98.

Lindsay, W.R., Olley, S., Baillie, N. & Smith, A.H.W. (1999). The treatment of adolescent sex offenders with intellectual disability. *Mental Retardation*, **37**, 320–33.

Lindsay, W.R., Olley, S., Jack, C., Morrison, F. & Smith, A.H.W. (1998c). The treatment of two stalkers with intellectual disabilities using a cognitive approach. *Journal of Applied Research in Intellectual Disabilities*, **11**, 333–44.

Lindsay, W.R. & Smith, A.H.W. (1998). Responses to treatment for sex offenders with intellectual disability: a comparison of men with one and two year probation sentences. *Journal of Intellectual Disability Research*, **42**, 346–53.

Lindsay, W.R., Smith, A.H.W., Law, J., Quinn, K., Anderson, A., Smith, A., Overend, T. & Allan, R. (2002). A treatment service for sex offenders and abusers with intellectual disability: characteristics of referrals and evaluation. *Journal of Applied Research in Intellectual Disabilities*, **15**, 116–74.

Luiselli, J.K. (2000). Presentation of paraphilias and paraphilia related disorders in young adults with mental retardation: two case profiles. *Mental Health Aspects of Developmental Disabilities*, **3**, 42–6.

Lund, J. (1990). Mentally retarded criminal offenders in Denmark. *British Journal of Psychiatry*, **156**, 726–31.

McKerracher, D.W., Street, D.R.K. & Segal, L.J. (1976). A comparison of the behaviour problems presented by male and female subnormal offenders. *British Journal of Psychiatry*, **112**, 891–7.

Marquis, J.N. (1970). Orgasmic reconditioning: changing sexual object choice through controlling masturbation fantasies. *Journal of Behaviour Therapy and Experimental Psychiatry*, **1**, 263–71.

Marshall, W.L. (1969). Cessation therapy: a procedure for reducing deviant sexual arousal. *Journal of Applied Behavioural Analysis*, **2**, 377–89.

Marshall, W.L., Anderson, D. & Fernandez, Y. (1999). *Cognitive Behavioural Treatment of Sex Offenders*. Chichester: John Wiley & Sons.

Marshall, W.L. & Barbaree, H.E. (1990). An integrated theory of sexual offending. In W.L. Marshall, D.R. Laws & H.E. Barbaree (eds) *Handbook of Sexual Assault: Issues, Theories and Treatment of the Offender* (pp. 257–75). New York: Plenum Press.

Marshall, W.L., Laws, D.R. & Barbaree, H.E. (eds) (1990). *Handbook of Sexual Assault: Issues, Theories and Treatment of the Offender*. New York: Plenum Press.

Murphy, G. & Clare, I. (1991). MIETS: a service option for people with mild mental handicaps and challenging behaviour or psychiatric problems. *Mental Handicap Research*, **4**, 180–206.

Murphy, G. Holland, A.J., Fowler, P. & Reep, J. (1991). MIETS: a service option for people with mild mental handicaps and challenging or psychiatric problems. 1 philosophy, service and service users. *Mental Handicap Research (Journal of Applied Research and Intellectual Disabilities)*, **4**, 41–66.

Myers, B.A. (1991). Treatment of sexual offences by persons with developmental disabilities. *American Journal on Mental Retardation*, **95**, 563–9.

Noble, J.H. & Conley, R.W. (1992). Toward an epidemiology of relevant attributes. In R.W. Conley, R. Luckasson & G. Bouthilet (eds) *The Criminal Justice System and Mental Retardation*. Baltimore, MD: Paul Brookes.

Nussbaum, D., Collins, M., Culter, J., Zimmerman, W., Farguson, B. & Jacques, I. (2002). Crime type and specific personality indicia: Cloninger's TCI impulsivity, empathy and attachment subscales in non-violent, violent and sexual offenders. *American Journal of Forensic Psychology*, **20**, 23–56.

O'Conner, W. (1996). A problem solving intervention for sex offenders with intellectual disability. *Journal of Intellectual and Developmental Disability*, **21**, 219–35.

Parry, C. & Lindsay, W.R. (2003). Impulsiveness as a factor in sexual offending by people with mild intellectual disability. *Journal of Intellectual Disability Research*, **47**, 483–7.

Pfaefflin, F. (2002). *What to do with sexual offenders*. Paper presented at Sexual Violence and Sexual Abuse: From Understanding to Protection and Prevention, 7th conference of the International Association for the Treatment of Sexual Offenders.

Plaud, J.J., Plaud, D.M., Colstoe, P.D. & Orvedal, L. (2000). Behavioural treatment of sexually offending behaviour. *Mental Health Aspects of Developmental Disabilities*, **3**, 54–61.

Rose, J., Jenkins, R., O'Connor, C., Jones, C. & Felce, D. (2002). A group treatment for men with intellectual disabilities who sexually offend or abuse. *Journal of Applied Research in Intellectual Disabilities*, **15**, 138–50.

Scorzelli, J.F. & Reinke-Scorzelli, M. (1979). Mentally retarded offender: a follow-up study. *Rehabilitation Counselling Bulletin*, September, 70–3.

Seghorn, T.K. & Ball, C.J. (2000). Assessment of sexual deviance in adults with developmental disabilities. *Mental Health Aspects of Developmental Disabilities*, **3**, 47–53.

Sequeira, H. & Hollins, S.A. (2003). Clinical effects of sexual abuse on people with learning disability. *British Journal of Psychiatry*, **182**, 13–19.

Sherak, D.L. (2000). Pharmacological treatment of sexually offending behaviour in people with mental retardation. *Mental Health Aspects of Developmental Disabilities*, **3**, 62–74.

Sundram, C. (1989). *Developmentally Disabled Offenders in New York State Prisons: An Interim Report*. Albany, NY: New York State Commission on Quality of Care for the Mentally Disabled.

Swanson, C.K. & Garwick, G.B. (1990). Treatment for low functioning sex offenders: group therapy and interagency co-ordination. *Mental Retardation*, **28**, 155–61.

Thompson, D. & Brown, H. (1997). Men with intellectual disabilities who sexually abuse: a review of the literature. *Journal of Applied Research in Intellectual Disabilities*, **10**, 140–58.

Vanhouche, W. & Vertommen, H. (1999). Assessing cognitive distortions in sex offenders: a review of commonly used versus recently developed instruments. *Psychologica Belgica*, **39**, 163–87.

Walker, N. & McCabe, S. (1973). *Crime and Insanity in England*. Edinburgh: Edinburgh University Press.

Ward, T., Hudson, S.M., Johnston, L. & Marshall, W.L. (1997). Cognitive distortions in sex offenders: an integrative review. *Clinical Psychology Review*, **17**, 479–507.

Ward, T., Keenan, T. & Hudson, S.M. (2000). Understanding cognitive, affective and intimacy deficits in sexual offenders: a developmental perspective. *Aggression and Violent Behaviour*, **5**, 41–62.

Wish, J.R., McCombs, K.F. & Edmonson, B. (1980). *The Socio-Sexual Knowledge and Attitude Test*. Wood Dale, IL: Stoelting.

Xenitidis, K.I., Henry, J., Russell, A.J., Ward, A. & Murphy, D.G. (1999). An in-patient treatment model for adults with mild intellectual disability and challenging behaviour. *Journal of Intellectual Disability Research*, **43**, 128–34.

Chapter 10

TREATMENT OF SEXUALLY AGGRESSIVE BEHAVIOURS IN COMMUNITY AND SECURE SETTINGS

Michael C. Clark,* Jay Rider,* Frank Caparulo[†] and Mark Steege[‡]

* Kern Regional Center, Bakersfield, California, USA
† Caparulo Associates, Connecticut, USA
‡ Steege and Associates, San Antonio, Texas, USA

The majority of sexual offenders with developmental disabilities live in community settings. Some may be unknown to the legal system, or law enforcement may determine not to prosecute because of developmental disability or the apparently minor nature of the offence. Some offenders may be unadjudicated, released from prison, or placed in community settings under various forms of legal supervision such as probation. Others may be referred by their family members or may be self-referred. This chapter describes programmes for sexual offenders with developmental disabilities living in community settings, open residential settings and secure settings in different areas of the United States of America.

GENERAL CONSIDERATIONS

Any consideration of the treatment of sexual offenders with developmental disabilities must begin with the recognition of their right to be sexual and be taught appropriate methods of attaining sexual satisfaction.

Before consideration of treatment techniques and management arrangements, it is essential to understand the importance of individual differences between offenders in order to select different forms of intervention since each type of offender presents a different dynamic. For example, some offenders have poor knowledge of sexual matters or standards of behaviour in public versus private settings. Some adults with developmental disabilities have sometimes been allowed behaviours in their home which, if practised outside the home, would result in problems with the law. Other offenders are socially and sexually curious. This is normal and

Offenders with Developmental Disabilities. Edited by W.L. Lindsay, J.L. Taylor and P. Sturmey.
© 2004 John Wiley & Sons, Ltd.

acceptable for 6–10-year-old children. However it is understood as offending by the general public when the same behaviour is practised by adults with developmental disabilities. Some offenders appear to be starved of intimacy and touch. No one is exempt from the need for touch, and so many adults with developmental disabilities are touch starved. Some repeat offenders were sexually molested by a trusted adult and then told the behaviour was normal. With limited reasoning ability, the client may repeat the offence. Finally, some offenders are predatory and have sexually deviant tendencies.

It is essential to begin with the concept that those who have offended are not always terrible people who behave in despicable ways. Rather they are unique and valuable human beings who have behaved in unacceptable ways. Treatment for the offender with developmental disability may take place either in groups or individually. Some may benefit a great deal from group treatment whereas others may benefit more from individual therapy.

There are also general goals and techniques that apply to all the groups. With each behaviour that is extinguished, a positive behaviour should be offered and taught. By focusing on the positive behaviours which they engage in and giving them added attention for those behaviours, they will be encouraged to be positive.

Treatment will be best done if we first decide which of the types of offender listed above best fits the individual with whom we are dealing. With the uninformed offender, sometimes all that is needed is effective sex education. Treatment for the curious offender must involve good and complete sex education. Treatment for the offender seeking intimacy must involve social skills training as well as the necessary steps towards developing friends. Treatment for the replicating offender must involve more empathy training even though they may not understand the concept. They can still be taught what it feels like to be hurt and can be helped to understand the emotional effects of sexual abuse. It is less likely that predatory offenders can be treated in the community. A locked ward facility where escort is available whenever the individual goes into the community may be more appropriate.

A REGIONAL FORENSIC SERVICE FOR SEX OFFENDERS WITH DEVELOPMENTAL DISABILITIES: A CALIFORNIAN EXPERIENCE (MICHAEL CLARK AND JAY RIDER)

Community services for persons with developmental disabilities in California are organised into a network of 21 Regional Centres. These Regional Centres were created by the landmark entitlement legislation called the Lanterman Developmental Disabilities Services Act (1991). The number of people with developmental disabilities who become involved with the criminal justice system is a serious and growing problem in California.

The Kern Regional Center (KRC) is a private, non-profit corporation which contracts from the California Department of Developmental Services (DDS). KRC provides forensic services to people with developmental disabilities in part of California. It uses an interdisciplinary approach in case management as the vehicle to ensure that appropriate advocacy and treatment occur. Services are based in both community and state developmental centres. These forensic services serve people with developmental disabilities who are charged with, or who have engaged in, criminal behaviour. KRC provides diagnostic evaluations, client programme management and lifelong planning services for persons with developmental disabilities and their families. KRC serves approximately 4,400 clients living in Kern, Inyo and Mono counties and is governed by a 16-member Board of Directors. The Board includes people with developmental disabilities, parents of individuals with developmental disabilities, professionals and community representatives.

Forensic Clients

The California Penal Code defines a person classified as forensic as one who:

> a) has engaged in a criminal offence with harm or loss to others or significant potential of same. This includes offences such as, but not limited to: murder, prostitution, theft, grand theft auto, assault on a Peace Officer, assault with a deadly weapon, rape, child molestation, drug trafficking, substance abuse, property destruction, indecent exposure, arson; or b) commits an offence described above while a resident in the Developmental Centre; or c) engages in pre-meditated aggressive acts which result in serious injuries and/or have life threatening potential (including suicide attempts); or d) has been court committed via California Penal Code (PC) Section 1370.1 for competency training; or e) is a California Youth Authority Ward who is a Regional Center consumer and who would more appropriately be served in a Developmental Center; or f) has been court committed as a term of probation or diversion from jail.

In order for services to be rendered by the Regional Center, a person must be diagnosed and eligible as defined in the above definition. It must be noted that while "forensic" clearly relates to the above six points there is by no means uniformity and consensus on what is and is not forensic around our state and system.

Community Resources for Forensic Clients

Specialised staff

The services needed by forensic clients may be extensive. Clearly specialised staff are required in order to provide adequate case management to those clients. We have a mandate to provide adequate case management and to this end, employ a Court Liaison who provides case management and coordinates all services directed at ameliorating the offence or behaviour which causes the client's arrest. The Court Liaison must have an extensive knowledge of all services provided by the Regional Center, courts and generic services, those available to all members of the community, and have a high tolerance for difficult clients.

Staff training is essential to a well coordinated and integrated case management plan that can address forensic issues. Ultimately, good services can only be obtained if the Regional Center recognises the problem in a timely fashion and devises an adequate comprehensive structure which addresses the problems of forensic clients. Although specialised staff and training are important, Regional Centers must also have services to be purchased available for forensic clients. All services are purchased by the Regional Center unless available as a generic service. Services will be described later.

Court liaison activities

The Court Liaison has the responsibility for providing case management services and advocacy within the judicial system for forensic clients. The Court Liaison writes reports, attends court on behalf of clients, provides programming and attends forensic team meetings, and provides other case management services as needed. The Court Liaison caseload ($n = 62$) is comprised of clients who have committed drug and alcohol offences ($n = 35$), robbery ($n = 15$), misdemeanour of sexual offences ($n = 3$) and a variety of other petty crimes. The caseload changes from day to day. Those clients who have completed their obligations to the court are returned to a regular case management status.

All court cases are reviewed by a multi-disciplinary forensic team. In this way difficult clinical issues such as advocacy and treatment, consequences for criminal conduct, the need for community safety as well as programming may be considered. The ongoing service coordinator may be responsible for providing forensic information at the forensic team meeting. The service coordinator contacts the Court Liaison directly when a client is arrested, has a court date, or in other legal circumstance which may require the Court Liaison's intervention. Upon receipt of information that a client has an upcoming court date or has been arrested, the Court Liaison will investigate the arrest or the upcoming legal circumstances prior to a forensic team meeting. The ongoing service coordinator, the Court Liaison, the director of clinical services and other staff as appropriate normally attend a forensic team meeting.

The Court Liaison reviews the legal status and court status of the client by contacting the appropriate court or jail. They request criminal record information, if needed. A meeting with the client and service coordinator to discuss the client's understanding of their legal circumstances currently outstanding is held. The Court Liaison also coordinates a forensic team meeting by inviting appropriate staff. The review will consider past arrest records, behaviours, substance usage, needed living arrangements, employment needs, willingness to cooperate and so on. The Court Liaison makes recommendations to the court by writing necessary reports, coordinates any psychological evaluation pertaining to the client's legal standing or requests by the court, attends court with the client and shares the forensic team recommendations with the court. Once courts have defined the client's legal status, the ongoing service coordinator will transfer the case to the Court Liaison for ongoing case management.

Residential services

A wide variety of residential services are available to forensic clients with developmental disabilities. They may vary depending on the assessments completed by the Regional Center and other pertinent data. Clients who require care and supervision may be placed in a community care facility which has been designated as having an appropriate programme design, staff experience and a desire to assist the offender. KRC uses facilities with designations of levels II, III or IV. Levels designate staffing ratios, behavioural programmes and security arrangements. Typically, level IV facilities provide the highest level of care, supervision and programming for clients. Not all forensic clients require residential placements. Individual living alternatives may be appropriate with good case management. Support living and family home agencies have offered another opportunity for some clients. With the potential of future institutional closures, we need to explore the development of secured residential options in the community.

Mental health services

Mental Health Services are necessary for forensic clients with dual diagnosis. Medication utilisation and monitoring is essential and we refer to the local mental health agency, access some psychiatric services via tele medicine and develop an individual programme plan for clients with a history of drug and alcohol abuse. We have developed a vendored programme which provides counselling and education based on the 12-step programme of Alcoholics Anonymous. Urine testing is also done to ensure that clients are not using drugs and alcohol. If clients continue to use drugs and alcohol they are returned to court to determine further disposition or services which are appropriate.

Day programmes

All forensic clients have access to day programmes. These programmes may include behavioural components, supported employment, work activity programmes and activity centres. An important but often overlooked consideration is that clients require transportation to day programmes and other activities. Bus passes and vendor transportation providers are used to enable clients to attend all necessary activities. Clients are also offered the opportunity to participate in social recreation programmes as part of their daily activities.

Client behaviours which are serious and prevent socialisation and day programme activities may be assessed by a behavioural intervention specialist, who may offer methods to extinguish or modify problematic behaviours. To provide health and dental care, clients are supported to access community hospitals and medical service providers.

California Laws Pertaining to People with Developmental Disabilities

Clients who commit crimes and have a developmental disability may or may not be competent to stand trial. The court may wish to evaluate a client to determine competency under California Penal Code Section 1370.1. Upon notification, the Court Liaison may coordinate evaluations with psychologists, who will determine if the client is competent. If found competent, the client may be returned to the court for further disposition. If the client is incompetent to stand trial, he/she may be placed on out-patient status if recommended by the forensic team. If they have committed a specific violent crime (California Penal Code 1600) or sexual offence (California Penal Code 2900) identified in the Penal Code, and are found incompetent, the client may be ordered by the court to a State Developmental Center for care and treatment. In any case, the forensic team shall make specific recommendations to the court through the Court Liaison. In some cases, these recommendations may be different to that of the psychologist who is doing the client evaluation. Clients who receive competency training at the State Developmental Center and return to a state of competency may face further court action.

Civil commitments

California Welfare and Institutions Code Section 6500 defines how Regional Centers may deal with clients who are a danger to self and others. The Regional Center prepares the request for commitment, along with supportive declarations and information, and submits this to the District Attorney's Office who will present it to court. Typically, a psychological evaluation by two psychologists will be done by reviewing the submitted documentation and complete psychological evaluation to determine if the client is a danger to self or others. The Court Liaison will attend any required court hearings. The forensic team findings may be shared with the identified psychologist prior to any evaluation. However, the court will determine the appropriate treatment and recommendations after considering all information.

Disposition

Diversion

Diversion relates to people with developmental disabilities who are charged with a misdemeanour. However, diversion may apply to some felony crimes which can be downgraded to misdemeanours. Diversion allows the Regional Center the opportunity to develop a plan for the client which addresses the offence for which the client was arrested. The Court Liaison, through the forensic team process, will document treatment needs and the recommendations for the length of diversion (6 months to 2 years) to the courts. The Court Liaison will provide case management services through the length of diversion including monitoring of the client's progress through the plan.

State prison

Regional Centers are not currently providing services to residents of the state prison system. However the Regional Center is expected to resume services when a client moves from prison back to the community.

Developmental Centers

Regional Centers and Developmental Centers work together to provide forensic services. The Department of Developmental Services (DDS) currently services about 3,940 individuals with developmental disabilities in its five Developmental Centers. At the present time, 355 of these persons with developmental disabilities (or 9% of the population) are considered to have forensic or severe behaviour issues.

Individual programme plans

A comprehensive assessment of the client's abilities, strengths and needs will lead to a programme to help them identify and acknowledge the reasons for their admission, accept responsibility for their actions and learn replacement behaviours that are more acceptable for meeting societal rules and laws. Services provide the opportunity for each individual to learn new skills and abilities, thereby increasing his or her repertoire of behaviours that will be more acceptable in community settings. The programme supports the empowerment of individuals through self-advocacy and the concept of self-direction, believing that individuals learn by having the opportunity to make good choices that will assist them in avoiding future offending. The challenge is to balance these freedoms and choices with the responsibility to address community safety and protection from harm for all individuals.

Treatment Modalities

We include the use of specific behaviour modification techniques, psychotropic medication, self-care training, education services, vocational training, socialisation training and competency training. Core courses that are provided include anger management and impulse control. In this intervention individuals learn to understand their feelings and learn techniques for managing anger and expressing emotions constructively. In victim awareness clients learn to identify victims and perpetrators, the feelings each is likely to have and an understanding of the rights of the victims. In social sexual development, clients learn appropriate social skills and acceptable behaviour in sexual relationships, including issues such as safe sex, consent, intimacy, risks and responsibility. In assertiveness training, they learn to express themselves positively and to understand the difference between assertive, aggressive and passive communication styles. Training in competency to stand trial is offered to clients who have been found incompetent by a court. They are taught to prepare for a return to court to dispose of the criminal charges against them. Substance abuse and substance abuse relapse is used to give an overview of commonly abused substances and gain an understanding of the dangers and long-term effects of their use. Finally, critical thinking/problem solving is used to teach effective ways of resolving problems.

In addition, based on security/escort considerations, more traditional activities are offered such as recreational opportunities, trips to the community, classes which build skills of daily living (social skills, home economic skills, independent living skills and communication skills). School services are provided for adolescents and other clients under the age of 22. Adult education is provided for those over 22 years of age. Sheltered workshop arrangements and work training services are provided for adults. Recreation and leisure activities are also available. In general, those are provided within the Developmental Center. To meet spiritual needs, weekly religious services are offered.

Clients are returned to the community once their commitment expires and the client is no longer thought to be dangerous by the courts, or through the filing of a writ of habeas corpus. Once released, the Developmental Center Liaison assists the client in finding appropriate services and coordinates those services while the client adjusts to the community living situation.

HIGH SECURITY SETTINGS FOR OFFENDERS WITH DEVELOPMENTAL DISABILITIES: A COMPOSITE EXAMPLE (FRANK CAPARULO)

This is an overview of several facilities that provide services to those individuals who present with criminal behaviour of a sexual nature. These services serve both adjudicated and non-adjudicated sexual abusers. While some correctional centres isolate this population for incarceration purposes and may even offer treatment, these sites are limited and provide less than adequate services due to many factors. The USA has several secure sites specifically designed to house offenders with intellectual disabilities, including mental retardation/developmental disabilities. What follows is an amalgam of the most exemplary features of several programmes currently in operation in the USA with suggestions by the author. This composite programme will be referred to as the secure treatment centre (STC).

This facility operates as an Intensive Care Facility/Mental Retardation (ICF/MR) site and is certified by the Health Care Financing Administration (HCFA) under the United States Department of Health and Human Services (HHS). As an ICF/MR facility there is the mandate to follow all the HHS guidelines that govern the lives of persons with developmental disabilities, in contrast to the rules and regulations that govern mental health centres and correctional institutions. In our estimation the level of oversight mandated by HHS ensures the highest quality of care along with respecting the rights of consumers. Therefore, in our opinion, secure sites that are most effective are those run by State Departments of Developmental Disabilities. The rights of persons with developmental disabilities in a facility for that population are totally different from those afforded prisoners in the correctional systems (Federal and State). Inspections of ICF/MR facilities occur once a year and are done by outside professionals. The principal focus of these inspections is the facilities' adherence to and implementation of ICF/MR requirements (Department of Health and Human Services, 1995). Inspectors assess a range of facilities, from the delivery of treatment services through staffing to the physical environment.

Site Description

The STC would have 100 beds, in 10 residencies housing 10 residents each. The STC serves individuals (men and women) with the highest levels of risk, i.e. the most violent and recidivistic; those individuals determined to be in need of the most comprehensive, intensive treatment and with the need for the highest level of security. The individuals in these facilities have not admitted themselves voluntarily, but have been mandated to these sites by the state's risk/forensic committee. They usually present with a high level of cognitive distortions, including denial, minimisation of the crime, and rationalisation of the crime up to and including blaming the victims. Treatment regime is one where the individual is immersed in group treatment. We recommend five days per week with as many as four groups per day. There is a vocational component and as persons move up on the security level system, they have the potential of earning minimum wage and learning a skill that can be transferred if they can be moved out into society. The individual in the highest level (lowest level of risk) can earn the privilege of residing in the house with more freedom of choice, more access to recreational areas etc.

Prior to admission, a departmental clinical psychologist, a court forensic examiner or a consulting certified forensic examiner with a background in developmental disabilities has evaluated the client. That report is forwarded to the state's risk/forensic committee and placement at one of the residential sites and the continuum of care including the STC is recommended. The stay at the latter site will average approximately 18 months.

In addition to the STC, this hypothetical state also has County Comprehensive Treatment Units (CCTU) that serve individuals who have been designated as high risk and in need of a secure facility, but not at the level that would warrant placement at the STC. Some individuals who have been at the STC may step down to this level of security. At these sites treatment is still intensive and offence specific. Other individuals (not transferred from an STC and placed directly into a CCTU) may have been engaged in treatment elsewhere, have exhibited some awareness of their offence and accepted some responsibility for their offence. Treatment is recommended five days per week, including offender-specific therapy. Focus is less acute than the STC and includes day-to-day issues (social readjustment), relapse prevention, changing negative behaviours to positive as well as vocational training. There are community outings, family involvement and preparation for an offence-free life outside of the secure site.

A step down in security from the CCTU are several less restrictive Area Intensive Treatment Units (AITU), which service individuals with a designation of moderate level of risk.

The Secure Treatment Centre (High Security)

There are 10 living units. In addition, there are several outdoor recreational areas that include a baseball field and basketball court. All lockable doors operate on a key card system. As the resident moves up the STC level system, he/she is given more accessibility to different areas of the campus and within the building. The levels progress from zero (most restrictive) to IV (community access and supervised outings).

Court Procedures and the Secure Treatment Centre

A typical scenario is as follows. An alleged offender is referred to the state risk/forensic committee. The committee calls for a comprehensive forensic evaluation that includes evaluation of both static and dynamic risk factors. Through this evaluation and one that determines department eligibility, the person may be deemed suitable for treatment in one of the residential sites operated by the agency in that state responsible for the care and treatment of persons with mental retardation. Bear in mind that the person who has been evaluated has committed a violent criminal act, and this has been adjudicated or not (due to lack of competency) by the criminal justice system, and may or may not be incarcerated. The Departments of Mental Retardation are faced with two questions. How can they provide for the safety of the community and the offender who has developmental disability? Will the criminal justice system release and allow these individuals to receive treatment if the safety of the community cannot be assured? In those states that have made provisions for this population, the response can be yes—community safety can be ensured by placing the offender in a secure and highly supervised setting.

We can no longer assume that the criminal justice system will always see the diagnosis of mental retardation as a sign of low or no culpability in any given case. For this reason, the criminal justice system must have the assurance that these alternatives to incarceration sites are secure. In addition, advocates for people with developmental disabilities must be convinced that there is strict adherence to the standards and policies that provide for the most humane treatment. It should be kept in mind, however, that the criminal justice system always has jurisdiction when a community's safety versus individual rights conflict arises. For example, in a recent situation, a resident (who was on probation) of a large institution was being moved from one side of the campus to another. The reason for this move was that his victim, another resident, was moving into the same area of the campus and under the terms of his probation the perpetrator could not live in the same area as the victim. Because the advocates for the perpetrator believed that his rights were being violated, they assisted him in filing a request not to be moved. The State Office of Probation responded by saying that if the individual were not moved within three hours, he would be in violation of his probation and would be remanded in jail. The advocates immediately appealed to the legal department of the agency and were told that the State Office of Probation had the right to do this.

Staff Training

STC provides staff with comprehensive training, qualified internal personnel and sometimes outside consultants. A description of the elements of training is given below:

- characteristics of the offender who has developmental disability;
- problems with the criminal justice system for offenders who have developmental disability;
- providing clinical information to the criminal justice system;
- developing a comprehensive approach to address the problems of offenders with developmental disability;

- basic principles of cognitive behaviour therapy for the treatment of maladaptive behaviour;
- introduction to the STC level system;
- overview of safety/security, clinical and treatment issues;
- individual counselling strategies;
- managing group interaction;
- the role of family/correspondent communication;
- introduction to the risk management system;
- stress management for high secure unit personnel;
- the duties and privileges of citizenship;
- basic principles of recreation;
- mentorship programme (identify the skills, knowledge, abilities and attitudes of the consumers to succeed in a job; identify the characteristics of good mentoring);
- decision-making techniques on a secure unit;
- substance abuse treatment;
- community skills;
- health skills for well-being;
- human sexuality;
- basic principles of security and supervision (entrance and egress, contra-band/searches, perimeter checks, safety security and supervision, religious and cultural subgroups and gangs, transport and furloughs, restraint and escape deterrent devices, staff responsibilities, sharp counts, missing persons).

The STC Level System

The level system includes five levels from most to least restrictive. Level 0 is the most restrictive with level IV the least restrictive, involving supervised community access. The level system also provides response costs for major, moderate and minor maladaptive behaviours. There is adequate opportunity for self-correction and response for "off bounds" infractions. All consumers can apply to the Level System Appeal Board if they feel they have been unjustly dealt with. Level IV consumers can work in supported employment for a minimum wage and receive mentoring.

Active Treatment

Both the State Department of Mental Retardation and Federal Inspectors mandate active treatment. Some consumers participate in four groups daily, including a sex offender specialised group treatment. This group addresses relapse prevention (Steen, 1999), victim empathy, values and choices in decision making, sex education, social skills, assertiveness and anger management, Alcoholics Anonymous and drug abuse education, impulse control, the level system, and dealing with the perpetrator's own victimisation. Groups for recreational skills address leisure time activities and skills, alternatives to offending, exploration of individual skills and capacities, and good sportsmanship.

Individualised counselling is also used. Much of the preparation for group work is done in individual counselling, e.g. terminology (rules, personal rules and societal laws), high-risk situations, cognitive distortions or denials (thoughts used to mitigate offences such as "she was asking for it"), and personal interventions designed to break the offence chain. Individual therapy may address such disorders as paraphilia, erotomania and other deviant sexual disorders.

CASE STUDY

James was a 35-year-old with mild ID who offended against both genders and is non-exclusive for age. He committed his index crime when he was 17 years old when he sexually assaulted a 14-year-old girl in his neighbourhood. This crime never came to light until the end of treatment seven years later after being arrested for sexual assault on a female peer. He then was placed on "line of sight" supervision and received minimal treatment of one hour per week. Over a period of 25 years he has committed 9 sex crimes, has had 10 victims and has been arrested four times.

In 1987, James was placed in a secure site for offenders and released one year later. He was released because a new commissioner disagreed with the high-security concept. The subject did well for several years until in 1993 he sexually assaulted a female peer, was arrested and placed on probation for 25 years. He was remanded back to the Department of Mental Retardation for placement and treatment. With the old commissioner gone and the return of the STC, the subject was admitted. The subject went in under a new director and a new curriculum that included comprehensive relapse prevention, victim empathy, values and choices in decision making, sexual education, social skills, assertiveness and anger management. James stayed at the STC for 24 months, moved through the level system and was placed at the next level of the continuum of care. Eventually he moved to a four-man ICF group home and was placed on one-to-one supervision. He received treatment all through this continuum. As of this writing he is living in the community in a specialised group home and has been incident-free for seven years, but still has 18 years of probation left to serve.

Focus of the Intervention for James

- Appropriate social interactions and on- and off-ground activities to substitute for illegal/inappropriate sexual contact.
- Appropriate requests used as a functional equivalent behaviour to replace arguing, manipulative behaviour and verbal abuse in the context of gaining access to items/activities.
- Appropriate acceptance of consequences to compete with arguing, manipulative behaviour, and verbal abuse in the context of escaping/avoiding consequences.

A response cost programme remained in place with restrictions to on- and off-ground activities, media, personal possessions, door alarms and restitution.

Target Behaviours to Decrease

- Illegal and/or inappropriate sexual behaviour—seduces or coerces underage or less able peers for sexual contact.
- Verbal abuse—will yell at, curse or make derogatory statements about others.
- Arguing—becomes agitated, defensive, is verbally oppositional or disputes others.
- Manipulative behaviour—attempts to exploit interpersonal contacts via lies, non-disclosure of relevant information, or setting up their environment for devious intent.

Target Behaviours to Increase

- Appropriate requests—asks politely for an item/activity/event without displaying verbal abuse, arguing or manipulative behaviour.
- Appropriate acceptance of consequences—accepts the consequences of his behaviour or the denial of a request/item activity without displaying verbal abuse, arguing or manipulative behaviour.
- Socially appropriate behaviour during on- and off-ground activities—attends activities and maintains an appropriate social distance of at least one foot from others and does not display any of the target behaviours to decrease.

Proactive Routines and Intervention

James needs one-to-one supervision at all times. His bedroom door will have an alarm that has a unique chime but should not be used as a primary means of supervision. On community access visits James requires one-to-one supervision. Staff need to accompany him to the bathroom. If James requests items or activities appropriately, thank him for asking politely and provide him with the requested item or activity if possible. If he makes the requests using verbal abuse, give him one prompt to ask for the item appropriately. If he responds thank him for asking politely and provide him with the item.

If James accepts the consequences of his behaviour or denial of the request, thank him for accepting the consequences so well. If he becomes verbally abusive, give him one prompt to act appropriately. Wherever James acts appropriately during an activity and keeps an appropriate personal distance from others, give him extra attention and activities. If he displays verbal abuse give him one prompt as above. If James continues to be verbally abusive he will be placed on immediate restriction for 14 days. If James is found having inappropriate sexual contact he is to be immediately placed on level I restriction.

Criteria for Movement to a Less-Restrictive Programme

James must have a recommendation from his individual therapist and sex offender coordinator. He must successfully complete all aspects of the sex offender treatment programme. He must demonstrate an ability to avoid triggers for abusive verbal situations or inappropriate sexuality, or to set up such situations. He must be able to show resolution for his abuse and victimisation. He should demonstrate appropriate social behaviour in planned *in vivo* experiences. He must demonstrate at least one year without any sexually related target behaviour, including setting up such situations. There must be a unanimous decision by the core treatment team that such action is appropriate.

CONCLUSIONS

This chapter has described a wide variety of treatment settings and the social and legal conditions under which such treatments are set up. Perhaps the most notable aspect is the way in which the different services described have responded to different local arrangements, legal context and client characteristics. On the one hand, the California example describes services for offenders delivered within the general context of services for people with developmental disabilities. On the other hand, the secure treatment centre describes a service delivered within a specific criminal justice context. The earlier part of the chapter describes a number of possible aetiologies for the development of sexually offending behaviour in particular clients. This allows the reader to consider their clients in a number of developmental contexts and also gives reference to a range of possible outcomes. There is little doubt that there can be no single solution for sex offenders with intellectual disability. The reasons why such problems might arise are multi-dimensional and require a range of treatment and management solutions. Furthermore, these problems and solutions must be considered by each of us within our own legislative context. The purpose of this chapter has been to draw attention to all of these issues through practical illustration.

ACKNOWLEDGMENT

Frank Caparulo was assisted by Dr Jill Niesen.

REFERENCES

Department of Developmental Disability Services (1991). *The Lanterman Developmental Disability Service Act.* Sacramento, CA: State Government of California.
Department of Health and Human Services (1995). *Summary of Procedures and Interpretative Guidelines: State Operations Manual.* Provider Classification, Department of Health and Human Services, Healthcare Functioning Administration, PO Box 26684, Baltimore, Maryland.
Steen, C. (1999). *The Relapse Prevention Workbook.* Brandon, VT: Safer Society Press.

Chapter 11

TREATMENT OF ANGER AND AGGRESSION

JOHN L. TAYLOR,* RAYMOND W. NOVACO,† BRUCE T. GILLMER,‡
AND ALISON ROBERTSON‡

* University of Northumbria, Newcastle upon Tyne and Northgate & Prudhoe NHS Trust,
  Northumberland, UK
† University of California, Irvine, California, USA
‡ Northgate and Prudhoe NHS Trust, Northumberland & University of Newcastle,
  Newcastle upon Tyne, UK

INTRODUCTION

There are a number of important epidemiological and clinical service reasons for giving attention to anger and aggression among offenders with developmental disabilities. Aggression is frequently activated by internal distress and can be expressive of thwarted needs. For persons with deficits in emotional expression, aggressive behaviour may be a default response in anger provoking situations. People with developmental disabilities have difficulty not only in expressing emotions, but also in recognising and encoding them (McAlpine, Kendall & Singh, 1991). When strong negative emotions such as anger are involved, it can be anticipated that such deficits are likely to lead to the exacerbation of conditions of distress and the production of a vicious cycle of antagonistic behaviour (Holt, 1994).

Taylor (2002) reviewed studies of the prevalence of aggression in populations of people with developmental disabilities conducted across three continents. They indicate prevalence rates for aggression of between 11% and 27% (Hill & Bruininks, 1984; Harris, 1993; Sigafoos, Elkins, Kerr & Attwood, 1994; Smith, Branford, Collacott, Cooper & McGrother, 1996). In those studies where they were compared, rates for aggression were consistently higher in institutional than in community settings—38% versus 11% in Harris' (1993) survey, for example. These studies empirically establish aggressive behaviour as a widely occurring problem, especially in institutional care facilities.

Aggressive behaviour, as noted by Lakin, Hill, Hauber, Bruininks and Heal (1983), is perhaps the most frequent reason for people with developmental disability being admitted or re-admitted to hospital. Aman, Richmond, Stewart, Bell

Offenders with Developmental Disabilities. Edited by W.L. Lindsay, J.L. Taylor and P. Sturmey.
© 2004 John Wiley & Sons, Ltd.

and Kissell (1987) found that aggression was the main reason for this client group to be prescribed antipsychotic and behaviour control drugs. As well as these very serious consequences for individuals with developmental disability, aggression carries high costs for staff and services working with them. Kiely and Pankhurst (1998), in their study of aggression experienced by staff working in a learning disability service of an NHS Trust in the UK, found that there were almost five times more incidents of patient violence than was recorded in the Trust's sister psychiatric service. Following such incidents, staff reported feeling more cautious and wary of the perpetrator, and less confident in their own abilities. Other studies have found that as a consequence of service-user aggression, staff feel annoyed, angry and fearful (Bromley & Emerson, 1995), and there are high rates of staff turnover and "burnout" (Attwood & Joachim, 1994).

The activation of aggression occurs both with and without anger. The arousal of anger is not sufficient for aggression, nor is anger a necessary precursor. Nevertheless, anger is strongly associated with aggression, particularly under conditions of high arousal intensity, which can serve to override inhibitory controls (Novaco, 1994). Anger has been shown to be predictive of aggression in psychiatric and forensic populations (Novaco, 1994; Novaco & Renwick, submitted). Recently, Novaco and Taylor (in press) showed that patient anger, as measured on a number of self- and staff-rated measures, was strongly associated with assaultiveness in hospital and violent offence histories for an in-patient population of male offenders with developmental disabilities.

In addition to being an important determinant of aggressive behaviour, anger is a common feature of personal distress and has been robustly linked to a variety of physical health problems, especially cardiovascular disorders (Chesney & Rosenman, 1985; Diamond, 1982; Dembroski, MacDougall, Williams, Haney & Blumenthal, 1985; Siegman & Smith, 1994). Novaco (1986) described the associations between anger and a range of mental health disturbances that can feature aggression as part of their clinical profiles. They include personality disorders, conduct disorder in children and adolescents, organic mental disorders, affective disorders, post-traumatic stress disorder, dissociative disorders such as amnesia and fugue, and explosive disorder. Although anger can be an adaptive human emotion that facilitates functioning in a number of spheres, it is also associated with many clinical disorders and dysfunctional syndromes in ways that are not helpful to affected individuals, those around them, or society at large, and this dysfunction would seem to begin at an early age. Gilliom, Shaw, Beck, Schonberg and Lukon (2002) found that deficits in anger regulation as toddlers were predictive of externalising behaviour problems among boys at pre-school age. In young offender populations, anger self-reported by incarcerated adolescents has been found to be significantly related to subsequent physical and verbal aggression (Cornell, Peterson & Richards, 1999) and to indicators of poorer general health (Swaffer & Hollin, 2001). There is no reason to suppose that people with developmental disabilities are not similarly affected by these psychological, physical and developmental correlates of chronic anger problems.

A further reason for addressing anger and aggression issues in this population is its salience for clients. Our clinical experience indicates that patients are often more willing to discuss temper control problems early in their rehabilitation, compared with, for example, sexual aggression. Therefore, by beginning with problems that have relevance for patients, therapeutic relationships can be built and developed that can form a bridge to, and facilitate, offence-related work in more threatening areas at a later stage of rehabilitation. In this chapter, we present essential features of our approach to the treatment of anger and aggression as applied to institutionalised forensic patients with developmental disabilities.

ASSESSMENT AND TREATMENT OF ANGER AND AGGRESSION

Despite the consequences that anger and aggression problems have for people with developmental disabilities directly, and for others around them, including direct care staff and systems concerned with their care and rehabilitation, there is little in the literature concerning the development of reliable and valid measures of these phenomena in this population (Novaco & Taylor, in press; Taylor, 2002). Studies by Benson and Ivins (1992) and Rose and West (1999) have indicated that modified self-assessment measures of *anger reactivity* can have some reliability and validity with people with developmental disability.

Novaco and Taylor (in press) sought to evaluate the reliability and validity of anger assessment procedures with 129 male in-patients with developmental disabilities, most of whom had forensic histories. The prevalence of anger among this patient group and its interrelationship with a range of demographic, cognitive and personality variables was examined, as well as the degree to which anger was retrospectively predictive of assaultive behaviour in the hospital. This study demonstrated that anger has validity and can be reliably assessed among clients with developmental disabilities and offending backgrounds, and a coherent pattern of findings supported anger construct validity. Almost half of the patients (46.5%) had been assaultive on at least one occasion following admission to specialist secure and semi-secure services marked by high levels of supervision, provided by staff with expertise in the care and management of very disturbed patients. High degrees of internal reliability and inter-measure consistency were obtained for self-rated measures of *anger traits*, *disposition* and *reactivity*, as well as some concurrent validity with staff ratings of anger.

In reviewing the literature on the treatment of anger and aggression in people with developmental disabilities, Taylor (2002) found that there were three distinct, if overlapping, areas. These were concerned with (a) psychopharmacological treatments, (b) behavioural treatments and (c) cognitive-behavioural therapies (CBT). Despite the apparently ubiquitous use of medication to reduce aggression in people with developmental disabilities, recent reviews by Baumeister, Sevin and King (1998), Brylewski and Duggan (1999) and Matson *et al.* (2000) indicate that there is no conclusive evidence to support the use of psychoactive medications as first-line treatments. Given their lack of specificity and variable effects, including significant dampening of adaptive behaviour, routine use of these compounds to treat aggression is not justified.

The greatest literature concerning treatment of aggression in people with developmental disability relates to behavioural interventions. Reviews by Lennox,

Miltenberger, Spengler and Efranian (1988), Scotti, Evans, Meyer and Walker (1991), Whitaker (1993) and Carr *et al.* (2000) included studies of the effectiveness of behavioural methods for aggression problems. The information presented in the reviews by Lennox *et al.* and Scotti *et al.* suggests that, to some extent, less intrusive and more constructive approaches can be more effective than more intrusive and restrictive techniques. The studies included in Whitaker's (1993) review suggest that contingency management techniques, which make up the bulk of the studies available, have been efficacious mainly with more disabled client groups. He concludes that these approaches have been shown to be effective for clients with relatively high-frequency aggression in highly controlled environments with high staff ratios. Such conditions contrast with those in services for offenders with developmental disabilities who are relatively high functioning and display low-frequency, yet very serious, aggression and violence.

A further potential limitation of behavioural approaches to the treatment of aggression is that they tend not to be presented as "self-actualising" in nature. That is, often they do not actively target self-regulation in behaviour control. In contrast, promoting internalised control over behaviour to facilitate transfer is intrinsic to the skills teaching in CBT approaches being used with clients with developmental disabilities (e.g. Williams & Jones, 1997). There is also some evidence available from studies in non-developmental-disability fields to show that the effects of CBT for a range of clinical conditions do maintain and increase over time compared to control conditions (e.g. Barrowclough *et al.*, 2001; Kuipers *et al.*, 1997; Oosterban, van Balkom, Spinhoven, van Oppen & van Dyck, 2001).

Perhaps for these reasons, there has been rising interest in CBT approaches to the aggression and anger problems of people with developmental disabilities. Reviews by Tafrate (1995), Edmondson and Conger (1996) and Beck and Fernandez (1998), although limited by their over-valuing college student studies and ignoring case studies, have concluded that the CBT treatment of anger is effective for adolescent and adult clinical and forensic groups, and for non-clinical samples. Both Whitaker (2001) and Taylor (2002) reviewed studies of cognitively based anger treatments specifically for people with developmental disabilities. Numerous authors, for example Murphy and Clare (1991), Black and Novaco (1993), Lindsay, Overend, Allan, Williams and Black (1998), Rose and West (1999) and Howells, Rogers and Wilcock (2000), have reported case and case-series studies involving people with histories of aggressive behaviour in hospital and community settings. Individual treatment and group therapy formats have yielded reductions in aggression levels. In addition, group studies by Moore, Adams, Elsworth and Lewis (1997) and King, Lancaster, Wynne, Nettleton and Davis (1999) using CBT anger treatments demonstrated clinically significant post-treatment gains for developmentally disabled clients living in the community.

Studies including treatment comparison groups of group-implemented anger treatment for community-based clients were conducted by Benson, Johnson Rice and Miranti (1986) and Rose, West and Clifford (2000). In the Benson *et al.* study, significant post-treatment changes were obtained across four treatment conditions (self-instruction, relaxation training, problem-solving and a combined condition), but there were no significant differences between conditions following treatment. Rose *et al.* (2000), using a waiting-list control design, found that a CBT approach resulted in significant reductions in self-reported anger for the treatment group compared with the control group. Both studies, however, used measures with limited psychometric evaluation, and the Rose *et al.* study was compromised by some of the waiting-list control group being included in the treatment group.

DEVELOPMENT OF A NEW ANGER TREATMENT PROTOCOL

None of the above CBT anger studies involving people with developmental disabilities included participants classified as forensic cases or convicted offenders, although some of the cases described were at risk of becoming convicted offenders given the severity of their aggressive and violent behaviour. Allan, Lindsay, MacLeod and Smith (2001) reported on a group cognitive-behavioural anger management intervention for a case series of five women with ID who had been involved with the criminal justice system because of violent assaults. Lindsay, Allan, MacLeod, Smart and Smith (2003) described a similar approach for six men with ID and convictions for assault. In both studies improvements were recorded for all participants at the end of treatment and these were maintained at 15 months follow-up. Until very recently, these were the only reports in the literature concerning anger treatments specifically for offenders with developmental disabilities.

Almost all of the existing anger treatment studies in the developmental disability field involve interventions broadly based on Novaco's (1975, 1993) anger treatment. This approach incorporates the stress inoculation paradigm (Meichenbaum, 1985) and has cognitive restructuring, arousal reduction and behavioural skills training as its core components. Novaco, Ramm and Black (2000) pointed out that *anger treatment* is targeted at modification of cognitive structures that maintain anger, enhancement of self-monitoring, and development of self-control strategies through therapeutically guided graded exposure to provocation. It is based on a detailed analysis and formulation of a client's anger problems and requires delivery by trained therapists on an individual basis. This level of intervention is differentiated from *anger management* approaches, which are less intensive, not driven by analysis and formulation, and generally involve psycho-educational approaches guided by cognitive-behavioural principles delivered in a group therapy format.

Anger treatment is recommended for people with chronic, deep-rooted anger problems that impair their interpersonal functioning and psychological well-being. The intensive individualised approach is intended to overcome clients' anxieties about change and resistance to engagement in the therapeutic process. Offenders with developmental disabilities can often exhibit such characteristics, and for these reasons a new treatment protocol designed specifically for use with this client group was developed (Taylor & Novaco, 1999).

Anger Treatment Protocol Development and Delivery

This new treatment protocol is based on the cognitive-behavioural approach developed by Novaco (1975, 1993). Treatment is delivered to individual patients by the same therapist over 18 sessions, this number of sessions approximating the average amount of therapy delivered to participants in published anger treatment studies involving people with developmental disabilities which had been successful with a small number of patients in a case-series pilot.

Whenever possible, treatment is delivered at the rate of two sessions each week, with a minimum of one session per week. Previous experience of using psy-chotherapeutic approaches with this patient group suggested that a more intensive treatment schedule would reduce clients' resistance to change by maintaining mo-mentum and preventing therapy drift. Also, a higher therapeutic dosage can offset some of the cognitive limitations of this client group which can result in problems with assimilation and recall of information from session to session.

Although treatment sessions routinely involve only the therapist and patient, the patient's keyworker nurse or a deputy is involved whenever possible at the end of each session to discuss the patient's progress and any "homework" to be completed between sessions. For example, from the second session onwards, patients are encouraged to complete daily anger logs to record the nature, fre-quency and intensity of any angry incidents. Anger logs are completed, when-ever possible, with assistance and support from the patient's keyworker nurse in order to promote a collaborative approach to treatment through open discus-sion, shared problem-solving and mutual reflection concerning anger-provoking incidents.

Content of Anger Treatment Protocol

Many offenders with developmental disabilities have personal histories that create barriers to their engagement in trusting therapeutic relationships. Physical, emo-tional and sexual abuse, as well as repeated failures in human service settings and perceived rejection by important others, are common experiences. Thus, a psycho-educational "preparatory phase" of anger treatment is provided in this new protocol. The need for such an introductory phase, to develop the skills and confidence required to successfully engage in and benefit from anger treatment, and to judge whether the individual can cope with the treatment, was discussed by Black, Cullen and Novaco (1997). A similar preparatory phase of treatment was implemented successfully by Renwick, Black, Ramm and Novaco (1997) in the treatment of chronic anger problems in four mentally disordered offenders in a high-security hospital setting in Scotland.

Preparatory phase

In this new treatment manual the preparatory phase comprises six sessions aimed at desensitising patients to any fears that they might have about embarking on intensive psychological therapy. The goals of this phase of treatment are: (a) to give the patient information on the nature and purpose of anger treatment; (b) to encour-age motivation to change current unhelpful anger coping responses by identifying the costs of this behaviour; (c) to develop some basic skills needed for success-ful treatment including self-disclosure, emotional awareness, self-monitoring and recording, and basic relaxation techniques; (d) to foster trust and confidence in the therapist and the therapeutic process; and (e) to emphasise the collaborative nature of the treatment that is aimed primarily at helping the patient achieve better self-control.

This preparatory phase has the added benefit of improving patients' understanding of the treatment process so that they are in a better position to give informed consent before moving on to the next phase of treatment.

Treatment phase

On successful completion of the preparatory phase, and if they wish to do so, patients proceed to the 12-session "treatment phase". The core components of this phase, which map onto the key domains of the cognitive model of anger proposed by Novaco (1994), are cognitive restructuring, arousal reduction and behavioural skills training. The approaches used in this phase of treatment include: (a) advanced self-monitoring and recording of anger frequency, intensity and triggers; (b) a detailed analysis and formulation of the individual's anger problems; (c) construction of a personal anger provocation hierarchy; (d) cognitive restructuring by shifting attentional focus, modifying appraisals and challenging expectations; (e) developing arousal reduction techniques; (f) training problem-solving using role-play rehearsal; (g) development of personalised self-instructions to prompt coping; and (h) use of the stress inoculation approach to practise effective coping while visualising anger-provoking scenes from the anger hierarchies.

The primary clinical focus of each of the 18 sessions of anger treatment making up this protocol is described in Table 11.1. The key components of the treatment (cognitive restructuring, arousal reduction and behavioural skills training) build during therapy in a logical step-wise manner through the classical cognitive preparation, skills acquisition and skills rehearsal/practice stages. In this way, towards the end of the 18 treatment sessions they are incorporated into practice *in vitro*, and if possible *in vivo*, as a sequential but integrated and comprehensive approach to coping effectively with anger problems.

Accommodating Individual Differences

There is variation in the focus, pace and emphasis of the therapy delivered by different therapists working with different patients depending on the analysis and formulation of their anger problems. The treatment is, by nature, collaborative and interactive. It is, therefore, applied in a manner that reflects these dynamics. Thus, while it is a manualised treatment, it is intended to provide a framework within which the therapists and patients can flexibly apply the therapeutic techniques described to meet the needs of individual patients. In this sense we make a clear distinction between *protocol-guided* and *protocol-driven* treatments. The latter tend to be applied rigidly, are not reflexive to needs of clients and tend not to lead to good outcomes when administered by experienced therapists.

Table 11.1   Primary focus of preparatory and treatment phase sessions of anger treatment

Preparatory phase	Session focus	Treatment phase	Session focus
Session 1	Explaining the purpose of anger treatment	Session 7	Introduction to the treatment phase sessions
Session 2	Feeling angry is OK—anger as a normal emotion	Session 8	Building an anger hierarchy
Session 3	Understanding our own and other peoples' feelings	Session 9	Introduction to stress inoculation
Session 4	How to control the physical feelings of anger— physiological arousal	Session 10	Beginning cognitive restructuring
Session 5	Reasons for changing the way we cope with angry feelings	Session 11	Developing cognitive restructuring
Session 6	Review of the preparatory phase and preview of treatment phase	Session 12	Perspective-taking and role-playing
		Session 13	Using self-instructions effectively
		Session 14	Problem-solving through effective communication
		Session 15	Development of problem-solving through effective communication
		Session 16	Dealing with rumination and escalation
		Session 17	Integration of skills and dealing with repeated provocation
		Session 18	Review and evaluation of anger treatment phase

Note: All sessions are guided by a detailed manual, delivered by qualified therapists to individual patients. Each session is of approximately 1-hour duration. Feedback is provided routinely to direct care staff at the end of the each session concerning the patient's presentation and progress within the session, and any homework that is to be completed between sessions.

Evaluation of the Anger Treatment Protocol

In a pilot study conducted by Taylor, Novaco, Gillmer and Thorne (2002) to evaluate the effectiveness of the newly designed anger treatment, 9 in-patient male offenders with developmental disabilities were allocated to an anger treatment (AT) condition and 10 matched cases were allocated to a routine care waiting-list control (RC) condition. All of the patients involved in this study were detained under sections of the Mental Health Act 1983, they were relatively young (mean age 29.2 years), and they were functioning towards the top of the mild mental retardation range of intelligence (mean full scale IQ assessed using the WAIS-R UK = 67.9, s.d = 5.2). Of the 19 study participants, 7 had convictions for violence. Following admission to hospital from the courts, 10 had been physically violent, 8 of the 10 on more than one occasion.

The main outcome measure in this study was a modification of the Provocation Inventory (PI). The PI (Novaco, 1988) is an anger reaction inventory made up of 25 items providing an index of anger intensity and generality across a range of

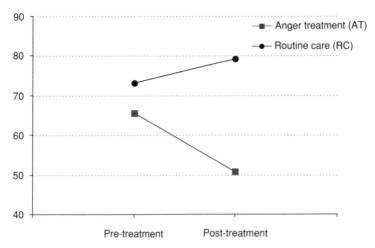

Figure 11.1 Mean Provocation Inventory (PI) scores over time.
Source: Taylor *et al.* (2002)

potentially provocative situations. Novaco and Taylor (in press) established the reliability and validity of this modified scale for this patient population. AT group patients' self-report of anger, as measured by the PI, was significantly lower following treatment with the new protocol compared to the RC group patients (Figure 11.1). Obviously there are problems (such as assessment reactivity) with relying solely on self-report measures to evaluate the effectiveness of the treatment. Therefore, direct care ward staff rated treatment participants' anger attributes and social behaviour relevant to anger coping skills, and following treatment changes in the anticipated direction were obtained. While these changes were convergent with patients' self-reporting of anger, they were not statistically significant.

PATIENT ENGAGEMENT, MOTIVATION AND SATISFACTION

Based on the results of the pilot study we concluded that people with developmental disabilities and histories of offending could benefit from a specially modified cognitive-behavioural anger treatment. However, prior to the development of this new approach, we were concerned about the ability of the treatment to engage and motivate clients sufficiently for them to benefit in a meaningful way from it. Numerous writers have commented on the special challenges, for both therapists and patients, that therapeutic interventions for anger problems present (Novaco & Welsh, 1989; DiGiuseppe, Tafrate & Eckhardt, 1994; Novaco, 1995). These difficulties are often related to the inherent threat such clients present, their impatience and impulsiveness, and the positive functions and reinforcement that their anger often holds, which causes it to be deeply embedded and difficult for them to release.

These and other issues can create significant difficulties in establishing therapeutic alliances, helping clients to see anger as a legitimate treatment target and motivating clients to contemplate change with respect to their anger-related

Table 11.2   Patients' ratings concerning their experience of the preparatory and treatment phases of anger treatment

		Numbers of patients responding (%)	
Question/response		Post-preparatory phase	Post-treatment phase
1.	Q. Overall, was it worthwhile for you to attend the [anger treatment] sessions?		
	R. Yes, most of the sessions	16 (89)	14 (78)
2.	Q. Have you enjoyed the sessions?		
	R. Yes, most of the sessions	17 (94)	15 (83)
3.	Q. Have the sessions been helpful to you?		
	R. Yes, in lots of ways	14 (78)	15 (83)
4.	Q. Do you think you have changed since you started your anger treatment?		
	R. Yes, a lot, for the better	4 (22)	12 (67)
5.	Q. Are you a more or less angry person now than before you started your anger treatment?	Not asked	
	R. Less angry	–	15 (83)

Note: Questions were put to 18 treatment completers at the end of the preparatory and treatment phases as part of the Patients' Evaluation of Anger Treatment—Preparatory Phase (PEAT-PP) and Patients' Evaluation of Anger Treatment—Treatment Phase (PEAT-TP) questionnaires. Each question had a 3-point Likert response scale.

difficulties. In addition to these characteristics, many of the participants in the current study have life histories characterised by trauma and repeated experiences of failure and rejection across a range of health and social care settings. Add to this list impaired intellectual functioning and associated limited psychological/emotional resources, and the scale of the task involved in successfully engaging these patients, in anger treatment becomes apparent. Despite these very substantial difficulties and challenges, the therapy is acceptable to patients, who have expressed high levels of satisfaction with it and found it to be helpful. The responses of the first two cohorts of patients to complete the programme to a number of questions put to them at the end of the two phases of treatment concerning their experiences of the therapy are presented in Table 11.2.

The broadly psycho-educational six-session preparatory phase of treatment highlights the normality of anger, but gently introduces the personal costs associated with recurrent maladaptive anger reactions. This appears to be successful in helping psychologically fragile participants form therapeutic relationships and become motivated to maintain them. This stage of treatment enables participants to gradually engage in the therapy process without feeling threatened. Even those patients who are initially most wary or suspicious generally choose to continue beyond the preparatory phase, despite being given an opportunity to opt out.

This treatment takes place within an institutional context that gives little consideration to the individual's past or their long-term future and emphasises the present (Heyman, Buswell Griffiths & Taylor, 2002). Similarly, our clients generally focus on the "here-and-now", avoid reflection of their emotionally painful and shame-inducing pasts, and have significant problems with planning for the future. Despite these difficulties, they are able to benefit from an intensive therapy that integrates past negative experiences into the here-and-now in order to be better prepared for future challenges. In spite of its more emotionally demanding qualities, the 12-session anger treatment phase does not induce any marked degree of anxiety or distress in participants. Very little additional work is required from therapists in supplementary sessions outside of the protocol. Therapists occasionally report in peer supervision sessions that particular patients appear to be engaging in treatment at a superficial level—the concern being that they are "playing along". However, almost without exception, for those patients who complete treatment, therapists report that at some point during the therapeutic process they begin to respond in a meaningful and beneficial way to the content and/or process. Patients' feedback through the questionnaires completed at the end of treatment provides evidence to support these clinical observations. That is, while the percentage of patients reporting enjoyment reduced slightly from post-preparatory to post-treatment (94% to 83%), the percentage of those indicating that the sessions had been helpful remained much the same (78% to 83%), and it increased markedly (from 22% to 67%) for patients' own estimates of positive personal change following the treatment phase (Table 11.2). This is not to say that it is always the case that individuals engage in treatment effortlessly and quickly become motivated to change their maladaptive anger coping responses. The case of Bill demonstrates some of the difficulties in working with this client group.

Case Study 1 (Bill)

Bill was a 43-year-old man with an index offence of causing serious damage to hospital property and having a knife in his possession. He had four previous convictions for offences involving violence. He had a history of alcohol and substance abuse that was presumed to trigger his aggressive outbursts. Originally it had been anticipated that a short hospital admission would address these dependency problems and that he would be discharged quickly. However, and perhaps unsurprisingly, his stay in hospital without alcohol and drugs did not reduce the anger he experienced, or the periods of depression he was found to suffer from—although he displayed little overt aggression. He became particularly angry about his continued detention, but he also felt provoked by other forms of frustration, and by people whom he perceived as being annoying.

Bill started anger treatment and completed four preparatory phase sessions before refusing further sessions, despite the therapist rating him highly in terms of engagement and communication. After approximately four months Bill was offered the anger treatment again, this time with a therapist better known to him, and he agreed to resume treatment. During the "costs and benefits" exercise in session 5, and at the session 6 post-preparatory evaluation, Bill expressed serious doubts about the effectiveness of the treatment for him. To give him adequate time and space to consider whether or not he wanted to continue with treatment, Bill was asked to consider this matter with his keyworker nurse over the next week. At the end of this period he opted out of treatment again. Another five months on, Bill asked if he could try anger treatment again. This time he omitted the preparatory sessions and worked through the 12 treatment-phase sessions. It was estimated that it would be counterproductive to repeat the six preparatory phase sessions, which, at an intellectual level, he had comprehended quite well.

It was noted during treatment that Bill's verbal memory was relatively poor and his motivation to do homework was not high. Despite this he seemed to engage in the therapy and worked well during the treatment-phase sessions. He was able to comprehend the "How Anger Works" model to a limited extent. By session 10, which addresses appraisal and expectations of situations, Bill was able to reflect on how he had used his earlier withdrawals from treatment as a way of expressing his anger about other issues. On both occasions he had experienced an adverse event, unrelated to the treatment or to the patient–therapist relationship. This resulted in Bill directing his anger indirectly at a different part of the system he perceived as constraining him unjustly, but over which he felt he *did* have some control. His first withdrawal from anger treatment followed a formal Mental Health Tribunal, the decision of which (continued detention) had angered him. His second withdrawal followed his girlfriend leaving him for someone else. Shortly before these connections were drawn and discussed, he had threatened to withdraw from treatment for a third time. However, by this stage he was able to see that this action was unlikely to resolve the issue that concerned and angered him. It seemed that his expressions of anger, albeit misdirected, supplanted the feelings he had previously directed inwardly in the forms of self-harm or expressions of suicidal intent.

Towards the end of the anger treatment sessions, Bill was able to acknowledge that he had a vested interest in maintaining an aggressive persona as a response to threat. He was a very small man, appearing younger than his years. He had a long history of being teased and bullied. His aggressive style seemed to be a survival strategy that was exacerbated by the disinhibiting effects of alcohol. On completion of the treatment phase Bill demonstrated some intellectual grasp of the model and strategies, but he still seemed ambivalent about committing himself to change at cognitive-emotional and behavioural levels. Given the complexity of Bill's case and his presentation in the therapy context, the fact that he had been able to tolerate and complete the treatment, develop some new insights and skills and build a good working relationship with the therapist indicated significant success.

At the end of treatment a "Patient Competency Checklist" completed by the therapist and his keyworker nurse suggested that Bill was either "competent" or had "limited competence" in most of the areas covered in the treatment. In a questionnaire completed at the end of treatment Bill rated most elements of the therapy as "a little" or "very helpful". Also, he commented that he had learned "how to control myself more" and "to think about relaxation" in angry situations. He also said that the treatment had been "better than I thought it would be". Post-treatment psychometric assessments indicated that Bill's self-rated anger disposition and reactivity had reduced markedly. While Bill remains in hospital and continues to be frustrated about his lack of progress towards discharge, he appears to be coping quite well. He talks less frequently about absconding, self-harm and suicide. He has engaged in further individual therapy to develop self-esteem and he has completed a drug and alcohol education programme.

THE CENTRALITY OF COGNITIVE RESTRUCTURING

A distinctive characteristic of the anger treatment described above is the modification of perceptual schemas and entrenched beliefs that maintain anger problems. A basic premise of cognitive-behavioural therapeutic approaches is that psychological distress is derivative of distortions in processing information about oneself and environmental demands, and this assumptive framework has certainly been articulated with regard to anger (Beck, 1999; Novaco & Welsh, 1989). Quite intrinsic to problems of anger and aggression are attentional biases and cognitive processing distortions associated with threat perception, as well as memory biases for distressing experiences. Cognitive-behavioural therapy strives to shift attentional focus, modify appraisals of events, restructure belief systems and self-schemas, and develop effective emotion regulation and behavioural coping skills. It is predicated on the human tendency to behave as guided by symbols, to seek meaning, and to formulate strategies to optimise quality of life.

Disconnecting the anger from threat perception and instilling self-control is central to anger treatment. People having serious anger difficulties have lost the capacity to self-regulate and are quick to perceive malevolence. Elementary CBT language encourages the client to recognise that consequences are closely linked to thoughts and beliefs about activating events and not directly to the events themselves. In anger treatment, the process begins by creating space and safety and by normalising the client's experience of anger. Constant support and validation of personal worth encourages the moderation of anger intensity, from which self-monitoring can be shaped and self-control augmented.

Taylor *et al.*'s (2002) pilot study demonstrated that offenders with developmental disabilities could benefit from a modified CBT anger treatment with cognitive restructuring as one of its core components. The putative role of cognitions in the experience of anger is given attention right from the start as part of the presentation of a simplified model of "How Anger Works". Cognitive restructuring techniques are infused in this treatment approach and are given the same amount of attention as arousal reduction and behavioural skills training. Sessions 10 through 17 of the treatment protocol are concerned with cognitive restructuring.

This defining feature of CBT is the hardest part of the process to communicate to clients with developmental disabilities and can deter many therapists from using a CBT framework. However, there is now some limited evidence for the application of CBT to a broad range of clinical problems among people with developmental disabilities (cf. Stenfert Kroese, Dagnan & Loumidis, 1997). The therapeutic process of inducing cognitive change can be seen in the following case illustration.

Case Study 2 (Joe)

Joe was a 30-year-old man who was functioning towards the lower end of the mild mental retardation range of intelligence. He had been convicted of rape and wounding and was detained in hospital under the Mental Health Act nine years before he began anger treatment. Prior to his index offence, he had a history of delinquency and minor offending. Following admission to hospital Joe was recorded as having carried out five physical assaults on staff and other patients. He was noted by ward staff as being argumentative, antagonistic and hostile in his relations with other patients. His characteristic response to provocation was confrontation and aggression.

Despite this background, Joe responded well to the preparatory phase and consented to move on to treatment-phase sessions. In session 10, cognitive restructuring was introduced. The therapist and Joe had selected salient incidents from his "anger logs" in which he described his thoughts at the time of an anger incident. Together they explored what he selectively perceived in the situation that led him to feel angry ("perceived intentionality"). Specific situations recorded in anger logs provide material for cognitive restructuring exercises that encourage patients to think differently about anger situations, to work through what actually happened from the patient's perspective and then to explore possible alternative explanations and perspectives.

In session 11, Joe was encouraged to think about anger situations in terms of attentional focus, expectations and appraisals that can cue angry feelings. He was also introduced to "perspective-taking" as a means of identifying and modifying his judgements. After review of his most recent anger logs, Joe was encouraged to identify recurring themes or patterns and to notice his selective attention to particular aspects of others' behaviour that he judges to be deliberately provocative or threatening, as well as the associated "self-talk".

THERAPIST: OK Joe, let's have a look at your anger logs. I see that you were at the recreation club. So what happened on Thursday night?
JOE: She really upset me.
T: Who upset you?
J: Rosie my girlfriend [a fellow patient who resides in the hospital].
T: And when this happened what were you thinking?
J: Why are you late? You can go to hell!
T: How angry were you with Rosie?
J: Lots [points to 4 on 5-point scale].
T: And what did you do?
J: You know. Shouted. Swore. Ran off.
T: How well do you think you handled her being late?
J: Not so good (points to 2 on a 5-point scale). I felt bad afterwards.

To facilitate cognitive restructuring, the therapist explored with Joe how he might think differently about this situation and whether this can help him to modulate his emotional, physical and behavioural responses. Joe was prompted to consider shifting his attentional focus and altering his expectations by encouraging him to view the situation from his girlfriend's perspective, to put himself "in her shoes".

THERAPIST: OK Joe, here you are at the recreation club. Your girlfriend Rosie is late. What are you thinking?
JOE: Why are you late again? You can go to hell.
T: And you are feeling?
J: Very angry [points to 4 on 5-point scale].
T: Your body—how is it feeling?

J: Tight chest [shows clenched fists].

T: And remind me, what did you actually do?

J: Like I said, shouted and ran off.

T: OK. Let's try and think why Rosie might have been late, and how she was feeling about it.

J: Why was she late? Maybe she got kept on the ward? How *does* she feel?

T: And how are *you* feeling now, right now?

J: OK. Sad [looks down].

[This is a crucial disconnection of Joe's characteristic "signature-anger" from his threat perceptions.]

T: And your body, right now?

J: OK. Heavy.

T: Thinking about it now what could you have done?

J: I could put my arm around her. But I never done that. Never [cries].

T: Just stay with that feeling, Joe ... what are you thinking right now?

J: I've got to protect myself.

[An explicit acknowledgement that Joe's signature-anger is functionally in-grained. His habitual anger responses are intrinsically linked to deep-rooted threat schemas.]

Following practice of generating alternative cognitions, patients are given new anger logs that prompt them to "think differently" about angry situations as they occur between treatment sessions. This is intended to dislodge rigid beliefs concerning the hostile quality of others' actions and to create space for more empathic appraisals.

At the end of treatment, Joe's self-rated anger disposition, reactivity and control scores improved markedly, and direct care staff noted improvements in his demeanour in the ward environment. He was considered to be less easily provoked and less hostile. A short time after finishing this treatment, Joe moved to a less secure unit within the hospital where he settled well and has not displayed any serious management problems. Plans for his resettlement into a community placement are now well advanced.

CONCLUSIONS

Anger, which is closely associated with aggression, is a significant clinical issue requiring concerted attention in offenders with developmental disabilities. Although little work has been completed in this area, there are encouraging signs that anger can be assessed in a reliable and valid fashion with this population. Also, the limited literature on the effectiveness of CBT for anger problems in offenders with developmental disabilities has yielded positive results that need to be followed up and replicated in future studies. The sustainability of treatment gains over time and their generalisabilty across different environments require particular consideration.

The case of Bill described above illustrates that this treatment approach can be successful in engaging and motivating even those people with developmental disabilities who have very serious histories of offending and violence, chronic anger problems and are highly resistant to the notion of psychological therapy as a way of helping them to develop more adaptive coping responses.

The mechanisms that facilitate good treatment outcomes also require further investigation. It has been suggested that the components of CBT anger treatment that benefit people with developmental disabilities are the non-cognitive elements such as relaxation and behavioural skills training (Rose *et al.*, 2000; Whitaker, 2001). The implication is that the cognitive elements of anger treatment are too difficult for people with developmental disabilities due to their intellectual and cognitive impairments. This conclusion appears to be premature. First, none of the CBT for anger outcome studies, with the possible exceptions of Allan *et al.* (2001) and Lindsay *et al.* (2003), appears to have cognitive restructuring as a core component. They tend to focus on the amelioration of cognitive skills deficits as opposed to exploration of the content of cognitions that are associated with and maintain maladaptive anger responses. This is a common phenomenon in the wider CBT and developmental disability literature (Stenfert Kroese, 1998). Further, the evaluation of the treatment protocol described in this chapter demonstrates that offenders with developmental disabilities can benefit from treatment that has cognitive restructuring based on individual analysis and formulation as a central feature. While anger arousal reduction and behavioural skills training techniques are given equal weight, the case of Joe illustrates the value of closely integrating these with work on the content of cognitions, even with relatively less able patients for whom it might be anticipated this aspect of treatment would have little to offer.

REFERENCES

Allan, R., Lindsay, W.R., MacLeod, F. & Smith, A.H.W. (2001). Treatment of women with intellectual disabilities who have been involved with the criminal justice system for reasons of aggression. *Journal of Applied Research in Intellectual Disabilities*, **14**, 340–7.

Aman, M.G., Richmond, G., Stewart, A.W., Bell, J.C. & Kissell, R. (1987). The Aberrant Behavior Checklist: factor structure and the effect of subject variables in American and New Zealand facilities. *American Journal on Mental Deficiency*, **91**, 570–8.

Attwood, T. & Joachim, R. (1994). The prevention and management of seriously disruptive behavior in Australia. In N. Bouras (ed.) *Mental Health in Mental Retardation: Recent Advances and Practice* (pp. 365–74). Cambridge: Cambridge University Press.

Barrowclough, C., King, P., Colville, J., Russell, E., Burns, A. & Tarrier, N. (2001). A randomized trial of the effectiveness of cognitive-behavioral therapy and supportive counseling for anxiety symptoms in older adults. *Journal of Consulting and Clinical Psychology*, **69**, 756–62.

Baumeister, A.A., Sevin, J.A. & King, B.H. (1998). Neuroleptics. In Reiss, S. & Aman, M.G. (eds) *Psychotropic Medications and Developmental Disabilities: The International Consensus Handbook* (pp. 133–50). Columbus, OH: Ohio State University.

Beck, A.T. (1999). *Prisoners of Hate*. New York: HarperCollins.

Beck, R. & Fernandez, E. (1998). Cognitive-behavioral therapy in the treatment of anger: a meta-analysis. *Cognitive Therapy and Research*, **22**, 63–74.

Benson, B.A., & Ivins, J. (1992). Anger, depression and self-concept in adults with mental retardation. *Journal of Intellectual Disability Research*, **36**, 169–75.

Benson, B.A., Johnson Rice, C. & Miranti, S.V. (1986). Effects of anger management training with mentally retarded adults in group treatment. *Journal of Consulting and Clinical Psychology*, **54**, 728–9.

Black, L., Cullen, C. & Novaco, R.W. (1997). Anger assessment for people with mild learning disabilities in secure settings. In B. Stenfert Kroese, D. Dagnan, & K. Loumidis (eds) *Cognitive Behaviour-Therapy for People with Learning Disabilities* (pp. 33–52). London: Routledge.

Black, L. & Novaco, R.W. (1993). Treatment of anger with a developmentally disabled man. In R.A. Wells & V.J. Giannetti (eds) *Casebook of the Brief Psychotherapies* (pp. 143–58). New York: Plenum Press.

Bromley, J. & Emerson, E. (1995). Beliefs and emotional reactions of care staff working with people with challenging behavior. *Journal of Intellectual Disability Research*, **39**, 341–52.

Brylewski, J. & Duggan, L. (1999). Antipsychotic medication for challenging behaviour in people with learning disability. *Journal of Intellectual Disability Research*, **43**, 360–71.

Carr, J.E., Coriaty, S., Wilder, D.A., Gaunt, B.T., Dozier, C.L., Britton, L.N., Avina, C. & Reed, C.L. (2000). A review of "noncontingent" reinforcement as treatment for the aberrant behavior of individuals with developmental disabilities. *Research in Developmental Disabilities*, **21**, 377–91.

Chesney, M.A. & Rosenman, R.H. (eds) (1985). *Anger and Hostility in Cardiovascular and Behavioral Disorders*. Washington, DC: Hemisphere.

Cornell, D.G., Peterson, C.S. & Richards, H. (1999). Anger as a predictor of aggression among incarcerated adolescents. *Journal of Consulting and Clinical Psychology*, **67**, 108–15.

Dembroski, T.M., MacDougall, J.M., Williams, R.B., Jr. Haney, T.L. & Blumenthal, J.A. (1985). Components of Type A, hostility, and anger-in: relationship to angiographic findings. *Psychosomatic Medicine*, **47**, 219–33.

Diamond, E.L. (1982). The role of anger and hostility in essential hypertension and coronary heart disease. *Psychological Bulletin*, **92**, 410–33.

DiGiuseppe, R., Tafrate, R. & Eckhardt, C. (1994). Critical issues in the treatment of anger. *Cognitive and Behavioral Practice*, **1**, 111–32.

Edmondson, C.B. & Conger, J.C. (1996). A review of treatment efficacy for individuals with anger problems: conceptual, assessment and methodological issues. *Clinical Psychology Review*, **16**, 251–75.

Gilliom, M., Shaw, D.S., Beck, J.E., Schonberg, M.A. & Lukon, J.L. (2002). Anger regulation in disadvantaged preschool boys: strategies, antecedents, and the development of self-control. *Developmental Psychology*, **38**, 222–35.

Harris, P. (1993). The nature and extent of aggressive behaviour amongst people with learning difficulties (mental handicap) in a single health district. *Journal of Intellectual Disability Research*, **37**, 221–42.

Heyman, R., Buswell Griffiths, C. & Taylor, J. (2002). Health risk escalators and the rehabilitation of offenders with learning disabilities. *Social Science and Medicine*, **54**, 1429–40.

Hill, B.K. & Bruininks R.H. (1984). Maladaptive behavior of mentally retarded individuals in residential facilities. *American Journal of Mental Deficiency*, **88**, 380–7.

Holt, G. (1994). Challenging behaviour. In N. Bouras (ed.) *Mental Health in Mental Retardation: Recent Advances and Practices*. Cambridge: Cambridge University Press.

Howells, P.M., Rogers, C. & Wilcock, S. (2000). Evaluating a cognitive/behavioural approach to anger management skills to adults with learning disabilities. *British Journal of Learning Disabilities*, **28**, 137–42.

King, N., Lancaster, N., Wynne, G., Nettleton, N. & Davis, R. (1999). Cognitive-behavioural anger management training for adults with mild intellectual disability. *Scandinavian Journal of Behaviour Therapy*, **28**, 19–22.

Kiely, J. & Pankhurst, H. (1998). Violence faced by staff in a learning disability service. *Disability and Rehabilitation*, **20**, 81–9.

Kuipers, E., Garety, P., Fowler, D., Dunn, G., Bebbington, P., Freeman, D. & Hadley, C. (1997). London–East Anglia randomised controlled trial of cognitive-behavioural therapy for psychosis. *British Journal of Psychiatry*, **171**, 319–27.

Lakin, K.C., Hill, B.K., Hauber, F.A., Bruininks, R.H. & Heal, L.W. (1983). New admissions to a national sample of public residential facilities. *American Journal on Mental Retardation,* **88**, 13–20.

Lennox, D.B., Miltenberger, R.G., Spengler, P. & Efranian, N. (1988). Decelerative treatment practices with persons who have mental retardation: a review of five years of the literature. *American Journal on Mental Retardation,* **92**, 492–501.

Lindsay, W.R., Allan, R., MacLeod, F., Smart, N. & Smith, A.H.W. (2003). Long-term treatment and management of violent tendencies in men with intellectual disabilities convicted of assault. *Mental Retardation,* **41**, 47–56.

Lindsay, W.R., Overend, H., Allan, R., Williams, C. & Black, L. (1998). Using specific approaches for individual problems in the management of anger and aggression. *British Journal of Learning Disabilities,* **26**, 44–50.

Matson, J.L., Bamburg, J.W., Mayville, E.A., Pinkston, J., Bielecki, J., Kuhn, D., Smalls, Y. & Logan, J.R. (2000). Psychopharmacology and mental retardation: a 10 year review (1990–1999). *Research in Developmental Disabilities,* **21**, 263–96.

McAlpine, C., Kendall, K.A. & Singh, N.N. (1991). Recognition of facial expression of emotion by persons with mental retardation. *American Journal of Mental Retardation,* **96**, 29–36.

Meichenbaum, D. (1985). *Stress Inoculation Training.* Oxford: Pergamon Press.

Moore, E., Adams, R., Elsworth, J. & Lewis, J. (1997). An anger management group for people with a learning disability. *British Journal of Learning Disabilities,* **25**, 53–7.

Murphy, G. & Clare, I. (1991). MIETS: a service option for people with mild mental handicap and challenging behaviour or psychiatric problems. 2. Assessment, treatment, and outcome for service users and service effectiveness. *Mental Handicap Research,* **4**, 180–206.

Novaco, R.W. (1975). *Anger Control: The Development and Evaluation of an Experimental Treatment.* Lexington, MA: Heath.

Novaco, R.W. (1986). Anger as a clinical and social problem. In R. Blanchard and C. Blanchard (eds) *Advances in the Study of Aggression,* vol. 2 (pp. 1–67). New York: Academic Press.

Novaco, R.W. (1988). Novaco Provocation Inventory. In M. Hersen & A.S. Bellack (eds) *Dictionary of Behavioral Assessment Techniques* (pp. 315–17). New York: Pergamon.

Novaco, R.W. (1993). Stress inoculation therapy for anger control: a manual for therapists. Unpublished manuscript, University of California, Irvine.

Novaco, R.W. (1994). Anger as a risk factor for violence among the mentally disordered. In J. Monahan & H.J. Steadman (eds) *Violence and Mental Disorder: Developments in Risk Assessment* (pp. 21–59). Chicago, IL: University of Chicago Press.

Novaco, R.W. (1995). Clinical problems of anger and its assessment and regulation through a stress coping skills approach. In W. O'Donohue & L. Krasner (eds) *Handbook of Psychological Skills Training: Training and Applications* (pp. 320–38). Boston, MA: Allyn & Bacon.

Novaco, R.W., Ramm., M. & Black, L. (2000). Anger treatment with offenders. In C.R. Hollin (ed.) *Handbook of Offender Assessment and Treatment* (pp. 281–96). Chichester: John Wiley & Sons.

Novaco, R.W. & Renwick, S.J. (submitted). Anger predictors and the validation of a ward behavior scale for anger and aggression.

Novaco, R.W. & Taylor, J.L. (in press). Assessment of anger and aggression in offenders with developmental disabilities. *Psychological Assessment.*

Novaco, R.W & Welsh, W.N. (1989). Anger disturbances: cognitive mediation and clinical prescriptions. In K. Howells & C.R. Hollin (eds) *Clinical Approaches to Violence* (pp. 39–60). Chichester: John Wiley & Sons.

Oosterban, D.B., van Balkom, A.J.L.M., Spinhoven, P., van Oppen, P. & van Dyck, R. (2001). Cognitive therapy versus moclobemide in social phobia: a controlled study. *Clinical Psychology and Psychotherapy,* **8**, 263–73.

Renwick, S.J., Black, L., Ramm, M. & Novaco, R.W. (1997). Anger treatment with forensic hospital patients. *Legal and Criminological Psychology,* **2**, 103–16.

Rose, J. & West, C. (1999). Assessment of anger in people with intellectual disabilities. *Journal of Applied Research in Intellectual Disabilities,* **12**, 211–24.

Rose, J., West, C. & Clifford, D. (2000). Group interventions for anger in people with intellectual disabilities. *Research in Developmental Disabilities,* **21**, 171–81.

Scotti, J.R., Evans, I.M., Meyer, L.H. & Walker, P. (1991). A meta-analysis of intervention research with problem behavior: treatment validity and standards of practice. *American Journal on Mental Retardation*, **96**, 233–56.

Siegman, A.W. & Smith, T.W. (1994). *Anger, Hostility, and the Heart*. Hillsdale, NJ: Lawrence Erlbaum Associates.

Sigafoos, J., Elkins, J., Kerr, M. & Attwood, T. (1994). A survey of aggressive behavior among a population of persons with intellectual disability in Queensland. *Journal of Intellectual Disability Research*, **38**, 369–81.

Smith, S., Branford, D., Collacott, R.A., Cooper, S.-A. & McGrother, C. (1996). Prevalence and cluster typology of maladaptive behaviours in a geographically defined population of adults with learning disabilities. *British Journal of Psychiatry*, **169**, 219–27.

Stenfert Kroese, B. (1998). Cognitive-behavioural therapy for people with learning disabilities. *Behavioural and Cognitive Psychotherapy*, **26**, 315–22.

Stenfert Kroese, B., Dagnan, D. & Loumidis, K. (1997). *Cognitive-Behaviour Therapy for People with Learning Disabilities*, London: Routledge.

Swaffer, T. & Hollin, C.R. (2001). Anger and general health in young offenders. *Journal of Forensic Psychiatry*, **12**, 90–103.

Tafrate, R.C. (1995). Evaluation of treatment strategies for adult anger disorders. In H. Kassinove (ed.) *Anger Disorders*. Washington, DC: Taylor & Francis.

Taylor, J.L. (2002). A review of assessment and treatment of anger in offenders with intellectual disability. *Journal of Intellectual Disability Research*, **46**, (Suppl. 1), 57–73.

Taylor, J.L. & Novaco, R.W. (1999). Treatment of anger control problems in people with developmental disability: a manual for therapists. Unpublished manuscript, Northgate & Prudhoe NHS Trust.

Taylor, J.L., Novaco, R.W., Gillmer, B. & Thorne, I. (2002). Cognitive-behavioural treatment of anger intensity among offenders with intellectual disabilities. *Journal of Applied Research in Intellectual Disabilities*, **15**, 151–65.

Williams, H. & Jones, R.S.P. (1997). Teaching cognitive self-regulation of independence and emotion control skills. In B. Stenfert Kroese, D. Dagnan & K. Loumidis (eds) *Cognitive-Behaviour Therapy for People with Learning Disabilities* (pp. 67–85). London: Routledge.

Whitaker, S. (1993). The reduction of aggression in people with learning difficulties: a review of psychological methods. *British Journal of Clinical Psychology*, **32**, 1–37.

Whitaker, S. (2001). Anger control for people with learning disabilities: a critical review. *Behavioural and Cognitive Psychotherapy*, **29**, 277–93.

Chapter 12

TREATMENT OF FIRE-SETTING BEHAVIOUR

JOHN L. TAYLOR,* IAN THORNE[†] AND MICHAEL L. SLAVKIN[‡]

* *University of Northumbria, Newcastle upon Tyne and Northgate & Prudhoe NHS Trust, Northumberland, UK*
[†] *Northgate & Prudhoe NHS Trust, Northumberland, UK*
[‡] *University of Southern Indiana, Evansville, USA*

INTRODUCTION

Arson is a growing problem in society. In 1997 there were 31,500 arson offences recorded by police in England and Wales. Reports by fire brigades suggest that these accounted for 28.6% of all fires attended (Arson Prevention Bureau, 2000). In the UK the numbers of arson fires in buildings increased by 40%, and the number of fires set in vehicles increased three-fold between 1990 and 2000. The direct costs of arson in the UK are estimated to be more than £2.1 billion per annum (Canter & Almond, 2002). In 2000 deliberate fires were thought to account for 90 deaths and 2,800 injuries in the UK. In 1998 it was estimated that fires set by children and juveniles resulted in 6,215 deaths, another 30,800 injuries, and $2 billion in property damage in the USA (National Fire Protection Association, 1999).

While investigative methods of arson detection continue to improve, in only a small number of cases is sufficient evidence generated to proceed to court. The number of offenders found guilty or cautioned has remained relatively static in recent years. In 1997, in England and Wales a total of 2,516 people were prosecuted for arson offences, with 1,574 convicted offenders receiving sentences ranging from fines or probation orders, to maximum custodial sentences of life imprisonment. Hospital Orders under section 37 of the England and Wales Mental Health Act (1983) were made in the case of 54 offenders, five of which were with section 41 Restriction Orders (Arson Prevention Bureau, 2000).

Offenders with Developmental Disabilities. Edited by W.L. Lindsay, J.L. Taylor and P. Sturmey.
© 2004 John Wiley & Sons, Ltd.

DEFINITIONS, TYPOLOGIES AND THEORETICAL PERSPECTIVES ON FIRE-SETTING BEHAVIOUR

Definitions

In DSM-IV (American Psychiatric Association, 1994) pyromania is classified as an impulse-control disorder. Somewhat confusingly, the defining features of the disorder include deliberate and purposeful setting of fires involving "considerable advance preparation" (p. 614). The definition also includes, as diagnostic criteria, fire fascination and pleasure and gratification associated with setting fires. These criteria make the definition very narrow and unlikely to apply to all but a very few arsonists. More pertinently, with regard to the population of interest in the context of this chapter, DSM-IV pyromania specifically excludes fire-setters with mental retardation as a group whose fire-setting is a result of impaired judgement.

Swaffer, Haggett and Oxley (2001) made the distinction between arsonists who are apprehended, charged and convicted of starting uncontrolled fires, and fire-setters who have committed acts of arson that may or may not have resulted in charges being brought or convictions. Health and other human services that work with people with developmental disabilities and offending histories frequently deal with offenders who have committed acts of arson that have not been processed through the criminal justice system. Therefore the term "fire-setters" is the most appropriate to describe the population discussed in this chapter.

Jackson (1994) distinguished between "pathological" and other types of fire-setters (p. 95). The five criteria for pathological fire-setting were recidivism, fire to property rather than fire against other people, fire-setting alone, or repetitively with a single identified accomplice, evidence of personality, psychiatric or emotional problems, and the absence of financial or political gain as a motive for setting fires. Jackson, Glass and Hope (1987) considered this to be a more clinically relevant and useful concept that takes into account the evidence available concerning the prevalence and development of fire-setting behaviour.

Typologies and Classification Systems

There have been many attempts over the years to organise information about fire-setters into different schemes to help our understanding of this phenomenon. Lewis and Yarnell (1951) and then Bradford (1982) suggested classifying arson by the motives of those setting fires. Bradford found that almost 30% of the sample in his study were motivated by the need for attention, and 13% by revenge. Alternatively, authors such as Geller (1992) classified arson by the characteristics of the perpetrators. Categories included arson associated with medical/neurological disorder, with mental disorder and with young age (juvenile fire-setting). Prins, Tennant and Trick (1985) and Fineman (1995), on the other hand, offer mixed typologies classifying arson by perpetrator characteristics, motives and other features. An outline of Fineman's detailed scheme is presented as an example in Table 12.1.

Table 12.1 Typology of fire-setters

Type of firesetter	Characteristics
1. Curiosity type	Younger children who do not understand consequences of their behaviour. Desire is to watch the flame. Hyperactivity or attention deficit may be present. No intent to cause harm. Traditional early childhood diagnosis.
2. Accidental type	Usually involves children under 11 years of age. Teenagers playing scientist. The fire results from no destructive motive to create fire.
3. The "cry for help" type	Includes those offenders who consciously or subconsciously wish to bring attention to an interpersonal dysfunction (depression). Not meant to harm people. Acceptable prognosis for treatment. Firefighter who sets fires or adult/juvenile "would-be hero types"—seeking the attention of peers or the community in order to discover or help put out fires they start. Traditional early childhood diagnosis for abused children.
4. Delinquent type	Includes the "fire for profit" type and the "cover another crime" type. Interest in vandalism and hate crimes is noteworthy. This type shows little empathy for others. They show little conscience. Juvenile types rarely harm others with fire. Significant property damage is common. As adults, a significant percentage harm others. Fire-setting behaviour is more easily extinguished than other personality and behaviour problems that usually accompany the fire-setting.
5. Severely disturbed type	Includes those who seek to harm themselves, paranoid and psychotic types, for whom the fixation of fire may be a major factor in the development of a mental disorder. Sensory aspects of the fire are sufficiently reinforcing to cause fires to be frequently set. Pyromaniac is a sub-type—sensory reinforcement is often powerful enough for significant harm to occur. Prognosis is guarded with this group.
6. Cognitively impaired type	Includes the retarded and the organically impaired types. Tends to avoid intentional harm, lack acceptable judgement. Significant property damage is common. Prognostically, they are acceptable therapy candidates. Also included in this group are persons with severe learning disabilities, and those affected by foetal alcohol syndrome or by drugs taken by their mother during pregnancy.
7. Sociocultural type	Includes the uncontrolled mass hysteria type, the attention to cause type, the religious type and the satanic type. Arsonists who set fires primarily for the support they get for doing so by groups within their communities. Those who may set fires in the midst of civil unrest, and are either enraged and enticed by the activity of others and follow suit, or set fires with deliberation in order to call attention to the righteousness of their cause. Frequently lose control and harm others. Most are amenable to treatment.

Source: Adapted from Fineman (1995, p. 34).

One limitation of schemes that categorise fire-setters, or fire-setting behaviour, is that they do not account for the diversity or heterogeneity of fire-setters, or the complex interaction of dispositional, situational and environmental factors that might lead to an individual setting a fire. Further, these schemes give little by way of clinically relevant information to help with formulation or to guide treatment interventions.

Explanatory Theories

Underlying the DSM-IV criteria for pyromania is the concept of an irresistible impulse or drive to set fires. Historically there are a number of theoretical approaches that underpin this notion of drive or impulse to act. These relate to the assumed associations between arson and fire fascination, sexual gratification, displaced aggression and psychoses. Jackson (1994) explored the evidence supporting each of these associations in detail. He concluded that there is very little in the research literature to support clear and straightforward relationships between arson and any of these factors.

An adequate understanding of fire-setting is contingent upon the simultaneous examination of individual and environmental factors (Barnett, Richter, Sigmund & Spitzer, 1997). Jackson et al. (1987) described recidivistic arson within a "functional analysis paradigm" (p. 175), with arsonists presented as a psychosocially disadvantaged group, impaired in their abilities to influence their environment. As such, arson is conceived as a (mal)adaptive response influenced by antecedents, positive and negative reinforcing contingencies and other learning processes. The triggering event is likely to be emotionally significant, for example, disappointment, stress, insult, leading to feelings of anger and negative affect (Bumpass, Fagelman & Brix, 1983). However, fire is likely to be selected as the weapon of choice because it provides a non-confrontational form of communication for these often under-assertive individuals (Harris & Rice, 1984; Jackson, Glass & Hope, 1987; Smith & Short, 1995). While there is an absence of a "person target", the action elicits quick, dramatic and reinforcing results in the form of avoidance, care giving, revenge or the amelioration of negative affective states. Thus, in the short term at least, the disenfranchised fire-setter attains some degree of control over their environment. This is what Jackson (1994) described as "The Only Viable Option Theory" (p. 107).

Jackson's (1994) theory provides an explanation for the development of fire-setting behaviour from childhood curiosity and experimentation to pathological arson. For example, arsonists, due to their socially deprived, disadvantaged and abusive early experiences, frequently have significant difficulties in interacting in a socially acceptable manner with family, schools and peers. This in turn reduces their opportunities for learning or engaging in pro-social means of emotional expression. This combination of factors leads to the expression of emotion, or attempts to resolve interpersonal problems, through the medium of fire. The choice of fire as the only viable option might be particularly relevant for people with developmental disabilities given the social and emotional problems often associated with such disabilities. One further benefit of this theoretical model is that it provides a framework for assessment, formulation and treatment interventions for pathological fire-setters.

TREATMENT OF FIRE-SETTING BEHAVIOUR

The bulk of the research literature on outcomes of treatment for fire-setters relates to children and adolescents (Barnett & Spitzer, 1994). A number of studies have described systemic and behavioural approaches to treatment for child and adolescent fire-setters. These have included family therapy (Eisler, 1974), implosion (Cowell, 1985) and aversion (Carstens, 1982) therapies, stimulus satiation (Wolff, 1984), covert sensitisation and combined approaches (McGrath, Marshall & Prior, 1979). However, it is possible that a high proportion of children can be expected to stop setting fires, even if they receive no intervention, due to the effects of maturation.

There are very few treatment outcome studies concerning adults who set fires (Smith & Short, 1995; Swaffer, Haggert & Oxley, 2001). The material that is available appears to offer few pointers to successful intervention (Barnett & Spitzer, 1994). Behavioural approaches, limited to single case studies, have been reported (Royer, Flynn & Osadca, 1971; Lande, 1980).

Hurley and Monahan (1969) reported some improvements in communication skills and tolerance of others, following participation in discussion groups. However, given the descriptive nature of their study, both treatment and assessment methods lacked validity. Rice and Chaplin (1979) addressed social skills deficits and found that assertion training was more effective than non-directed group psychotherapy in improving the social skills of ten male arsonists. Furthermore, they found that there were no known acts of fire-setting among those discharged at one year follow-up. Theoretically, training in such skills could enable individuals to express their emotions more effectively and have more control over their environment. However, the description and systematic evaluation of group-based treatment packages remain largely absent from the literature. A recent UK government report (Canter & Almond, 2002) concluded that arson treatment programmes have not to date been evaluated in a consistent or objective manner. In terms of future research and development, it recommends a number of steps to be taken to improve the evidence base supporting these interventions.

FIRE-SETTING AND DEVELOPMENTAL DISABILITIES

The prevalence of arson, like other forms of offending among people with developmental disabilities, is difficult to estimate with any degree of confidence. A number of methodological problems in studies in this field contribute to this difficulty. These include the location of the study sample (community, courts, prison, etc.), and different methods of identifying the presence and level of developmental disability (educational history, IQ test) (Holland, Clare & Mukhopadhyay, 2002; Simpson & Hogg, 2001). Variations in the inclusion criteria applied can also affect the reported prevalence rates—a particular issue being whether or not those functioning in the "borderline intelligence" range are included. Because of these difficulties there are different views among researchers about whether arson is more prevalent among people with developmental disability than in the general population, or whether people with developmental disabilities are over- or under-represented in the arson offender population (Day, 1993; Holland et al., 2002; Prins et al., 1985; Robertson, 1981; Simpson & Hogg, 2001).

Irrespective of the size and scope of the problem, there is no disagreement that it exists and that people with developmental disabilities and histories of arson and fire-setting present significant challenges and require attention from relevant agencies. In particular, health and correctional services are required to develop effective methods for intervention and management. Unfortunately, there is little available in the research literature to guide such developments. Fire-setting was excluded from a recent Department of Health sponsored review of the evidence base in the intellectual disability field (Fraser & Taylor, 2002) as there was so little research literature available.

Murphy and Clare (1996) developed a Fire-Setting Assessment Schedule (FSAS) which they administered to 10 fire-setters with developmental disabilities regarding their recollection of their cognitions and feelings immediately before and after setting fires. The development of the FSAS was consistent with the proposal by Jackson *et al.* (1987) that a functional analytical approach to fire-setting was clinically useful. Murphy and Clare found that the participants in their study identified antecedents to their fire-setting more reliably then consequences. Anger, followed by not being listened to, and then feelings of depression or sadness were most frequently mentioned as antecedents. Anger and then not being listened to were most often reported as having been helped by setting fires.

The only developmental-disability-specific study in the UK to report on the outcome of fire-setter treatment was by Clare, Murphy, Cox and Chaplin (1992). This was a single case study involving a man with mild intellectual disability who had been transferred from a maximum security hospital to a specialist in-patient unit. He had prior convictions for arson and a history of making hoax telephone calls to the fire services. He underwent a comprehensive treatment package that included assertiveness and social skills training, coping skills training, covert sensitisation and surgery for a severe facial disfigurement. Significant clinical improvements were observed following treatment, and 30 months post-discharge to a community placement there had been no reports of fire-setting or associated offending behaviour.

In North America, Rice and Chaplin (1979) delivered a social skills training intervention to two groups of five fire-setters in a maximum security psychiatric facility. One of the groups were reported to be functioning in the mild-borderline intellectual disability range. Both treatment groups improved significantly on an observational rating scale of role-played assertive behaviour. Following treatment, the treated patients were discharged from hospital and none had been convicted or suspected of setting fires at 12-month follow-up.

DEVELOPMENT OF A GROUP TREATMENT FOR ARSONISTS WITH DEVELOPMENTAL DISABILITIES

As so little research concerning fire-setters with developmental disability has been reported in the literature, it was decided to develop a fire-setters group treatment programme to be delivered in the low secure areas of an NHS Trust in the UK that specialises in working with clients with developmental disabilities and histories of offending. The hospital forensic service has beds for 159 patients, 22 women and 137 men. At the point at which the fire-setters programme was developed, 51 (32%) patients had histories of fire-setting; 31 (19%) had arson convictions and 20 (13%) had documented histories of, but no convictions for, fire-setting.

Delivery of Treatment

Psychologist and qualified nurse co-facilitators used a therapy manual to deliver the fire-setters treatment programme. The treatment is guided by the manual, rather than driven by it. There are variations in the pace and emphasis of treatment delivery depending on the characteristics of the patients. While guidance is provided regarding how long (how many sessions) a particular aspect of the treatment may take, this is varied if the judgement of the therapists, and feedback from patients, indicates that more or less time is required. In this way the procedure is reflexive to the needs of individual participants and the group as a whole.

The treatment is delivered in a group therapy context as such settings can provide safe environments for participants to explore problems, challenge attitudes and contemplate change. When facilitated by skilled therapists, group therapy settings can also be effective in that participants can learn that others have experienced similar problems in controlling their behaviour and are motivated to improve their control. Offenders' peers are often best placed to suggest credible alternative coping strategies and they facilitate modelling, practice and development of alternative interpersonal skills within a structured and contained environment. Generally, between 30 and 40 sessions are required to work through the programme depending on the abilities of the participants, their levels of motivation and the ease with which group cohesion is established. Each session lasts for about two hours, with a coffee break of approximately half an hour in the middle. Ideally, treatment sessions are delivered twice weekly to maintain therapeutic momentum, avoid drift and to ameliorate difficulties with recall of recently completed work associated with participants' cognitive limitations.

Treatment Rationale

The approach to treatment draws on the "what works" literature in terms of the features of successful and effective interventions in the offender and delinquency fields (McGuire, 1995; Skett, 1995). This suggests that interventions should be theoretically sound, cognitive-behavioural in nature, multi-faceted in terms of the problem areas targeted, and orientated towards skills development. Interventions should be responsive to the learning needs, styles and preferences of both clients and therapists and focus on the criminogenic aspects of the clients' presenting problems that are proximal, rather than distal, to offending behaviour(s). Interventions should also take into account the level of risk presented by clients by increasing the therapeutic "dosage" proportionately for those judged to be higher risk in terms of recidivism, and attend to issues of programme integrity by reducing or eliminating therapeutic drift, treatment gain reversal and non-compliance with regard to the delivery of programmes by therapists. Finally, intervention should be delivered by trained staff and evaluated independently.

The treatment is a comprehensive and multi-faceted programme based on the approach outlined by Jackson (1994). This approach is consistent with Jackson *et al.*'s (1987) "functional analysis paradigm" for recidivistic arson. Within a broad cognitive-behavioural framework, clients' offence cycles are analysed with regard to (1) antecedent setting factors and triggers; (2) the cognitions, emotions and behaviour they experienced at the time fires were started; and (3) the positive and negative consequences of their fire-setting behaviour. Clients receive education concerning the dangers and costs associated with setting fires. The acquisition and rehearsal of skills to enhance future coping with emotional and interpersonal problems associated with previous fire-setting behaviour are emphasised. The development of personalised plans to prevent relapse are also an important aspect of the treatment package.

Programme Components

The main aims of the treatment are: (1) for patients to show improvement on factors closely associated with fire-setting such as inappropriate levels of interest in and attitudes towards fire, and distorted beliefs concerning responsibility for and risks factors associated with fire-setting; (2) to improve self-esteem and personal effectiveness; (3) to consider the functions served by their fire-setting; (4) to develop alternative, more effective, emotional coping skills; (5) to receive education regarding the potential effect of fires, and (6) to learn coping strategies to avoid reoffending.

In order to achieve these aims, the main components of the treatment package involve the following:

Review of offence cycle

This component, utilising a functional analysis framework, enables an individualised examination of the purposes served by offending—in particular, the causation, triggering and maintenance factors—and facilitates an understanding of offenders' perceptions of themselves in relation to others. Thus, cognitions, emotions and events surrounding the fire-setting are explored, consistent with Jackson et al.'s (1987) model. Cognitive distortions and misconceptions are identified, together with any coping strategies previously used in relation to interpersonal problem solving. The collation of such details also facilitates risk assessment.

Education and information

Given that arsonists often perceive their fire-setting to be a victimless crime, involving no direct, face-to-face contact, in which supposedly empty buildings are targeted, the dangers of fire, its potential human and financial costs, need to be made explicit. Arson involves more than damage or destruction of property. It poses a danger to human life, with the potential for multiple and unwitting victims. Thus there is a need to develop victim awareness. In addition, some basic education regarding fire prevention and environmental hazards may help to develop pro-social attitudes towards fire.

Skills acquisition and development

The risks associated with arson lie not in the nature of fire-setting *per se*, but in the underlying psychological and situational factors that lead to the fire-setter feeling frustrated, distressed and helpless. A strong focus should be given to developing patients' capacity to both cope with and express their feelings in more adaptive and appropriate ways. The acquisition and development of interpersonal skills is essential, with particular emphasis on communication and socially adaptive modes of expressing emotions, interpersonal problem solving and handling conflict in an assertive manner. Use of modelling, role-played practice and behavioural feedback offer useful techniques in terms of generalising learning and developing a sense of personal effectiveness.

Relapse prevention

Based upon offenders' understanding of their own offence cycle, the relapse prevention model (Marlatt & Gordon, 1985) reinforces the point that treatment does not result in a "cure", rather it emphasises the behavioural and cognitive skills that may prevent relapse from occurring, or minimise the extent of relapse. Essentially it is a maintenance model, successfully used in relation to substance abusers (Marlatt & Gordon, 1985) and sex offenders (Pithers Marques, Gibat & Marlatt, 1983; Pithers, Kashmina, Cumming & Beal, 1988), but also helpful in the management of recidivistic arson (Bumpass, Brix & Preston, 1980). Group members are encouraged to continue to monitor their cognitions, feelings and behaviours, in order to avoid, control or escape from previously identified high-risk situations. Furthermore, they are encouraged to recognise the need to seek support when they feel that their capacity to avoid reoffending is failing. As such, emphasis is placed upon the individual's responsibility for themselves and others within their environment.

Treatment Modules

1. Establishing the group (approximately two sessions)

Initial sessions are structured to help group members get to know each other and to introduce them to a mutually agreed set of ground rules. In order to desensitise participants to any anxieties that they might have about embarking on group therapy, the purpose of the group is outlined and the methods and techniques to be used are explained.

2. Group cohesion exercises (approximately three sessions)

Yalom (1975) asserted that cohesiveness is the primary and most important curative factor in group psychotherapy. Participants remain members of successful groups because of their cohesion, as well as the benefits that they derive from them. Establishing a safe, secure and confidential environment provides a context in which group members can begin to disclose basic information about themselves, including "good and bad things" that have occurred since the last session. During these discussions, group members are encouraged to identify their thoughts and feelings about such events.

Enhancement of self-esteem is the central aim of therapy, underlying all aspects of the programme. Specific exercises, in which group members are encouraged to identify and share positive things about themselves (strengths, achievements, successes and personal qualities), and to show appreciation of positive qualities of other participants are introduced at this point, in order to bolster self-image and confidence.

3. Family and related issues (approximately four sessions)

Having established some degree of trust and confidentiality in the preceding modules, group members are asked to trace their personal histories and identify key life events in the form of a "Life Map". Therapists encourage participants to discuss their feelings about these events. This locates patients' position within various social systems (familial, educational, institutional, relationships and support networks) and provides some context for their offending behaviour. In addition, this process can help the therapists to gain some basic insights into cognitive schemas and beliefs associated with group members' offending behaviour.

4. Offence analysis (approximately 13 sessions)

A detailed analysis of events before, during and after the fire-setting behaviour is completed with each group member over about four sessions. A BARE-PIT acronym was developed for such assessment—breaking each stage down in terms of Behaviour, Attitudes, Relationships, Emotions, Physical state, (fire-related) Interests and Thoughts. Participants are encouraged to support each other by identifying and challenging any cognitive distortions that other members display concerning their fire-setting behaviour.

At the end of this module group members are given a typed copy of their functional analysis. With the support of direct care nurse colleagues, participants are asked to undertake a homework exercise in which they are required to identify high-risk situations, feelings, thoughts and behaviours associated with their fire-setting. This preliminary analysis is developed further in module 7.

5. Information and education (approximately two sessions)

Links were established with Northumberland Fire & Rescue Service, such that they were able to develop a custom-made presentation illustrating the role of the Fire Service, the chemistry of fires and the rapidity with which they spread, the way in which hoax calls serve to divert potentially life-saving services, and the human cost of fires. The latter involves distressing, but not gruesome, film of a house fire in which two children died. Discussion, led by operational firemen, takes place around each issue, and a quiz is administered further emphasising the human and financial costs of fires.

6. *Alternative skills training (approximately 13 sessions)*

In this module, anger and self-esteem are targeted specifically as participants' scores on the FSAS (Murphy & Clare, 1996) indicated these to be salient issues with regard to the antecedents to and consequences of their fire-setting. This module begins at a micro-behavioural level, focusing on aspects of non-verbal communication and why individuals might choose to mask their feelings. Emphasis then shifts towards anger management, drawing heavily upon the treatment developed by Taylor and Novaco (1999) (see Chapter 11). Initial sessions point out the normality of the emotion, helping group members to recognise what makes them angry, and explaining the sequential process (situations, cognitions and feelings) by which individuals experience anger.

Anger provoking incidents are identified from group members' maintenance of "anger logs" and discussion exercises. Attention is then given to different methods for controlling anger. These include arousal reduction through relaxation and use of calming imagery, perspective-taking and the generation of alternative reasons for others' behaviours to counteract the cognitive component of anger, and the use of calming self-statements as technique to combat maladaptive reactions to anger.

Assertiveness training emphasises the distinctions between passive, aggressive and assertive behaviours and the likely outcomes of each. Moreover, it raises awareness of personal rights in relation to self and others. Subsequent sessions integrate and further consolidate techniques learned and focus on coping effectively with criticism, insults and group pressures.

All sessions in this module are underpinned by training of participants' behavioural skills using modelling, rehearsal (using role-play) and feedback, in order to improve performance and aid generalisation to other settings.

7. *Risk management/relapse prevention (approximately four sessions)*

Group members are reminded that their fire-setting is likely to show a characteristic pattern or signature, and they are re-acquainted with their own offence cycle and individual risk factors (identified in module 4) with a view to further development and discussion. Remaining sessions focus on the active deployment of self-management strategies including relaxation, self-talk and cognitive restructuring. External supports are also identified as a means of maintaining treatment gains and self-control. It is acknowledged throughout this module that while lapses will occur, participants can recover, without reoffending, through use of the techniques discussed.

CASE REPORTS

Patients with fire-setting histories admitted to the service are administered a newly designed Pathological Fire-Setters Interview (PFSI). This is a structured interview, augmented with collateral information from patients' records, that gathers information in a functional analytic framework concerning (a) personal and offending details, (b) personal setting conditions, (c) situational setting conditions, (d) antecedents to fire-setting, (e) motives for setting fires, and (f) consequences (thoughts, feelings and actual) of setting fires.

Outcome Measures

Before beginning, and immediately after completing the fire-setter group therapy programme, participants complete a number of fire-specific and psychological assessment measures. These include:

- *Fire Interest Rating Scale (FIRS)* (Murphy & Clare, 1996). This scale consists of 14 descriptions of fire-related situations. Respondents are asked to rate how they would feel in each situation using a 7-point scale from "most upsetting/absolutely horrible" to "very exciting, lovely, nice".
- *Fire Attitude Scale (FAS)* (Muckley, 1997). This is a self-report measure that consists of 20 statements such as "The best thing about fire is watching it spread".
- *Goal Attainment Scales (GAS).* Six GASs were developed based on the method described by Kiresuk and Sherman (1968). Based on clients' responses in a semi-structured interview, a group therapist and an independent rater use GASs to score clients in relation to four offence-related treatment targets: "acceptance of guilt", "acknowledgement of responsibility", "understanding of victim issues" and, "understanding of high-risk elements of offence cycle". In addition two GASs ("appropriate expression of emotion" and "ability to form and maintain relationships") are completed independently by direct-care staff who know the clients well and have day-to-day contact with them.
- *Novaco Anger Scale (NAS)* (Novaco, 1994). A 48-item self-report instrument containing cognitive, arousal and behavioural subscales, which comprise a total score for anger disposition.
- *Culture-Free Self-Esteem Inventory—2nd Edition, Form AD (CFSEI-2)* (Battle, 1992). A widely used and reliable measure of self-esteem. It comprises general, social and personal subscales, which can be summed to give a total summary index score.

Case Descriptions

The following four case descriptions illustrate treatment participants' functioning, backgrounds and offence profiles. They also provide a synopsis of their progress through a fire-setters treatment group that ran for 31 sessions. In order to protect anonymity, participants' names have been changed and potentially identifying details have been modified appropriately. Patients' pre- and post-treatment scores on fire-specific and psychological assessment measures are presented in Table 12.2.

Case 1—Robson

Robson was a 40-year-old single man with a diagnosis of Asperger syndrome in addition to his mild intellectual disability (full scale IQ = 71). He had a history

Table 12.2 Patient self-report and clinicians' scores for fire-specific and psychological measures

Measure	Client 1		Client 2		Client 3		Client 4	
	Pre	Post	Pre	Post	Pre	Post	Pre	Post
Fire Interest Rating Scale (FIRS)	59	57	44	37	33	42	56	36
Fire Attitude Scale (FAS)	45	44	26	26	27	26	39	25
Goal Attainment Scales (GAS)								
GAS total	6	11	14	18	9	13	4	8
Acceptance of guilt	2	2	3	3	2	2	1	2
Personal responsibility	2	2	2	3	2	3	1	1
Victim issues	0	2	2	3	1	2	0	1
Emotional expression	1	2	2	3	2	2	1	2
Relationships	0	1	3	3	1	2	1	1
Understanding of risks	1	2	2	3	1	2	0	1
Novaco Anger Scale (NAS) total	89	69	92	84	113	100	140	90
Culture-Free Self-Esteem Inventory total	25	23	13	18	7	13	15	9

of general developmental delay and was educated in residential special schools from the age of 7 years. With the exception of his parents divorcing when he was in his mid-teens, Robson's personal and family history appeared to have been relatively stable.

Robson was detained under section 37 of the England & Wales Mental Health Act (MHA) 1983, and had a Home Office restriction order (section 41). When he was 25 years old, Robson was convicted of arson with intent to endanger life. Acting alone, Robson set fire to furniture in the living room of a hostel where he was living with other people with intellectual disabilities and mental health problems because of "bad feelings" in his head. Having started the fire, Robson alerted the officer-in-charge and serious harm to vulnerable hostel residents was averted. He had one conviction for arson, but it is documented that he had set at least two fires previously. Following conviction Robson was detained in a high-security hospital for 11 years before his transfer to a medium/low secure facility where he accessed the fire-setters group treatment programme.

Robson attended all 31 sessions and was rated highly throughout by the therapists in terms of his levels of attention, participation, self-disclosure and the form and content of his communication within sessions. In fact he began as a quiet, somewhat shy group member. However, as sessions progressed he became more relaxed and comfortable in the group. Most strikingly, for a person with a diagnosis of Asperger syndrome, Robson's "empathic" interest and concern for other participants increased markedly during the course of the programme. His level of communication waned a little during the alternative skills module. This is perhaps due to Robson's feeling that these aspects of treatment were not particularly relevant to him, a view supported to some extent by his relatively good scores on the pre-treatment assessments of anger and self-esteem.

In terms of fire interest and fire attitudes, Robson's self-rated scores indicated no change following the intervention. However, therapist and independent ratings of arson-related GASs suggest that he showed modest improvements in all areas, reaching a satisfactory level 2 on all but one scale. He showed particular improvement in his understanding of the impact of fires on victims. He remained below a satisfactory level on the relationships GAS, which may be due to difficulties with making and maintaining relationships that are often associated with Asperger syndrome. At the beginning of treatment Robson scored at the 44th percentile on the self-esteem measure, indicating that he had an appropriate degree of self-esteem. This did not change markedly following treatment. Before starting the programme his self-reported NAS anger score was around the mean of 92.4 (S.D. = 16.2) for the male forensic hospital population of which he was part. Following treatment this had fallen by just over one standard deviation to a sub-clinical level.

Case 2—Bobby

Bobby was a 37-year-old single man with a diagnosis of mild intellectual disability (full scale IQ = 68) and "psychopathic disorder" as defined within the MHA 1983. His mother was known to have intellectual disabilities and his father was an alcoholic who died at a young age. Following his father's death, Bobby was adopted by a stable family including adoptive siblings. Bobby had a long history of mental health difficulties and alcohol problems. He had previous convictions for violence that resulted in admission to a high-security hospital, and concerns had been expressed and recorded in the past concerning sexual aggression.

Bobby was detained in a special hospital under sections 37/41 of the MHA 1983 following convictions for assault and attempted robbery when in his mid-twenties. His index arson offence occurred while he was conditionally discharged from this section to a community placement in the early 1990s. Bobby was living in a specialist housing project for people with intellectual disabilities when, together with two fellow residents, he set fire to a barn causing serious damage to the building and its contents. Bobby had consumed a large amount of alcohol when he set the fire, in which turpentine was used as an accelerant. This is the only fire that Bobby is known to have set. Following his arrest he was remanded in custody and transferred to a medium/low secure facility prior to his arson conviction when a section 37/41 was reapplied.

Bobby attended all 31 group treatment sessions offered to him. He was highly motivated, positive and enthusiastic throughout the programme. He was keen to try to understand his offending and learn how to help himself so that he could move on. Although he was a quiet member of the group to begin with, therapists' ratings indicate that Bobby showed high levels of attention, concentration, self-disclosure, communication skills and empathic interest in other group members from the outset. This high degree of group involvement was maintained during the offence analysis and risk and coping strategies phases of the treatment, where Bobby increased in confidence and became more active.

Bobby's self-rated fire interest and fire attitudes scores hardly changed at all following treatment. Before he started the fire-setters treatment programme, Bobby's ratings on the GASs were either at or above satisfactory levels. Post-treatment ratings did suggest, however, that he had improved through treatment from "satisfactory" to "better than expected" outcomes for acknowledgement of personal responsibility, understanding of victim issues, appropriate expression of emotion and understanding of high-risk situations. Before the group began Bobby scored at the 8th percentile on the self-esteem measure, and following treatment he moved up to the 21st percentile, reflecting the increased self-confidence observed in group sessions. Bobby's pre-treatment NAS anger disposition score was slightly above the clinically significant threshold of 90. Post-treatment this fell over half a standard deviation to a sub-clinical level, consistent with his good performance in the alternative skills training module of the programme.

Case 3—Graham

Graham was a 44-year-old single man with a diagnosis of mild intellectual disability (full scale IQ = 66). Graham was brought up by his parents and attended special schools from the age of 8 years. Until he was in his early thirties, Graham lived with his parents in a stable family environment. Around this time his father died and his mother needed the support of a nursing home. Graham moved to supported accommodation at this point, but was expelled after a short time because of "behavioural problems". He then lived an itinerant lifestyle, drinking heavily, with only intermittent contact with services.

Graham was convicted of four counts of arson in the mid-1990s after which he was detained in a local secure treatment service under sections 37/41 of the MHA 1983. Acting alone he set fire to rubbish skips on three occasions and then involved himself to some degree in fighting the fires. However, following an argument with a woman car driver, he set fire to her car later the same day. He suggests that this was because of the anger he felt following the earlier confrontation, which he had ruminated about, as well as a desire to get his own back on the car owner. He observed this fire from some distance and did not involve himself in any attempt to fight the fire. In addition to excessive drinking, there was some suggestion that at the time the index arson offences occurred, Graham was depressed following his father's death and the break-up of his family. Prior to these convictions Graham had no other recorded offences, although minor incidents of sexually inappropriate behaviour have been noted at various points during his stays in residential settings.

Graham attended 30 of the 31 group sessions and was probably the least able member of the group in terms of intellectual/cognitive functioning. However, therapists considered him to function at quite a high level within the group context in terms of his levels of attention, concentration and self-disclosure. As the sessions progressed and became more complex and demanding intellectually in the offence analysis, risk and coping strategies phases, Graham sometimes found it difficult to understand particular concepts and issues. This difficulty was reflected in the quality of his communication, which became variable. Despite these problems, Graham continued to be motivated to be an active group member and his empathic interest in others increased slightly as the group progressed.

Graham's self-reported fire interest and attitudes scores changed very little following treatment. His GAS ratings showed only minor improvements in the areas of personal responsibility for setting fires, understanding of victim issues, relationship formation and maintenance, and understanding of risks associated with fire-setting. However, all GASs reached satisfactory levels, which is encouraging given

Graham's cognitive limitations and difficulties with some of the programme content. Encouragingly, given the central role anger appears to have played in his most serious arson offence, Graham's self-rated NAS anger score reduced by almost one standard deviation following treatment, although it remained in the clinically significant range. His self-esteem score increased modestly from the 1st to the 8th percentile at the end of the group therapy.

Case 4—George

George was a 22-year-old single man with a diagnosis of mild intellectual disability (full scale IQ = 72). He had a very disturbed developmental history including evidence of intra-familial physical and sexual abuse. In the past he had been aggressive and destructive. He had a long-standing history of serious sexually inappropriate and aggressive behaviour towards young children of both sexes, both within and outside of the family setting. George's father was absent throughout his childhood and he was taken into foster care when he was 10 years old. He then attended residential special needs schools until he was expelled at the age of 13 due to sexually inappropriate and predatory behaviour towards younger students.

George's index offence of arson with intent to cause harm occurred in his family home when he was 16 years old. George's older sister found him in the family home engaging in sexually inappropriate behaviour with his younger brother. His sister challenged George about this and in response he became angry and abusive. After his brother had left the scene George set fire to the sitting room and then quit the house. Although he set the fire to cause harm to and to get his own back on his sister, after a while he telephoned her to tell her what he had done. By this time his sister had discovered the fire and had alerted the emergency services. This is the only fire that George is known to have set. Following his arrest he was remanded in prison briefly before being transferred under section 35 of the MHA 1983 to a medium and low secure hospital facility for management and treatment.

George attended 29 of the 31 fire-setters group therapy sessions. During the initial stages of the group work, George was rated positively by the therapists in terms of attention, concentration, self-disclosure and level of communication. Despite his relatively young age within the group, he was noted to be enthusiastic and keen to contribute during these early stages of the programme. However, as the group progressed to work on more emotionally demanding areas such as self-disclosure concerning offending behaviour, George had difficulty coping, became less willing to contribute and missed two sessions as his behaviour became generally unsettled. It was felt that the linkage between his index arson offence and sexually inappropriate behaviour with his brother caused him to feel anxious and defensive. As the focus of the treatment was fire-setting, he was not pressed to disclose details of any sexual misdemeanour, and he rejoined the group, began to participate effectively once again and completed the group successfully.

In terms of fire interest and attitudes, George's self-rated scores reduced markedly following treatment, indicating reduced fire interest and improved attitudes towards fire-related issues. However, he made less obvious progress on the

GASs, achieving satisfactory levels on only two scales—acceptance of guilt and appropriate emotional expression. The latter area of improvement was reflected in a very large reduction of more than $3\frac{1}{2}$ standard deviations on his NAS anger disposition score following treatment. His post-treatment score of 90 is at the threshold for a clinically significant anger problem. This is possibly quite important for George given the role that anger played in his arson offence. Somewhat curiously, George's self-esteem score fell following treatment. This was possibly related to his increasing, if limited, acknowledgement of guilt for his offending during the treatment programme.

SUMMARY AND CONCLUSIONS

Fire-setting, including arson, is a significant and growing criminal and economic problem for society. It is also an increasing problem for human services working with those who set illegal fires. In particular, clinical services that deal with adult clients who might be described as pathological fire-setters are hampered by a dearth of evidence to guide assessment and therapy procedures. This gap in the research literature is even more apparent when fire-setters with developmental disabilities are considered. In response to this lack of information, a multi-faceted group treatment programme that uses a functional analytic framework was devised and implemented in a clinical service that specialises in work with detained offenders with developmental disabilities, a significant proportion of whom are fire-setters.

The clinical and assessment data provided by the evaluation of the progress of a group of four men with mild intellectual disabilities and arson convictions who worked through this programme are illuminating. The therapy was able to successfully engage patients with developmental disabilities and serious offending histories, with life experiences of abuse, deprivation and repeated failures in service settings. All four participants completed the 31 session programme delivered over a period of four months, with very few sessions missed by any one patient. Despite their intellectual and cognitive limitations, all participants responded positively to the group environment, showing quite high levels of motivation and commitment, which translated into strong group cohesion that sustained individual patients through challenging and difficult phases of the programme. The group met twice weekly whenever possible. It is felt that this fairly intensive schedule helped to promote therapeutic momentum, limit drift and ameliorated the recall difficulties that are often associated with impaired cognitive function.

With the exception of George, the group therapy participants did not demonstrate clear improvements with regard to the fire-specific self-report measures, FIRS and FAS. The reasons for this are not clear. However, it is possible that for these particular patients inappropriate fire interest and attitudes had little to do with their arson offences. Alternatively, the FIRS and FAS may not be sensitive to clinical change over a relatively short period of time. Neither have psychometric evaluation data available to help judge their utility in this regard. Following treatment, all four participants improved markedly on the NAS anger measure, and two of the four also showed modest increases on the CFSEI self-esteem inventory. Given that anger is a frequent antecedent to, and therefore appears to be an activator of fire-setting behaviour, the impact of the treatment on self-reported anger disposition for group participants is encouraging.

Apart from George, participants reached satisfactory or better than expected outcomes on the staff- and independent-rated GASs. However, only one participant (Bobby) was rated above the satisfactory outcome level concerning their understanding of the high-risk elements of their fire-setting behaviour. This was reflected in the content of the risk management/relapse prevention plans that participants drew up for themselves. Generally, their strategies for avoiding risk, and for dealing with risks when they arise, were somewhat superficial, not always practicable and heavily reliant on others to spot problems and apply external controls. This could reflect the difficulty in attempting to do work relating to "real-life" situations in an artificial context where external controls are a structural component of the environment. On the other hand, for the participants in this particular group, these plans may be an accurate indication of their abilities at this point to take responsibility for their future actions, and their need for ongoing support and supervision in order to remain safe. Alternatively, while the intervention might be a good starting point for work with this client group, it may not be potent enough in this specific area of treatment and requires development and improvement in this regard.

Even within this small group, George's profile in terms of his response to the programme stands out. As he was significantly younger than the other group members, his interest in and attitudes towards fire at the outset of treatment might have been more consistent with those often associated with children and adolescents. Therefore, the marked improvement that he showed on the FIRS and FAS may be due to George's lack of maturity having been ameliorated to some extent through his involvement in the programme. Perhaps his very limited improvements on the GASs were also linked to his immaturity, making it difficult for him to take more responsibility for his actions and better understand the impact of his behaviour on others. George's very significant improvement on the NAS anger measure is to be welcomed, although it was so high before treatment it could only move in one direction. That said, direct-care ward level staff did independently rate George's emotional expression as improving to a satisfactory level during the course of the programme.

A largely clinical account of the application and evaluation of a fire-setters group therapy programme has been presented in this chapter. The limitations of this account and the programme evaluation are clear. However, given the paucity of the research literature in this field, this description and preliminary evaluation of a programme for seriously challenging fire-setters with developmental disabilities is aimed at providing practitioners in this area with some guidance for practice. In addition, pointers are given for future research that might involve more robust and controlled evaluations of treatment effectiveness.

ACKNOWLEDGEMENTS

The work of Alison Robertson and Ginny Avery, who helped to coordinate the programme, and collected and collated the information on which much of this material is based is greatly appreciated. Special thanks go to Dr Kath Featherstone and Lee Anderson who organised and delivered the treatment to the men whose case reports are included in this chapter. Thanks also to Dr Bruce Gillmer for his comments on earlier drafts of this chapter.

REFERENCES

American Psychiatric Association (1994). *Diagnostic and Statistical Manual of Mental Disorders*, 4th edn. Washington, DC American Psychiatric Association.

Arson Prevention Bureau (2000). Statistics on the arson problem: http://www.arsonpreventionbureau.org.uk.

Barnett, W., Richter, P., Sigmund, D. & Spitzer, M. (1997). Recidivism and concomitant criminality in pathological firesetters. *Journal of Forensic Sciences*, **42**, 879–83.

Barnett, W. & Spitzer, M. (1994). Pathological fire-setting 1951–1991: a review. *Medicine, Science and the Law*, **34**, 4–20.

Battle, J. (1992). *Culture-Free Self-Esteem Inventory*. Austin, TX, Pro-Ed.

Bradford, J.M.W. (1982). Arson: a clinical study. *Canadian Journal of Psychiatry*, **27**, 188–92.

Bumpass, E., Brix, R. & Preston, D. (1980). A community-based program for juvenile firesetters. *Hospital and Community Psychiatry*, **36**, 529–33.

Bumpass, E.R., Fagelman, F.D. & Brix, R.J. (1983). Intervention with children who set fires. *American Journal of Psychotherapy*, **37**, 328–45.

Canter, D. & Almond, L. (2002). *The Burning Issue: Research Strategies for Reducing Arson*. London: The Office of the Deputy Prime Minister.

Carstens, C. (1982). Application of a work penalty threat in the treatment of and care of juvenile firesetting. *Journal of Behaviour Therapy and Experimental Psychiatry*, **13**, 159–61.

Clare, I.C.H., Murphy, G.H., Cox, D. & Chaplin, E.H. (1992). Assessment and treatment of fire-setting: a single-case investigation using a cognitive-behavioural model. *Criminal Behaviour and Mental Health*, **2**, 253–68.

Cowell, P. (1985). Implosive therapy in the counselling of a pupil who sets fires. *British Journal of Guidance and Counselling*, **13**, 157–65.

Day, K. (1993). Crime and mental retardation: a review. In K. Howells & C.R. Hollin (eds) *Clinical Approaches to the Mentally Disordered Offender* (pp. 111–44). Chichester: John Wiley & Sons.

Eisler, R.M. (1974). Crisis intervention in the family of a fire-setter. *Psychotherapy: Theory, Research and Practice*, **9**, 76–9.

Fineman, K. (1995). A model for the qualitative analysis of child and adult fire deviant behavior. *American Journal of Forensic Psychology*, **13**, 31–60.

Fraser, W.I. & Taylor, J.L. (eds) (2002). Forensic learning disabilities: the evidence base [supplement 1]. *Journal of Intellectual Disability Research*, **46**.

Geller, J. (1992). Pathological fire-setting in adults. *International Journal of Law and Psychiatry*, **15**, 283–302.

Harris, G.T. & Rice, M.E. (1984). Mentally disordered fire-setters: psychodynamic versus empirical approaches. *International Journal of Law and Psychiatry*, **7**, 19–43.

Holland, T., Clare, I.C.H. & Mukhopadhyay, T. (2002). Prevalence of 'criminal offending' by men and women with intellectual disability and the characteristics of 'offenders': implications for research and service development. *Journal of Intellectual Disability Research*, **46** (suppl. 1), 6–20.

Hurley, W. & Monahan, T.M. (1969). Arson: the criminal and the crime. *British Journal of Criminology*, **9**, 4–21.

Jackson, H.F. (1994). Assessment of fire-setters. In M. McMurran & J. Hodge (eds) *The Assessment of Criminal Behaviours of Clients in Secure Settings* (pp. 94–126). London: Jessica Kingsley.

Jackson, H.F., Glass, C. & Hope S. (1987). A functional analysis of recidivistic arson. *British Journal of Clinical Psychology*, **26**, 175–85.

Kiresuk, T. & Sherman, R. (1968). Goal attainment scaling: a general method of evaluating comprehensive mental health programmes. *Community Mental Health Journal*, **4**, 443–53.

Lande, S.D. (1980). A combination of orgasmic reconditioning and covert sensitisation in the treatment of a fire fetish. *Journal of Behaviour Therapy and Experimental Psychiatry*, **11**, 291–6.

Lewis, N.D.C. & Yarnell, H. (1951). *Pathological Firesetting (Pyromania)*, New York: Nervous and Mental Disease Monographs, no 82.

McGrath, P., Marshall, P.G. & Prior K. (1979). A comprehensive treatment program for a fire setting child. *Journal of Behaviour Therapy and Experimental Psychiatry*, **10**, 69–72.

McGuire, J. (1995). *What Works: Reducing Reoffending: Guidelines from Research and Practice.* Chichester: John Wiley & Sons.

Marlatt, G.A. & Gordon J.R. (1985). *Relapse Prevention: Maintenance Strategies in the Treatment of Addictive Behaviours.* New York: Guilford Press.

Muckley, A. (1997). *Firesetting: addressing offending behaviour.* Unpublished manual. Redcar and Cleveland Psychological Service.

Murphy, G.H. & Clare, I.C.H. (1996). Analysis of motivation in people with mild learning disabilities (mental handicap) who set fires. *Psychology, Crime and Law*, **2**, 153–64.

National Fire Protection Association (1999). Statistics on the national fire problem. Citation found at http://www.fema.gov/nfpa.

Novaco, R.W. (1994). Anger as a risk factor for violence among the mentally disordered. In J. Monahan & H.J. Steadman (eds) *Violence and Mental Disorder: Developments in Risk Assessment* (pp. 21–59). Chicago, IL: University of Chicago Press.

Pithers, W.D., Kashima, K.M., Cumming, G.F. & Beal, L.S. (1988). Relapse prevention: a method of enhancing maintenance of change in sex offenders. In A.C. Salter (ed.) *Treating Child Sex Offenders and Victims: A Practical Guide* (pp. 131–70). Newbury Park, CA: Sage.

Pithers, W.D., Marques, J.K., Gibat, C.C. & Marlatt, G.A. (1983). Relapse prevention with sexual aggressives: a self-control model of treatment and the maintenance of change. In J.G. Greer & I.R. Stuart (eds) *The Sexual Aggressor: Current Perspectives on Treatment* (pp. 214–39). New York: Van Nostrand Reinhold.

Prins, H., Tennant, G. & Trick, K. (1985). Motives for arson (fireraising). *Medicine, Science and the Law*, **25**, 275–8.

Rice, M.E. & Chaplin, T.C. (1979). Social skills training for hospitalised male arsonists. *Journal of Behaviour Therapy and Experimental Psychiatry*, **10**, 105–8.

Robertson, G. (1981). The extent and pattern of crime amongst mentally handicapped offenders. *Apex, Journal of the British Institute of Mental Handicap*, **9**, 100–3.

Royer, F.L., Flynn, W.F. & Osadca, B.S. (1971). Case history: aversion therapy for firesetting by a deteriorated schizophrenic. *Behaviour Therapy*, **2**, 229–32.

Simpson, M.K. & Hogg, J. (2001). Patterns of offending among people with intellectual disability: a systematic review. Part I: methodology and prevalence data. *Journal of Intellectual Disability Research*, **45**, 384–96.

Skett, S. (1995). What works in the reduction of offending behaviour? *Forensic Update*, **42**, 20–7.

Smith, J. & Short, J. (1995). Mentally disordered firesetters. *British Journal of Hospital Medicine*, **53**(4), 136–40.

Swaffer, T. Haggett, M. & Oxley, T. (2001). Mentally disordered firesetters: a structured intervention programme. *Clinical Psychology and Psychotherapy*, **8**, 468–75.

Taylor, J.L. & Novaco, R.W. (1999). *Treatment of anger control problems in people with developmental disability: a manual for therapists.* Unpublished manuscript, Northgate & Prudhoe NHS Trust.

Wolff, R. (1984). Satiation in the treatment of inappropriate firesetting. *Journal of Behaviour Therapy and Experimental Psychiatry*, **15**, 337–40.

Yalom, I. (1975). *The Theory and Practice of Group Psychotherapy*, 2nd edn. New York: Basic Books.

Chapter 13

OFFENDERS WITH DUAL DIAGNOSIS

Anne H.W. Smith* and Gregory O'Brien[†]
* NHS Tayside, Dundee, UK
[†] Northgate & Prudhoe NHS Trust, Northumberland and University of Northumbria, Newcastle upon Tyne, UK

Dual diagnosis refers to the co-occurrence of a mental illness and intellectual disability. The recognition of the existence of mental illness in this population and interest in the understanding of its clinical presentation and treatment have been described over the past three decades. Although it is accepted that mental illnesses are more common than in the general population, prevalence rates reported vary depending largely on the population studied.

This chapter reviews the relationship between intellectual disability, mental illness and offending. It falls in two parts. The first part deals with major mental illness, and drug and alcohol abuse. The second part reviews neuropsychiatric considerations and pervasive developmental disorders, such as autism and attention deficit hyperactivity disorder.

MENTAL ILLNESS, AND DRUG AND ALCOHOL ABUSE

This section will begin by reviewing the prevalence of mental illness and intellectual disability separately in offenders. We will then review the prevalence of mental illness in people with intellectual disabilities and further review the prevalence of mental illness in the population of offenders with intellectual disabilities. We will then investigate separately the clinical aspects of offenders with intellectual disabilities who are dually diagnosed with mood disorder, schizophrenia or substance abuse. Throughout this part of the chapter we will comment on the management of these clients and note the tolerance in the community of mental illness and intellectual disability in offenders.

Offenders with Developmental Disabilities. Edited by W.L. Lindsay, J.L. Taylor and P. Sturmey.
© 2004 John Wiley & Sons, Ltd.

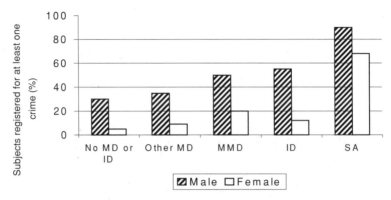

Figure 13.1   The results of Hodgins (1992) showing the relationship between gender and mental disorder (MD), major mental disorder (MMD), intellectual disability (ID) and substance abuse (SA) on prevalence of offending

Prevalence of Dual Diagnosis

For decades professionals and others have accepted the premise that individuals with mental illness or intellectual disability are more likely to offend than others. Hodgins (1992) conducted a large-scale study in Sweden which gave some support to this hypothesis. Hodgins prospectively studied a birth cohort of 15,117 individuals for 30 years. He made comparisons between men and women with no mental disorder or intellectual disability, those with major mental disorders (mood disorder and schizophrenia), other mental disorders, intellectual disability and substance abuse. Subjects were classified based on the main psychiatric diagnosis made following an episode of in-patient care. Individuals categorised as having an intellectual disability were defined as those people included in special classes in high school with no admission to a psychiatric ward.

The results of this study are shown in Figure 13.1. Men with major mental disorders were 2.5 times more likely to commit crime than men with no disorder. They were also 4.5 times more likely to be violent offenders. Similarly, women with mental illness were over-represented 5-fold for all offences and 27-fold for violent offences. Male offenders with intellectual disability were over-represented 3-fold for any offence and 5-fold for a violent offence as compared with non-intellectually disabled offenders. Women offenders were over-represented 4-fold for any offence among those with intellectual disability and 25-fold for a violent offence.

While this is an extremely useful piece of research in estimating the relevance of mental illness and intellectual disability to offending, it inevitably oversimplifies. People with intellectual disability, mental illness and problems with substance abuse do not represent mutually exclusive groups. In addition, the definition of intellectual disability (i.e. attending special classes in high school) is an inexact one. It may have been that a proportion of these individuals had an IQ in the borderline or low normal range which would place them outside the range of intellectual disability.

The increased prevalence of serious mental illness in the population of people with intellectual disabilities is also well documented. Estimates of the prevalence of mood disorder have been reasonably consistent. Reid (1972) found a prevalence of 1.2% in a hospital population of over 500 patients. Wright (1982) studied 1,507 adult residents and found a prevalence of 2.8%. Lund's (1985) community survey of 302 adults reported a prevalence of 1.7%. These figures compare with point prevalence figures in the general population of 4% for mood disorder (Kallman, 1953).

Epidemiological studies have also found reasonably consistent prevalence rates for schizophrenia in this client group. Turner (1989) reviewed nine English language studies published between 1968 and 1985 which reported point prevalences of 1.3% to 3.7%. For example, Heaton Ward (1977) found 3.4% of adults from an in-patient population of 1,251 to be suffering from schizophrenia. Reid (1972) reported a prevalence of 3.2%. Epidemiological studies of schizophrenia in the general population often yield a prevalence of approximately 0.5% (e.g. Jablensky, 2000; Jeffreys et al., 1997).

The literature suggests that offenders with intellectual disability have an even higher prevalence rate of mental illness than the population with intellectual disability who are not offenders. According to Day (1997), between 25% and 33% of sex offenders with intellectual disabilities have a history of mental illness. He comments further that the possibility of mental illness should always be explored since in a small proportion of such cases treatment of the illness may be all that is required to resolve the offending behaviour. Noriek and Grunfield (1998) reported an analysis of 3,343 forensic psychiatric examinations conducted between 1980 and 1996. They found that of the 294 patients diagnosed with intellectual disability, 25% also had a psychiatric disorder. Lindsay et al. (2002) studied 62 sex offenders and abusers with intellectual disability. They found that 32% had a psychiatric diagnosis of major mental illness. Smith, Quinn and Lindsay (2000) examined 153 consecutive referrals over an 8-year period. All patients were referred for sexual offences, sexual abuse, assault or aggressive behaviour or other severe challenging behaviours. The average IQ was 66.8 and the average age was 36.6 years; 22% of the sample had a serious mental illness. This rate is 7-fold higher than in non-offender populations with intellectual disability. They found 12% of the sample had a diagnosis of mood disorder and 10% had a diagnosis of schizophrenia.

Mood Disorders

The prevalence of mood disorder per se in this population is greater than that found in the general population and more prevalent in those who offend. Most offenders suffer from mild or moderate intellectual disability and the clinical presentation of depression and mania is similar to that observed in general psychiatric patients. Fundamental to a diagnosis of a mood disorder is a change in mood, which may be either depressed or elated. There is a wide range of associated signs and symptoms critical in recognising the condition.

Depressed patients may not describe depression but show signs of misery and be unable to maintain their usual mood state throughout the day. Mood change can be inferred from loss of interest or pleasure in activities previously enjoyed or from social withdrawal. Irritability is invariably present when there are no signs suggestive of depressed mood (Royal College of Psychiatrists, 2001). In addition they may be mentally or physically slowed, have poor concentration, or slowed thought processes. They may have other physical signs such as poor sleep with early morning wakening, a poor appetite and constipation. Patients may complain of a variety of physical symptoms and may neglect themselves. Aggression is common and has been observed in up to 40% of intellectually disabled depressed individuals (Reiss & Rojahn, 1994). Rarely, when at their deepest level of depression, they may experience delusions consonant with their mood, such as a belief that they are dying or that something catastrophic might happen. Those with mild disability may describe hallucinations, which are usually auditory but hardly ever visual. They may report hearing derogatory statements. It is usually difficult for individuals to convey directly all but the simplest symptoms apart from the most intellectually able. Concrete thinking, limited ability to conceptualise and limited communication skills may limit their ability to report symptoms. Sovner and Hurley (1990) labelled this "intellectual distortion". Usually symptoms have to be inferred from behaviour, particularly when there is a change from their norm.

In mainstream forensic psychiatry depression is linked with shoplifting, where no attempt is made to cover up the crime, and to altruistic extended suicide, both of which are rare (Guze, 1976). Neither has been reported in the forensic learning disability literature. The agitation and aggression commonly found with depression in the latter group can result in conflict with the law via aggressive behaviour, usually provoked by minor incidents. The disturbance and aggression may also be self-directed and result in self-injury or suicide attempts in those with mild disability.

Dysthymia, a lowering of mood not amounting to clinical depression, is a relatively common disorder in this population group (Day, 1990). It may be interrupted by episodes of major depression usually precipitated by acute stress (Dosen & Gielen, 1993). This may occur as a reaction to their predicament or a response to the stress of confronting their offences. It is important that this is recognised and understood. It should not be construed as the development of insight or guilt. Treatment with antidepressant medication may be indicated and necessary to allow continued useful participation in therapeutic programmes.

Hypomanic patients present with an elevated or expansive mood often with an irritable demeanour. The irritability may present as verbal or physical aggression to minor real or perceived affronts (Royal College of Psychiatrists, 2001). In addition, individuals are commonly mentally and physically overactive and may experience impaired attention and concentration, often with rapid and disjointed speech. They may be overconfident, sometimes to the point of grandiosity. They need little sleep and may be too active or inattentive to eat or take care of themselves. Often loss of inhibitions lead to social over-familiarity and disinhibited behaviour. If severely mentally ill, they may experience delusions expressed in a simple form and of a grandiose or religious nature. They rarely have visual hallucinations. Poor judgement is also very common.

Some patients may present with an admixture of both manic and depressive symptoms. Mood may swing from high to low at intervals of varying frequency of days or weeks (Glue, 1989; Sovner & Pary, 1993). While it is difficult to miss the diagnosis in severely ill individuals, mild and moderate forms are much more common. The fluctuating nature of the condition may mean the individual may seem well when examined on one occasion but not on another. This might suggest an element of self-control, which may actually be absent. It is therefore essential that a careful corroborative history is taken as well as a detailed scrutiny of past records and close informed observation of behaviour over time if this diagnosis is not to be missed.

Hypomanic patients in mainstream forensic psychiatry commonly commit public order offences, theft and assault. This picture is also reflected in people with intellectual disabilities. Smith *et al.* (2000) compared 19 offenders diagnosed with mood disorder, 16 offenders diagnosed with schizophrenia and 115 subjects with no diagnosis of major mental illness. They found that mood disordered offender patients presented at an older age than other offenders. This is similar to findings in the general forensic psychiatry literature, where it is suggested that inmates with major mental disorders commit crimes later in life than those with no such disorder (Hodgins & Cote, 1990). These patients also had a lower IQ than offenders with no mental illness. Also, those diagnosed with mood disorder had an average performance IQ of 57, which was approximately 10 IQ points lower than those diagnosed with schizophrenia and those with no mental illness diagnosis. It is intriguing that the opposite was found in a sample of intellectually disabled sex offenders (Murray *et al.*, 2001). In this study non-offenders' verbal IQ was higher than the offenders' verbal IQ. There was no difference between the two groups' non-verbal IQs. Although the group with mood disorder were tested when thought to be mentally well, it may be that there were residual symptoms which affected their performance. This study also observed that in the group without mental illness the sex ratio was 7.5:1 in favour of males, whereas in the group with a mood disorder it was 4:1.

Smith *et al.* (2000) reported that those subjects with a diagnosis of hypomania who committed assault were less likely to reoffend than offenders with no mental illness. This suggests that there may have been an influence of the illness on reoffending. Reoffending rates in the group without mental illness was 17% for sex offenders and 42% for other types of offenders. In the group with mood disorders 11% reoffended. The difference in non-sexual offending was considerable. Although the mood disordered patients were less likely than others to commit a sexual offence and had a reduced chance of reoffending, that was not the case with offences against children. The reoffending rates in these cases were equal to those with intellectual disability alone. This suggests that the illness was, if at all, only in part relevant to the crime.

In those individuals with rapid cycling mood disorder the crime of sexual harassment is substantially over-represented. Smith *et al.* (2000) found that three of seven reported cases of severe and repeated harassment had this diagnosis. In many ways there are clinical similarities in intensity of interest to cases of stalking described in the mainstream forensic field with an intense interest and drive to repeat the offence. McGuire and Wraith (2000) found an associated psychiatric diagnosis to be unusual in individuals convicted of stalking, although Kienlen, Birmingham, Solberg, O'Regan and Meloy (1997) also found a diagnosis of serious psychiatric disorder in 8 out of 26 cases.

Treatment of mood disorders

Treatment of mood disorders in offenders with intellectual disabilities should follow that used in conventional psychiatric practice. The prescription of mood stabilising drugs for those patients whose mood remains elevated or fluctuating represents the treatment of choice. Where compliance is problematic depot neuroleptic medication is a useful alternative. Anti-depressant medication is indicated if clinical signs of depression persist. Once recovered, supportive psychotherapy, to help gain an understanding of the illness and issues related to offending, is vital if symptoms are to be recognised in the future and their possible relevance to further offending understood. This is particularly so for sex offenders, but also for those guilty of assault. Although reoffending rates are better in mood disordered than non-mentally-ill patients, other than sex offences against children, a significant proportion of clients continue to offend once well (Smith *et al.*, 2000).

Case example

Mr Bergman was the youngest of six children. His parents separated during his infancy and he ended up in many and varied homes. He was bullied, exposed to violence and sexually abused in at least one setting during his adolescence. He was a farm worker for three years and became itinerant with several brief in-patient spells in learning disability hospitals. Medical records described him variously as happy and outgoing, likeable, a seeker of self-gratification, showing unpredictable and aggressive outbursts.

He settled in a local authority flat. Two local boys were found there and reported to the police that he had masturbated in front of them. He was described in a court report as theatrical, loud and disinhibited, but with no psychiatric illness. He was jailed for six months. He did not adjust well and was referred for a psychological opinion. Assessment revealed a full scale IQ of 69, a verbal IQ of 63 and a performance IQ of 70. He talked a lot with no content. A sexual attitudes questionnaire revealed a high score for paedophilia and homosexual rape. After challenging Mr Bergman's account of his actions his probation officer described him as one of the most frightening and aggressive men he had ever seen. He felt that Mr Bergman would target young boys.

During assessment Mr Bergman was jolly and composed. However, after a few weeks he became edgy for no apparent reason. He was easily offended, overactive and restless. His sleep was disturbed and he lost weight. He became increasingly uncooperative. Finally, he exploded over a minor issue involving a train ticket, was physically restrained and detained under the Mental Health Act. His old notes gave a history of symptoms of hypomania, a positive family history of mood disorder and schizophrenia in his estranged maternal family and a more recent history of episodic disturbance. He was treated with major tranquillisers and a mood-stabilising drug and made a slow but sure response. His probation officer, so struck by the force of his previous aggressive behaviour, refused to accept the diagnosis and persisted in challenging him, to his cost. He was involved in sex offender and anger management programmes with a definite shift in attitudes. He quickly picked up a basic level of domestic skills. He was discharged two years later to his own flat. This was unsuccessful due to financial exploitation. He remains a vulnerable and easily led man. However, he has married, lives in a makeshift but acceptable manner and remains mentally well with no hint to date of a significant recurrence of mental illness or offending. Continued contact with the service is encouraged.

Schizophrenia

The diagnosis of schizophrenia in its early stages can be difficult in both the general population and in people with intellectual disabilities. Often, it is only with the benefit of hindsight that earlier unusual behaviour can be recognised as part of a schizophrenic process. Reiss and Szyszko (1983) demonstrated that even experienced professionals were more likely to miss the diagnosis of schizophrenia in the presence of intellectual disability. Psychiatric symptoms were often attributed to circumstantial or constitutionally driven behaviour. During adolescence schizophrenia often presents as poor performance in the educational system, irritability and aggression. Truanting is often misconstrued as being due to intellectual or adjustment difficulties. There may be no overt psychotic symptoms, such as hallucinations. The individual may progress to a highly disorganised lifestyle, including criminal activity, before coming to the attention of services. Even then the diagnosis may be missed and any vulnerability or oddness may only be first noticed within the prison setting.

Classical clinical features are present in acute psychotic states, with delusions and hallucinations being common. Their simplicity may reflect the limited life experience of this population, which is described by Sovner and Hurley (1990) as psychological masking. Auditory hallucinations are the most frequent symptom. Meadows *et al.* (1991) reported that 90% of patients with intellectual disabilities and schizophrenia presented with auditory hallucinations. Ideas of reference, especially from the television, are common. Those patients who are paranoid may in the early stages display an unusual degree of touchiness or super-sensitivity. This can extend to full-blown delusional beliefs of persecution. A delusion is defined as a false belief which is firm and unshakeable (Royal College of Psychiatrists, 2001). However the level of compliance common in the learning disabled population can mean that an individual may be persuaded of the apparent nonsense of their ideas. They will, however, repeatedly return to their beliefs and an open approach must be taken at interview. It is understandable that such patients will respond badly to cajoling or teasing if, driven by their beliefs, they make bizarre statements or behave strangely. Thought disorder may present as disorganised thinking or apparent lack of attention or interest with sudden breaks in speech or attention. It requires skilled observation to elicit thought disorder in this population. The patient's mood is often incongruent and it may be wrongly perceived as lacking empathy or understanding in the context of offending. In many patients the diagnosis is not evident at the time of referral. It may only become clear during contact with services months or even years later, a finding reflected in criminals of average intellectual ability (Taylor, 1985).

Short-term psychotic states lasting days or weeks with sudden onset in response to stress are well recognised in the general population. They are much more common in young patients with intellectual disability (Sovner, 1986). The pattern is of full recovery and frequent recurrence in susceptible individuals. The possibility of this diagnosis must be borne in mind when seeking a diagnosis in the offender group.

Smith *et al.* (2000) found that offenders with schizophrenia referred to their service were, as expected, younger than other offenders. They found no difference in IQ when compared with non-mentally-ill offenders with intellectual disabilities. This was in spite of the reported cognitive decline in established schizophrenia (Cannon *et al.*, 1994). This suggests that referral should be made at as early a stage in the illness as possible. Violence, often of a severe nature, is known to be associated with schizophrenia. Humphreys, Johnstone, MacMillan and Taylor (1992) also found that at first admission, non-intellectually-disabled offenders with schizophrenia presented at a young age and were particularly violent. Smith *et al.* (2000) reported that offenders with intellectual disability and schizophrenia were more likely than those with mood disorder to have committed a violent offence. This group had a lower but significant reoffending rate compared to those violent offenders with no psychiatric diagnosis. This suggests that treatment of the illness is an important, but not sufficient, intervention.

General forensic psychiatry literature suggests that the presence of acute symptoms, rather than their nature, and the early years of the illness rather than the later years seem to be related to more violence. This observation might be relevant and worthy of consideration and investigation in offenders with intellectual disability (McNeill, 1994). Steadman *et al.* (1998) noted the associations between schizophrenia, drug abuse and violence. (This is discussed later in the context of substance abuse.)

Smith *et al.* (2000) found that 44% of schizophrenic patients compared with 52% of those with no diagnosis had committed a sexual offence, but were marginally less likely to reoffend (12% versus 17%). As with mood-disordered patients, those who had committed sex offences involving children were as likely to reoffend as the non-mentally-ill group. As with mainstream sex offenders with schizophrenia (Craissati & Hodes, 1992), the offences took place in the early part of the illness when more florid symptoms were not evident. This raises the possibility of an early breakdown of inhibitory controls.

Treatment of schizophrenia

Once the diagnosis has been made, standard psychiatric treatment should be instituted. This should include anti-psychotic medication, especially the newer anti-psychotic drugs. Response to medication is variable. Individual recovery from the first episode is usual with active treatment, but there is a risk of relapse. A good initial response may not persist and a series of medications may have to be tried. Each drug should be introduced slowly. The dose should be increased depending on response and tolerance and only changed after several weeks of non-response. Clozapine should be prescribed for those who fail to respond to two or three other psychotropic medications. Unfortunately, a small proportion of individuals prove treatment resistant. Some may show a rapid decline with the onset of negative symptoms while still in their twenties. These individuals will require long-term care. Whenever their mental state permits, patients should continue to be involved in all aspects of a comprehensive offender programme for both offences involving violence and sex offences since the relationship between illness and offending is not simple.

Case example

Mr Allen first came to the attention of the offender service when he was referred at the age of 17. He was referred for assessment of his mental state from the medical wing of the local prison. It was his second stay on remand and the prison officer had noticed deterioration in his condition, with social withdrawal and intense anxiety. Mr Allen offered no specific symptoms other than a free-floating anxiety and feeling of intense unease. He was prescribed a major tranquilliser, settled and claimed to feel better than he had for some considerable time.

He had a history of childhood behavioural difficulties and delayed milestones. He truanted from special classes at school for several years, ran a way from home and slept rough. He survived largely by prostituting himself with older men. He was placed in a children's home at the age of 15. When there he was observed to make shrieking noises. He spoke to himself, made inappropriate sexual advances to young children and intimidated staff. He was finally charged after approaching young girls in the city and placed on probation. One year later he was charged again after stalking an older woman.

Attempts to manage him as a day patient failed. He continued to offend and was admitted for assessment. Initially no clear diagnosis was made. He was prescribed anti-psychotic medication on a clinical basis. He responded well, although he could only tolerate small doses of the older anti-psychotic medications. When off medication, his thinking became muddled and he became threatening and aggressive. He became preoccupied by a female patient. He reported obsessive thoughts about her with sexual and aggressive content. At times he held beliefs, not substantiated by fact and bordering on the delusional, about her infidelity. This led to aggressive acts towards her and those he felt were involved with her.

He was detained under the Mental Health Act. He was treated with a variety of newer medications and took part in anger management and sex offender groups when his thought processes were clear enough. He made good progress. When he was 21 years old he was assessed as suitable for discharge to staffed accommodation and a day patient programme in the community. He ostensibly looked forward to discharge. However, without any warning he left the ward and seriously sexually assaulted a young teenager in broad daylight in full view of the public. Since being detained through the courts his mental state has continued to fluctuate with an overall pattern of steady deterioration.

This man suffers from early onset schizophrenia presenting as a serious conduct disorder in childhood with teenage offending. The course of the illness was fluctuating and deteriorating. His most serious offence took place when he was apparently at his best from the psychiatric and psychological perspective.

Substance Misuse

Hodgins (1992) describes the influence of substance abuse on offending. It is noteworthy that 90% of offenders were found to abuse substances. Substance abuse is predominant when considered against other factors such as mental illness and intellectual disability. The association between alcohol and drugs and crime is well known. Offenders who abuse substances turn to crime to feed their habit: as many as 70% of habitual criminals have been reported to misuse alcohol (Persilia, Greenwood & Lavin, 1978).

Habitual drunken offenders pose particular problems in mainstream forensic psychiatry (Higgins, 2001). This is directly reflected in clinical experience in those patients who have learning disability, abuse alcohol and offend. Alcohol education is critical for individuals who may have had little, if any, opportunity to learn about alcohol use during their development (Lindsay, Allen, Walker, Lawrenson & Smith, 1991). Unfortunately, those who persist with heavy drinking may continue to offend repeatedly and become unmanageable in current community treatment settings.

Problems of substance abuse are common in offender populations (Davidson, Humphreys, Johnstone & Ovens, 1995). The co-existence of schizophrenia, substance misuse and offending is a common finding worldwide (Chiswick, 2000). The adverse influence of substance abuse on the management and treatment of serious mental illness, the increasing prevalence of drug-induced psychosis and the precipitation or exacerbation of co-existent schizophrenia will all further influence an already complex picture. The higher prevalence of schizophrenia in the intellectually disabled population as a whole, and even higher prevalence in offenders with intellectual disability, is a cause for concern.

In a study of 294 forensic examinations of offenders with intellectual disability, Noriek and Grunfield (1998) found substance abuse to be rare. However, in a review by Ashton (2002), involving young people between the ages of 18 and 25 years in the UK, the USA, New Zealand, and some European countries, some 40–60% have some experience of cannabis use. She reported that the age of first experience is falling and the dose and frequency of abuse is increasing. It seems likely that substance abuse of this type will become more prevalent in people with intellectual disability. Several studies have now reported illegal and problematic use of alcohol and use of illicit substances among teenagers with mild and moderate intellectual disabilities (Pack, Wallander & Browne, 1998). Many cannabis users quit in their mid-twenties (Von Sydow *et al.*, 2001), but this pattern may not necessarily be reflected in people with intellectual disability, whose opportunities for stability and broadening of interest and responsibility in early adulthood are often restricted. In addition to the deleterious effects on mental health, the association between mental illness and substance abuse with violent behaviour is now well established (Steadman *et al.*, 1998), further increasing the risk of offending in an already vulnerable group. Treatment of substance-related disorders in people with intellectual disabilities may take place in some community and in-patient settings. For some clients in-patient treatment may be necessary to ensure their safety and to provide supervised treatment.

Tolerance of Offending and Psychiatric Symptomatology

In our experience, there is an acceptance and an under-reporting of inappropriate sexual behaviour in children and young people with intellectual disability. It is often not until the young person reaches late adolescence or young adulthood that concerns are voiced. At this point such behaviour has either persisted or escalated; an opportunity for treatment has been missed. Lyall, Holland and Collins (1995) found extremely high tolerance of levels of offending in some hostels, group homes and day centres. The majority of staff indicated that they would not report a major assault. Only a very small minority would report a sexual offence. Some staff would not report rape or would do so only after serious consideration. Charman and Clare (1992) reported on men who had committed multiple offences and the criminal justice system had failed to respond to these early offences.

In a similar way, there can be an acceptance of even extensive psychiatric symptomatology by those caring for clients with intellectual disability. Bizarre behaviour or delusions can be accepted and tolerated as eccentricity or just part of having an intellectual disability. Sovner (1986) described four factors that may minimise the recognition of mental illnesses in people with intellectual disabilities. Intellectual distortion includes concrete thinking and impaired communication skills. Psychosocial masking includes impoverished social skills and life experiences. Stress-induced disruption of information processing can lead to cognitive disintegration, which can present as mental illness. Finally, baseline exaggeration refers to an increase in severity of pre-existing cognitive deficits and maladaptive behaviours. These factors can lead to a missed diagnosis. This can often be a highly relevant factor in the offending pattern. It can lead to further under-reporting of criminal activity.

Day (1993) speculated that there may be a rise in offending by people with intellectual disability as the freedom of community care gives rise to greater opportunities and as offences that were hidden, tolerated or under-reported in institutions become more visible. The unintentional disregard of this issue may become increasingly common as inexperienced carers are employed in rapidly expanding community developments caring for increasingly complex individuals.

Case example

Mr Torrence came to the notice of the adult offender service when the Children's Panel asked for a report from clinical psychology. He was 17 years old and lived alone in a flat with a substantial professional supportive network. He had committed innumerable offences over many years dating from his early teens. These offences were mainly breach of the peace and assault leading to special residential schooling with contact with adolescent social work and psychiatry services.

His presentation at interview for preparation for the report was perplexing to the psychologist. His concentration was variable and his demeanour odd. The most disconcerting feature was an inappropriate affect with episodes of incongruent but humourless laughter leading to referral for a psychiatric opinion. Prior to the assessment staff described him as likeable, limited, variably cooperative and un-usual. They went on to describe fluctuating mood with unpredictable episodes of aggression: he had a routine which they tampered with at their peril. He talked of aggressive acts and fire-raising. He was fascinated by September 11th, creating models and re-enacting the event. He was preoccupied by a television series, fanta-sising that he was the most aggressive character. On one occasion he had barricaded a female member of staff in his flat, said that he was chosen by God and was invin-cible. He had made disturbing sexual inferences in conversation with female staff. It later transpired that he had done the same in the past with elderly females relatives although they never felt threatened by him. He became extremely disturbed and aggressive when the assessment was arranged. He had to be detained under the Mental Health Act to allow the assessment to proceed. A diagnosis of schizophre-nia was made. Shortly after his admission to hospital, a meeting of those involved in his community care decided to terminate his tenancy, leaving him homeless.

This example illustrates a case of early onset schizophrenia with an early history of multiple crimes, often involving violence from early teenage years. He developed acute, florid psychotic symptoms, the seriousness of which was missed without appreciation of the very real danger he presented if untreated. He was tolerated but not treated. Once diagnosed, he lost his home and community support. In our experience, such withdrawal of domestic placement and community services for offenders who have mental illness is not uncommon.

Management of Offenders with Dual Diagnosis

There are new challenges to be met in the management of offenders with intel-lectual disability and mental illness. Some are positive, as in the advances in the management of major mental illness with, for example, the evidence base for the newer anti-psychotic drugs. Others are negative, such as the potential influence of substance abuse on both offending and mental health. Since it is likely that any intellectual disability offender service has a significant minority of patients likely to be suffering from mental illness at any one time, these challenges cannot be ig-nored. They need to be met imaginatively in any service dealing with this particular complex group of individuals.

Best psychiatric practice is germane to the management of the individual with intellectual disability and mental illness who offends. Effective treatment may re-duce and sometimes obviate the risk of offending, but it does not eradicate it. Although when acutely ill patients may not be accessible to psychological treat-ment approaches due to impaired concentration or thought disorder, this is likely to be for relatively short periods of time in the context of offender programmes. Apart from the minority of clients who offend only when ill, there is another poten-tially worrying group who may be disorganised when ill. They may be more likely to be apprehended, but are more organised when well and therefore potentially more dangerous on recovery. It is worth reiterating that Smith, Quinn and Lindsay (2000) found that both patients with mood disorder and schizophrenia and those with intellectual disability alone are equally likely to offend against children and with the same amount of violence. Even after successful psychiatric treatment many continued to offend. Other than in the very small number of cases of severe psychosis, it is critical that patients remain responsible for their offence.

In a literature review of men with intellectual disabilities who sexually abuse, Brown and Thompson (1997) found no direct correlation with mental illness and offending. They questioned a role for the medical model in this field. However, Krakowski, Jaeger and Volvaka (1988) showed that in an eight-week stay psychotic patients showed a reduction in violent behaviour as symptoms subsided for the first four weeks but not the second half. This improvement in social functioning was paralleled by a decrease in violence throughout the eight weeks. It would seem that an integration of models rather than an artificial demarcation between them should prevail.

Staff should include those with the awareness and ability to both diagnose and treat mental illness. They should also address other issues, such as sex offending, anger and substance abuse and maintaining. Occupational, social and educational interventions are also important elements of a service. There should be the flexibility to withdraw and re-enter patients to specific psychological treatments when necessary. This is particularly important in view of the lengthy spells of treatment required for any useful change to occur in a regime, which can of itself be stressful (Lindsay & Smith, 1998). There should be an educational component, so that those involved with this group in the community are sufficiently aware of psychiatric symptomatology to recognise when to seek advice at as early a stage as possible.

There is current debate regarding attempts to disentangle what is the effective component in treatment programmes, particularly those aimed at managing sex offenders (Jahoda, 2002). Jahoda pointed out that the model proposed by Lindsay *et al.* (2002) renders the elucidation of the effective component in treatment programmes for offenders impossible. Perhaps empirical research will focus on the development of prospective studies as new innovative treatment approaches are introduced.

Summary and Conclusions

This section has reviewed issues involved in those offenders with the dual diagnosis of intellectual disability and mental illness. Studies have revealed that mental illness is several times over-represented in the population of people with intellectual disability as a whole. This over-representation is even greater among offenders with intellectual disability. Effective treatment may remove but usually reduces the risk of offending. Therefore, pharmacological treatment of the illness is not sufficient for the effective management of most offenders, particularly sex offenders involving children and offenders convicted of arson. Indeed, effective pharmacological treatment may allow the individual to be better organised when well and therefore potentially more risky in that they are more able to plan an offence. The management of problems related to the interplay between drug addiction, offending and mental illness requires to be addressed now in anticipation of a growing problem reflected in that scene in mainstream offenders. The detrimental effect of tolerance of offenders with intellectual disability, including those without mental illness, needs to be recognised at both an individual and policy making level. Also noted in this section is a less reported tendency for particularly problematic offenders with intellectual disability to lose their community placement and community support when admitted to hospital for protracted periods of treatment. The literature and our experience would suggest that management of these patients should be in an inclusive interdisciplinary setting.

NEUROPSYCHIATRIC CONSIDERATIONS

In this section, it is proposed that a neuropsychiatric approach to the clinical assessment of adult offenders with intellectual disability can yield useful insights into the understanding of offending behaviour in this population. Such a neuropsychiatric approach is introduced through consideration of two major common neuropsychiatric disorders: autism and attention deficit hyperactive disorder (ADHD). In the general population these disorders are more familiar in child rather than adult practice, but they are also seen in the population of adults with intellectual disabilities. Through consideration of the behaviour and social functioning of affected individuals, the role of such disorders in the aetiology of offending behaviour is explored. In addition, the importance of giving attention to the cause of the individual's intellectual disability is emphasised by the potential contribution to offending of behavioural phenotypes and neurodegenerative disorders. Throughout this section, it is emphasised that attempts to identify simple direct links between such medical disorders and antisocial behaviour are unhelpful. As demonstrated in the present text, much of the clinical response to the offending behaviour of adults with intellectual disability is informed by consideration of other influences on behaviour, which in turn operate at personal, family, wider environmental and societal levels. In addition, a holistic clinical approach to the offending behaviour of adults with intellectual disabilities is enhanced by attention to any predisposition to offending behaviour. The contribution of any coincident organic brain syndrome, which may exert an influence on behaviour, and the role of diagnosable disorders, such as autism and ADHD, should also be considered.

Autism

Autism and the associated autistic spectrum disorders are characterised by three core pathognomonic features: impaired social reciprocity, impaired communication, and the presence of a restricted, repetitive repertoire of interest or behaviours (WHO, 1992). While autism commonly occurs in individuals with intellectual disability, the diagnosis relies on the triad of impairments being of a greater magnitude than can be explained or expected by the given degree of intellectual disability. The available evidence suggests a prevalence of around 5–10% in people with mild intellectual disability (IQ 50–69), and up to 30% in those with moderate to severe intellectual disability (Steffenburg, Gillberg & Steffenburg, 1996). In line with the move towards higher prevalence rates among the general population (Le Couteur et al., 1996; Rutter, 1982), more recent studies of autism in people with intellectual disabilities have reported higher prevalence rates than previous estimates (Wolf-Schein, 1996).

Autism and offending

Violence, aggression and other antisocial offending behaviours are not uncommon in autism (Baron-Cohen, 1988; Scragg & Shah, 1994). One longstanding impression, based partly on the classical clinical descriptions of autistic spectrum disorder (Asperger, 1944; Kanner, 1943), is that offending by people affected by autism has a bizarre quality which may reflect the core features of the disorder. Some of the notable contributions to the understanding of offending behaviour in autism have been made by Wing (1982). She emphasised the lack of empathy inherent in the condition, which may be important in the genesis of offending in autism. Tantam (1988) commented on the apparent unaccountability of many of the aggressive episodes of people with autism. The actions of people with autism are not easily understandable.

A useful synthesis has been elaborated by Howlin (1997), who has proposed that offending and aggression in autism might arise by four means. First, people with autism, because of their social naivete, may be led into criminal acts by others. For example, in the movie *Rain Man*, the card counting in the casino is carried out by the autistic individual at the suggestion of his brother. Second, aggressive behaviours can arise from a disruption of routines or changes in daily circumstances in individuals with autism. This is commonly seen in clinical practice with adults with intellectual disability who are affected by autism. There are many examples of family and professional carers who have borne the brunt of severe assaults when an autistic individual's daily routine is disturbed. Third, antisocial behaviours in autism can relate to a lack of understanding or misinterpretation of social cues. One scenario is where an autistic individual misinterprets a polite social encounter as a wish to form a friendship, to which (s)he replies with an awkward or clumsy attempt to form a relationship, only to be rebuffed. Such a rebuttal can quickly provoke violence. Finally, antisocial or criminal behaviours in autism may result from obsessions. This phenomenon is largely responsible for the longstanding observation that some of the offending behaviour of autism has a bizarre or inexplicable quality. For example, a man with autism had a lifelong interest in cars which led to him having in excess of 20 convictions for theft of vehicles. Sadly, he also fits into the first category described above. Much of his theft of vehicles had been suggested by others—indeed, had been to others' material advantage, rather than his own. Offending behaviour which arises from obsessions may be a cause for great concern and where this does present, the behaviour can be particularly refractory and enduring.

Management of the individual offender with intellectual disability and autism

The diagnosis of autism may be an aid to understanding how the offending behaviour has arisen. It may also be a pointer towards appropriate therapeutic intervention and case management. If we consider Howlin's (1997) typology of offending behaviour in autism, there are important implications for intervention and case management. The following will follow the categories outlined above. First, where there is good evidence that the individual with intellectual disability and autism has been steered into criminal acts through the direction of others, primed by innate social naivete and lack of empathic understanding of the consequences of their actions, then this is important. It can often be argued that the greatest need in such cases, and the most effective intervention, is to redirect the individual into a new peer group. While in normal circumstances this may be difficult to implement, it is quite conceivable to do this as part of the response to a criminal offence. Through the instigation of a new pattern of personal supervision and escort, expedited by a statutory legal order such as a probation order or equivalent, the client may be facilitated towards more socially acceptable patterns of behaviour. Second, where aggression has arisen as a result of disruption of obsessional behaviour or routine, then all concerned are well advised to avoid this, unless there is a structured behavioural plan to address modifying routines. When dealing with such cases, it is well to remember that obsessions can often be shaped. Many routines can be changed. It is equally important not to attempt to do this suddenly, but gently, accepting the individual's own potential pace for change and to anticipate that some routines in individual cases will endure.

Third, where offending appears to be closely linked to a major misunderstanding of social cues, one element of a coherent service response might be based on a social skills development programme. Such an intervention may not be straightforward in an individual who is both of low intelligence and lacks empathic appreciation of the needs of others. One useful strategy is to focus on the need for the individual to accept social rules and act upon them. This may seem to be at variance with certain more orthodox social skills acquisition-based approaches to offending behaviour, which often rely on the individual's capacity to take the perspectives of others. But given the inherent incapacities of the individual, such an approach is more pragmatic and liable to succeed. Finally, where offending is driven by obsessions, and where behaviour is particularly antisocial or dangerous this can be the most difficult to treat and only a very structured directive regime may succeed. Occasionally, it is possible to reduce obsessional thinking and behaviour through therapeutic intervention. One possibility may be to employ cognitive behavioural approaches, as described elsewhere in the present text. Another option is to use medication. Here the most recent evidence is that even refractory obsessional thinking may be reduced through the use of more recently introduced atypical anti-psychotic drugs (Barnard, Young, Pearson, Geddes & O'Brien, 2002).

In summary, understanding the mechanisms at play in the offending behaviour of any one individual with intellectual disability affected by autistic spectrum disorder relies on an appreciation of the nature of autism. Here, Howlin's contribution has been pivotal and facilitates the development of an appropriate service response.

Intellectual Disability and ADHD

A high prevalence of ADHD might be expected among people with intellectual disability. Deficits in concentration and attention are present in many people with

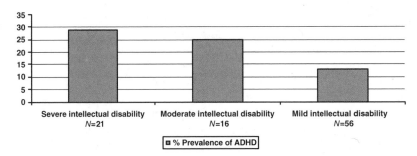

Figure 13.2 The percentage prevalence of ADHD in young adults with a history of childhood intellectual disability ($N = 93$)

intellectual disabilities. However, some individuals may have deficits in attention which are substantially in excess of that which can be accounted for by their more widespread general intellectual disability. Such deficits are identifiable on detailed neuropsychological assessment. Furthermore, restless, overactive behaviour is much more common than in the general population. This is increasingly so in more individuals with more severe intellectual disabilities. Any pattern of overactive behaviour to be included as a diagnostic criterion for ADHD must substantially exceed that to be expected for the individual's level of disability. For the diagnosis of ADHD to be made in the adult with intellectual disability, there must be a clinical syndrome of inattention, impulsivity and overactivity, which is out of keeping with the overall developmental level.

Much of the available data on prevalence of ADHD comes from child research. While the prevalence of ADHD among children of average IQ has been found to lie between 3% and 9% (Anderson, Williams, McGee & Silva, 1987; McArdle, O'Brien & Kolvin, 1995; Taylor, Sandberg, Thorley & Giles, 1991), one major American study (Epstein, Cullinam & Gadow, 1986) found the prevalence of ADHD in children with intellectual disability aged 6 to 11 years to be approximately 20%. O'Brien (2000) looked at rates of hyperactivity in a community sample of 148 young adults aged 18–22 years old who had a childhood diagnosis of intellectual disability. The rates of hyperactivity among these young adults increased markedly with increasing severity of intellectual disability as identified in childhood, from 13% in the mild intellectual disability group (IQ 50–69), through 25% in the moderate intellectual disability group (35–49), to 29% in the most severely disabled (IQ under 35) group (see Figure 13.2).

ADHD and offending

There is widespread evidence that individuals affected by ADHD are at higher risk for offending behaviour. Given the prevalence of ADHD in people with intellectual disability, and in particular the evidence of high rates persisting into adulthood, these considerations are of importance. Data here comes principally from studies of the comorbidity of ADHD, especially the co-occurrence of ADHD and conduct problems, and from studies of the outcome of ADHD, especially where outcome studies have included consideration of antisocial behaviour and offending.

There has been a century-long notion that hyperactivity, inattention and a wide variety of developmental disabilities and learning problems are linked in a meaningful way (Rutter, 1982; Sandberg, 1996). This broadly-based putative syndrome has been proposed to include not only those whose developmental disabilities constitute intellectual disability, but also other motor control deficits, and speech and language disorders. This theme has been developed and refined in Swedish studies, which have shown that attention deficits are usually comorbid with motor control problems, speech and language deficits, specific learning disorders, perceptual abnormalities and with other behavioural and psychiatric problems (Gillberg, 1983; Gillberg, Gillberg & Groth, 1989; Hellgren, Gillberg, Bagenholm & Gillberg, 1994). The Scandinavian concept of DAMP (deficits in attention, motor control and perception) is applied to conditions comprising both marked cross-situational attention deficits and motor control/perceptual problems (Gillberg, 1998). All cases of DAMP meet criteria for ADHD. Recent reports (Gillberg, 1998) of the long-term consequences of the DAMP group as identified in childhood have clarified that affected individuals are at a high risk for the development of antisocial behaviour and criminality in adulthood. Notably, all of these studies have emphasised the high rates of intellectual disability found among those diagnosed as DAMP. These studies suggest that ADHD is a risk factor for antisocial and offending behaviour among people with intellectual disability, and stress the importance of detection and diagnosis of this condition in clinical practice among adult offenders with intellectual disability. Given the occurrence of ADHD among adults with intellectual disability, it follows that careful consideration should be given to the possible role of ADHD in the offending behaviour of individual cases.

Management of offenders with intellectual disability and ADHD

Just as it was earlier argued in connection with the diagnosis of autism, the diagnosis of ADHD is an aid to understanding how the offending behaviour has arisen. On making the diagnosis, the first consideration is treatment of the condition. Where symptoms are situation-specific or transient, drug treatment is usually not warranted. Also, it is crucial to consider carefully the concept of developmental equivalence before embarking on drug treatment. In other words it is important to consider whether what is being observed is a reflection of overall developmental level and not a disorder as such. For adults with intellectual disability who are prone to be overactive and who have poor concentration, and where such a picture does not constitute ADHD, then drug treatment is not warranted. However, in classical cases of ADHD a trial of stimulant medication is warranted. Fortunately, it is now accepted that the response to medication is equally good in cases where an underlying syndrome is known to be the cause of both the individual's intellectual disability and ADHD (Harris, 1998).

In opting for a trial of stimulant medication, such as methylphenidate, for adults with intellectual disability who have offended, it is wise to recognise certain precautions and logistic issues. These include standard general medical considerations of individual metabolic tolerance of stimulant medication and the possibility of interactions with other prescribed medications. First, it should be emphasised to all concerned that this will be a trial and medication will only be continued if benefit has been seen. In our experience, less than half of all adults with intellectual disability who have ADHD will respond to stimulant medication. Helpfully, those cases who respond at all will usually show some response by two weeks into the medication trial. Improvements are commonly seen in levels of restlessness and in the capacity of the individual for sustained attention. In order to be clear about these effects, it is recommended that standard mechanisms of behavioural recording are adopted. It is also helpful to avoid other changes in the therapeutic plan while drug effects are being investigated. If no improvements are seen within, say, four weeks, then there is little point in continuing medication. On the other hand, where some significant benefit has been identified, but not perhaps fully sustained over time, then there is scope for adjustment of regime by increasing dose of medication, within the recommended standard prescribing limits of the preparation in question.

In opting to employ stimulant medication in the management of the adult with intellectual disability who has offended, it is crucial to emphasise that this will not in any sense be a panacea. However, just as ADHD predisposes to conduct disorder and offending, amelioration of ADHD symptoms renders the individual more amenable to the other therapeutic influences reviewed in the present text, notably offence-related therapies. Recognition and treatment of this condition is therefore recommended as part of the holistic management of the adult with intellectual disability who has offended.

Behavioural Phenotypes and Neurodegenerative Disorders

There are many examples of causes of intellectual disability which carry with them predispositions to more or less specific patterns of behaviour. This proposition can be of importance when we come to consider the predisposing factors to behaviour construed as offending. Such suggestions may have legal significance, might inform our general understanding of behaviours, such as antisocial acts, which constitute offences and might in some way contribute to our thinking in case management planning.

Aggression and aggressive propensities have been reported as a feature of the behavioural phenotype of certain causal syndromes of intellectual disability. There have been reports in respect of a few rare genetic conditions including Sotos (O'Brien, 2002) and Smith-Magenis (Greenberg et al., 1991) syndromes. Perhaps more than most other putative genotype–phenotype links, claims of this kind must be scrutinised very carefully, for the proposition that aggression might have such a genetic basis is highly controversial. What is clear is that in other situations, the site of intellectual disability, in terms of focal brain damage, may be an important predisposing factor to aggression. Where there is focal damage, in particular acquired frontal brain damage, aggression is a common problem. Also, aggression is commonly seen where brain damage is acquired or progressive. In clinical practice, a period of aggressive propensities may be seen over the course of neurodegenerative disorders as brain damage progresses, such as tuberous sclerosis (Hunt & Dennis, 1987). However, here it is the nature, site and disinhibiting effect of the central neurodegeneration which is implicated, rather than there being evidence of aggressive traits as part of the behavioural phenotype.

Problems identified in this way may not be remediable, in that even with careful management, the constitutional predispositions endure. However, this in turn can be crucially important for case management and therapeutic intervention. In some cases we may need to consider very carefully the possibility of the presence of enduring behavioural traits or propensities with underlying organic bases. Long-term plans should include limit setting accordingly. In others, the identification of specific cognitive or linguistic deficits of the behavioural phenotype in question may serve to emphasise the need to design interventions to suit the skills and deficits of the individual case.

Conclusion

A neuropsychiatric contribution to the clinical care of offenders with intellectual disability is described. It is proposed that consideration of two major, persistent disorders which are common in this population—autism and ADHD—can be informative in understanding offending, and can also inform the construction of a rational service response to some of the complex challenges posed by these individuals. This may be enhanced by consideration of the behavioural phenotype of the intellectual disability of the individual in question.

REFERENCES

Anderson, C., Williams, S., McGee, R. & Silva, P. (1987). DSM III disorders in preadolescent children: prevalence in a large sample from the general population. *Archives of General Psychiatry*, **44**, 69–76.

Ashton, H. (2002). Cannabis or health? *Current Opinion in Psychiatry*, **15**, 247–53.

Asperger, H. (1944). Die autischen psychopathen im kindesalter. *Archives fur Psychiatrie und Nervenkrankheiten*, **117**, 76–136.

Barnard, L., Young, A.H., Pearson, J., Geddes, J. & O'Brien, G. (2002). A systematic review of the use of atypical antipsychotics in autism. *Journal of Psychopharmacology*, **16**, 93–101.

Baron-Cohen, S. (1988). An assessment of violence in a young man with Asperger's syndrome. *Journal of Child Psychology and Psychiatry and Allied Disciplines*, **29**, 351–60.

Brown, H. & Thompson, D. (1997). The Ethics of research with men who have learning disabilities and abusive sexual behaviour: a minefield in a vacuum. *Disability and Society*, **12**, 695–708.

Cannon, T.D., Zorilla, L.E., Schase, D., Gur, R.E., Gur, R.C., Marco, E.J., Moberg, P. & Price, A. (1994). Neuropsychological functioning in siblings discordant for schizophrenia and healthy volunteers. *Archives of General Psychiatry*, **51**, 651–61.

Charman, T. & Clare, I.C.H. (1992). Education about the laws and social rules relating to sexual behaviour. *Mental Handicap*, **20**, 74–80.

Chiswick, D. (2000). Associations between psychiatric disorder and offending. In M.G. Gelder, J.J. Lopez-Ibor & N.C Andreason (eds) *New Oxford Textbook of Psychiatry* (pp. 2037–8). Oxford: Oxford University Press.

Craissati, J. & Hodes, P. (1992). Mentally ill sex offenders the experience of a regional secure unit. *British Journal of Psychiatry*, **161**, 846–9.

Davidson, M., Humphreys, M.S., Johnstone, E.C. & Ovens, D.G.C. (1995). Prevalence of psychiatric morbidity among remand prisoners in Scotland. *British Journal of Psychiatry*, **167**, 545–8.

Day, K. (1990). Depression in mildly and moderately retarded adults. In A. Dosen & F. Menlolascino (eds) *Depression in Mentally Retarded Children and Adults* (pp. 129–54). Leiden: Logon.

Day, K. (1993). Crime and mental retardation: a review. In K. Howells & C. R. Hollin (eds) *Clinical Approaches to the Mentally Disordered Offender* (pp. 111–43). Chichester: John Wiley & Sons.

Day, K. (1997). Sex offenders with learning disability. In G. Read & S.G. Pub (eds) *Psychiatry in Learning Disability* (pp. 278–306.) London: W.B. Saunders.

Dosen, A. & Gielen, J. (1993). Depression in persons with mental retardation: assessment and diagnosis. In R. Fletcher & A.Q. Dosen (eds) *Mental Health Aspects of Mental Retardation* (pp. 70–97). New York: Lexington Books.

Epstein, M.H., Cullinan, D. & Gadow, K.D. (1986). Teacher ratings of hyperactivity in learning disabled, emotionally disturbed and mentally retarded children. *Journal of Special Education*, **20**, 219–29.

Gillberg, C. (1983). Perceptual, motor and attentional deficits in Swedish primary school children: some child psychiatric aspects. *Journal of Child Psychology and Psychiatry*, **24**, 377–403.

Gillberg, C. (1998). Hyperactivity, inattention and motor control problems: prevalence, co-morbidity and background factors. *Folia Phoniatrica et Logopaedica*, **50**, 107–17.

Gillberg, I.C., Gillberg, C. & Groth, J. (1989). Children with pre-school minor neurodevelopmental disorders. V. Neurodevelopmental profiles at age 13. *Developmental Medicine and Child Neurology*, **31**, 14–24.

Glue, P. (1989). Rapid cycling affective disorders in the mentally retarded. *Biological Psychiatry*, **26**, 250–6.

Greenberg, F., Guzzetta, V., Mondes de Oca-Luna, R., Magenis, R.E., Smith, A.C.M, Richter, S.F., Kondo, I., Dobyns, W.B., Patel, P.I. & Lupski, J.R. (1991). Molecular analysis of the Smith-Magenis syndrome: a possible contiguous gene associated with del(17)(p11.2p11.2) in nine patients. *American Journal of Medical Genetics*, **24**, 393–414.

Guze, S.B. (1976). *Criminality and Psychiatric Disorders*. New York: Oxford University Press.

Harris, J.C. (1998). *Developmental Neuropsychiatry, vol. II: Assessment, Diagnosis and Treatment of Developmental Disorders*. Oxford: Oxford University Press.

Heaton Ward, W.A. (1977). Psychosis in mental handicap. *British Journal of Psychiatry*, **130**, 524–33.

Hellgren, L., Gillberg, I.C., Bagenholm, A. & Gillberg, C. (1994). Children with deficits in attention, motor control and perception (DAMP) almost grown up: psychiatric and personality disorders at age 16 years. *Journal of Child Psychology and Psychiatry*, **35**, 1255–71.

Higgins, J. (2001). Crime and mental disorder II: Forensic aspects of psychiatric disorder. In: D. Chiswick & R. Cope (eds) *Seminars in Practical Forensic Psychiatry* (pp. 52–86). London: Royal College of Psychiatrists.

Hodgins, S. (1992). Mental disorder, intellectual deficiency, and crime; evidence from a birth cohort. *Archives of General Psychiatry*, **49**, 476–83.

Hodgins, S. & Cote, G. (1990). The prevalence of mental disorders among penitentiary inmates. *Canada's Mental Health*, **38**, 1–5.

Howlin, P. (1997). *Autism: Preparing for Adulthood*. London: Routledge.

Humphreys, M.S., Johnstone, E.C., MacMillan, J.F. & Taylor, P.J. (1992). Dangerous behaviour preceding first admission for schizophrenia. *British Journal of Psychiatry*, **161**, 501–5.

Hunt, A. & Dennis, J. (1987). Psychiatric disorder in children with tuberous sclerosis. *Developmental Medicine and Child Neurology*, **29**, 190–8.

Jablensky, A. (2000). Epidemiology of schizophrenia: the global burden of disease and disability. *European Archives of Psychiatry and Clinical Neurosciences*, **250**, 274–85.

Jahoda, A. (2002). Offenders with a learning disability: the evidence for better services? *Journal of Applied Research in Intellectual Disabilities*, **15**, 175–8.

Jeffreys, S.E., Harvey, C.A., McNaught, A.S., Quale, A.S., King, M.B. & Bird, A.S. (1997). The Hampstead schizophrenia survey 1991. 1. The prevalence and service use comparison in an inner London health authority, 1986–1991. *British Journal of Psychiatry*, **70**, 301–6.

Kallman, F.J. (1953). *Heredity in Health and Mental Disorder*. New York: W.W. Norton.

Kanner, L. (1943). Autistic disturbances of affective contact. *Nervous Child*, **2**, 217–50.

Kienlen, K.K., Birmingham, D.L., Solberg, K., O'Regan, J. & Meloy, J.R. (1997). A comparative study of psychotic and non-psychotic stalking. *Journal of American Academy of Psychiatry and Law*, **25**, 317–34.

Krakowski, M., Jaeger, J. & Volvaka, J. (1988). Violence and psychopathology: a longitudinal study. *Comprehensive Psychiatry*, **29**, 174–81.

Le Couteur, A., Bailey, A., Goode, S., Pickles, A., Robertson, S., Gottesman, I. & Rutter, M. (1996). A broader phenotype of autism: the clinical spectrum. *Journal of Child Psychology and Psychiatry*, **37**, 785–802.

Lindsay, W.R., Allan, R., Walker, P.J., Lawrenson, H. & Smith, A.H.W. (1991). An alcohol education service for people with learning difficulties. *Mental Handicap*, **19**, 3.

Lindsay, W.R. & Smith, A.H.W. (1998). Responses to treatment for sex offenders with a learning disability: a comparison of one-year and two-year probation sentences. *Journal of Intellectual Disabilities Research*, **42**, 346–53.

Lindsay, W.R., Smith, A.H.W., Law, J., Quinn, K., Anderson, A., Smith, A., Overend, T. & Allan, R. (2002). A treatment service for sex offenders with intellectual disability; characteristics of referrals and evaluation. *Journal of Applied Research and Intellectual Disability*, **15**, 166–74.

Lund, J. (1985). The prevalence of psychotic morbidity in mentally retarded adults. *Acta Psychiatrica Scandinavica*, **72**, 562–70.

Lyall, I., Holland, A.J. & Collins, S. (1995). Offending by adults with learning disabilities and the attitudes of staff to offending behaviour; implications for service development. *Journal of Intellectual Disabilities Research*, **39**, 501–8.

McArdle, P., O'Brien, G. & Kolvin, I. (1995). Hyperactivity: prevalence and relationship with conduct disorder. *Journal of Child Psychology and Psychiatry*, **36**, 279–303.

McGuire, B. & Wraith, A. (2000). Legal and psychological aspects of stalking: a review. *Journal of Forensic Psychiatry*, **112**, 316–27.

McNeil, D. (1994). Hallucinations and violence. In J. Monohan & H.J. Steadman (eds) *Violence and Mental Disorder: Developments in Risk Assessment* (pp. 183–202). Chicago, IL: University of Chicago Press.

Meadows, G., Turner, T., Campbell, L., Lewis, S.W., Reveley, M.A. & Murray, R.M. (1991). Assessing schizophrenia in adults with mental retardation; a comparative study. *British Journal of Psychiatry*, **158**, 103–5.

Murray, G.C., McKenzie, K., Quigley, A., Matheson, E., Michie, A.M. & Lindsay, W.R. (2001). A comparison of the neurological profiles of adult male sex offenders and non-offenders with a learning disability. *Journal of Sexual Aggression*, **72**, 57–64.

Noriek, K. & Grunfield, B. (1998). Forensic psychiatric examinations of the mentally retarded. *Tidsskrift for Den Norske Laegeforening*, **14**, 2149–51.

O'Brien, G. (2000). Learning disability. In C. Gillberg and G. O'Brien (eds) *Developmental Disability and Behaviour*, Clinics in Developmental Medicine No. 149. (pp. 12–26). London: MacKeith Press.

O'Brien, G. (2002). *Behavioural Phenotypes and their Clinical Phenotypes*, Clinics in developmental medicine. London: MacKeith Press.

Pack, R.P., Wallander, J.L. & Browne, D. (1998). Health risk behaviors of African-American adolescents with mild mental retardation: prevalence depends on measurement method. *American Journal on Mental Retardation*, **102**, 409–20.

Persilia, J., Greenwood, P.W. & Lavin, M. (1978). *Criminal Careers of Habitual Felons*. National Institute of Law Enforcement and Criminal Justice. Washington, DC: Government Printing Office.

Reid, A.H. (1972). Psychosis in adult mental defectives. *British Journal of Psychiatry*, **120**, 205–18.

Reiss, S. & Rojahn, J. (1994). Joint occurrence of depression and aggression in children and adults with mental retardation. *Journal of Intellectual Disability Research*, **7**, 287–94.

Reiss, S. & Szyszko, J. (1983). Diagnostic overshadowing and professional experience with mental retarded persons. *American Journal of Mental Deficiency*, **87**, 396–402.

Royal College of Psychiatrists (2001). Diagnostic criterion for psychiatric disorders for use with adults with learning disabilities/mental retardation (DC-LD). Occasional paper, 48. London: Gaskell.

Rutter, M. (1982). Syndromes attributed to minimal brain dysfunction in childhood. *American Psychiatry*, **139**, 21–33.

Sandberg, S. (ed.) (1996). *Hyperactivity Disorder*. Cambridge: Cambridge University Press.

Scragg, P. & Shah, A. (1994). Prevalence of Asperger's syndrome in a secure hospital. *British Journal of Psychiatry*, **16**, 679–82.

Smith, A.H.W., Quinn, K. & Lindsay, W.R. (2000). Influence of mental illness on the presentation and management of offenders with learning disabilities. *Journal of Intellectual Disability Research*, **44**, 360–1

Sovner, R. (1986). Limiting factors in the use of DSM III criteria with mentally ill/mentally retarded persons. *Psychopharmacology Bulletin*, **22**, 1055–9.

Sovner, R. & Hurley, A. (1990). Assessment tools which facilitate psychiatric evaluation of treatment *Habilitative Mental Health Care Newsletter*, **9**, 11.

Sovner, R. & Pary, R. (1993). Affective disorders in developmentally disabled persons. In J.L. Matson & R. Barrett (eds) *Psychology in the Mentally Retarded* (pp. 87–148). Boston, MA: Longwood.

Steadman, H.J., Mulvey, E.P., Monahan, J., Robbins, P.C., Appelbaum, P.S., Grisso, T., Roth, L.H. & Silver, E. (1998). Violence by people discharged from acute psychiatric inpatient facilities and by others in the same neighbourhoods. *Archives of General Psychiatry*, **55**, 393–401.

Steffenburg, S., Gillberg, C. & Steffenburg, U. (1996). Psychiatric disorders in children and adolescents with mental retardation and active epilepsy. *Archives of Neurology*, **53**, 904–12.

Tantam, D. (1988). Lifelong eccentricity and social isolation. 1. Psychiatric, social, and forensic aspects. *British Journal of Psychiatry*, **153**, 777–82.

Taylor, E., Sandberg, S., Thorley, G. & Giles, S. (1991). *The Epidemiology of Childhood Hyperactivity*. Maudsley monograph no. 33. Oxford: Oxford University Press.

Taylor, P.J. (1985). Motives for offending amongst violent and psychotic men. *British Journal of Psychiatry*, **147**, 491–8.

Turner, T.H. (1989). Schizophrenia and mental handicap: an historical review with implications for further research. *Psychological Medicine*, **19**, 301–314.

Von Sydow, K., Lieb, R., Pfister, H. Hogger M., Sountag, H. & Wittchen, H.U. (2001). The natural course of cannabis use and dependence over four years: a longitudinal community study of adolescents and young adults. *Drug and Alcohol Dependency*, **64**, 347–61.

Wing, L. (1982). Asperger's syndrome: a clinical account. *Psychological Medicine*, **11**, 115–29.

Wolf-Schein, E.G. (1996). The autistic spectrum disorder: a current review. *Developmental Disabilities Bulletin*, **24**, 33–55.

WHO (1992). *The ICD-10 Classification of Mental and Behavioural Disorders*. Geneva, Switzerland: World Health Organization.

Wright, E.C. (1982). The presentation of mental illness in mentally retarded adults. *British Journal of Psychiatry*, **141**, 469–502.

Chapter 14

FEMALE OFFENDERS OR ALLEGED OFFENDERS WITH DEVELOPMENTAL DISABILITIES: A CRITICAL OVERVIEW

KATHLEEN KENDALL
University of Southampton, Southampton, UK

INTRODUCTION: FEMINIST CRIMINOLOGY AND ANTI-OPPRESSIVE PRACTICE

The National Association for the Care and Resettlement of Offenders (NACRO) recently published a report entitled *Women Who Challenge* (Kesteven, 2002). This document aims to provide a comprehensive overview of issues relevant to women offenders with mental health issues. More specifically, it considers the situation of female offenders who are "mentally disturbed" in England and Wales. While the definition of mental disturbance adopted by the author includes those with intellectual disabilities, there is no further mention of this population in the report. The failure to consider women offenders with intellectual disabilities is emblematic of the larger literature (Hayes, 2004; Holland, Clare & Mukhopadhyay, 2002). Yet, there is growing international concern over both the possible disproportion of people with intellectual disabilities inside the criminal justice system (Hayes, 2004; Mason & Murphy, 2002) and the dramatic rise in women's imprisonment (Gelsthorpe & Morris, 2002; Cook & Davies, 2000). Pate (2001) suggests that the co-existence of these two patterns has meant that while the rate of offending among women with intellectual disabilities is actually very low, this group nonetheless appears to be increasingly over-represented within the penal system.

While explanations for this situation are complex and muddied by definitional and methodological issues, they include: the closure of institutions housing large numbers of people with intellectual disabilities without adequate alternative provisions; vulnerability at all stages of the criminal justice system; challenging behaviour which brings some women into contact with the criminal justice system; the unavailability of services to address challenging behaviour at an earlier juncture;

Offenders with Developmental Disabilities. Edited by W.L. Lindsay, J.L. Taylor and P. Sturmey.
© 2004 John Wiley & Sons, Ltd.

changes in sentencing patterns; alterations in the type and severity of women's crimes; shifts toward purportedly equal treatment between male and female offenders; and increased social and economic deprivation (Gelsthorpe & Morris, 2002; Holland *et al.*, 2002; Lewis & Hayes, 1998; Lindsay, 2002a, b; Linhorst, Bennett & McCutchen, 2002).

Work in the fields of feminist criminology (e.g. Cain, 1989; Carlen, 1998; Chesney-Lind, 1997; Dobash, Dobash & Gutteridge, 1986; Faith, 1993; Howe, 1994; Rafter & Heidensohn, 1995) and anti-oppressive practice (Dalrymple & Burke, 1995; Dominelli, 2002; Payne, 1997) suggests that in addition to these factors any attempt to understand women offenders or alleged offenders with intellectual disabilities must address sexism, racism, ableism and other oppressions.

As defined by Dominelli (2002, p. 8), "Oppression involves relations of domination that divide people into dominant or superior groups and subordinate or inferior ones". Those deemed inferior are devalued and excluded from the social resources available to the dominant group. This does not imply that oppressed groups are simply passive victims but rather that their ability to exercise agency is constrained by disadvantage and the exercise of power over them by others. Furthermore, people occupy various social positions, such as gender, race, class and sexuality. This means that they can simultaneously be in dominant and subordinate groups and therefore both oppress others and be oppressed by others. Recognising oppression means that in order to understand behaviour we must take into account the relations of power and social structures within which individuals are situated.

Women, people with intellectual disabilities, and offenders have all been recognised as groups who experience oppression. Therefore, women offenders with intellectual disabilities are situated within various networks of oppressions. This chapter rests on the assumption that it is necessary to take into account the social context, including relations of domination and exclusion, when considering women offenders or alleged offenders with intellectual disabilities. It is further assumed that while this group has a shared experience of oppression, each woman's own situation is unique, informed by her particular circumstance and social position. It will be argued that while very little is known about women offenders with intellectual disabilities, great caution must be exercised in attempts to fill this void through research, programming and evaluation. Without such consideration and awareness of our own power, we may contribute to the further oppression of these women.

This chapter largely focuses upon the situation of women offenders with intellectual disabilities in England and Wales, but draws on relevant literature from elsewhere.

INTELLECTUAL DISABILITY AND OFFENDING

In 2002 a review of the evidence base in the field of forensic intellectual disability was commissioned by the Department of Health National Programme on Forensic Mental Health Research & Development (Fraser & Taylor, 2002). The review was informed by a recognition that this area is poorly researched (Taylor, 2002a). As Holland *et al.* (2002) suggest, the relationship between criminal offending and intellectual disability is a difficult area of study. A number of methodological and definitional problems make it very difficult to determine the prevalence of offending among people with intellectual disabilities (see Chapter 2). Holland *et al.* (2002, p. 16) argue that because of these complications, "issues relating to prevalence are extremely difficult to establish and unlikely to be of great value". Similarly, Lindsay (2002a) states that "the methodological differences between studies are so great that it is extremely difficult to draw firm conclusions" (p. 114). In their systematic and comprehensive overview of literature on mentally disordered offenders, Badger, Nursten, Williams and Woodward (1999) confirm that no British studies adequately describe the epidemiology of mentally disordered offenders, including intellectual disability.

These methodological problems are compounded by the questions researchers ask. In this regard, there has been very little epidemiological work seriously addressing cultural differences among offenders with intellectual disabilities. In particular, while gender and ethnicity have been identified as key issues in studies of crime patterns among the general population, they remain neglected in research on people with intellectual disabilities (Hayes, 2004; Holland *et al.*, 2002; Maden, 1996). Issues related to gender and ethnicity will be discussed in greater detail below.

THE HISTORICAL TREATMENT OF OFFENDERS OR ALLEGED OFFENDERS WITH INTELLECTUAL DISABILITIES

The foregoing discussion suggests that the extent to which people with intellectual disabilities offend is unknown (Clare & Murphy, 1998). Although there is very little evidence to indicate an association between developmental disabilities and a predisposition toward criminality (Health Evidence Bulletin Wales, 2000), "more has been written about the association between low intelligence and criminal behaviour than any other factor" (Bluglass, cited in Maden, 1996, p. 28).

In the early part of the twentieth century it was commonly believed that *feeble-mindedness* was hereditary and was associated with criminality (see Chapter 2), and that female *mental deficients* were especially sexually promiscuous and morally degenerate (Zedner, 1991). These social anxieties were based on gendered expectations (Cox, 1996), and fed into the eugenics movement, a loose collection of scientists, reformers and others united by a desire to improve the genetic quality of the population. Attempts to achieve such ends took different shapes, including institutionalisation and forced sterilisation in Canada, the United States, the United Kingdom and other countries (Barker, 1983; Digby, 1996; McLaren, 1990; Trent, 1994). These policies were successful, at least in part, because scientific views were consistent with respectable fears (Holland *et al.*, 2002; Pearson, 1983). That is, eugenics targeted populations already regarded by society as dangerous and frightening.

A review of the history emphasises the need to examine associations between crime and intellectual disability with great caution. It also affirms the need to consider the social and political context as well as the ideological assumptions within which such examinations occur. Indeed, the growing popularity of evolutionary psychology and behavioural genetics, as well as recent calls for the reassessment and re-implementation of eugenics policies, suggests that events of the past have a very real resonance for the present (e.g. Lynn, 2001; Pinker, 2003).

GENDER DIFFERENCES IN OFFENDING

While the evidence base around intellectual disability and crime remains weak, it is the case that people do not commit crime simply because of their intellectual disability, but rather that the same complex, multi-faceted processes around offending behaviour and the regulation of offending apply equally to this group as to others (Conley, Luckasson & Bouthilet, 1992). Importantly, crime and other *challenging behaviours* are social phenomena and any analysis of them must take into account the environmental context as well as social relationships (Health Evidence Bulletin Wales, 2000). As McGee and Menolascino (1992) state, like most offenders, a disproportionate percentage of people with intellectual disabilities appear to be "poor, living at the margin and powerless . . . They are the last to be served, the least likely to be served, and the most subjected to abuse, neglect and social abandonment" (pp. 55–6). They are also typically young and male (Clare & Murphy, 1998). Day (1993) emphasises the gendered nature of offending among intellectually disabled people, stating that "Female offenders are uncommon and differ significantly from male offenders" (p. 17).

This gendered difference is reflected in crime patterns more generally. As numerous studies have concluded, females have a much lower rate of criminality at every stage of the justice process—from suspicion through apprehension, prosecution, conviction and imprisonment (Harvey, Burnham, Kendall & Pease, 1992). For example, in the year 2000, females accounted for only 19% of those cautioned or found guilty of an offence in England and Wales. Females also commit many fewer serious crimes: those crimes that they do commit are perpetrated under different circumstances (Carlen, 1998). The most common offence resulting in a custodial sentence for women is theft and handling, which accounted for 42% of the female prison population in England and Wales during 2000. This compared to a figure of 23% for males (Kesteven, 2002). Furthermore, women are given shorter sentences and have less persistent criminal careers (Home Office, 2000a).

The vast majority of women have not committed a violent crime and do not pose a danger to the public (Carlen, 1998; HM Inspectorate of Prisons, 1997). This is important to keep in mind given the upsurge in the prison population, where the numbers of women have increased disproportionately. Between 1993 and 2000, there was an increase of 115% in the female prison population, compared to a 43% rise among the male population (Kesteven, 2002). Gelsthorpe and Morris (2002) outline possible explanations for this increase in female incarceration: changes in sentencing patterns, differences in the *type* of women sentenced to prison, increased sentence lengths, shifts toward equal treatment between males and females, and more serious crime being committed by females. The authors conclude that these explanations are inadequate because they do not take into account the complexity of female imprisonment. They argue that women's pathways into imprisonment are many and varied. If we wish to understand women's incarceration we must carefully consider the different social positions and experiences of women. At the same time, Gelsthorpe and Morris maintain that women prisoners share a common experience of economic and social deprivation.

Ethnic minority women are particularly vulnerable to deprivation and more likely to come into contact with the criminal justice system (Hudson, 2002). For example, minority ethnic UK nationals in women's prisons are over-represented. While they comprise only 6% of the whole UK population, they make up 12.7% of the female prison population (Home Office, 2000a). Rates of incarceration among female minority ethnic groups are also disproportionate as compared to ethnic minority male prisoners (Kesteven, 2002). Kesteven states that this difference is accounted for to a large extent by the greater percentage of foreign nationals in the female population (15%) than the male population (8%). Most black sentenced women (68%) are imprisoned for drugs offences. When foreign national women are excluded, 50% of black women are serving sentences for drugs offences, compared to 25% of white women and 19% of black men. Kesteven concludes that it is not possible to draw any significant conclusions from these figures because the context within which these offences were committed is unknown. However, Hudson (2002) argues that racialised and gendered assumptions operating throughout the criminal justice system mean that black women are more likely than others to be severely dealt with.

Carlen (2002a, p. 8) states that while there is no statistical evidence to indicate that women are sentenced more harshly than men overall, certain groups of women— "those who have been brought up in the state's institutional care, have transient lifestyles, have their own children already in state guardianship, are living without family and male-related domesticity, or are members of ethnic minority groups"— are more likely to receive harsher treatment. Thus, the effects of gender upon sentencing are filtered through ideological assumptions and realised within structural inequalities. This again demonstrates the importance of recognising the varied social positions and experiences among women.

A key issue for many women prisoners is parenthood, since it is estimated that 55% of this group have at least one child under the age of 16 (Home Office, 2000a). This situation partially accounts for the assertion that imprisonment is more damaging to women than men, with additional harm caused to their children, for whom they are often the primary carer (Kesteven, 2002). Further injury is imposed through an increasingly punitive prison environment (HM Inspectorate of Prisons, 2001). Restraint and body searches may particularly affect women, who might experience them as repeats of earlier violations (Carlen, 2002a). Indeed, research indicates that many female prisoners have experienced physical, sexual and emotional abuse. The Chief Inspector of Prisons, Sir David Ramsbotham, stated that control and restraint were unnecessarily used against women prisoners (HM Inspectorate of Prisons, 1997). In a follow-up report four years later the Chief Inspector stated that punitive measures were actually being used more often (HM Inspectorate of Prisons, 2001).

WOMEN OFFENDERS OR ALLEGED OFFENDERS WITH INTELLECTUAL DISABILITIES

As different writers have argued, studies of alleged or convicted offenders with intellectual disabilities have neglected to seriously consider the particular situation of females (Hayes, 2004; Holland et al., 2002). Where data exists, it tends to focus upon prison populations. In their comprehensive and systematic review of the literature, Lart, Payne, Beaumont, MacDonald and Mistry (1999) cite the work of a team of researchers investigating psychiatric disorders among prisoners as the only British study to really address intellectual disabilities (Gunn, Maden & Swinton, 1991; Maden, 1996; Maden, Swinton & Gunn, 1994). This research comprised a survey among a representative, cross-sectional sample of 301 females (adults and youths) serving a prison sentence in England and Wales and a sample of 1,769 males (adults and youths) in the same position. This meant that one-quarter of the entire female prison population and 5% of the male population were included. However, following exclusions the study sample analysed comprised 258 female and 1,751 male prisoners.

The study was conducted between 1988 and 1990, and included women from Her Majesty's Prisons Holloway, Styal, Drake Hall and Durham. Maden (1996) found the greatest gender disparity to be among those found to have a "mental handicap", defined as "a disadvantage for a given individual, resulting from a disability that limits or prevents the fulfilment of a role that is normal for that individual" (p. 29). Their definition thus contains a social component but does not involve any assessment of IQ. With this method, Maden found that 2.3% ($n = 6$) of non-overseas women and 0.6% ($n = 11$) of non-overseas men were diagnosed with mental handicaps.

Three of the women with intellectual disabilities were convicted of arson, one for shoplifting, one for indecent assault and the sixth woman was incarcerated for aggravated burglary. Case histories of the six women diagnosed as mentally handicapped indicate a common, although not entirely shared, experience of physical, sexual and emotional abuse, deprivation, institutionalisation, self-injury and psychiatric treatment (Maden, 1996; Maden et al., 1994). General population studies indicate a high rate of sexual abuse among women with intellectual disabilities (McCarthy, 1999a, 2000; Millard, 1994). The findings of Maden's team are similar to Canadian research demonstrating histories of deprivation, institutionalisation and violence among female prisoners with intellectual disabilities (Rivera, 1996; Warner, 1998). Therefore, many offenders with intellectual disabilities are also victims. As discussed above, this is also true for the female prison population generally.

Lindsay et al. (in press 2004) reported on a cohort of female offenders with intellectual disabilities referred to a Scottish community-based service for severe challenging behaviour and forensic problems between 1990 and 2001. Of the 179 individuals, 18 (approximately 10%) referred for offence-related behaviour were female. The mean IQ for these women was 67.1. No one single offence predominated, although assault-related offences were most frequent. Offences included the following: prostitution (22%), assault (16.5%), alcohol-related assault (16.5%), breach of the peace (16.5%), theft and breach of the peace (11%), attempted murder (5.5%), infanticide (5.5%), and procurement for the purposes of sexual assault (5.5%). In addition to assault, two of the women were also charged with wasting police time.

MENTAL HEALTH ISSUES FOR WOMEN OFFENDERS WITH INTELLECTUAL DISABILITIES

Three of the six women with mental handicaps in the study by Maden et al. (1994) were given diagnoses of schizophrenia or another psychosis, and two were prescribed neuroleptic medication. Maden (1996) concludes that at least three of the women would have been better placed in a psychiatric hospital. Yet, he also notes that all of the women with intellectual disabilities were held in the same prison, and the doctor in charge actively opposed transfer to hospital. The NACRO recent report calls for a standardised prescription protocol following its findings that half of all women prisoners were treated with psychotropic drugs, while only 17% were prescribed these prior to their sentences (Kesteven, 2002). Others suggest that prescription protocols must acknowledge gender differences because women and men may react differently to various medications (Department of Health, 2002).

Rates of psychiatric diagnoses and prescription drug use may be even more prevalent among people with intellectual disabilities in the community. A recent review of research findings concerning psychiatric disorder among offenders with intellectual disabilities concludes that despite varied methodologies and prevalence rates identified across studies, there is a common agreement that psychiatric disorder is common in people with intellectual disabilities, and "increasingly so with more severe intellectual delay and in those with evidence of epilepsy or organic brain disease" (O'Brien, 2002, p. 22). However, the author of the review does not identify gender or other differences.

In a retrospective Swedish study, Hodgins (1992) studied the criminal convictions of more than 15,000 children born in 1953. People with intellectual disabilities were distinguished on the basis of school registers noting that they had been placed in special classes. Those who had received psychiatric treatment in hospital were excluded from the study. It found that the likelihood of a criminal conviction by age 30 was three times greater for men and four times greater for women with intellectual disabilities than those of the same gender but without intellectual disabilities. The disparity was even more apparent for violent offences, where men with intellectual disabilities were four times as likely to have a criminal conviction and women with intellectual disabilities were twenty-five times more likely. However, as Holland et al. (2002) warn, the reliance upon official records and the inability to distinguish cause from effect limit the findings.

In Lindsay et al.'s (in press 2004) study of 179 women referred to a community-based service for challenging and offending behaviour, 78% had a diagnosis of mental illness, and only 22% were not on any psychotropic drug. At least 61% of the women had suffered sexual abuse, and 38.5% experienced physical abuse. This sample comprised women referred from criminal justice services (44%), from community intellectual disability teams (27.5%) and from other services including psychology or child psychiatry (27.5%). Half of the referrals occurred on suspicion of mental illness with a request for a psychiatric assessment. The majority of assessments were for multiple problems related to anger and aggression (55.5%), sexual and relationship problems (44%), anxiety (33%), alcohol (27%) and daily living problems (11%). The authors conclude that mental illness is a key intervening variable in the women's offending behaviour. Therefore they suggest that a significant reduction in offending should occur with the treatment of mental illness.

Rates of psychiatric disorder appear to be higher among female than male offenders with intellectual disabilities. This is consistent with the broader criminological literature, including NACRO's recent report, which states that two-thirds of all women prisoners experience some form of mental health problem (Kesteven, 2002).

This report also cites research indicating that 40% of female prisoners compared to 20% of male prisoners sought psychiatric help prior to incarceration, suggesting that the degree of psychiatric morbidity was much higher among women than men prior to imprisonment (Singleton *et al.*, cited in Kesteven, 2002, p. 10). However, caution is warranted in the interpretation of these findings. Much debate surrounds the finding that women in general are more likely than men to have a mental health problem (Meltzer, Gill, Pettigrew & Hinds, 1995).

The disproportion of psychiatric diagnoses among women may not simply be accounted for by the fact that they have more mental health problems than men. Rather, a complex interplay of factors contributes to this disparity. A number of studies suggest that women offenders are even more likely than women in general to have their experiences pathologised since not only have they violated or allegedly violated the law, they have also challenged cultural expectations of female passivity and innocence (Chan, 2001; Faith, 1993; Sim, 1990). Because they are female and because they are offenders, women criminals are regarded as "doubly deviant" (Lloyd, 1995). Female offenders are therefore perceived as unruly—a group whose cognitions, emotions and behaviours are out of control, extreme and potentially dangerous (Kendall, 2000; Pollack, 2000; Shaw, 1999; Warner, 2001).

Stereotypes of people with intellectual disabilities have typically fitted into two socially constructed categories: the innocent *eternal child* or the dangerous, uncontrollable and oversexed deviant (McCarthy, 1999a). The fit between cultural representations of female criminality and the latter typology of people with intellectual disabilities may serve to conflate the two categories so that women with intellectual disabilities are also assumed to be offenders. This could further mean that women offenders with intellectual disabilities are viewed as 'triply deviant' and are more likely than others to have their actions pathologised and criminalised.

More recently, Hannah-Moffat (2000) and Kendall (2000) have argued that Canadian women prisoners labelled as mentally disordered, including those with intellectual disabilities, are being over-classified as security risks and treated with undue force and restraint. These women appear to have eluded attempts at rehabilitation and are regarded as difficult to manage. Rather than acknowledging the limitations prison imposes upon rehabilitation as well as the distress it creates, the penal system identifies the problem as lying within individual women. Yet, as discussed in the next section, imprisonment is particularly difficult for women and even more so for those with intellectual disabilities.

TRUTH IN PUNISHMENT

In the research carried out by Maden and his colleagues, women with intellectual disabilities did not mix well with other prisoners and some were bullied by them (Maden, 1996; Maden *et al.*, 1994). Warner (1998) found that attempts at shared accommodation between women with intellectual disabilities and other prisoners in Canada proved problematic, and concluded that distinctive sets of needs among different groups of prisoners made them incompatible with one another.

People with intellectual disabilities may experience frustration, anger, helplessness and injustice in relation to oppressive secure environments and through difficulties in communication (Taylor, 2002b). This suggests that challenging behaviour, however potentially threatening, can be viewed as purposeful once it is contextualised. Furthermore, because it may serve to signal that something is wrong, attempts to merely contain challenging behaviour without considering its meaning could create further harm. Damage could be caused both through a continuation of the setting conditions and through the sense of powerlessness that is created and reinforced (Jahoda, Trower, Pert and Finn, 2001). Similarly, criminological work suggests that volatile situations erupt within prison largely as a consequence of legitimate grievances and poor management (Mandaraka-Sheppard, 1986; Shaw, 1999).

Prisons are founded upon unequal relationships and the imposition of high levels of control. Whatever autonomy women bring to prison is largely lost within an institution which determines nearly every move and often appears to enforce rules arbitrarily (Eaton, 1993; Kendall, 1994). The pains of imprisonment are particularly felt by women for the reasons cited above and because prisons are designed primarily for men. Numerous writers have argued that because men comprise the vast majority of those incarcerated, prison classification, assessment, security, programming and healthcare have all been designed with male prisoners in mind. Consequently, women's unique experiences and needs are neglected (Carlen, 1998; Hannah-Moffat & Shaw, 2001; Prison Reform Trust, 2000).

Additionally, because there are fewer women's prisons, women are more likely than men to be incarcerated at a greater distance from their homes, and this has serious implications for the ability of prisoners to keep in touch with family and friends. Given the prevailing male orientation of prisons and their operation, women prisoners tend to be punished for behaviour considered acceptable among men and are more likely to be punished for trivial transgressions (Bosworth, 1999; Eaton and Humphries, 1996).

The more damaging effects of prison upon women as well as the sexist attitudes of staff may partially account for the relatively high proportion of women prisoners charged for breach of prison discipline. In 2000, for example, 256 offences were committed per 100 female prisoners compared to 159 offences per 100 male prisoners (O'Brien, Mortimer, Singleton & Meltzer, 2001). As a consequence of these charges, Kesteven (2002, p. 21) argues that "women prisoners are more likely than men to receive forfeiture of privileges, stoppage or reductions in earnings and cautions". Similarly, there is some evidence that women with intellectual disabilities housed in institutions experience greater restrictions and controls as well as more intrusive intervention in the form of punishment and medication than do men of similar ability (McCarthy, 1999a; Scotti, Evans, Meyer & Walker, 1991). Given this, women prisoners with intellectual disabilities may experience particularly harsh control and discipline.

Lewis and Hayes (1998) suggest that because women with intellectual disabilities often have a reduced verbal ability and their coping strategies are more limited, other means of coping, such as self-harm, substance use and binge eating, are therefore employed. Unfortunately, these actions are often dealt with through punishment rather than support (Eaton, 1993; Heney & Kristiansen, 1998; Warner, 2000, 2001). Prison conditions, therefore, may create, exacerbate and perpetuate mental health problems.

As Hannah-Moffat (2002) suggests, we must remind ourselves of the unpleasant-ness of incarceration, or the "truth in punishment", in order that we do not become complacent about the pains of imprisonment and underestimate the obstacles to reform and rehabilitation. This is important to keep in mind in discussions of al-ternatives to incarceration, since some writers argue against diversion schemes for people with intellectual disabilities. They suggest that such a process is patronising and denies people with intellectual disabilities their right to a normal dispensation of justice (Linhorst et al., 2002; Murphy & Clare, 1998; New South Wales Law Re-form Commission, 1996). However, this is to miss the point that prison is *not* a normal situation for anyone. The appropriateness of prison for everyone should be questioned.

COMMUNITY PENALTIES AND WOMEN WITH INTELLECTUAL DISABILITIES

United Kingdom government policy recommends that convicted offenders with intellectual disabilities should, as far as possible, be treated in the community, rather than in institutional settings, under conditions of no greater security than is justified by the danger they pose to others and to themselves. Additionally, services should maximize the opportunity for rehabilitation and an independent life (Department of Health, 1993; Department of Health and Home Office, 1992; Home Office, 1995). Similarly, a recent strategic report by the Department of Health (2002) identified women as a high priority group for movement out of high security facilities and stated that custody for women offenders should only be "used as a last resort for the most serious offences, and where it is necessary for the protection of the public" (p. 20). The report also identified a need for improving community-based mental health care and access to it by women in the criminal justice system, including those with intellectual disabilities.

In fact, Mason and Murphy (2002) and Murphy and Clare (1998) note that it is likely that many people with intellectual disabilities are already diverted into non-custodial sentences, or we would see greater numbers in prison. The term "diversion" is used to refer "to the process of securing appropriate health and so-cial care for offenders with mental disorder at the earliest stage possible" (Barron, Hassiotis & Banes, 2002, p. 456). They note that diversion from custody is possible through several routes in England and Wales. Kesteven (2002) states that there are approximately 200 court diversion schemes in operation as well as a range of psy-chiatric disposals. However, very little is currently known about the numbers and location of offenders with intellectual disabilities who are diverted from custody and treated in the community (Mason & Murphy, 2002).

Barron et al. (2002) report that most diversion schemes developed over the past ten years focus on the court stage of the criminal justice system. Despite court schemes being partially developed to prevent mentally disordered people from being sent to prison unnecessarily, there appears to be a low recognition rate of offenders with intellectual disability at this stage. Similarly, Murphy and Clare (1998) note that few people who are referred to court diversion schemes have an intellectual disability.

In an attempt to ascertain the prevalence of intellectual disability among people on probation, Mason and Murphy (2002) administered an assessment tool— Learning Disabilities in the Probation Service (LIPS)—to probationers in the Kent region of England. LIPS was designed especially to screen people in the probation service for social functioning and cognitive ability. The tool was administered to 90 probationers, of whom 97% were Caucasian and 86% were male. The results showed that for 19% of the total sample there was some evidence of an intellectual disability or borderline intellectual disability. Not one individual within this group had reported being in contact with services for people with intellectual disabilities and they were more likely than those without an intellectual disability to have been in prison more frequently. Probationers with intellectual disabilities had similar outcomes to those who did not. Noting the limitations of their study, the authors cautiously conclude that probation is, at least in some respects, an appropriate sentence for offenders with intellectual disabilities.

Denney (1998) recommends that the role of the probation service should be to identify and divert people with intellectual disabilities from custody. However, he notes that work in this area is "conspicuously absent" (p. 196) and that care in the community is patchy. Identification of offenders may assist in diverting people from custody, but is of little consequence if there are not adequate services to redirect them to. Denney argues that there are few formalised links between health and social services, prison and probation, and poor aftercare upon release. Murphy and Clare (1998) similarly state that many intellectual disability teams and services do not have links with diversion schemes. Furthermore, many people who are diverted from custody are placed in hospitals without appropriate treatment.

Maden (1996) recommends that women with mental disorders, including those with intellectual disabilities, be transferred from prisons into hospitals. Yet, Holland *et al.* (2002) argue that diversion to hospital should have only a very limited role as it could further increase the risk of social exclusion. They maintain that the long-term nature and quality of social care is important if the likelihood of future offending is to be minimised. However, community-based intellectual disability teams offer only very limited services, and some may provide no service at all to those with mild intellectual disabilities if they are not seen to meet the eligibility criteria (Murphy & Clare, 1998).

Murphy, Estien and Clare (1996) interviewed 26 people with mild intellectual disabilities and challenging behaviour, including 12 women, who had been service users at a specialist, hospital-based unit. On average, the research occurred $4\frac{1}{2}$ years after the service users had left the unit. While about half of those interviewed (56%) had thought that their problems had improved, 16% felt they remained the same. Almost one-third of those interviewed stated that they preferred the specialist unit to their current and previous placement. Of those sharing this view, two were currently in hospital and one was in prison. However, five people living in the community stated that they preferred their placement on the unit to their current arrangement. In three of these cases, provision was very poor, another person found community life stressful and a fifth was living in very isolated and poor circumstances, with inadequate levels of support. While the service had largely met its aim of resettling people into the community, such placements were woefully inadequate for a significant number of people. This highlights the need to put greater resources into community support. Integration into the community is important if offenders are to desist from crime.

GENDER-SENSITIVE INTERVENTION PROGRAMMES AND EVALUATIONS

In a recent literature review, Barron *et al.* (2002) conclude that "[Generally] the efficacy of virtually all of the proposed interventions for offenders with ID [intellectual disability] is patchy and based on small-scale uncontrolled studies of people with challenging behaviour and sex offenders" (p. 460). Increasingly, much of the work done in this area is based on a broadly cognitive behavioural approach (see Barron *et al.*, 2002; Lindsay, 2002b; Taylor, 2002b for reviews).

A number of studies have focused on men with intellectual disabilities and histories of sexual aggression (see Chapter 9; Lindsay, 2002b; Taylor, 2000). Taylor, Novaco, Gillmer and Thorne (2002) conducted the first controlled study of individual cognitive-behavioural anger treatment for detained men with intellectual disabilities and histories of offending. This small pilot study showed that following the intervention, treatment group participants had significantly lower levels of self-reported anger compared with routine-care control group participants. Allen, Lindsay, Macleod and Smith (2001) similarly found success with their group anger management programme for a case series of five women convicted offenders with aggressive and violent histories. Recently, Taylor, Thorne, Robertson and Avery (2002) reported on an evaluation of a broad-based cognitive-behavioural group intervention for convicted arsonists with mild and borderline intellectual disabilities. They found that participants, including a group of six convicted women, improved significantly following treatment on arson-specific measures as well as on clinical measures relating to self-esteem and anger.

While research on treatment programmes for offenders with intellectual disabilities is limited, that which addresses the particular treatment needs of females offenders with intellectual disabilities is even more sparse (Hayes, 2004; Holland *et al.*, 2002). The paucity of research addressing the needs of female offenders is reflective of the criminological literature more generally. As Bloom (2000, p. 120) states, "little data exist to help us identify and evaluate appropriate and effective programs for females under criminal justice supervision". Since females have different personal histories than men and because their pathways to offending differ, it should not be assumed that programmes designed for males are suitable for women. Therefore, effective programmes for women and girls must adopt approaches that are sensitive to the reality of their lives. The Department of Health (2002) has recently recommended that mental health services be gender-sensitive. Such programmes would emphasise the context of female lives, including racism, sexism, ableism, economic marginalisation, abuse and parenthood. Furthermore, they would acknowledge the differences which exist among women such as race, ethnicity, sexuality and physical and cognitive ability (Bloom, 2000; Covington, 2000). The task is to acknowledge similarities and differences between men and women and among women while avoiding either simple distinctions or broad universalisms. Here the concept of "intersection" illustrates the notion that each individual's location and experience in the world is fashioned by traversing networks of gender, race, sexuality, class, ability, nation and so on (Daly & Maher, 1998).

Given that there are few programmes designed specifically for female offenders, it is unsurprising that evaluations of programmes for this group are scarce. Unfortunately, the programme evaluations which have been carried out are typically poorly designed. Not only do they fail to distinguish which particular components correlate with success, they also tend not to identify specific outcome or process measures. Furthermore, both the context within which programmes are delivered and the diversity among participants are neglected (Kendall, 1998). Despite these failings, a number of writers have identified what appear to be elements of effective programming for female offenders. For example, based upon the experiences and impressions of American programme participants, programme administrators and correctional administrators, Koons, Burrow, Morash and Bynum (1997) found general agreement on attributes of effective programmes for incarcerated women. These include a comprehensive and holistic strategy aimed at addressing women's multiple needs in a continuum of care. Other components were: specific training relevant to women's family responsibilities and/or work; staff characteristics such as a caring attitude and personal experience with criminal activity; peer interaction and a safe and comfortable environment.

Austin, Bloom and Donahue (1992) analysed innovative strategies and programmes for American female offenders in the community and concluded that the best programmes "combined supervision and services to address the specialized needs of female offenders in highly structured, safe environments where accountability is stressed" (p. 22). The most promising programmes were also multidimensional, dealt specifically with women's issues, and included a continuum of care, coordination of community resources and aftercare. Young (1994) suggests that programmes can better meet the needs of the women for whom they are designed if participants are actively involved in programme development and evaluation design.

It has been argued that the gender of people with intellectual disabilities is seldom acknowledged (Tait & Genders, 2002). However, writers in the field of intellectual disability are beginning to acknowledge the importance of gender in programme service and delivery (Brown, 1996; McCarthy, 1999a; Traustadóttir & Johnson, 2000). For example, in their examination of gender and challenging behaviour, Clements, Clare and Ezelle (1995, p. 426) state that "there is a high cost to be paid if a person is perceived to be gender-free in a gendered world". The authors suggest that challenging behaviour may be partially understood as an expression of unidentified needs resulting from a failure to acknowledge gender-related issues. Others writers argue that gender-blind service provision has resulted in programmes which inappropriately place together women who have been abused by men with men who have abused women (McCarthy, 1999b). The Department of Health (2002) acknowledges the need to have women-only programmes and accommodation available to women. Programmes which fail to address gender and other social inequalities may mask the asymmetry of power existing between users and providers, thereby allowing abuses and discrimination to go unnoticed (Williams, Scott & Waterhouse, 2001).

CRIME DESISTANCE

Within criminology more generally, there is a growing literature on the process of *desistance*. In particular, researchers are identifying those factors which help prevent offenders from becoming further involved in crime. The elements which appear to be most helpful in avoiding further offending are those related to changes in the social context within which people live, including employment, personal relationships, and home environment. That is, *desisters* are more likely to have employment, stable relationships and a safe accommodation (Farrall, 2002; Farrall & Bowling, 1999; Rex, 2002). As Farrall (2002) suggests, while gaining employment is associated with reduced offending, finding a job is not simply a matter of an individual's motivation "but also of that work actually *being there* to be found, and an employer being prepared to offer a job to the probationer concerned" (p. 225). The social environment, and its structural barriers, in which offenders live must therefore be addressed.

Unfortunately, the key elements identified by the desistance literature are ones in which people with intellectual disabilities are known to fare particularly badly. For example, people within this group experience a relative lack of partners and friendships (Emerson & Hatton, 1994). Murphy *et al.* (1996) suggest that this is due to frequent placement moves and related disruptions, lack of carer support in building relationships and difficulty in sustaining relationships. Discrimination in this area is particularly evident for women, where assumptions about their sexuality have contributed toward practices preventing them from establishing partner relationships. These same beliefs, underpinned by a denial or distortion of women's sexuality, also contribute toward the sexual abuse of women. Policies and guidelines should both offer support to women with their relationships, including sexual ones, and prevent abuse (McCarthy, 1999a, 2000).

With regard to accommodation, offenders with intellectual disabilities fare even worse than offenders more generally, because they are extremely difficult to place in the community. Often, they are rejected by both services for offenders and those for people with intellectual disabilities (Lindsay, 2002a). The rate of homelessness is high among people with intellectual disabilities (Lewis & Hayes, 1998). Homelessness is furthermore a risk factor for imprisonment, since the availability of a stable place of residence may help determine whether an accused will be given a custodial sentence or be remanded into custody. People with intellectual disabilities may find it even more problematic than other offenders to manage living with insecure accommodation because they do not have the same range of coping strategies available to negotiate difficult circumstances.

Finally, fewer than 10% of people with intellectual disabilities are in paid employment (Department of Health, 2001). Denney (1998) argues that the Probation Service has been neglectful in assisting offenders with intellectual disabilities to find employment. He states that equal opportunities legislation must be introduced more thoroughly if positive changes are to occur. Such policies should ensure that people with intellectual disabilities are offered a wide range of employment opportunities and that they are paid on equal terms with others. The low levels of income currently received by those in paid work, as well as through state benefits, limit economic independence. This, in turn, limits the availability of choice in other aspects of people's lives.

Taken together, the key factors which prevent people with intellectual disabilities from further involvement in crime lie within the social structure rather than particular individuals. This is not to deny individual differences and agency, but to acknowledge that people's capacity to exercise agency is circumscribed by various networks of power and social structural arrangements which frequently disadvantage them.

CORRECTIONAL COGNITIVE-BEHAVIOURALISM AND NEO-LIBERALISM

As discussed above, many contemporary treatment programmes for offenders, including those with intellectual disabilities, adopt a cognitive-behavioural model. Simply stated, cognitive-behaviouralism assumes that thoughts produce emotions, mood and behaviour. Offending behaviour is largely understood to be a consequence of faulty or deficit thinking. Programmes, therefore, aim either to inculcate thinking skills or restructure thoughts (Home Office, 2000b). However, the efficacy of the cognitive component of cognitive-behavioural interventions has not been adequately demonstrated in clients with intellectual disabilities (Taylor, 2002b; Willner, Jones, Tams and Green, 2002).

Nonetheless, a cognitive-behavioural model is central to current programme schemes for all offenders within British prison and probation services. Taken together, these developments are referred to as the *what works* initiative, an attempt to ensure that all programmes are based upon hard evidence that they reduce offending. Only those programmes adopting proven methods will receive official accreditation and run nationally (Home Office, 2000b). *The Government's Strategy for Women Offenders* (Home Office, 2000a) has meant that a cognitive-behavioural framework now governs approved treatment for females within the prison and probation services (Carlen, 2002a; Rex, 2002).

Yet, the effectiveness of cognitive-behavioural programmes in reducing offending is in fact actually highly contested on methodological as well as ethical grounds (Farrall, 2002; Kemshall, 2002b; Kendall, 2002; Merrington & Stanley, 2000; Robinson, 2001). While undoubtedly helpful to many individual offenders, the effectiveness of cognitive-behaviouralism appears to be overstated. Its incorporation within corrections has transformed its utility from a technique or model of practice to a panacea for practice. Key among criticisms is the concern that correctional cognitive-behaviouralism focuses almost exclusively on individuals to the exclusion of social factors contributing to crime (Farrall, 2002; Kemshall, 2002a, Kendall, 2002; Hannah-Moffat & Shaw, 2000). In locating the problem within individuals' thought processes, offenders are pathologised, their protests de-legitimised and social structural issues and inequalities are largely denied.

Such a process is likely to further exclude already vulnerable populations. Stenfert Kroese (1997) emphasises this point in her discussion of cognitive-behavioural programmes for people with intellectual disabilities. She suggested that cognitive-behavioural programmes may cause damage to individuals if delivered in an oppressive environment. This occurs when the purported aims of enhancing self-determination and self-regulation are contradicted and undermined by the environment. Even when programmes are delivered in a warm and supportive environment, achievements can be undone when individuals leave them only to enter an unwelcoming, threatening world. In essence, these situations create a cognitive dissonance. The delivery of cognitive-behavioural programmes within prisons and other institutions may therefore be particularly problematic if the coercive context is not taken into account.

Writers are beginning to argue that the dominance of cognitive-behaviouralism within corrections has largely occurred, not because it has been proven effective, but because it is consistent with the broader political climate (e.g. Farrall, 2002; Hannah-Moffat & Shaw, 2001; Kendall & Pollack, 2003; Kendall, 2002, 2004). There is currently a shift in governmental practice and policy from *welfarism* to *neo-liberalism*. While the former aims to meet the basic needs of all citizens through state-centred, universal benefits and services, the latter maintains that economic, political and social arrangements should be primarily determined by the market economy. Under neo-liberalism, well-being is purportedly established through competition and entrepreneurialism, and genuine need is targeted through means-testing and auditing (Dominelli, 2002; Kemshall, 2002a).

Under neo-liberalism law and order is purportedly achieved not by repressive and overt means, but rather through self-governance. This occurs as individuals internalise the rationalist, economic tenets of neo-liberalism and become prudent consumers making wise choices in their everyday lives. Since free-will and a level playing field are assumed, individuals are held almost entirely responsible for making bad choices or for not availing themselves of the opportunities that are purportedly available. Social problems, including crime, become individualised and de-contextualised (Kemshall, 2002b; Kendall, 2004; Robinson, 2001).

In constructing a group of criminals whose thinking purportedly makes them different from non-criminals, cognitive-behaviouralism legitimises both rehabilitative treatment for offenders amenable to treatment and more punitive practices with those who appear recalcitrant. The former group are conceptualised as entrepreneurial criminals—as responsible and rational consumers—whose thinking led them to make poor choices but who are now taking advantage of the opportunities offered to them through prison or probation. The latter group are demonised as risky, fearsome and dangerous criminals for whom heightened security and punishment are deemed necessary for public protection (Hannah-Moffat, 2000; Garland, 1996; Kendall, 2004).

These concerns may be especially relevant to offenders with intellectual disabilities. While programmes for this group increasingly use a cognitive-behavioural model, practitioners emphasise the non-cognitive aspects such as relaxation and skills training because it is assumed that people with intellectual disabilities lack the cognitive ability required for more intensive cognitive work such as restructuring (Jahoda *et al.*, 2001; Taylor, 2002b). When such an assumption is coupled with correctional cognitive behaviouralism, wherein criminals are regarded as cognitively faulty or deficient, and it is believed that the worst criminals cannot or will not restructure their thinking, there is the potential for harm. That is, because assumptions about people with intellectual disabilities coincide with current characterisations of the worst kind of criminals there is the possibility that the two groups will simply be seen as one and the same. As noted earlier, women offenders with intellectual disabilities may already be regarded as triply deviant—a group whose cognitions, emotions and behaviour are out of control. This socio-political process may help to account for the apparent increased imprisonment and punitive practices toward women, particularly those with intellectual disabilities.

On the surface, correctional cognitive-behaviouralism appears to contradict the social model embedded within *Valuing People: A New Strategy for Learning Disability for the 21st Century* (Department of Health, 2001). This White Paper emphasises four key principles: legal and civic rights, independence, choice and inclusion. The language used suggests that this strategy is progressive, even liberating. Yet, language is a social phenomenon and as such it is "embedded within wider social processes and relationships of power. The way we acquire and use language not only reflects our relationship to the wider social world, it also reproduces it" (Priestly, 1999, p. 92). The flexibility and fluidity of language means that a single word can hold multiple and even contradictory meanings. The particular significance of any given word depends upon how it is used, by whom and under what conditions. Thus a word or phrase can simultaneously convey the dominant discourse as well as resistance to it. Recent feminist work has demonstrated that within the criminal justice system, the principles of 'empowerment', 'choice' and 'need' have become co-opted and mobilised in such a way as to undermine their radical usage by feminists and to further mask oppression (e.g. Carlen, 2002b; Hannnah-Moffat & Shaw, 2001; Townsend, 1998). This has been particularly true of language employed in correctional treatment and rehabilitation (Kendall, 1994).

Similarly, some writers within the disability literature suggest that the term *choice* can mask the fact that opportunities for intellectually disabled people are often very narrow, constrained or even non-existent. This practice obscures unequal power relations which underlie the lack of real choice and further perpetuates disablism. False notions about choice can also result in victim blaming. That is, individuals may be held responsible for their perceived inability to avail themselves of the opportunities supposedly afforded them (Marsden, 2002; Wareing & Newell, 2002).

Such a critique does not suggest that the *Valuing People* strategy be dismissed. Rather, it is important to recognise the potential for varied interpretations of the strategy's components and the implications which follow. Furthermore, the strategy must be assessed alongside the other many and varied, often contradictory, initiatives competing for money and resources at a time when efficiency, means-testing, and targeting are being emphasised. In this regard, Harris (2001) argues that the *Valuing People* strategy greatly underestimates the economic and material resources needed for successful implementation of services.

At a broader level, Holland *et al.* (2002) suggest that the current emphasis upon crime reduction has informed proposed mental heath legislation, endorsing a greater and broader reliance upon compulsory detention and institutionalisation, rather than an exploration of alternatives for offenders. They warn of a return to a political agenda similar to that at the height of the eugenics movement. At the same time, many parts of the welfare state are being restructured in accordance with market forces. Because they are often reliant upon service provision, vulnerable people such as those with intellectual disabilities are particularly affected by these changes. A number of writers argue that neo-liberal policies have created economic hardship, growth in unemployment and poverty as well as the erosion of services for socially excluded groups. This in turn has contributed toward a decrease in public tolerance and the further exclusion and criminalisation of marginalised groups (Dominelli, 2002; Drakeford & Vanstone, 2000; Kemshall, 2002a; Kendall, 2004).

This does not suggest that cognitive-behavioural programmes should not be run. Rather, it implies that for *any* rehabilitative programme to work, the social context within which offenders are situated and the broader political climate shaping available opportunities and services, as well as public perceptions, must be acknowledged in programme design, implementation and evaluation.

CONCLUSION

Women offenders or alleged offenders with intellectual disabilities are a woefully neglected group. Yet, as this chapter has argued, attempts to fill the void must exercise great caution and sensitivity. Research and programming which fails to consider the social, economic and political context within which this group is situated is not only methodologically flawed, but may contribute toward its further exclusion and oppression. Proponents of anti-oppressive practice and feminists insist that researchers and practitioners be aware of their own power and the social contexts within which they operate, for these shape their understandings of the world, the work they do and their interactions with other people (Dominelli, 2002; Pollack, in press). Such an epistemological position implies that we are never completely objective and value-free. However, by making visible the positions we occupy, the assumptions we hold, and the contexts within which we operate, we can become more accountable for the outputs of our research, our programmes and to those with whom we work (Kendall & Pollack, 2003). Such self-reflexivity and transparency is particularly crucial for people working with vulnerable groups. We can be further accountable to women offenders with intellectual disabilities by ensuring their active participation in the design, implementation and evaluation of research and programmes.

REFERENCES

Allen, R., Lindsay, W., Macleod, F. & Smith, A. (2001). Treatment of women with intellectual disabilities who have been involved with the criminal justice system for reasons of aggression. *Journal of Applied Research in Intellectual Disabilities*, **14**, 340–7.

Austin, J., Bloom, B. & Donahue, T. (1992). *Female Offenders in the Community: An Analysis of Innovative Strategies and Programs*. Washington, DC: National Institute of Corrections.

Badger, D., Nursten, J., Williams, P. & Woodward, M. (1999). *Systematic Review of the International Literature on the Epidemiology of Mentally Disordered Offenders*. York: NHS Centre for Reviews and Dissemination, University of York.

Barker, D. (1983). How to curb the fertility of the unfit: the feeble-minded in Edwardian Britain. *Oxford Journal of Education*, **9**, 197–211.

Barron, P., Hassiotis, A. & Banes, J. (2002). Offenders with intellectual disability: the size of the problem and therapeutic outcomes. *Journal of Intellectual Disability Research*, **46**, 454–63.

Bloom, B. (2000). Beyond recidivism: perspectives on evaluation of programs for female offenders in community corrections. In M. McMahon (ed.) *Assessment to Assistance: Programs for Women in Community Corrections* (pp. 107–38). Lanham, MD: American Correctional Association.

Bosworth, M. (1999). *Engendering Resistance: Agency and Power in Women's Prisons*. Aldershot: Ashgate.

Brown, H. (1996). Ordinary women: issues for women with learning disabilities. *British Journal of Learning Disabilities*, **24**, 47–51.

Cain, M. (ed.) (1989). *Growing Up Good. Policing the Behaviour of Girls in Europe*. London: Sage.

Carlen, P. (1998). *Sledgehammer*. London: Macmillan.

Carlen, P. (2002a). *Women and Punishment: The Struggle for Justice*. Cullompton: Willan.

Carlen, P. (2002b). Controlling measures: the repackaging of common-sense opposition to women's imprisonment in England and Canada. *Criminal Justice*, **2**, 155–72.

Chan, W. (2001). *Women, Murder and Justice*. Houndmills: Palgrave.

Chesney-Lind, M. (1997). *The Female Offender. Girls, Women and Crime*. London: Sage.

Clare, I. & Murphy, G. (1998). Working with offenders or alleged offenders with intellectual disabilities. In E. Emerson, C. Hatton, J. Bromley & A. Caine (eds) *Clinical Psychology and People with Intellectual Disabilities* (pp. 154–76). Chichester: John Wiley & Sons.

Clements, J., Clare, I. & Ezelle, L.A. (1995). Real men, real women, real lives? Gender issues in learning disabilities and challenging behaviour. *Disability and Society*, **10**, 425–35.

Conley, R., Luckasson, R. & Bouthilet, G. (1992). *The Criminal Justice System and Mental Retardation. Defendants and Victims*. Baltimore, MD: Paul H. Brookes.

Cook, D. & Davies, S. (eds) (2000). *Harsh Punishment: International Experiences of Women's Imprisonment*. Boston, MA: Northeastern University Press.

Covington, S. (2000). Helping women to recover: creating gender-specific treatment for substance-abusing women and girls in community corrections. In M. McMahon (ed.) *Assessment to Assistance: Programs for Women in Community Corrections* (pp. 171–234). Lanham, MD: American Correctional Association.

Cox, P. (1996). Girls, deficiency and delinquency. In D. Wright & A. Digby (eds) *From Idiocy to Mental Deficiency: Historical Perspectives on People with Learning Disabilities*. London: Routledge.

Dalrymple, J. & Burke, B. (1995). *Anti-Oppressive Practice: Social Care and the Law*. Buckingham: Open University Press.

Daly, K. & Maher, L. (1998). Crossroads and intersections: building from feminist critique. In K. Daly & L. Maher (eds) *Criminology at the Crossroads. Feminist Readings in Crime and Justice* (pp. 1–17). Oxford: Oxford University Press.

Day, K. (1993). Crime and mental retardation: a review. In K. Howells & C.R. Hollin (eds) *Clinical Approaches to the Mentally Disordered Offender*. Chichester: John Wiley & Sons.

Denney, D. (1998). People with learning difficulties and criminal justice—a role for the probation service. *Probation Journal*, **45**, 194–201.

Department of Health (1993). *Services for People with Learning Disabilities and Challenging Behaviour or Mental Health Needs* (Mansell Report). London: HMSO.

Department of Health (2001). *Valuing People: A New Strategy for Learning Disability for the 21st Century*. London: DOH. http://www.archive/official-documents.co.uk/document/cm50/5086/5086.htm.

Department of Health (2002). *Women's Mental Health: Into the Mainstream. Strategic Development of Mental Health Care for Women. Summary*. London: DOH. http://ww.doh.gov.uk/mentalhealth/wmh-summary.pdf.

Department of Health and Home Office (1992). *Review of Health and Social Services for Mentally Disordered Offenders and Other Requiring Similar Services* (Reed Report). London: HMSO.

Digby, A. (1996). Contexts and perspectives. In D. Wright & A. Digby (eds). *From Idiocy to Mental Deficiency: Historical Perspectives on People with Learning Disabilities*. London: Routledge.

Dobash, R.P., Dobash, R.E. & Gutteridge, S. (1986). *The Imprisonment of Women*. Oxford: Blackwell.

Dominelli, L. (2002). *Anti-Oppressive Social Work Theory and Practice*. Houndmills: Palgrave Macmillan.

Drakeford, M. & Vanstone, M. (2000). Social exclusion and the politics of criminal justice: a tale of two administrations. *The Howard Journal*, **39**(4), 369–81.

Eaton, M. (1993). *Women After Prison*. Buckingham: Open University Press.

Eaton, M. & Humphries, J. (1996). *Listening to Women in Special Hospitals*. Twickenham: St Mary's University College.

Emerson, E. & Hatton, C. (1994). *Moving Out: Relocation from Hospital to Community*. London: HMSO.

Faith, K. (1993). *Unruly Women: The Politics of Confinement and Resistance*. Vancouver: Press Gang.

Farrall, S. (2002). *Rethinking What Works With Offenders. Probation, Social Context and Desistance From Crime*. Cullompton: Willan.

Farrall, S. & Bowling, B. (1999). Structuration, human development and desistance from crime. *British Journal of Criminology*, **39**, 252–67.

Fraser, W.I. & Taylor, J.L. (eds) (2002). Forensic learning disabilities: the evidence base [supplement 1]. *Journal of Intellectual Disability Research*, **46**.

Garland, D. (1996). The limits of the sovereign taste: strategies of crime control in contemporary society. *British Journal of Criminology*, **36**(4), 445–71.

Gelsthorpe, L. & Morris, A. (2002). Women's imprisonment in England and Wales: a penal paradox. *Criminal Justice*, **2**(3), 277–301.

Gunn, J., Maden, T. & Swinton, M. (1991). *Mentally Disordered Prisoners*. London: Home Office.

Hannah-Moffat, K. (2000). Prisons that empower: neo-liberal governance in Canadian women's prisons. *British Journal of Criminology*, **40**, 510–31.

Hannah-Moffat, K. (2002). Creating choices: reflecting on the choices. In P. Carlen (ed.) *Women and Punishment* (pp. 199–219). Cullompton: Willan.

Hannah-Moffat, K. & Shaw, M. (2000). Thinking about cognitive skills? Think again! *Criminal Justice Matters*, **39**, 8–9.

Hannah-Moffat, K. & Shaw, M. (2001). *Taking Risks: Incorporating Gender and Culture into the Classification and Assessment of Federally Sentenced Women in Canada*. Ottawa: Status of Women Canada.

Harris, J. (2001). Valuing people: a response from BILD on implementation. http://www.bild.org.uk/general/white_paper/response_to_valuing_people.htm.

Harvey, L., Burnham, R.W., Kendall, K. & Pease K. (1992). Gender differences in criminal justice: an international comparison. *British Journal of Criminology*, **32**, 208–17.

Hayes, S. (2004). Interaction with the criminal justice system. In E. Emerson, C. Hatton, T. Parmenter & T. Thompson (eds) *International Handbook of Applied Research in Intellectual Disabilities* (chapter 24). Chichester: John Wiley & Sons.

Health Evidence Bulletin Wales (2000). *Learning Disabilities*. Cardiff: National Assembly for Wales. Available from http://hebw.uwcm.ac.uk:9080/learningdisabilities/intro.htm. Downloaded 4 December 2002.

Heney, J. & Kristiansen, C. (1998). An analysis of the impact of prison on women survivors of childhood sexual abuse. In J. Harden & M. Hill (eds) *Breaking the Rules: Women in Prison and Feminist Therapy*. New York: Harrington Park Press.

HM Inspectorate of Prisons (1997). *Women in Prison: A Thematic Review*. London: Home Office.

HM Inspectorate of Prisons (2001). *Follow-Up to Women in Prison*. London: Home Office.

Hodgins, S. (1992). Mental disorder, intellectual deficiency and crime: evidence from a birth cohort. *Archives of General Psychiatry*, **49**, 476–83.

Holland, T., Clare, I.C.H. & Mukhopadhyay, T. (2002). Prevalence of "criminal offending" by men and women with intellectual disability and the characteristics of "offenders": implications for research and service development. *Journal of Intellectual Disability Research*, **46** (suppl. 1), 6–20.

Home Office (1995). *Provision for Mentally Disordered Offenders*, Home Office Circular 12/95. London: Home Office.

Home Office (2000a). *The Government's Strategy for Women Offenders*. London: Home Office. http://www.hmprisonservice.gov.uk/filestore/189_610.pdf.

Home Office (2000b). *What Works? Reducing Re-Offending: Evidence-Based Practice*. London: Home Office.

Howe, A. (1994). *Punish and Critique: Towards a Feminist Analysis of Penality*. London: Routledge.

Hudson, B. (2002). Gender issues in penal policy and penal theory. In P. Carlen (ed.) *Women and Punishment* (pp. 21–46). Cullompton: Willan.

Jahoda, A., Trower, P, Pert, C. & Finn, D. (2001). Contingent reinforcement of defending the self? A review of existing models of aggression in people with mild learning disabilities. *British Journal of Medical Psychology*, **74**, 305–21.

Kemshall, H. (2002a). *Risk, Social Policy and Welfare*. Buckingham: Open Universitiy Press.

Kemshall, H. (2002b). Effective practice in probation: an example of "advanced liberal" responsibilisation? *The Howard Journal*, **41**(1), 41–58.

Kendall, K. (1994). Therapy behind prison walls: a contradiction in terms? *Prison Service Journal*, **96** (November), 2–11.

Kendall, K. (1998). Evaluation of programs for female offenders. In R. Zaplin (ed.) *Female Offenders. Critical Perspectives and Effective Interventions* (pp. 361–79). Gaithersburg, MD: Aspen.

Kendall, K. (2000). Psy-ence fiction: inventing the mentally disordered female prisoner. In K. Hannah-Moffat & M. Shaw (eds) *An ideal prison? Critical essays on women's imprisonment in Canada* (pp. 82–93). Halifax, Nova Scotia: Fernwood Publishing.

Kendall, K. (2002). Time to think again about cognitive behavioural programmes. In P. Carlen (ed.) *Women and Punishment* (pp. 182–98). Cullompton: Willan.

Kendall, K. (2004). Dangerous thinking: a critical history of correctional cognitive-behaviouralism. In G. Mair (ed.) *What Matters in Probation Work* (pp. 53–89). Collompton, Devon: Willan.

Kendall, K. & Pollack, S. (2003). Cognitive behaviouralism in women's prisons: a critical analysis of therapeutic assumptions and practices. In B. Bloom (ed.) *Gendered Justice: Addressing Female Offenders* (pp. 69–96). Durham, NC: Carolina Academic Press.

Kesteven, S. (2002). *Women Who Challenge: Women Offenders and Mental Health Issues*. London: NACRO.

Koons, B., Burrow, J., Morash, M. & Bynum, T. (1997). Expert and offender perceptions of program elements linked to successful outcomes for incarcerated women. *Crime and Delinquency*, **43**(4), 512–32.

Lart, R., Payne, S., Beaumont, B., MacDonald, G. & Mistry, T. (1999). *Women and Secure Psychiatric Services: A Literature Review*. York: NHS Centre for Reviews and Dissemination, University of York.

Lewis, K. & Hayes, S. (1998). Intellectual functioning of women ex-prisoners. *Australian Journal of Forensic Sciences*, **30**(1), 19–28.

Lindsay, W.R. (2002a). Integration of recent reviews of offenders with intellectual disabilities. *Journal of Applied Research in Intellectual Disabilities*, **15**, 111–19.

Lindsay, W.R. (2002b). Review of research and literature on sex offenders with intellectual and developmental disabilities. *Journal of Intellectual Disability Research*, **46** (suppl. I), 74–85.

Lindsay, W.R., Smith, A., Quinn, K., Anderson, A., Smith, A., Allan, R. & Law, J. (in press 2004). *Women With Intellectual Disability Who Have Offended: Characteristics and Outcome*. *Journal of Intellectual Disability Research*.

Linhorst, D., Bennett, L. & McCutchen, T. (2002). Development and implementation of program for offenders with developmental disabilities. *Mental Retardation*, **40**, 41–50.

Lloyd, A. (1995). *Doubly Deviant, Doubly Damned*. London: Penguin.

Lynn, R. (2001). *Eugenics: A Reassessment*. Westport, CT: Praeger.

McCarthy, M. (1999a). *Sexuality and Women With Learning Disabilities*. London: Jessica Kingsley.

McCarthy, M. (1999b). Gender matters. *British Institute of Learning Disabilities Bulletin*, **112** (3).

McCarthy, M. (2000). Consent, abuse and choices. Women with intellectual disabilities and sexuality. In: R. Traustadóttir & K. Johnson (eds) *Women with Intellectual Disabilities. Finding a Place in the World* (pp. 132–56). London: Jessica Kingsley.

McGee, J. & Menolascino, F. (1992). The evaluation of defendants with mental retardation in the criminal justice system. In R. Conley, G. Luckasson & G. Bouthilet (eds) *The Criminal Justice System and Mental Retardation. Defendants and Victims* (pp. 55–77). Baltimore, MD: Paul H. Brookes Publishing.

McLaren, A. (1990). *Our Own Master Race. Eugenics in Canada, 1885–1945*. Toronto: Oxford University Press.

Maden, A. (1996). *Women, Prisons and Psychiatry. Mental Disorders Behind Bars*. Oxford: Butterworth-Heinemann.

Maden, A., Swinton, M. & Gunn, J. (1994). A criminological and psychiatric survey of women serving a prison sentence. *British Journal of Criminology*, **34**, 172–91.

Mair, G. (2000). Credible accreditation? *Probation Journal*, **47**, 268–71.

Mandaraka-Sheppard, A. (1986). *The Dynamics of Aggression in Women's Prisons in England and Wales*. London: Gower.

Marsden, D. (2002). Critical policy. *Learning Disability Practice*, **5**, 20–3.

Mason, J. & Murphy, G. (2002). Intellectual disability among people on probation: prevalence and outcome. *Journal of Intellectual Disability Research*, **46**, 230–8.

Meltzer, H., Gill, B., Pettigrew, M. & Hinds, K. (1995). *The Prevalence of Psychiatric Morbidity Among Adults Living in Private Households*. London: Office of Population Censuses and Surveys/HMSO.

Merrington, S. & Stanley, S. (2000). Reflections: doubts about the what works initiative. *Probation Journal*, **47**, 272–5.

Millard, L. (1994). Between ourselves: experiences of a woman's group on sexuality and sexual abuse. In A. Craft (ed.) *Practice Issues in Sexuality and Learning Disability*. London: Routledge.

Murphy, G. & Clare, I. (1998). People with learning disabilities as offenders or alleged offenders in the UK criminal justice system. *Journal of the Royal Society of Medicine*, **91**, 178–82.

Murphy, G., Estien, D. & Clare, I. (1996). Services for people with mild intellectual disabilities and challenging behaviour: service user views. *Journal of Applied Research in Intellectual Disabilities*, **9**(3), 256–83.

New South Wales Law Reform Commission (1996). *People with an Intellectual Disability and the Criminal Justice System*. Sydney: New South Wales Law Reform Commission.

O'Brien, G. (2002). Dual diagnosis in offenders with intellectual disability: setting research priorities: a review of research findings concerning psychiatric disorder (excluding personality disorder) among offenders with intellectual disability. *Journal of Intellectual Disability Research*, **46** (suppl. 1), 21–30.

O'Brien, M., Mortimer, L., Singleton, N. & Meltzer, H. (2001). *Psychiatric Morbidity Among Women Prisoners in England and Wales*. London: Office for National Statistics.

Pate, K. (2001). Why should we form an international coalition against women's imprisonment? Paper presented at the Sisters Inside Conference, Brisbane Australia, 29 November, 2001. http://www.elizabethfry.ca/confernc/nov29-01/1.htm.

Payne, M. (1997). *Modern Social Work Theory*, 2nd edn. Chicago, IL: Lyceum Books.

Pearson, G. (1983). *Hooligan. A History of Respectable Fears*. London: Macmillan.

Pinker, S. (2003). The blank slate: the modern denial of human nature. *The Skeptical Inquirer*, **27**(2), 37–41.

Pollack, S. (2000). Reconceptualizing women's agency and empowerment: challenges to self-esteem discourse and women's lawbreaking. *Women and Criminal Justice*, **12**, 75–89.

Pollack, S. (in press). Anti-oppression social work practice with women in prison: discursive reconstructions and alternative practices. *British Journal of Social Work*.

Priestly, M. (1999). Discourse and identity: disabled children in mainstream high school. In M. Corker and S. French (eds) *Disability Discourse* (pp. 92–102). Buckingham: Open University Press.

Prison Reform Trust (2000). *Justice for Women: The Need for Reform* (Wedderburn Report). London: Prison Reform Trust.

Rafter, N.H. & Heidensohn, F. (eds) (1995). *International Perspectives in Criminology: Engendering a Discipline*. Buckingham: Open University Press.

Rex, S. (2002). Beyond cognitive behaviouralism? Reflections on the effectiveness literature. In A. Bottoms, L. Gelsthorpe & S. Rex (eds) *Community Penalties. Change and Challenges* (pp. 67–86). Cullompton: Willan.

Rivera, M. (1996). *Giving Us a Chance. Needs Assessment: Mental Health Resources For Federally Sentenced Women in the Regional Facilities*. Ottawa: Correctional Service of Canada.

Robinson, G. (2001). Power, knowledge and "what works" in probation. *The Howard Journal*, 40(3), 235–54.

Scotti, J.R., Evans, I.M., Meyer, L. & Walker, P. (1991). A meta-analysis of intervention research with problem behavior: treatment validity and standards of practice. *American Journal of Mental Retardation*, 96, 233–56.

Shaw, M. (1999). Knowledge without acknowledgement: violent women, the prison and the cottage. *Howard Journal of Criminal Justice*, 38(3), 252–66.

Sim, J. (1990). *Medical Power in Prisons: The Medical Service in England 1774–1989*. Milton Keynes: Open University Press.

Stenfert Kroese, B. (1997). Cognitive-behaviour therapy for people with learning disabilities. Conceptual and contextual issues. In B. Stenfert Kroese, D. Dagnan & K. Loumjidis (eds) *Cognitive-Behaviour Therapy for People with Learning Disabilities*. London: Routledge.

Tait, T. & Genders, N. (2002). *Caring for People with Learning Disabilities*. London: Arnold.

Taylor, J.L. (2000). Northgate sex offender project [abstract]. *Journal of Intellectual Disability Research*, 44, 483–4.

Taylor, J.L. (2002a). Preface. *Journal of Intellectual Disability Research*, 46 (suppl. 1), vii.

Taylor, J.L. (2002b). A review of the assessment and treatment of anger and aggression in offenders with intellectual disability. *Journal of Intellectual Disability Research*, 46 (suppl. 1), 57–73.

Taylor, J.L., Novaco, R.W., Gillmer, B.T. & Thorne, I. (2002). Cognitive-behavioural treatment of anger intensity among offenders with intellectual disabilities. *Journal of Applied Research in Intellectual Disabilities*, 15, 151–65.

Taylor, J.L., Thorne, I., Robertson, A. & Avery, G. (2002). Evaluation of a group intervention for convicted arsonists with mild and borderline intellectual disabilities. *Criminal Behaviour and Mental Health*, 12(4), 282–93.

Townsend, E. (1998). *Good Intentions Overruled: A Critique of Empowerment in the Routine Organisation of Mental Health Services*. Toronto: University of Toronto.

Traustadóttir, R. & Johnson, K. (eds) (2000). *Women With Intellectual Disabilities: Finding a Place in the World*. London: Jessica Kingsley.

Trent, J.W., Jr (1994). *Inventing the Feeble Mind: A History of Mental Retardation in the United States*. Berkeley, CA: University of California Press.

Wareing, D. & Newell, C. (2002). Responsible choice: the choice between no choice. *Disability and Society*, 17(4), 419–34.

Warner, A. (1998). *Implementing Choices at Regional Facilities: Program Proposals for Women Offenders with Special Needs*. Ottawa: Correctional Service of Canada.

Warner, S. (2000). Women and child sexual abuse: childhood prisons and current custodial practices. In R. Horn and S. Warner (eds) *Issues in Criminological and Legal Psychology* 2: *Positive Directions for Women in Secure Environments* (pp. 11–16). Leicester: British Psychological Society.

Warner, S. (2001). Disrupting identity through visible therapy: a feminist post-structural approach to working with women who have experienced sexual abuse. *Feminist Studies*, 68, 115–35.

Williams, J., Scott, S. & Waterhouse, S. (2001). Mental health services for "difficult women": reflections on some recent developments. *Feminist Review*, **68**, 89–104.

Willner, P., Jones, J., Tams, R. & Green, G. (2002). A randomised controlled trial of the efficacy of a cognitive-behavioural anger management group for clients with learning disabilities. *Journal of Applied Research in Intellectual Disabilities*, **15**, 224–35.

Young, I. (1994). Punishment, treatment, empowerment: three approaches to policy for pregnant addicts. *Feminist Studies*, **20**, 33–57.

Zedner, L. (1991). *Women, Crime and Custody in Victorian England*. Oxford: Clarendon Press.

Chapter 15

THE RELATIONSHIP OF OFFENDING BEHAVIOUR AND PERSONALITY DISORDER IN PEOPLE WITH DEVELOPMENTAL DISABILITIES

ANDREW H. REID,* WILLIAM R. LINDSAY,[†] JACQUELINE LAW[‡]
AND PETER STURMEY[§]

* NHS Tayside and University of Dundee, Dundee, UK
[†] The State Hospital, Carstairs; NHS Tayside & University of Abertay Dundee, Dundee, UK
[‡] HM Prison Service, Edinburgh, UK
[§] Queens College, City University of New York, USA

The concept of personality disorder has a long and chequered history. An early landmark was the description by Pritchard (1837) of the condition of "moral insanity" in which there was no apparent mental illness but a gross disturbance of behaviour. A few years later Esquirol (1845) drew the seminal distinction between intellectual disability and mental illness as follows:

> A man in a state of dementia is deprived of advantages which he formerly enjoyed: he was a rich man who had become poor. The idiot, on the other hand, has always been in a state of want and misery.

The judgmental view of personality disorders was perpetuated in the latter part of the nineteenth and early part of the twentieth century. Maudsley (1868) described a group which was of "inherently vicious propensities" (p. 329). The pejorative tone continued with Partridge (1930), with personality disorder being classified into three categories. The first category was labelled as being inadequate and included people with insecure, depressive, weak-willed and asthenic characteristics. The second group were the egocentrics. These were contentious, paranoid, explosive and excitable individuals. Subjects enter Partridge's final category simply on the basis of criminal behaviour. He describes them as liars, swindlers, vagabonds and sexual perverts.

Gradually the concept of psychopathic personality emerged from this literature. Henderson (1939) described three main types of psychopathic personality:

Offenders with Developmental Disabilities. Edited by W.L. Lindsay, J.L. Taylor and P. Sturmey.
© 2004 John Wiley & Sons, Ltd.

the predominately inadequate, the predominately aggressive and the predominately creative. Batchelor (1964) commented of aggressive psychopaths that "those who constitute this group exhibit disorder of conduct which may reach the highest degree of violence either directed towards themselves or others".

Psychopathic personality found its way into the 1959 English Mental Health Act and there was a seminal monograph by Craft (1965) entitled *Ten Studies into Psychopathic Personality*. At a clinical level, if no more, a link between psychopathic personality and criminality had been established. Hare (1980) refined the association through the development of an instrument, "The Psychopathy Checklist", which is based on a structured clinical interview leading to a diagnosis of psychopathic disorder. The Hare Checklist is widely used in penal institutions to identify those among the criminal population who exhibit the core traits of psychopathic personality and its value is in its predictive power.

The concept remained in the 1983 English Mental Health Act (Bluglass, 1990), where psychopathic personality disorder was defined as "a persistent disorder or disability of mind (whether or not including significant impairment of intelligence) which results in abnormally aggressive or seriously irresponsible conduct on the part of the person concerned". In the 1984 Scottish Act (Whatmore, 1990), however, the term did not appear as such, although if a person is diagnosed as suffering from a mental disorder which is persistent and manifested by abnormally aggressive or seriously irresponsible conduct, compulsory powers for hospital admission can be used if the patient is likely to benefit from treatment (Whatmore, 1990). In ICD-10 (WHO, 1992) psychopathic personality is categorised in terms of a callous unconcern for the feelings of others; a gross and persistent attitude of irresponsibility and disregard for social norms, rules and obligations; an incapacity to maintain enduring relationships, though having no difficulty in establishing them; a very low tolerance to frustration and a low threshold for discharge of aggression, including violence; an incapacity to experience guilt or to profit from experience, particularly punishment; and a marked proneness to blame others, or to offer plausible rationalisations, for the behaviour that has brought the patient into conflict with society.

DSM-IV-TR (American Psychiatric Association, 1998) includes both personality disorders and mental retardation as an Axis II diagnosis. Personality disorders include paranoid, schizoid, schizotypal, antisocial, borderline, histrionic, narcissistic, avoidant, dependent, obsessive compulsive and personality disorder not otherwise specified. Those most closely associated with criminality, and associated with concepts discussed later in this chapter, are Cluster B personality disorders—antisocial, borderline and to a lesser extent histrionic and narcissistic. The diagnostic criteria for antisocial personality disorder have parallels with the Hare Psychopathy Index, which is discussed later: disregard for and violation of the rights of others resulting in a tendency to lack empathy, be callous, cynical, and glib with superficial charm. Failure to conform with social norms, deceitfulness, impulsiveness, aggressiveness, irresponsibility and lack of remorse are also mentioned as features. In borderline personality disorder, instability in interpersonal relationships and marked impulsivity are mentioned along with instability of mood, recurrent suicidal behaviour and inappropriate intense anger or difficulty controlling anger. These are generally features which are mentioned in relation to psychopathy although DSM-IV-TR itself does not mention this concept.

Table 15.1 Personality disorder in adults with intellectual disability

	Number	Percentage
Paranoid	4	4.0
Schizoid	2	2.0
Impulsive	15	15.0
Immature/unstable	48	47.5
Anxious	23	22.5
Explosive	9	9.0
Total	101	100

The status of personality disorder in the latest revision of the Scottish Mental Health Act remains to be seen—present indications are that it is likely to persist as one of the categories of mental disorder.

In contrast to the situation in the population of average intelligence, there has been very little research into personality disorder in people with intellectual disability. One of the few systematic studies was by Earl (1961) in his kindly book on *Subnormal Personalities*. His classification into "weakness, simplicity, immaturity, instability, schizoidia, viscosity, neurosis, psychopathy and psychosis" was idiosyncratic but his clinical vignettes are illuminating and shrewd.

Subsequently Corbett (1979), in his Camberwell study, which was essentially the first systematic investigation into personality disorder in adults with intellectual disability, reported a prevalence rate of personality disorder of over 25% in a large community sample of 402 persons, categorising them as shown in Table 15.1.

Eaton and Menolascino (1982) found a prevalence rate for personality disorder of 27.1% in a community-based sample of 115 people with intellectual disabilities. Gostasson (1987) commented on the difficulty in applying diagnostic criteria for personality disorder to individuals with severe intellectual disability. Reid and Ballinger (1987) then carried out a further study of personality disorder in 100 adults with mild or moderate intellectual disability using Mann's Standardised Assessment of Personality (SAP) questionnaire (1981). Ballinger and Reid (1987) had previously demonstrated the applicability of the questionnaire to a population with intellectual disabilities through an inter-rater reliability study. They found a similar high rate of severe personality disorder in 22% of the population studied with a predominance of explosive personality disorder in males, cyclothymic personality disorder in females, and an approximately equal distribution of hysterical personality disorder between males and females. Reid and Ballinger (1987) were of the view that the diagnostic criteria for personality disorder did not really apply to people with severe mental retardation and suggested that a typology rooted more in developmental concepts might be more applicable with them.

Khan, Cowan and Roy (1997) completed a similar study on 101 individuals with mild, moderate and severe intellectual disability. They employed a modified version of the Standardised Assessment of Personality (Mann, Jenkins, Cutting & Cowan, 1981) and the disability assessment schedule (Holmes, Shah & Wing, 1982). They also employed an ICD-10 multi-axial diagnosis where it was possible to interview the subject. They found that 31% of the population had sufficient impairment to warrant a diagnosis of personality disorder and a further 19% had abnormal personality traits, totalling 50% of the population. Goldberg, Gitta and Puddephatt (1995) also report very high levels of personality disorder in samples of people with intellectual disability. Using DSM-III-R diagnostic criteria and two other screening measures for psychiatric symptomatology, they found abnormal personality traits in 57% of individuals in an institutional sample and an astonishing 91% of individuals in a community sample.

Flynn, Mathews and Hollins (2002) studied a hospital in-patient sample of 36 cases. They employed ICD-10 diagnostic criteria using the SAP and reported that 92% of participants were diagnosed with personality disorder and 39% with severe personality disorder. On the other hand, Naik, Gangadharan and Alexander (2002), also working with ICD-10 criteria, found personality disorder in 7% of participants in a community sample and 58% in a hospital in-patient sample. Alexander and Cooray (2003) review a number of studies and comment on the lack of reliable diagnostic instruments, differences between ICD-10 and DSM-IV diagnostic systems, confusion of definition and personality theory, and the difficulties of distinguishing personality disorder from other problems integral to intellectual disabilities, e.g. communication problems, sensory disorders and developmental delay. They conclude that "the variation in the co-occurrence of personality disorder in learning disability with prevalence ranging from 1% to 91% . . . is too large to be explained by real differences". They recommend tighter diagnostic criteria and greater use of behavioural observation and informant information.

With greater interest being taken in the diagnosis of personality disorder in intellectual disabilities, some initial consensus is developing among clinicians and researchers. Clearly diagnostic criteria should be tightened and made more explicit: because of developmental delays, a diagnosis of personality disorder should not be made until the individual reaches 21 years of age, and the diagnosis of personality disorder in people with severe and profound intellectual disability is unlikely (Royal College of Psychiatrists, 2001; Lindsay, Gabriel, Dana, Young & Dosen, 2003).

Personality disorder has certainly been diagnosed in people with intellectual disabilities and may indeed be a significant problem among certain populations of this client group. While these prevalence rates are variable, and in many cases extremely high, it should be noted that a majority of studies report rates similar to the results from studies on psychiatric populations. Pilgrim and Mann (1990), in a study of subjects admitted to psychiatric hospital, found that 36% were judged to have personality disorder and a further 14% were considered to have abnormal personality traits.

Personality Disorder and Offenders

In certain ways there is a fundamental tension in the work on personality disorders and criminality and this is no less true in the field of intellectual disabilities. Experimental research on personality has developed apace over the past twenty years with the emergence of the five-factor personality model. On the other hand, work on criminality has tended to focus on the concept of personality disorder or psychopathology. There has been little work aimed at synthesising these strands, although some authors have made attempts (Blackburn, 1995, 2000).

In relation to criminality, the concept of psychopathic personality disorder is most often considered, although there are clearly problems about the reliability of the diagnosis, with several authors (Blackburn, 1995; McMurran, 2001) noting that it is based more on intuition and judgement rather than sound evidence. Others, notably Quinsey, Harris, Rice and Cormier (1998) have written that psychopathy can be an extremely useful predictive variable when measured systematically using the Hare Psychopathy Checklist—Revised (PCL-R). Indeed, these authors have written that the PCL-R is the most powerful predictor of response to treatment yet reported in the area of criminal behaviour and recidivism. Notwithstanding the views of Quinsey *et al.* (1998), most studies which have looked at risk factors and prognostic indicators have found that the best indicator for future offending is previous offending (Robertson, 1989; Nagayama-Hall, 1990). The PCL-R (Hare, 1991) contains a large number of items which do not relate to actual criminal activity although there are a few which do record amount and nature of previous offending. It also correlates reasonably highly with the diagnosis of abnormal personality disorder defined in DSM-IV (Hare, Hart and Harpur, 1991; Skeem & Mulvey, 2001). Therefore, it would seem that there might be some merit in considering psychopathy when dealing with the issues of personality disorder in offenders with intellectual disability.

Hare (1991) notes that the term *psychopathy* has a varying use between Europe and North America. He writes that "In Europe the term psychopathy often refers to personality deviation . . . (while) . . . in Great Britain the situation is complicated by the fact that 'psychopathic disorder' is a medico-legal category that bears little resemblance to the North American construct [for] most North American clinicians and researchers, psychopathy refers to a rather specific constellation of deviant traits and behaviours, . . . [which form] . . . the clinical basis for the PCL and the PCL-R" (Hare, 1991, p. 2).

Developments in Work on Personality

It is difficult to review the work on personality measurement and intellectual disabilities since the most active and influential group have developed their work from a completely different perspective than that of mainstream researchers. First, we shall review this large body of work in intellectual disabilities.

Over the course of forty years, Zigler and his colleagues have conducted extensive research into personality and intellectual disabilities. Contending that the emphasis on cognitive aspects of intellectual disabilities is an incomplete account of the person, they used a variety of experimental tasks comparing the performance of people with developmental disabilities with chronological and mental age matched controls. Their work has mostly, but not exclusively, involved persons without organic causes of developmental disabilities.

Zigler's early work demonstrated that although children with cultural–familial developmental disabilities appeared to pass through the same developmental stages as other children, their experience of development was significantly different from other children. Specifically, he hypothesised that their repeated experience of failure on academic and other tasks changed their style of problem solving. He hypothesised that their repeated experience of failure led them to avoid novel, challenging tasks, expect to fail these tasks, and look to others for cues as to how to solve these tasks (Hodapp, 1999; Zigler & Bennett-Gates, 1999).

In order to evaluate these hypotheses Zigler's group would compare the performance of children with cultural–familial developmental disabilities with chronological and mental age matched controls on a variety of experimental tasks designed to evaluate their problem solving style and motivation. For example, when asked to make a picture children with intellectual disabilities are more likely to imitate models in making that picture than chronological and mental age matched controls. This illustrates greater dependency on external cues to solve an ambiguous and novel task.

This earlier developmental work led Zigler and colleagues to hypothesise *five* personality traits that might differentiate persons with cultural–familial developmental disabilities from their peers. Zigler, Bennett-Gates, Hodapp and Henrich (2002, pp. 181–2) describe these traits as follows:

- *Positive reaction tendency*: "heightened motivation . . . to both interact with, and be dependent upon, a supportive adult"
- *Negative reaction tendency*: "initial wariness shown . . . when interacting with strange adults"
- *Expectancy of success*: "the degree to which one expects to succeed or fail when presented a new task"
- *Outerdirectedness*: "tendency . . . to look to others for the cues to solutions of difficult or ambiguous tasks"
- *Efficacy motivation*: "the pleasure derived from tackling and solving difficult problems".

When compared to their typically developing peers, people with intellectual disabilities tend to have lower expectancy of success and efficacy motivation and higher positive and negative reaction tendencies and outerdirectedness.

Based on their earlier developmental work, Zigler *et al.* (2002) reported on the empirical development of a new measure of personality in people with intellectual disabilities. This measure is known as the *EZ-Yale Personality Questionnaire* (EZPQ). A pool of 115 items was generated which may have measured the five traits discussed above. This was then reduced by panel consensus and data reduction to a final pool of 37 items. The EZPQ was administered to 661 children with cultural–familial developmental disability aged between 5 and 20 years. Their IQs ranged from 45 to 75.

The results of a factor analysis identified seven factors. Five of these factors appeared to be those described above. Additionally, two more factors, named obedience and curiosity/creativity, were identified. Test/retest reliability and a measure of internal consistency were all high. There was also good evidence of validity. Scores of the EZPQ correlated reasonably well with performance on the experimental tasks previously used to measure these traits. There were also statistically significant differences between children with intellectual disabilities and typically developing children on all seven traits.

The EZPQ is a psychometrically well developed instrument with good evidence of reliability and validity. To date there is no research relating scores on this instrument to criminal behaviour or linking extreme scores on these scales to personality disorders. However, some research has linked personality variables to the development of psychopathology in people with intellectual disabilities (Zigler & Burack, 1989) and in people with mental health disorders (Zigler & Glick, 1986). Future research could investigate these possibilities using the EZPQ, as it is a promising instrument.

Having established that personality disorder is considered within the population of individuals with intellectual disability, it seems logical, then, to review work in the field of personality to consider both developments in the field and their relevance to intellectual disabilities and to the concept of personality disorder. As has been noted, psychopathy has been considered extensively in relation to criminality in mainstream offenders. Despite a series of criticisms on the intuitive use of the concept, structured assessment using the PCL-R has found that it may be a more valid and reliable concept than has previously been considered. In addition, it is closely related to diagnoses of personality disorder defined according to DSM-IV.

Recent developments in the field of personality research have centred on the concept of traits which make up the total of what is considered to be personality. This approach assumes that all individuals share the same basic personality structure but differ from each other in the extent to which they display particular traits. Cattell (1965) instituted a complex system of sixteen personality factors which was highly influential in the development of trait theory. Eysenck (1970) developed a much simpler system of two and then three super factors—neuroticism, extroversion and psychoticism. He felt these super factors to be much more statistically robust than Cattell's sixteen factors. When Cattell's variables were analysed by orthogonal rotational methods, only five and occasionally six factors emerged from subsequent studies (Tupes and Christal, 1961; Norman, 1963; Howarth, 1976).

The generality of the five factor solution was demonstrated by Goldberg (1990) in three disparate studies employing differing methodologies and subject samples. He found that where another factor might emerge, it did not generalise across methodologies or sample groups whereas the five orthogonal factors remained robust. Digman (1990) reviews a large number of studies and attempts to classify these five factors. The first two accord with Eysenck's (1947) description of personality dimensions. Extroversion/introversion emerges from all of the work, as does neuroticism/emotional stability. Digman (1990) writes that the other three are more difficult to define, with a larger variety of scale items compiling them. The third dimension has been called "Agreeableness" although such a description may be somewhat pallid for a factor that involves characteristics such as altruism, nurturance, caring and emotional support at one end of the scale, with hostility, indifference to others, self-centredness, spitefulness and jealousy at the other end. The fourth factor is generally called "Conscientiousness", although Digman (1990) suggests that "will to achieve" is a better term. Finally, a factor of "Openness" has been identified although from time to time this has been related to culture, intelligence, readiness to indulge in fantasy, educational aptitude and creativity.

For the purposes of this chapter, it should be noted that arguments over the existence of five factors still continue. In a study employing the *Eysenck Personality Profiler*, Jackson, Furnham, Forde and Cotter (2000) found little persuasive evidence to support a five-factor solution. Rather their data on 655 participants favoured a three-factor solution similar to that proposed by Eysenck.

Despite the arguments among trait theorists regarding the adequacy of a three-, five- or seven-factor solution to personality assessment, there remains no doubt whatsoever that structured assessment of personality characteristics, employing sophisticated statistical techniques, is beginning to clarify the important variables which make up personality. The five-factor solution has been replicated on numerous occasions, and Costa and McCrae (1985) have used the model to develop an inventory to assess the five trait dimensions that make up these robust personality factors. The *NEO Personality Inventory* (NEO-PI) assesses these five personality factors—neuroticism, extroversion, openness, agreeableness and conscientiousness. This personality inventory has been used extensively both in clinical and research work and has been employed by the present authors to investigate the feasibility of using a structured assessment for personality in offenders with intellectual disability.

Assessments

The NEO-Personality Inventory (NEO-PI)

This assessment was originally developed by Costa and McCrae (1985) and included the neuroticism, extroversion and openness personality dimensions. It was later revised to include the dimensions of agreeableness and conscientiousness. It now consists of 240 individual item scales rated from "strongly agree" through "agree", "neutral", "disagree" and "strongly disagree". Permission was granted to the authors by the publishers to simplify, where necessary, the item scales so that they would be more easily understood by people with intellectual disabilities. Examples of item simplification were as follows:

NEO item   "Some people think I am selfish and egotistical"
Revised item   "Some people think I am selfish and only think of myself"
NEO item   "I work hard to accomplish my goals"
Revised item   "I work hard to get what I want"
NEO item   "Sometimes when I am reading poetry or looking at a work of art I feel a chill or wave of excitement"
Revised item   "Sometimes a bit of poetry or a painting makes me feel excited"

All the items which had been altered were then given to three experienced clinical psychologists to ensure that the essential issue contained within each item scale had not been altered. For all but four of the 240 items it was agreed that the essential meaning of the scale had not been changed.

The NEO-PI is structured so that each of the five factors is made up of six facets. Each facet is made up of six individual item scales. Therefore, the neuroticism factor is made up of the six facets: anxiety, depression, obsessionality, anger, impulsiveness and vulnerability.

The NEO-PI has two distinct forms: one filled out by the individual themselves and one filled out by a respondent who is familiar with the subject. Because of this latter option, it was considered particularly suitable for the current study where it might prove to have wider applicability. Since many individuals with intellectual disability are lacking in language skills, if the current series of studies suggest that it is feasible to assess individuals from this client group, then it is helpful to have an assessment which does not depend solely on the responses of the subject themselves.

The Hare Psychopathy Checklist—Revised (PCL-R)

The PCL-R consists of twenty items which are rated by a professional rater (psychologist or psychiatrist) on a scale of 0, 1 and 2, with 0 indicating that the person shows none of these characteristics, 1 indicating that they show some of the characteristics or all of the characteristics some of the time, and 2 indicating that they show all of the characteristics all of the time. Ratings can be made from case notes although it is advised that the subject is well known to the rater. The manual contains extensive notes and guidelines for ratings. For the subjects to follow, ratings were made by both a psychologist and a psychiatrist who each had at least 20 years of experience in the field.

The PCL-R is made up of 20 items organised into two factors, the first of which Hare (1991) describes as "selfish, callous and remorseless use of others" and the second of which he describes as "chronically unstable and antisocial lifestyle; social deviance" (p. 38). The items also reveal a total psychopathy score. In Hare's (1991) technical manual, he recommends that a total score of over 30 indicates a significant score of psychopathy. Cooke (1995), working on a Scottish prison population of 124 prisoners, found that a lower cut-off of 25 was probably more indicative of psychopathy in the Scottish population. Since the current assessments were conducted on a population of Scottish men with intellectual disabilities, this lower cut-off should be borne in mind. In addition, Quinsey et al. (1998) consider that a PCL-R score of over 25 gives a positive score in risk assessment on the Violence Risk Appraisal Guide.

Some authors (Blackburn 1998, 2000) have indicated that there is some evidence that psychopathy as measured by the PCL-R has an association with the big five personality factors represented by low agreeableness and low conscientiousness. In a study of two assessment systems for specific traits relating to personality disorder, Clark, Livesley, Schroeder and Irish (1996) reported a five-factor structure which, again, broadly resembled the dimensions of the five-factor approach to personality. The third factor was marked most strongly by rejection, callousness and manipulativeness, which had parallels with the concept of psychopathy and indicated a pattern of low agreeableness and low conscientiousness. Therefore, there is some evidence that low A and C factors may be associated with high PCL-R scores. The following examples illustrate the employment of these measures with offenders with intellectual disability.

Examples of Personality Assessment

High PCL-R respondents

Mr M had a measured IQ of 66 (WAIS-III). He was 23 at the time of the assessment and until the age of 18 had lived with his father. His parents had split up during his childhood. He had a brother and a sister both of whom had severe alcohol- and drug-related problems. At the ages of 15 and 16 years Mr M was charged with a series of sexual offences against children. He was referred to the second author (WL) for assessment and treatment and was considered such a serious offender that he was admitted to hospital for treatment. His progress through treatment has been conspicuously poor. He began by letting staff know that he was aware of how to get them sacked, insinuating that if he made allegations of sexual abuse then they would be suspended. Throughout the subsequent years he refused treatment for thoughts and behaviour consistent with sexual offending against children and has continued to insist that given the opportunity he would offend again.

Assessment on the PCL-R revealed a score of 26, which is above the cut-off point suggested by Cooke (1995) for psychopathy in populations of Scottish men. His self-assessment on the NEO-PI revealed that he fell into the category of very high for neuroticism, average for extroversion and low for openness, agreeableness and conscientiousness. On the respondent assessment he fell into the categories of very high for neuroticism, average for extroversion and openness, and very low for agreeableness and conscientiousness.

A further two subjects scoring high in the PCL-R are noted in Table 15.2. Mr S was a 21-year-old man with a measured IQ of 69 (WAIS-III) and charged with three offences of sexual assault against teenage girls. He had lived all his life with his family until the offences occurred, when they felt they were unable to cope with him at home. Mr D was a 32-year-old man with physical disabilities who had a measured IQ of 66 (WAIS-III). He lived at home with his mother and father for most of his life and had been charged with a series of assaults against a variety of individuals, including his parents, the police, ambulance drivers and passers by. He had also made several suicide attempts and made dozens of unsubstantiated claims of attempted suicide.

It can be seen from Table 15.2 that both of these individuals show a similar pattern to Mr M with low scores both on the self-recording and respondent recording on the agreeableness and conscientiousness scales. The trends which are shown in the self-recording scales are more marked on the respondent scales.

Examples of low PCL-R respondents

Mr P was a 34-year-old man with a measured IQ of 66 (WAIS-III) who had lived with his parents all of his life. He attended special school and special college courses but was unable to hold down occupational placements because he complained re- peatedly of ill health. He was convicted of several non-penetrative offences against children resulting in a disposal of 3 years probation. His assessment on the PCL-R

Table 15.2 Examples of personality assessment

	Self-Reports					PCL			Respondent Reports				
	N	E	O	A	C				N	E	O	A	C
Low													
Mr G	103(H)	106(A)	106(A)	153(A)	109(L)	0	4	5	86(H)	78(L)	60(VL)	135(A)	120(A)
Mr P	126(VH)	113(A)	92(L)	129(H)	131(A)	0	1	3	107(VH)	109(A)	87(L)	151(H)	137(A)
Mr C	111(VH)	127(H)	122(H)	121(A)	102(L)	1	4	5	110(VH)	110(A)	108(A)	118(A)	81(VL)
	340	346	320	454	342				303	297	255	394	338
Average	113(VH)	115(A)	106(A)	151(A)	114(L/A)			4.3	101(H)	99(A)	85(L)	131(A)	113(L/A)
High													
Mr M	116(VH)	110(A)	89(L)	111(L)	109(L)	14	9	26	129(VH)	95(A)	102(A)	53(VL)	74(VL)
Mr S	109(VH)	117(A)	97(L)	98(L)	107(L)	9	11	22	119(VH)	73(L)	83(L)	56(VL)	56(VL)
Mr D	146(VH)	139(VH)	110(A)	115(A)	96(L)	10	13	23	112(VH)	94(A)	107(A)	52(VL)	51(VL)
	361	366	296	324	312				360	262	292	161	181
Average	120(VH)	122(H)	99(A)	108(L)	104(L)			23.6	120(VH)	87(VL)	97(L)	54(VL)	60(VL)

Note: N, Neuroticism; E, extroversion; O, openness; A, agreeableness; C, conscientiousness. VH, Very high; H, high; A, average; L, low; VL, very low.

revealed a score of 3, which is very low. His responses on the NEO-PI place him in the bands of very high for neuroticism, average for extroversion, low for openness, high for agreeableness and average for conscientiousness. Although the scores differ somewhat, the bands are the same for the respondent's ratings. The immediate and obvious difference between the scores of Mr P and those of Mr M are in the areas of agreeableness and conscientiousness, where Mr P has scored average or high and Mr M has scored low or very low.

Two other subjects with low scores on the PCL-R make up the final entries to Table 15.2. Mr G was a 44-year-old man with a measured IQ of 72 (WAIS-III). He lived on his own and worked as an assistant to a carpenter. He drank alcohol to excess and had a few close regular friends. His work record was exemplary. He was charged with sexual offences against a 7-year-old girl whereby he abducted her for a short period of time for purposes of masturbation in a public toilet. He was charged with offences against children and given 3 years probation. Mr C was 34 years old with a measured IQ of 65 (WAIS-III). He went to school for people with intellectual disabilities and lived with his father. He complained of a series of somatic complaints over the years but managed to stay at home with the help of short periods of admission to hospital for people with intellectual disabilities. He was charged with violent offences and theft and given a 1-year probation sentence.

As can be seen, all three of these individuals had low scores on the PCL-R. On the self-respondent scale they all scored very high or high on the neuroticism factor, average or high on the extroversion factor, they were variable on the openness factor, average or high on the agreeableness factor, and low or average on the conscientiousness factor. On the other respondent form they were considered to be high or very high on the neuroticism scale, low or average on the extroversion scale, very low to average on the openness scale, average or high on the agreeableness scale, and two were average and one very low on the conscientiousness scale.

While comparisons with such small numbers are obviously unreliable, it is interesting that structured assessment such as this allows hypotheses to be set up which might guide or inform future investigation. There would appear to be a difference between those scoring high and low on the PCL-R in relation to the agreeableness and conscientiousness scales on the NEO-PI. There is a tendency for those scoring high on the PCL-R to score lower on the agreeableness scale. This trend is accentuated in the profiles calculated from the other respondents. The same is true for the conscientiousness scale apart from Mr C. Indeed, if we average the raw scores of both groups and compare them on the profiles completed by the other respondents, the findings are interesting. The differences between the two groups on the N, E and O dimensions are less than 20 points. On the A and C dimensions the differences are more than 50 points.

It is not the purpose of such a comparison to suggest that this is a substantive finding since the numbers here are small. However, the results do accord with those reported by Blackburn (2000). Such work does demonstrate that systematic assessment can enable us to set up hypotheses about the way in which personality characteristics might vary and relate to each other. In this way, we may begin to investigate the relationship between intellectual disabilities, personality, offending, response to treatment and recidivism.

CONCLUSION

This chapter is one of the first attempts to integrate work on personality, personality disorder, psychopathy and intellectual disabilities. The authors are acutely aware that the areas of research are disparate, are developed from distinct and diverse backgrounds and based on separate principles and assumptions. As such, integration is at best interpretative and at worst guesswork. And yet personality has become such an important variable in the field of criminality that it is timely to begin to establish parameters for assessment and review, which will be of aid to clients and clinicians.

An early task is to make some integration of the work of Zigler and colleagues with the more general work on personality. Zigler's original five personality traits are considerably less complex than the five general factors derived in mainstream personality research. Three of the five traits are related to problem solving and two to interaction with others. The two further traits added more recently, obedience and curiosity, are again person and task oriented, respectively. It is noticeable that none is related to mood or emotion, which is one of the most enduring factors in personality research. Some investigation of the reason for differences in these research findings would seem required especially in the context of work on offenders with intellectual disability where emotions such as anger seem so salient in the profiles of a range of clients (see Chapters 9 and 11).

Early sections of this chapter illustrated that knowledge of personality disorder is as important when working with people with intellectual disability as it is with any other population. The assessment of psychopathy is increasingly used in the judgement of risk of violent recidivism in offenders. The case studies reported in this chapter would suggest that such developments may be relevant and useful in work with offenders with intellectual disability. Personality assessment may provide broad guidelines for treatment as we develop more information about the relationship between personality, response to treatment, treatment modalities and recidivism.

REFERENCES

Alexander, R. & Cooray, S. (2003). Diagnosis of personality disorders in learning disability. *British Journal of Psychiatry*, **182** (suppl. 44), S28–S31.

American Psychiatric Association (1998). *Diagnostic and Statistical Manual of Mental Disorders*, 4th edn, text revised. Washington, DC: American Psychiatric Association.

Ballinger, B.R. & Reid, A.H. (1987). A standardised assessment of personality in mental handicap. *British Journal of Psychiatry*, **150**, 108–9.

Batchelor, I.R.C. (1964). Psychopathic states. In I.R.C. Batchelor (ed.) *Henderson and Gillespie's Textbook of Psychiatry*, 10th edn. London: Oxford University Press.

Blackburn, R. (1995). *The Psychology of Criminal Behaviour: Theory, Research and Practice*. Chichester: John Wiley & Sons.

Blackburn, R. (1998). Psychopathy and personality disorder: implications of interpersonal theory. In D.J. Cooke, S.J. Hart & A.E. Forth (eds) *Psychopathy: Theory Research and Implications for Society* (pp. 269–301). Amsterdam: Kluwer.

Blackburn, R. (2000). Classification and assessment of personality disorders in mentally disordered offenders: a psychological perspective. *Criminal Behaviour and Mental Health*, **10** (suppl.), 8–32.

Bluglass, R. (1990). The Mental Health Act, 1983. In R. Bluglass & P. Bowden (eds) *Principles in Practice of Forensic Psychiatry*. London: Churchill Livingston.

Cattell, R.B. (1965). *The Scientific Analysis of Personality*. London: Penguin.

Clark, L.A., Livesley, W.J., Schroeder, M.L. & Irish, S.L. (1996). Convergence of two systems for assessing specific traits of personality disorder. *Psychological Assessment*, **8**, 294–303.

Cooke, E.D. (1995). Psychopathic disturbance in the Scottish prison population: the cross cultural generalisability of the Hare Psychopathy Checklist. *Psychology, Crime and Law*, **2**, 101–8.

Corbett, J.A. (1979). *Psychiatric Illness in Mental Handicap*. London: Gaskell Press.

Costa, P.T., Jr, & McCrae, R.R. (1985). *The NEO Personality Inventory*. Odessa, FL: Psychological Assessment Resources.

Craft, M. (1965). *Ten Studies into Psychopathic Personality*. Bristol: John Wright & Sons.

Digman, J.M. (1990). Personality structure: emergence of the five factor model. *Annual Review of Psychology*, **41**, 441–77.

Earl, C.J.C. (1961). *Subnormal Personalities: Their Clinical Investigation and Assessment*. London: Bailliere, Tindall & Cox.

Eaton, I.F. & Menolascino, F.J. (1982). Psychiatric disorders in the mentally retarded: types, problems and challenges. *American Journal of Psychiatry*, **139**, 1297–1303.

Esquirol, J.E.D. (1845). *Mental Maladies: A Treatise on Insanity*, translated by E.K. Hunt. Philadelphia, PA: Lea & Blanchard.

Eysenck, H.J. (1947). *Dimensions of Personality*. New York: Praeger.

Eysenck, H.J. (1970). *The Structure of Human Personality*. London: Methuen.

Flynn, A., Mathews, H. & Hollins, S. (2002). Validity of the diagnosis of personality disorder in adults with learning disability and severe behaviour problems. *British Journal of Psychiatry*, **180**, 543–6.

Goldberg, B., Gitta, M.Z. & Puddephatt, A. (1995). Personality and trait disturbance in an adult mental retardation population: significance for psychiatric management. *Journal of Intellectual Disability Research*, **39**, 284–94.

Goldberg, L.R. (1990). An alternative "description of personality". The big five factor structure. *Journal of Personality and Social Psychology*, **59**, 1216–29.

Gostasson, R. (1987). Psychiatric illness among the mildly mentally retarded. *Journal of Medical Science*, **44**(suppl.), 115–24.

Hare, R.D. (1980). The assessment of psychopathy in criminal populations. *Personality and Individual Differences*, **1**, 111–19.

Hare, R.D. (1991). *The Revised Psychopathy Checklist*. Toronto, Ontario: Multi-Health Systems.

Hare, R.D., Hart, S. & Harpur, T. (1991). Psychopathy and the DSM-IV criteria for antisocial personality disorder. *Journal of Abnormal Psychology*, **100**, 391–8.

Henderson, D.K. (1939). *Psychopathic States*. New York: Norsson.

Hodapp, R.M. (1999). *Developmental Disabilities. Intellectual Sensory and Motor Impairments*. New York: Cambridge University Press.

Holmes, N., Shah, A. & Wing, L. (1982). The disability assessment schedule: a brief screening device for use with the mentally retarded. *Psychological Medicine*, **12**, 879–90.

Howarth, E. (1976). Were Cattell's Personality Sphere Factors correctly identified in the first instance? *British Journal of Psychology*, **67**, 213–30.

Jackson, C.J., Furnham, A., Forde, L. & Cotter, T. (2000). The structure of the Eysenck Personality Profiler. *British Journal of Psychology*, **91**, 223–39.

Khan, A., Cowan, C. & Roy, A. (1997). Personality disorders in people with learning disabilities: a community survey. *Journal of Intellectual Disability Research*, **41**, 324–30.

Lindsay, W.R., Gabriel, S., Dana, L., Young, S. & Dosen, A. (2003). Personality disorders. In R. Fletcher, E. Loschen & P. Sturmey (eds) *Diagnostic Manual of Psychiatric Disorders for Individuals with Mental Retardation*. Kingston, NY: National Association for Dual Diagnosis.

McMurran, M. (2001). Offenders with personality disorders. In C.R. Hollin (ed.) *Handbook of Offender Assessment and Treatment* (pp. 467–79). Chichester: John Wiley & Sons.

Mann, A.H., Jenkins, R., Cutting, J.C. & Cowan, P.J. (1981). The development and use of a standardised assessment of abnormal personality. *Psychological Medicine*, **11**, 839–47.

Maudsley, H. (1868). *The Physiology and Pathology of Mind*, 2nd edn. London: Macmillan.

Nagayama-Hall, G.C. (1990). Prediction of sexual aggression. *Clinical Psychology Review*, **10**, 229–45.

Naik, B.I., Gangadharan, S.K. & Alexander, R.T. (2002). Personality disorders in learning disability—the clinical experience. *British Journal of Developmental Disabilities*, **48**, 95–100.

Norman, W.T. (1963). Towards an adequate taxonomy of personality attributes: replicated factor structure in the peer nomination personality ratings. *Journal of Abnormal and Social Psychology*, **66**, 574–83.

Partridge, G.E. (1930). Personality disorder. *American Journal of Psychiatry*, **10**, 53.

Pilgrim, J. & Mann, A. (1990). Use of ICD-10 version of the Standardized Assessment of Personality to determine the prevalence of personality disorder in psychiatric in-patients. *Psychological Medicine*, **20**, 985–92.

Pritchard, J.C. (1837). *A Treatise on Insanity and Other Diseases Affecting the Mind*. Philadelphia, PA: Harwell, Barrington & Howell.

Quinsey, V.L., Harris, G.T., Rice, M.E. & Cormier, C.A. (1998*). Violent Offenders: Appraising and Managing Risk*. Washington, DC: American Psychological Association.

Reid, A.H. & Ballinger, B.R. (1987). Personality disorder in mental handicap. *Psychological Medicine*, **17**, 983–7.

Robertson, G. (1989). Treatment for offender patients: how should success be measured? *Medicine, Science and the Law*, **29**, 303–7.

Royal College of Psychiatrists (2001). *Diagnostic Criteria in Learning Disability (DC-LD)*. London: Gaskell.

Skeem, J.L. & Mulvey, E.P. (2001). Psychopathy and community violence among civil psychiatric patients: results from the MacArthur Violence Risk Assessment Study. *Journal of Consulting and Clinical Psychology*, **69**, 1–23.

Tupes, E.C. & Christal, R.E. (1961). Recurrent personality factors based on trait ratings. USAF ASD Technical Report, 61–97.

Whatmore, P. (1990). The Mental Health (Scotland) Act 1984. In R. Bluglass & P. Bowden (eds) *Principles in Practice of Forensic Psychiatry*. London: Churchill Livingston

WHO (1992). *The ICD-10 Classification on Mental and Behavioural Disorders: Clinical Descriptions and Diagnostic Guidelines*. Geneva: World Health Organization.

Zigler, E. & Bennett-Gates, D. (1999). *Personality Development in Individuals with Mental Retardation*. Boston, MA: Cambridge University Press.

Zigler, E., Bennett-Gates, D., Hodapp, R. & Henrich, C.C. (2002). Assessing personality traits of individuals with mental retardation. *American Journal on Mental Retardation*, **107**, 181–93.

Zigler, E. & Burack, J.A. (1989). Personality development and the dually diagnosed persons. *Research in Developmental Disabilities*, **10**, 225–40.

Zigler, E. & Glick, M. (1986). *A Developmental Approach to Adult Psychopathology*. New York: John Wiley & Sons.

PART V

SERVICE DEVELOPMENT, PROFESSIONAL AND RESEARCH ISSUES

Chapter 16

STAFF SUPPORT AND DEVELOPMENT

Anthony F. Perini

Northgate & Prudhoe NHS Trust, Northumberland, UK

In few areas of psychiatry is staff support and development as critical as in the field of forensic mental health. Unlike other areas of health care, forensic psychiatry stands at an uneasy interface between the health care system, with its therapeutic aspirations, and the criminal justice system, whose necessary focus is on deterrence of offenders and protection of the public.

Health care staff work with vulnerable, often challenging and sometimes dangerous individuals, often in relatively closed settings. As well as carrying out their therapeutic work there are the additional administrative overheads of preparing reports, attending various hearings and being subjected to cross-examination by legal colleagues. In addition, the nature of forensic services is such that patients are often taken from geographically distant referring agencies, which increases the difficulties of coordination of the care plan, particularly when arranging transfer. Navigating geographic, agency and administrative barriers to continuity of care adds to the stress of the health care team, usually under pressure from other stakeholders to deliver an optimum care plan.

The management of a patient is scrutinised by numerous external agencies and other clinical and non-clinical professionals, often with different agenda. These can include the patient, relatives, carers, solicitors, advocates, hospital authorities, external health authorities and social services, the courts, the Prison Service, the Home Secretary (UK), the Mental Health Review Tribunal, the Mental Health Act Commission, charity/pressure groups, the media, politicians and the public. In many cases the scrutiny is adversarial in nature and the clinical team has to justify the management plan, steering a course which addresses the clinical needs of the patient while recognising and responding to the needs of other legitimate stakeholders and society at large.

Offenders with Developmental Disabilities. Edited by W.L. Lindsay, J.L. Taylor and P. Sturmey.
© 2004 John Wiley & Sons, Ltd.

STAFF SELECTION

Clinical staff working in hospital or community forensic settings have additional challenges in their work as compared with their colleagues in other specialties. In-patients are detained under various sections of the Mental Health Act, and for restricted patients, decisions about discharge and transfer are made by government departments rather than the clinical team. The patient's trust has to be won and therapeutic alliances made. Patient anxieties about the indeterminate length of stay (often compared by the patient with the determinate sentence he would have received had the court opted for a prison disposal) have to be managed.

Staff must adapt to a climate of increased scrutiny, challenge and comment on their work, often of an adversarial nature, by various interested parties. While this may sometimes stimulate new ways of thinking about the therapeutic challenges, such attention can also be demoralising, leading to a "damned if you do, damned if you don't" way of thinking which can divert attention from the primary task of treating the patient. Media interest, which in the experience of the majority of forensic services, rarely succeeds in portraying a balanced and accurate picture of the situation or event of interest, can have similar effects on staff and service-user morale.

In addition to the professional qualifications and experience necessary for a particular post, most services would look for some of the following qualities: a non-judgmental, positive, empathic approach to patients, focusing on the patient's needs; a level-headed and pragmatic personality, able to diffuse tense situations and act proportionately; the ability to see both sides of an argument, to justify decisions and actions, to be flexible and accept alternative viewpoints; resilience in coping with challenging patients and maintaining a positive attitude in a service which is unlikely to be understood or appreciated by the public; a "team player", able to relate to a wide variety of professionals; high ethical standards of care, confidentiality and respect for patients; and the ability to work within the constraints and restrictions imposed by the requirements of providing a safe environment for patients, staff and the public.

STAFF TRAINING AND DEVELOPMENT

Specialist services for people with intellectual disability are by nature few and far between, and in many countries non-existent. In such cases, people with intellectual disability utilise generic psychiatric units, either by design, for example in Sweden (Gustafsson, 1995, 1997) or by default, for example in Canada (Puddephatt & Sussman, 1994). Where such services exist, such as in the UK, the issue arises as to when it is appropriate to use specialist services for people with intellectual disability and when it is appropriate to use generic psychiatric services like other citizens (Gravestock & Bouras, 1997; O'Brien, 1990). In countries with specialised services the trend is to encourage the use of generic services as much as possible and to reserve specialist services for people whose intellectual disability results in needs that can only be met within specialist provision (UK Department of Health, 2001).

As well as a need for more widespread knowledge and experience of intellectual disability issues within general health and psychiatric services, and the inherent problems in achieving such expertise in such situations where people with intellectual disability will be a small minority of the population using the services (Day, 2001), the trend to fewer and more specialised units for people with intellectual disability requires organisations to recruit, train and retain effectively if they are to acquire, develop and maintain the specialist skills they need.

Developing and maintaining a skilled and highly motivated workforce is important to any organisation but essential in human organisations such as health and social care providers, where at least 70% of the running costs are invested in the staff. In highly specialised services with a small pool of potential recruits to draw from, these issues are critical to the success of the organisation.

It takes many years for an organisation to build up a core of highly skilled staff. Retention as well as recruitment of high-calibre personnel is thus of paramount importance. An organisation will be attractive if it offers a reputation for high quality services, stimulating posts with well-defined roles, a clear career structure, opportunities for training and development (including teaching and research), a collaborative culture between clinical professions and management, excellent terms and conditions of service, a high-quality working environment, and staff welfare facilities such as recreation and child care. Some of these attributes may not be readily definable in print, but in such a specialised area, reputation quickly spreads by word of mouth. The best organisations to work in are those with a culture that is patient centred, where inter-professional relationships are collaborative, and where management, support and clinical staff communicate effectively and share common goals.

Hertzburg (1966) relates job satisfaction to *extrinsic* factors (such as salary, job security, working conditions, status, policies and procedures, quality of supervision and quality of interpersonal relationships with colleagues) and *intrinsic* factors (such as recognition, achievement, advancement, responsibility, the work itself, opportunity for growth). According to this model, job satisfaction depends on how well the job meets the needs of the worker. Individuals tend to compare themselves with those close to them and become dissatisfied if they feel that they are unfavourably treated. Extrinsic rewards, such as salary and status, are more satisfying if they lead to intrinsic rewards such as greater autonomy, responsibility or recognition (Edward & Lawler, 1977). A more recent review, looking at enhanced roles among nurses and professions allied to medicine across 40 UK National Health Service Trusts, concluded that such factors increased job satisfaction, provided that adequate training was available and that new roles were clearly defined (Collins et al., 2000).

Training and development start with an organisational culture which values learning and which encourages and provides opportunities for staff at all levels to undertake further training. This should include "unqualified" staff such as nursing assistants, as well as professionally qualified staff. In the UK for example, the government recognised in the early 1980s that a competency-based certification system would be a valuable way of recognising and developing work-based skills in otherwise unqualified workers. The National Council for Vocational Qualifications was established in 1986 to set up a framework of National Vocational Qualifications based on agreed National Occupational Standards covering all occupations and industries. There are five levels in the system that can be linked to academic qualifications up to degree level.

In most countries intellectual disability is not recognised as a psychiatric speciality. The UK, however, has a long tradition of psychiatrists specialising in this field, with national training schemes administered by the Royal College of Psychiatrists, which include three to four years of higher training in the psychiatry of intellectual disability, following a similar period of postgraduate general psychiatric training (Day, 1999, 2001). In contrast, many countries employ nurses and psychologists in intellectual disability. In the UK, however, the shift towards community social care has, over the past two decades, altered the nurse training curriculum to reflect this changing service provision, to the detriment of psychiatric knowledge needed for specialised psychiatric services, such as those working with intellectually disabled offenders. The problem has been recognised by the UK government (Department of Health, 1995). Additional training is needed, either as in-service training or additional mental health qualifications. For psychologists, the UK model is a three-year postgraduate clinical training course with experience in relevant psychiatric specialties, leading to a higher degree. For comprehensive reviews of staff training issues for services working with people who have the dual diagnoses of mental health problems and mental retardation, see Day (2001), Hastings (1996) and Thomas (1995).

The organisation should encourage and foster a "learning culture", where clinical audit and research activity are a routine part of the work. Training programmes should be based on research evidence, modified as the evidence base changes (Brooker, 2001), and should be delivered in a "staff friendly" manner in order to maximise dissemination across a wide range of services (Jewell et al., 2001). There should also be appropriate information processing facilities in the workplace such as library facilities and access to computers and the internet. Specific training will need to be given in areas such as audit and research methods, literature reviews and ethics of research. Training in the use of computer technology will be needed for many staff, to support life-long learning as well as for use in day-to-day duties, where computers are an increasingly essential part of health-care delivery. In a recent study looking at attitudes of 309 mental health staff to computers, Walter, Cleary and Rey (2000) found that although a majority of staff had positive attitudes to computers, about half thought that they had insufficient access and very few had received training in their use.

Communications skills is another example of a key area which deserves attention within services for people with intellectual disabilities. Support and training for staff, particularly front-line staff who spend most time with the client group, can make a large difference to the quality of care, particularly a combination of direct work with a client and a "communication partner" and training courses for staff (Money, 1997). The use of communications workshops is associated with increased staff responsiveness to client communication as well as improvements in the quality and duration of staff–client interaction (Purcell, McConkey & Morris, 2000; Chatterton, 1999). Recent UK Department of Health publications relating to services for people with learning disabilities have recognised communication as a major barrier to delivery of services to people with learning disabilities

(Lindsay, 1998; Lindsay & Russell, 1999; Secretary of State for Health, 2001). In a climate of increasingly consumer-led health services, it is vital that staff have good communication skills across a wide range of professionals and other interested parties such as carers and relatives. Many organisations find that a significant proportion of complaints result from badly handled communication, which had it been better handled, would have saved much time, resource and stress in unnecessary investigation.

As well as general communication, staff working in forensic settings will not infrequently find themselves communicating in the very specialised setting of the court, whether as an expert witness in a trial or as a witness in a Mental Health Review Tribunal (MHRT). Although the latter are more informal, with a combination of inquisitorial and adversarial styles of examination, there are occasions, in certain cases, when Tribunals are conducted in a similar fashion to a criminal court, with cross-examination by members of the Bar. Training in this area should be part of the personal development of all health and social service professionals likely to have to appear in court or at MHRTs, or who need to provide legal reports in the course of their work. A handbook by Carson (1990) provides concise advice on these matters.

Continuous professional development is increasingly a compulsory requirement for professionally qualified staff, often with a requirement for documentary evidence. For example, medical staff in the UK must now undergo annual appraisal (Department of Health, 2000, 2001). A system of five-yearly revalidation is also currently being developed by the Department of Health in association with the General Medical Council and the medical profession. Each member of staff should have a Personal Development Plan, reviewed at least annually. This should be agreed between the individual and the organisation, reflecting the needs of both, along with an appropriately funded implementation plan. The personal development plan should include the following elements: continuous professional development required by the individual's professional body; training and development needed by the organisation in order to deliver its service plan and strategic direction; development in anticipation of the future needs of the organisation, for example, leadership development and management training; and training and development primarily related to the individual's personal professional interests, which may also have benefits to the organisation

The implementation of training commitments presents different challenges for different staff groups. For example, medical staff and psychologists can arrange their clinical and administrative duties to fit around periods of study leave, and, if away for short periods, can make reciprocal arrangements with their colleagues to cover for emergencies during their absence. Such arrangements, plus the fact that such staff groups are small in number relative to the overall clinical staff, allow flexibility for both the professional and the organisation. The costs are confined to the actual costs of the study plus travel and subsistence, which are relatively small, compared with the total financial impact should it have been necessary to replace the professional during the absence. The disadvantage is that the professional has to catch up on their routine work when he or she returns from study leave.

In contrast, clinicians such as nurses, who form the majority of staff in most organisations, cannot in many cases be released from their work area without finding a replacement, either through overtime work by the existing staff pool or by recruiting additional staff. The costs, in human resource as well as financial terms, place constraints on implementing training and development programmes for these staff groups. On-site learning and training facilities such as library and classroom facilities, and a "quiet room" on the ward which can accommodate a variety of learning aids such as video and audio tape, computer assisted learning, internet access, key textbooks and an intranet link to on-site electronic information bases, are of particular benefit to ward-based staff such as nurses who have less flexibility in building learning time into their working day.

Self-paced learning has been used, particularly in the USA, as a cost-effective method of staff development (O'Very, 1999). Modules are first pilot tested on a small group, then advertised by leaflet, email, poster and newsletter, or added to existing training programmes. A system of documentation is incorporated, allowing students to receive a certificate of completion, and feedback informs a continuous process of improvement. An additional benefit is that the method can be applied to mandatory training, for example, Fire, and Control of Substances Hazardous to Health, with dramatic improvements in compliance (Lipe, Reeds, Prokop, Menousek & Bryant, 1994). Other tools for staff development include secondment into another service area or organisation to gain experience, mentoring by a senior colleague (often working in a different organisation) and "action learning sets", where individuals with similar roles in different organisations meet to discuss issues of common interest and the progress of particular projects which they are leading in their respective services.

STAFF SUPERVISION AND SUPPORT

Traditionally, organisations have been better at providing supervision and support for staff in training grades, where, increasingly, professional bodies insist on specific supervision arrangements, as compared with trained or unqualified staff, where more reliance is placed on line management arrangements and adherence to policies and procedures. A sense of therapeutic optimism must be maintained and imparted to others, not least the patient, and the highest professional standards of treatment and care must be maintained, often in the face of stressful circumstances. Working for long periods with a challenging client group that responds slowly, if at all, to intensive therapeutic input can demoralise the most stoical of clinicians.

In addition, staff are asked to cope with frequent service reconfigurations and developments, changes in legislation, therapeutic developments and changes in working practices across a range of clinical professionals, with uncertainties and redefinition of roles. The effects of uncertainty and change on the way people relate and cooperate within organisations can have major effects both on the performance of the organisation and the well-being of the staff (Sylvester & Chapman, 1997; Stolte, 1994). Different professionals operate under different pressures and all can be at risk of so-called "burnout" (emotional exhaustion, depersonalisation and lack of personal achievement) (Jackson, Schwab & Schuler, 1986). Direct-care staff work in prolonged contact with patients/clients, often in circumstances where they have little ability to control this, as for example, a nurse having to work a shift on a ward. Such staff groups, many of whom are not professionally qualified, are often the most vulnerable to the effects of stress. Moreover, any adverse reactions to stress may impact directly on the patient.

Organisational support, to clarify policies and procedures, encourage the maintenance of high standards of care, as well as to identify and remedy problems at an early stage, is particularly important for this group (Dychawy-Rosner, Eklund & lsacsson, 2000). Active support training has been shown to improve staff–resident interaction and resident behaviour in community learning disability services (Felce et al., 2000). The issue of clinical supervision of nursing staff in an intellectual disability forensic service has been reviewed by Minto and Morrow (1999). Other professionals such as psychiatrists and psychologists may have the added burdens of indirect patient care, such as report writing, Tribunal and court attendance as well as general management, professional and service commitments, but they also have greater control in structuring their working day and in contact time with patients.

Perceived control and flexibility over the work environment and tasks can be a powerful moderator of work-related stress. Schmitz, Neumann and Oppermann (2000) studied 361 staff nurses from nine units in five German hospitals using the 22-item Maslach Burnout Inventory, the Levenson Locus of Control Scale and the Nursing Stress Questionnaire. High levels of burnout were associated with high levels of perceived work stress and a lack of control over events, surroundings or other people. The study had limitations in that it relied on the self-report of a postal sample (the response rate was 65%). However, the authors noted that similar results had been obtained in other studies looking at burnout and internal control, and recommended that specific training in practical problem solving and interpersonal skills should be part of nurse training, with the aim of increasing their internal locus of control, as well as further studies of social, psychological and environmental factors contributing to burnout.

Ito, Kurita and Shiiya (1999) studied 3,774 staff members in 216 Japanese social welfare facilities for people with intellectual disability using the Pines' Burnout Scale and found significantly higher burnout scores among direct care staff. Significantly lower scores were found where direct care staff were supported by supervisors with whom they could discuss work and personal problems. Some organisations have developed dedicated staff support departments to work both proactively and reactively (Lockhart, 1997). Informal discussion with colleagues is also an important source of support for both hospital and community staff (Reid et al., 1999).

In community services, the importance of direct care staff is paramount as poor job performance, low morale and stress can be much more hazardous to the service and its users due to the smaller scale of such services and their community location. The interface between psychiatry, the legal system and society is also much more acute in such services, and professionals need to balance care, supervision and social control (Mason & Mercer, 1996).

Up to a third of staff working in community residential settings for people with intellectual disability report high levels of stress (Hatton, Brown, Caine & Emerson, 1995; Hatton et al., 1998). In a study of 450 staff (therapeutic, managerial, administrative and domestic), working in five UK community residential services for people with intellectual disability, Hatton *et al.* (1999, 2001) used a questionnaire battery of some 18 scales looking at job activities, control, decision making, support, role conflict and organisational culture, and their effect on measures of stress, job strain and job satisfaction. Stress and lack of job satisfaction were linked to *wishful thinking* (an emotional coping strategy based on hope rather than action), lack of supervisor support, *alienative commitment* (negative feelings about the organisation coupled with behaviour indicating a strong desire to belong to it), role ambiguity, low status, lack of influence over work decisions, long hours and older staff age.

Other studies, such as Dyer and Quine (1998) and Rose, Jones and Fletcher (1998), again highlight role conflict and ambiguity, work overload, resident characteristics and lack of participation in decision making as demand factors contributing to occupational stress in community intellectual disability services. Caseload size is significantly correlated with stress levels in community forensic services (Coffey & Coleman, 2001). Hatton *et al.* (1999) recommended increased training and stress management for staff, focusing on problem solving, more flexible working hours, clear roles, providing more support and fostering a positive commitment to the organisation by democratic decision making and the promotion of clear organisational values.

So-called "challenging behaviour" (usually aggressive and antisocial) is also a frequent factor in relation to staff stress and poor mental health (Jenkins, Rose & Lovell, 1997; Mitchell & Hastings, 2001; Reid *et al.*, 1999; Hastings & Brown, 2002), particularly in community-based services. Appropriate training in the management of behaviour problems is essential for high-quality care and to maintain the morale of the staff. Training can help staff to understand the behaviour and to respond in ways that normalise the client's interactions rather than maintaining problems, to the benefit of both client and carer (Berryman, Evans & Kalbag, 1994). One of the roles of direct care staff is that of counsellor and teacher, helping clients to behave in ways that are conducive to community integration (Killu, 1994). Staff need training, not only in understanding challenging behaviour as a client communication issue but to deal with the complex emotional responses involved, to guard against negative reactions and to be open-minded about alternative ways of managing the problem (Brown & Brown, 1994).

Training may be delivered in a variety of ways. Didactic teaching increases knowledge but not necessarily the implementation of that knowledge (Milne, 1986; Hastings, 1996). Distance learning packages (e.g. Campbell *et al.*, 1993) again are strong in imparting knowledge but cannot control its implementation in a specific care setting. Interactional staff training, (Corrigan, 1998; Corrigan *et al.*, 1997; Corrigan & McCracken, 1997) is likely to be more effective, as it requires participation by the whole team, including the manager. Group cohesiveness and shared learning establish an environment where a need for information is accepted, where skills can be brought up to a consistent level across members of the team and where a consensus can be reached about the introduction of new practices. Gentry, Iceton and Milne (2001) reported favourable results from a three-day interactional staff training programme, with significant improvements in knowledge, core skills, job clarity and confidence, as well as practical outputs such as guidelines to manage challenging behaviours with specific clients.

Staff skills and performance need to be maintained over time, and training programmes will need to be repeated at intervals in order to maintain their benefits. Effects of training on staff behaviour, however, can persist for many months (Baker, 1998). In addition to direct supervision, and involving staff in decision making, performance feedback by managers to direct care staff is an effective mechanism for maintaining staff performance, valued by staff as well as managers (Green & Reid, 1991; Hrydowy & Martin, 1994). Self-monitoring by staff may be used, supported by other mechanisms (Richman, Riordan, Reiss, Pyles & Bailey, 1988).

The results of these studies suggest that some common-sense approaches are likely to be effective in combating stress and burnout. These include appropriate skills and training and regularly updating skills. Avoidance of excessive working hours is specified in the European Working Time Directive, which limits working hours to 48 hours per week (averaged over 17 weeks) and a minimum break of 30 minutes in a 7.5-hour period (The Council of the European Union, 1993). Family friendly personnel policies which allow staff to balance their work and personal commitments as parents and carers may also be helpful. Avoidance of prolonged direct contact with patients, healthy shift patterns, staffing levels which allow variation in the working day between direct and indirect clinical work and periodic rotation of staff roles may also be effective. Administrative factors such as clear staff roles, policies and procedures, facilitation of decision making within the role, participation in service issues and consultation on organisational issues may reduce staff stress. Peer support, staff sensitivity groups, team meetings, learning groups, appropriate workloads, stress management, training, workshops and "listening groups" may also be important. High quality management support and supervision, personal clinical support, supervision and performance feedback, recognition of value to the organisation, prompt attention to concerns and requests and a regularly reviewed personal development plan for each individual may be helpful. Finally, an external counselling service provided free of charge for any staff with work or personal problems may be appropriate for some staff members.

Organisations and agencies working in demanding fields such as the care and treatment of people with intellectual disabilities must take a more proactive approach to the support of their staff, their most valuable resource, and actively monitor their morale through good communications and management, and the use of tools such as the General Health Questionnaire (Goldberg & Williams, 1988) and the Staff Support and Satisfaction Questionnaire, a measure of organisational and personal support for staff working with mentally retarded people (Harris & Rose, 2002; Harris & Thompson, 1993).

Individual work-related stress overlaps with and may be symptomatic of the way in which the organisation works as a whole; for example, the pace of change, rising public expectations, and prioritising service development against limited resources. Senior management should be alert to this "organisational stress" as a barometer of the well-being, or otherwise, of the organisation. Guidance on planning and implementing a programme to address organisational stress has been developed by the UK Health Education Authority (1996).

THE CONFLICT BETWEEN THERAPY AND SECURITY

Working with offenders inevitably raises the issue of balancing the needs of the individual for therapy against society's need for protection from the individual's dangerousness. As a general principle, therapy and security should go hand in hand and should be proportionate; in other words, security and containment arrangements should match the level of the patient's assessed dangerousness (see Chapter 7), which of course may change with time and treatment. If therapy is to progress, some level of risk has to be accepted and managed. Security can be divided into three main areas (Kingsley, 1998).

Relational Security

Arguably the most important aspect of security is the detailed professional knowledge and understanding of the patient, which comes from a therapeutic relationship. An understanding of security aspects of therapeutic care should be an integral part of training and guidance given to all staff working in forensic settings. All staff carry a responsibility for security. Managers must ensure that clinical areas are staffed with appropriate numbers and that staff receive proper training and guidance in awareness, assessment and management of security issues.

Procedural Security

These are policies and procedures, which govern the way in which patients and their visitors are managed. Examples include movement of patients within and outside the hospital or unit, screening of goods and people entering the hospital or unit, searching of patients and patient areas, policies for the management of violence and aggression, policies on safe staffing levels, policies on visiting, and reporting of untoward incidents. Such policies and procedures support staff and patients and protect the public. They need to be simple, clearly understood and applied reliably. They also need to be revised regularly in response to changing needs.

Physical Security

Physical security refers to the environment where the patient can be safely contained without presenting a risk to the public in order that treatment can be carried out. Needless to say, it is equally important for the environment to be safe for the patient and the staff working with him/her as well as for the public at large. In general, the more physically secure the buildings are the more relaxed and "therapeutic" the internal environment can be made. An inevitable consequence, however, is that this also renders movement in and out of the setting, for therapeutic or rehabilitative purposes, more difficult. It is important, therefore, to provide a range of facilities with varying levels of physical security to suit the needs of patients both at onset and during the course of their treatment and rehabilitation.

As one moves along the spectrum from high, through medium and low security and eventually into care in the community, relational security becomes more critical as physical and procedural security are necessarily much reduced or absent. Success depends on not only providing an appropriate environment for community reintegration, but on careful selection and risk assessment of residents. In most cases, such residents will have spent considerable periods of time in other, more secure settings, and they will have been extensively investigated, assessed and treated.

However, a margin of uncertainty and risk will remain and this needs to be managed on a daily basis by the supporting staff. Day to day risk management, coupled with the relative lack of back-up should something go wrong, may place community staff under additional pressure as compared with their colleagues in a hospital unit, even though they are (or should be) managing clients who present much lower risks to themselves or others. The importance of careful selection, training and support for staff working in such settings cannot be overemphasised. In the author's opinion, these issues require even greater attention when developing community treatment and rehabilitation facilities and networks than for institutionally based provision providing higher levels of security.

Multi-Disciplinary Working

Multi-professional input to patient care has always been central to the practice of psychiatry, and is particularly well developed in intellectual disability services. The benefits of multi-disciplinary working are also increasingly being recognised and acknowledged as an education and training issue (SCOPME, 1997), and in UK government health strategy documents (Secretary of State for Health, 2000, 2001). The multi-disciplinary team is a confederation of professionals working together with the common aim of meeting the therapeutic, social and emotional needs of the patient under their collective care. The composition of the team may vary from patient to patient and at different stages of treatment, depending on need (and available resources). There are also areas such as risk assessment where the whole team can contribute to a single piece of work (Fuller & Cowan, 1999).

In order to function, the team needs to coordinate its efforts, communicate effectively, recognise and respect the professional contribution of each of its members and manage areas where the expertise of members overlaps. Issues of professional accountability need to be acknowledged and respected, especially in situations where opinions conflict. The coordination of such a disparate group, each with a greater or lesser degree of professional autonomy, requires skilled leadership. In hospital settings and particularly in forensic services, this is usually the consultant psychiatrist who, under current UK health legislation, is required to take final responsibility for a hospitalised patient, and for patients detained under the Mental Health Act, is also designated the "Responsible Medical Officer" (RMO). While it would be illogical to argue that the RMO is always the best person to lead the team, it is difficult to devolve leadership and the ability to make the final decision, while remaining in the position of having ultimate clinical responsibility for the patient. Such issues have tended to perpetuate medical leadership in hospital care, particularly in forensic settings, sometimes to the irritation of professionals such as psychologists and nurses who may be delivering the bulk of the professional input to the patient. The proposed new English Mental Health Act opens up the possibility of non-medical professionals having overall responsibility for the patient (Secretary of State for Health and Home Secretary, 2000).

In community settings, leadership and coordination may be carried out by the community nurse or social work care manager, who make direct referrals to other professionals, as required. The involvement of patients and carers is increasingly encouraged but there is still considerable room for improvement (Barker and Walker, 2000). Whatever the composition or leadership arrangements in place, teams work successfully where there is a range of professional and interpersonal skills, where communication is open and efficient and where members are in sufficient contact with each other to develop personal rapport and trust. Discussions of the roles of professionals in multi-disciplinary teams in forensic, intellectual disability and general psychiatry settings can be found in Cordess et al. (1996), Bregman and Gertz (1995) and De Silva, Dodds, Rainey and Clayton (1995) respectively.

Managing the Culture

The development and maintenance of a healthy culture among staff is important for any organisation but particularly so in human organisations dealing with vulnerable groups, whether in the health care, social care or criminal justice system. A substantial part of the management of offenders with intellectual disabilities is carried out in specialist units, often set apart from other services and even if not set apart, the necessary security measures limit the movement of staff and others in and out of these units. Staff working in forensic units are often seen as "different" by their colleagues, and may also see themselves as an elite, dealing with the most difficult and dangerous patients. Pay differentials may also set them apart and may discourage staff turnover. To varying degrees, forensic units are at risk of adopting some of the well-known characteristics of "total institutions" (Goffman, 1961). Over time, a unique and separate culture may develop and value systems may drift, often in a downward direction, with detrimental effects on patient care.

In cases where services have gone badly wrong, similar themes usually emerge: there has often been a lack of interest by management. The service has been underfunded, with poor buildings and inadequate staffing both in numbers and skill mix. Clinical leadership has been weak and front-line staff have been left to cope with difficult patients with little supervision, support or training. Staff members become demoralised and disinterested, professional standards start to slip and patient care suffers. Minor untoward incidents go unreported and unchallenged, and standards continue to deteriorate until a major scandal erupts which brings everything to a head, leading to a major inquiry. The organisation and its staff are blighted and the service may take decades to recover, if it recovers at all.

This depressing scenario is of course not unique to forensic health care services; any service which has a tendency, either by its nature or circumstances, to become isolated is at higher risk. The main issues to be addressed are investing in highquality, well-motivated staff, valuing staff and patients with a good living and working environment, investing in training and development of staff, providing opportunities for advancement, providing high-quality management support and supervision, encouraging research, critical evaluation of care, and encouraging participation of a wide range of staff in decision making about the service and patient care. An open culture can be encouraged through training placements, external review and accreditation, contact, comparison and collaboration with other similar services, robust mechanisms for incident reporting, periodically rotating staff to and from other services and encouraging new staff recruitment, and zero tolerance of professional misconduct.

ATTITUDES TOWARDS CLIENT GROUP

In common with many other walks of life, a health professional must maintain a balance between professional detachment and empathy with his or her client or patient, in order to function. Emotional involvement clouds professional judgement and lack of empathy tends to antagonise the client; neither is helpful to either party. In situations, such as working with offenders, where the professional is helping a client to overcome a problem or illness which has or may have resulted in harm to others as well as to himself, maintaining the balance is more difficult due to a number of factors (Gresswell & Kruppa, 1994; Roundy & Horton, 1990). These factors include details of the offence, which may be emotionally disturbing for the professional. For example, the circumstances of the offence may be identified with some aspect of the professional's own life history. Some staff may have difficulty in maintaining an appropriate therapeutic relationship with the offender while rejecting the offending behaviour itself. Some may have bias due to knowledge of the background history of the offender, particularly when, as is frequently the case, there are issues which increase the professional's empathy, such as deprivation, cruelty and rejection. This can lead to insipid collusion, by the therapist, with the patient's denial of personal responsibility for the offence. Some staff may experience frustration and demoralisation due to unrealistic expectations of success. Indifferent, misinformed or even hostile attitudes on the part of colleagues, society and the press to therapeutic work with offenders may sap morale and confidence of the professional in his or her abilities. Therapists need to acknowledge their own feelings and to share them with colleagues within their professional network inside and outside of the organisation. A task orientated approach, focusing on information gathering, helps to maintain emotional distance. Resistance and minimisation by patients should be seen as a stage in therapy and not *prima face* evidence of untreatability. However, it is illogical to engage in therapy with a patient unless the therapist believes that benefit is likely, and pressure to do otherwise must be resisted. Realistic measurable goals should be set as evidence of progress for patient and therapist alike.

MANAGEMENT OF VIOLENCE AND AGGRESSION

Dealing with violent and aggressive patients is an unavoidable part of health care in forensic settings, and is sadly becoming a feature of many other areas of medicine, notably accident and emergency departments and even general practice. However, in contrast to these front-line areas of practice, staff working within forensic settings will usually have some prior knowledge of the patients under their care as well as working in a protected and well-staffed environment. The ever-present risk of the eruption of violence inevitably adds to the stress on staff as well as disrupting the lives of the patients under their care. Clearly those staff members having the most contact time with patients are most at risk. Often these will be the most junior members of the staff team, with the least experience and training.

Violence to staff should neither be accepted by the organisation nor by staff themselves as "part of the job". Such acceptance debases the gravity of such behaviour, in the eyes of patients and staff, encouraging a culture tolerant of violence, detrimental to patients and staff alike. All incidents of violence must be carefully recorded and reported so that monitoring and analysis can take place with a view to reducing the behaviour. Prosecution of the offender should be considered in all but the most trivial of assaults, with active encouragement and support for the victim by the organisation. An assault on a patient by a member of staff should be dealt with by immediate suspension followed by disciplinary action and notification of the police.

Support for staff who are victims of violence, however, is not in itself sufficient. The organisation should provide the working conditions and training which reduce the risk of violence erupting in the first place. The UK Royal College of Psychiatrists Research Unit (1998) researched the literature on violence in clinical settings as well as canvassing opinions from those affected by violence. The result was a set of guidelines on the management of violence addressing a number of key areas:

- *Providing a calm environment.* The environment should be clean, light and airy and welcoming. Noisy areas should be controlled, there should be private spaces and safe indoor and outdoor activity areas as well as separate smoking areas.
- *Providing a secure environment.* There should be a safe room for disturbed patients. Furniture and fittings should be designed for reduced potential to cause injury if used as weapons. Clinical areas should have good sight lines, accessible doors and alarms, and visible entrances and exits. Response to alarms should be consistent and practised.
- *Accommodation and activities.* Sleeping and day areas should be separate. There should be a choice for the patient between a single sex and a mixed day ward. Facilities for physical exercise as well as more private activities should be provided. There should be structured timetable and collaboration with service users in planning clinical environments, policies and practices.
- *Effective care.* There should be open lines of communication between staff and management and clear operational policies should be in place. Staff training and development should be regularly updated and monitored and multi-disciplinary working encouraged. Staff numbers and skill mix, as well as gender and ethnicity, should be appropriate for the client group. Sufficient overlap for adequate handover should be built into the duty roster. Mechanisms should be in place to record and subsequently review any incident, and intervention such as restraint, PRN medication or seclusion.
- *Service-user concerns.* Staff should be supported in fostering communication with patients, anticipating risk and avoiding confrontation. Patients should be

encouraged to discuss their feelings with staff and should be treated with respect and dignity. Patient complaints should be taken seriously and staff should be encouraged to take action if they believe that the patient's needs are not being met.

- *Assessment and management of imminent violence.* Staff should be trained to recognise the warning signs of violence and to monitor their own body language and verbal response. Training should include techniques of de-escalation as well as management by restraint, medication or, as a last resort, seclusion. It is also advisable for clinicians to be trained and familiar in the use of cardiopulmonary resuscitation.

There is evidence that training in the management of violence improves staff confidence as well as leading to a reduction in the use of invasive interventions such as restraint and seclusion (Allen & Tynan 2000; Forster, Cavness & Phelps, 1999). In the Forster *et al.* study, a 20% reduction in staff injuries was observed after a period of 12 months.

The experience of violence can have serious psychological consequences for the victim (Wykes & Whittington, 1994) and is a significant source of occupational stress, particularly when the clinician, often a nurse, has to try to maintain a professional therapeutic relationship with the assaulter. Feelings of anger are common in the short term and reactions may last many months. Longer-term sequelae include depression and post-traumatic stress disorder (Lenehan & Turner, 1984; Ryan & Postner, 1989). There is, however a prevailing culture in many forensic services that violence is "part of the job" and that admitting to being upset by an assault is an admission of weakness or failure. An organisation that encourages a supportive culture needs to work actively to counteract such beliefs. Support can be given informally, or as part of a formal system such as Critical Incident Stress Debriefing (Mitchell & Everly, 1993). However, in a recent review of the literature, Paterson, Leadbetter and Bowie (1999), suggest that the benefits or otherwise of such formal support systems have not been conclusively demonstrated.

SUMMARY

Forensic intellectual disability services must achieve effective treatment for the service user while minimising risk to the individual, the staff and society at large. They must do so while upholding the human rights of individual patients, and conforming to a variety of legislation, guidance and policy, across health, social and legal agencies impacting on the patient's contact with the service. In order to achieve these aims, the organisation must necessarily invest heavily in its human resources and their support and development. The service must be patient focused and promote and encourage the highest ethical, clinical and care standards.

Services must attract and retain the highest quality of clinical and supporting staff by minimising organisational causes of staff stress and developing the staff in order to maximise the skills to work to the highest standards and to cope with the stresses inherent in working with a vulnerable but demanding client group.

REFERENCES

Allen, D. & Tynan, H. (2000). Responding to aggressive behaviour: impact of training on staff members' knowledge and confidence. *Mental Retardation*, **38**, 97–104.

Baker D.J. (1998). Effects of video-based staff training with manager-led exercises in residential support. *Mental Retardation*, **36**, 198–204.

Barker, P. & Walker, L. (2000). Nurses' perception of multidisciplinary teamwork in acute psychiatric settings. *Journal of Psychiatric and Mental Health Nursing*, **7**, 539–46.

Berryman, J., Evans, I.M. & Kalbag, A. (1994). The effects of training in non-aversive behaviour management on the attitudes and understanding of direct care staff. *Journal of Behaviour Therapy and Experimental Psychiatry*, **25**, 241–50.

Bregman, J.D. & Gertz, J. (1995). Psychiatry. In B.A. Thyer & N.P. Kropf (eds) *Developmental Disabilities: A Handbook for Interdisciplinary Practice* (pp. 160–71). Cambridge, MA: Brookline Books.

Brooker, C. (2001). A decade of evidence based training for work with people with serious mental health problems: progress in the development of psychosocial interventions. *Journal of Mental Health*, **10**, 17–31.

Brown, H. & Brown, V. (1994). *Understanding and Responding to Difficult Behaviour*. Brighton: Pavilion Publishing.

Campbell, M., Cullen, C., Connolly, D., Hutton, B., Beattie, K. & Robb, G. (1993). *Approaches to People with Challenging Behaviour—A Distance Learning Package for Direct Care Staff*. Brighton: Pavilion Publishing.

Carson, D. (1990). *Professionals and the Courts: A Handbook for Expert Witnesses*. Birmingham: Venture Press.

Chatterton, S. (1999). Communication skills workshops in learning disability nursing. *British Journal of Nursing*, **8**, 90–6.

Coffey, M. & Coleman, M. (2001). The relationship between support and stress in forensic community mental health nursing. *Journal of Advanced Nursing*, **34**, 397–407.

Collins K., Jones, M.L., McDonnell, A., Read, S., Jones, R. & Cameron, A. (2000). Do new roles contribute to job satisfaction and retention of staff in nursing and professions allied to medicine? *Journal of Nursing Management*, **8**, 3–12.

Cordess, C., Killian, M., Clarke, N., Flannigan, E., Wrench, M. & Hilton, M. (1996). The multi-disciplinary team. In C. Cordess & M. Cox (eds) *Forensic Psychotherapy: Crime, Psychodynamics and the Offender Patient*. Vol 2: *Mainly Practice* (pp. 97–132). Bristol: Jessica Kingsley.

Corrigan, P.W. (1998). Building teams and programs for effective rehabilitation. *Psychiatric Quarterly*, **69**, 193–209.

Corrigan, P.W. & McCracken, S.G. (1995). Psychiatric rehabilitation and staff development: educational and organisational models. *Clinical Psychology Review*, **1**, 699–719.

Corrigan, P.W. & McCracken, S.G. (1997). *Interactive Staff Training*. New York: Plenum Press.

Corrigan, P.W., McCracken, S.G., Edwards, M., Kommana, S. & Simpatico, T. (1997). Staff training to improve implementation and impact of behavioural rehabilitation programs. *Psychiatric Services*, **48**, 1336–8.

The Council of the European Union (1993). European Union Directive 93/104/EC of 23 November 1993. *Concerning certain aspects of the organisation of working time*. Brussels: The Council of the European Union.

Day, K. (1999). Professional training in the psychiatry of mental retardation in the United Kingdom. In N. Bouras (ed.) *Psychiatric and Behavioural Disorders in Developmental Disabilities and Mental Retardation*, (pp. 439–57). Cambridge: Cambridge University Press.

Day, K. (2001). Service provision and staff training: an overview. In A. Dosen & K. Day (eds) *Treating Mental Illness and Behaviour Disorders in Children and Adults with Mental Retardation* (pp. 469–92). Washington, DC: American Psychiatric Press.

De Silva, P., Dodds, P., Rainey, J. & Clayton, J. (1995). Management and the multidisciplinary team. In D. Bhugra & A. Burns (eds) *Management for Psychiatrists*, 2nd edn (pp. 121–38). London: Royal College of Psychiatrists.

Department of Health (1995). *The Health of the Nation: A Strategy for People with Learning Disabilities*. London: Department of Health.

Department of Health (2000). *Consultants' Contract: Annual Appraisal for Consultants*. Advance Letter (MD) 6/00. Department of Health, Quarry House, Leeds, UK.

Department of Health (2001). *Consultants' Contract: Annual Appraisal for Consultants*. Advance Letter (MD) 5/01. Department of Health, London.

Dychawy-Rosner, I., Eklund, M. & Isacsson, A. (2000). Direct care staff's need for support in their perceived work role in day activity units. *Journal of Nursing Management*, **8**, 39–48.

Dyer, S. & Quine, L. (1998). Predictors of job satisfaction and burnout among the direct care staff of a community learning disability service. *Journal of Applied Research in Learning Disabilities*, **11**, 320–32.

Edward, E. & Lawler, I.I.I. (1977). Reward systems. In J.R. Hackman & J.L. Suttle (eds) *Improving Life at Work* (pp. 163–226). Santa Monica, CA: Goodyear.

Felce, D., Bowley, C., Baxter, H., Jone, E., Lowe, K. & Emerson, E. (2000). The effectiveness of staff support: evaluating active support training using a conditional probability approach. *Research in Developmental Disabilities*, **21**, 243–55.

Forster, P.L., Cavness, C. & Phelps, M.A. (1999). Staff training decreases use of seclusion and restraint in an acute psychiatric hospital. *Archives of Psychiatric Nursing*, **13**, 269–71.

Fuller, J. & Cowan, J. (1999). Risk assessment in a multi-disciplinary forensic setting: clinical judgement revisited. *Journal of Forensic Psychiatry*, **10**, 276–89.

Gentry, M., Iceton, J. & Milne, D. (2001). Managing challenging behaviour in the community: methods and results of interactive staff training. *Health and Social Care in the Community*, **9**, 143–50.

Goffman, E. (1961). *Asylums*. London: Penguin.

Goldberg, D. & Williams, P. (1988). *A User's Guide to the General Health Questionnaire*. Windsor: NFER-Nelson.

Gravestock, S. & Bouras, N. (1997). Survey of services for adults with learning disabilities. *Psychiatric Bulletin*, **21**, 197–9.

Green C.W. & Reid D.H. (1991). Reinforcing staff performance in residential facilities: a survey of common managerial practices. *Mental Retardation*, **29**, 195–200.

Gresswell, D.M. & Kruppa, I. (1994). Special demands of assessment in a secure setting: setting the Scene. In M. McMurran & J. Hodge (eds) *The Assessment of Criminal Behaviours of Clients in Secure Settings* (pp. 35–52). London, Jessica Kingsley.

Gustafsson, C. (1995). Developments in providing services to people with mental retardation and psychiatric disorders in Sweden. In *Proceedings of the International Congress II on the Dually Diagnosed* (pp. 107–8). New York: National Association for the Dually Diagnosed.

Gustafsson, C. (1997). The prevalence of people with intellectual disability admitted to general hospital psychiatric units: the level of handicap, psychiatric diagnosis and care utilisation. *Journal of Intellectual Disability Research*, **41**, 519–26.

Harris, P. & Rose, J. (2002). Measuring staff support in services for people with intellectual disability: the Staff Support and Satisfaction Questionnaire, Version 2. *Journal of Intellectual Disability Research*, **46**(Pt 2), 151–7.

Harris, P.E. & Thompson, G. (1993). The Staff Support Questionnaire: a means of measuring support among staff working with people with challenging behaviour. *Mental Handicap*, **21**, 122–7.

Hastings, R.P. (1996). Staff training and management in services for people with learning disabilities. *British Journal of Clinical Psychology*, **35**, 480–2.

Hastings, R.P. & Brown, T. (2002). Coping strategies and the impact of challenging behaviours on special educators' burnout. *Mental Retardation*, **40**, 148–56.

Hatton, C., Brown, R., Caine, A. & Emerson, E. (1995). Stressors, coping strategies and stress related outcomes among direct care staff in staffed houses for people with learning disabilities. *Mental Handicap Research*, **8**, 252–71.

Hatton, C., Emerson, E., Rivers, M., Mason, H., Mason, M.L., Swarbrick, R., Kiernan, C., Reeves, D. & Alborz, A. (1999). Factors associated with staff stress and work satisfaction in services for people with intellectual disability. *Journal of Intellectual Disability Research*, **43**, 253–67.

Hatton, C., Emerson, E., Rivers, M., Mason, H., Swarbrick, R., Mason, L., Kiernan, C., Reeves, D. & Alborz, A. (2001). Factors associated with intended staff turnover and job search behaviour in services for people with intellectual disability. *Journal of Intellectual Disability Research*, **45**, 258–70.

Hatton, C., Rivers, M., Mason, H., Mason, L., Kiernan, C., Emerson, E., Alborz, A. & Reeves, D. (1998). *Staff in Services for People with Learning Disabilities*. Manchester: Hester Adrian Research Centre.

Hertzburg, F. (1966). *Work and the Nature of Man*. New York: World Publishing.

Hrydowy, E.R. & Martin, G.L. (1994). A practical staff management package for use in a teaching program for persons with developmental disabilities. *Behaviour Modification*, **18**, 66–88.

Ito, H., Kurita, H. & Shiiya, J. (1999). Burnout among direct-care staff members of facilities for persons with mental retardation in Japan. *Mental Retardation*, **37**, 477–81.

Jackson, S.E., Schwab, R.L. & Schuler, R.S. (1986). Toward an understanding of the burnout phenomenon. *Journal of Applied Psychology*, **71**, 630–40.

Jenkins, R., Rose, J. & Lovell, C. (1997). Psychological well-being of staff working with people who have challenging behaviour. *Journal of Intellectual Disability Research*, **41**, 502–11.

Jewell, T.C., Corry, R., Snyder, S., Kulju, K., Stewart, D.A. & Silverstein, S.M. (2001). A new initiative to enhance services for people with severe mental illness. *New York State Psychologist*, **13**(1), 25–30.

Killu, K. (1994). The role of direct care staff. *Behavioural Interventions*, **9**, 169–76.

Kingsley, J. (1998). Security and therapy, In C. Kaye & A. Franey (eds) *Managing High Security Psychiatric Care* (pp. 75–84). London: Jessica Kingsley.

Lenehan, G.P. & Turner, J. (1984). Treatment of staff victims of violence. In J. Turner (ed.) *Violence in a Medical Care Setting: A Survival Guide* (pp. 251–60). Rockville, MD: Aspen.

Lindsay, M. (1998). *Signposts For Success in Commissioning and Providing Health Services for People with Learning Disabilities*. Catalogue 98CC0156. London: Department of Health.

Lindsay, M. & Russell, O. (1999). *Once a Day*. Catalogue 98C114/173B. London: Department of Health.

Lipe, D.M., Reeds, L.B., Prokop, J.A., Menousek, L.F. & Bryant, M.M. (1994). Mandatory in-service programs using self-learning modules. *Journal of Nursing Staff Development*, **10**, 167–72.

Lockhart, K. (1997). Experience from a staff support service. *Journal of Community and Applied Social Psychology*, **7**, 193–8.

Mason, T. & Mercer, D. (1996). Forensic psychiatric nursing: visions of social control. *Australia and New Zealand Journal of Mental Health Nursing*, **5**, 153–62.

Milne, D.L. (1986). *Training Behaviour Therapists: Methods, Evaluation and Implementation with Parents, Nurses and Teachers*. London: Croom-Helm.

Minto, C. & Morrow, M. (1999). Clinical supervision in a learning disability forensic service. In D. Mercer, T. Marron, T. McKeown & G. McCann (eds) *Forensic Mental Health Care Planning: Direction and Dilemmas* (pp. 341–8). Edinburgh: Churchill Livingstone.

Mitchell, J. & Everly, G. (1993). *Critical Incident Stress Debriefing: an Operations Manual for the Prevention of Traumatic Stress among Emergency Services and Disaster Workers*. Ellicott City, MD: Chevron.

Mitchell, G. & Hastings, R.P. (2001). Coping with burnout and emotion in staff working in community services for people with challenging behaviours. *American Journal of Mental Retardation*, **106**, 448–59.

Money, D. (1997). A comparison of three approaches to delivering a speech and language therapy service to people with learning disabilities. *European Journal of Disorders of Communication*, **32**, 449–66.

O'Brien, G. (1990). Current patterns of service provision for the psychiatric needs of mentally handicapped people: visiting centres in England and Wales. *Psychiatric Bulletin*, **14**, 6–7.

O'Very, D.I. (1999). Self paced: the right pace for staff development. *Journal of Continuing Education in Nursing*, **30**, 182–7.

Paterson, B., Leadbetter, D. & Bowie, V. (1999). Supporting staff exposed to violence at work. *International Journal of Nursing Studies*, **36**, 479–86.

Puddephatt, A. & Sussman, S. (1994). Developing services in Canada: Ontario vignettes. In
    N. Bouras (ed.) *Mental Health in Mental Retardation* (pp. 353–64). Cambridge: Cambridge
    University Press.
Purcell, M., McConkey, R. & Morris, I. (2000). Staff communication with people with intel-
    lectual disabilities: the impact of a work based training programme. *Journal of Language
    and Communication Disorders*, **35**, 147–58.
Reid, Y., Johnson, S., Morant, N., Kuipers, E., Szmukler, G., Bebbington, P., Thornicroft, G.
    & Prosser, D. (1999). Improving support for mental health staff: a qualitative study. *Social
    Psychiatry and Psychiatric Epidemiology*, **34**, 309–15.
Richman, G.S., Riordan, M.R., Reiss, M.L., Pyles, D.A. & Bailey, J.S. (1988). The effects of
    self-monitoring and supervisor feedback on staff performance in a residential setting.
    Journal of Applied Behavior Analysis, **21**, 401–9.
Rose, J., Jones, F. & Fletcher, B. (1998). Investigating the relationship between stress and
    worker behaviour. *Journal of Intellectual Disability Research*, **42**, 163–72.
Roundy, L.M. & Horton, A.L. (1990). Professional and treatment issues for clinicians who
    intervene with incest perpetrators. In *The Incest Perpetrator: A Family Member No-one Wants
    to Treat* (pp. 164–89). Newbury Park, CA: Sage.
Royal College of Psychiatrists Research Unit (1998). *Management of Imminent Violence: Clinical
    Practice Guidelines*. London: Royal College of Psychiatrists.
Ryan, J.A. & Postner, E.C. (1989). The assaulted nurse: short term and long term responses.
    Archives of Psychiatric Nursing, **3**, 323–31.
Schmitz, N., Neumann, W. & Oppermann, R. (2000). Stress burnout and locus of control in
    German nurses. *International Journal of Nursing Studies*, **37**, 95–9.
SCOPME (1997). *Multiprofessional Working and Learning: Sharing the Educational Challenge*.
    London: SCOPME.
Secretary of State for Health (2000). *The NHS Plan: A Plan for Investment. A Plan for Reform*.
    Cm 4818-1. Norwich: The Stationery Office.
Secretary of State for Health and Home Secretary (2000). *Reforming the Mental Health Act.
    Part I: The New Legal Framework; Part II: High Risk Patients*. Cm 5016I/5016II. Norwich:
    The Stationery Office.
Secretary of State for Health (2001). *Valuing People: A New Strategy for Learning Disability for
    the 21st Century*. Cm 5086. Norwich: The Stationery Office.
Stolte, K. (1994). Adjustment to change: basic strategies. *Nursing Management*, **25**, 90–2.
Sylvester, J. & Chapman, A.J. (1997). Asking "Why" in the workplace: causal contributions
    and organisational behaviour, In C.L. Cooper & D.M. Rousseau (eds) *Trends in Organisa-
    tional Behaviour*, vol. 4. (pp. 1–14). New York: John Wiley & Sons.
Thomas, J.R. (1995). Individuals with dual diagnoses of mental retardation and mental illness
    in Illinois community based vocational programs: services provided and staff training
    needs. *Dissertation Abstracts International, A (Humanities and Social Sciences)*, **56** (1-A).
Walter, G., Cleary, M. & Rey, J.M. (2000). Patterns of use, attitudes and expectations of mental
    health staff regarding computers. *Journal of Quality and Clinical Practice*, **20**, 20–23.
Wykes, T. & Whittington, R. (1994). Reactions to assault. In T. Wykes & G. Mezey (eds)
    Violence and Health Professionals (pp. 105–26). London: Chapman & Hall.

Chapter 17

RESEARCH AND DEVELOPMENT

PETER STURMEY,* JOHN L. TAYLOR† AND WILLIAM R. LINDSAY‡

* Queens College, City University of New York, USA
† University of Northumbria, Newcastle upon Tyne and Northgate & Prudhoe NHS Trust, Northumberland, UK
‡ The State Hospital, Carstairs; NHS Tayside & University of Abertay Dundee, Dundee, UK

This volume has gathered together a considerable amount of research and development in the area of offenders with developmental disabilities. Yet it can only be considered as a beginning. The range of research and development issues that could and should be addressed is extensive. In this chapter we will outline the main areas to which attention should be directed in future. One of the fundamental issues in clinical research in the area of criminal behaviour is that we do not know how this clinical research relates to offenders with developmental disabilities. Therefore, when one reviews research concerning criminality in people of average intelligence, one should ask, "how might this apply to people with developmental disabilities?".

This chapter considers several broad areas in which further research and development would be enlightening. These areas include prevalence of offending, service development and organisational considerations, risk assessment and management issues, social, developmental and psychological influences on offending behaviour, research method, design and paradigm problems, research on victims, and ethical issues.

PREVALENCE OF OFFENDING

It is not at all clear if people with developmental disabilities commit more or less crime than those without a developmental disability, or whether the type and frequency of crimes committed by offenders with developmental disabilities differ from general populations of offenders. Several contributors to the present volume have indicated the methodological problems that contribute to this issue. The inclusion criteria used for any prevalence study sample will affect the offending rates obtained (Lindsay, 2002; Taylor, Thorne, Robertson & Avery, 2002b). This is especially true when attempting to ascertain and define those functioning in the

Offenders with Developmental Disabilities. Edited by W.L. Lindsay, J.L. Taylor and P. Sturmey.
© 2004 John Wiley & Sons, Ltd.

borderline and mild levels of intellectual disabilities. Classification trends in the United States have steadily moved toward labelling children and adolescents who meet the criteria for mild mental retardation and who have significant academic and social problems as emotionally disturbed or learning disabled (Macmillan, Gresham, Siperstein & Bocian, 1996). Increased use of diagnoses that are perhaps more acceptable than mental retardation, such as speech and language delays, autism and other pervasive developmental disabilities, might also account for less frequent use of the classification of mild mental retardation. There may also be a reluctance to label non-white students and students for whom English is a second language as mentally retarded. These and other factors are perhaps in part responsible for the large decrease in the use of the label mental retardation in the United States education system. Between the mid-1970s and late 1990s the number of children served by the American education system with the label mental retardation dropped by 30–40% from just under a million to approximately 600,000 (Beirne-Smith, Ittenbach & Patton, 2002; Polloway & Smith, 1983.) Similar problems occur in defining mild mental retardation in adulthood. Many students within special education and labelled as mildly retarded are not served in adult mental retardation services when they graduate from high school. Given these problems in defining mild mental retardation and the ambiguity that this concept now has in both educational and adult services, it may not be possible to answer questions relating to epidemiology of offending in people with mild mental retardation.

Another factor influencing offending rates among people with developmental disabilities is the source and location of the study sample. Studies on offending in people with developmental disabilities have been conducted at different stages of the criminal justice system. Studies may take place in police stations, courts, with remand and convicted prisoners, in secure hospital units and probation services. These studies may find different prevalence rates due to sampling bias and "filtering" effects (Holland, Clare & Mukhopadhyay, 2002; Mason & Murphy, 2002). These "filtering" mechanisms occur at different stages of the criminal justice system, are not well understood and merit future research. For example, the implementation of policies, such as diversion from custody, will have significant effects on observed prevalence rates for this client group.

The methods and measures used to determine participants' level of functioning are also factors that affect the reported prevalence of offending in people with developmental disabilities. Variations in the intelligence test, adaptive behaviour measure, education history and screening assessments selected will affect the observed prevalence rates (McBrien, 2003; Simpson & Hogg, 2001a, b). The decision making process, clinical skills and biases of the clinician making the diagnosis may also affect whether or not someone is labelled as having a developmental disability. Of course, these factors will have the largest effect on whether or not someone is labelled mentally retarded for people with borderline and mild intellectual disabilities, but will probably have a much lesser effect for labelling people with moderate through severe intellectual disabilities. It may also be possible that offending or certain kinds of offences may create biases as to whether or not someone with borderline or mild intellectual disabilities is referred for assessment or how a clinician behaves when conducting an assessment.

These methodological problems occur in the context of sometimes quite rapid changes in social, health care and criminal justice system policies. Definitions of both developmental disabilities and criminality may change significantly and quickly. These changes influence the apparent incidence, reporting and visibility of offending behaviour by people with developmental disabilities (Holland *et al.*, 2002; Lindsay, 2002; Macmillan *et al.*, 1996).

A final major gap in the literature is the dearth of well-controlled studies in which the prevalence of offending in whole populations of people with developmental disabilities is compared with that in general populations of non-disabled people using the same methods in both populations. Also, it is widely acknowledged that many offences committed by people with developmental disabilities are not reported, or not processed by the criminal justice system (Holland *et al.*, 2002). Therefore studies need to take into account convicted and non-convicted offences when investigating the prevalence of offending by people with developmental disabilities.

SERVICE DEVELOPMENT AND ORGANISATION

As has been mentioned in several places, the advent of deinstitutionalisation across the Western world has fundamentally altered services for offenders with developmental disabilities. In the mid-1970s it is likely that each large facility for people with developmental disabilities would have had a number of wards dedicated to forensic cases. Most of these facilities have now closed or reduced greatly in size (Coucouvanis, Polister, Prouty & Lakin, 2003). Thus, there are now few institutional beds into which forensic cases can be diverted. The impact of deinstitutionalisation on disposal of forensic cases with developmental disabilities is unknown. It is unknown if the number of people with developmental disabilities cases coming before the courts has increased or decreased after deinstitutionalisation. It might be the case that local generic services are directing significant resources at managing this client group.

The development of markets for service provision and separation of the functions of service authorities or managers from service providers has been a major change in service provision over the past 15 years. Thus, the numbers of extra-contractual referrals made by many local service commissioners may have increased. It would appear that some local service commissioners in the UK deal with forensic cases by referring them to out-of-area medium secure services. These out-of-area forensic services may be National Health Service (NHS) facilities, or private establishments that operate independently outside the NHS. Key research questions concern the pathways that convicted and alleged offenders with developmental disabilities follow prior to carrying out their offences and how different types of services respond to the needs of these clients once their offending behaviour has been identified. It is also important that the impact of client and service characteristics on client outcomes are identified for this population. In the UK the NHS National Research and Development Programme on Forensic Mental Health has recently commissioned a study, *Pathways into Forensic Learning Disability Services, Service Responses and Outcomes*, to begin researching these issues.

A related issue for services in areas where forensic clients are routinely exported to out-of-area facilities is that local staff may not develop a range of expertise in assessment, treatment and management skills to enable them to deal with clients who may present a relatively high degree of risk. Taylor, Keddie and Lee (2003) found evidence that staff working with sex offenders with developmental disabilities often have very little specific training concerning clients' offending behaviour and its management. Other consequences of such a policy might be re-institutionalisation by the back door. Cases that might otherwise be safely managed within local services might be exported to specialist forensic facilities because local staff are de-skilled and lack confidence in dealing with the risks associated with clients' offending behaviour. Perhaps some local service providers are motivated to refer challenging forensic clients out of area in order to shift the risk of challenging cases to other providers. The financial impact on local services is another consequence. On the one hand it may be cost effective under some circumstances to purchase external services for specific individual clients. However, an evaluation of the cost-benefits when the numbers become significant would be interesting and illuminating. For some clients who are difficult to serve and high risk, service providers may be able to demand a high rate from service commissioners.

RISK ASSESSMENT AND MANAGEMENT

Criminological issues cut across all areas, but perhaps risk assessment in violent offenders is most germane to the area of criminal behaviour. In Chapter 7 Quinsey reviewed research with reference to developmental disabilities and risk assessment. He provided strong evidence of the validity of risk assessment with this client group. Developments in this area are important, indeed urgent, since they relate closely to issues around the provision of services. The UK Government's Home Office has recently commissioned research aimed specifically at investigating the utility, reliability and validity of a range of established and emerging risk assessment measures in populations of offenders with developmental disabilities.

A pressing research question concerns the level of security and the nature of services required for different levels of risk. One methodological approach would be to investigate services for offenders that employ different methods and levels of security and compare the clients on standardised risk assessments. An interesting aspect of any such investigation would be the way in which services deal with individuals of similar levels of risk, if any differences were in fact identified. The risk assessment project funded by the Home Office will look at this particular issue.

Quinsey's work on risk assessment also suggested the interesting notion that dynamic risk assessment might be of significant value with offenders with developmental disability. He reported that the dynamic risk assessment scale was a significant predictor of violent incidents in a cohort of offenders. Lindsay, Elliot and Astell (submitted) also reported pilot results that suggest that dynamic risk assessment may be as important as static, historical factors in the prediction of sexually abusive incidents in this client group. These are areas of research which are not only intrinsically interesting because they add to our knowledge of which risk factors function for different client groups, but they are also of immediate practical value in the planning and day to day organisation of services.

There is a long research history on the effects of different forms of court disposal on outcomes for a range of offenders. Wilson, Gallacher and McKenzie (2000) reviewed the effects of diversion systems for adults, and Fass and Pi (2002) reviewed more recent effects of juvenile systems. We have little idea of the broad effects of these large-scale court disposal options on offenders with developmental disabilities. We do have some evidence that disposal options which do not allow for interventions such as cognitive-behaviour therapy, social skills training, sex education and day programming for at least two years may be ineffective with this client group (Day, 1994; Klimecki, Jenkinson & Wilson, 1994; Lindsay & Smith, 1998).

Linhorst, McCutchen and Bennett (2003) reviewed five American programmes serving convicted offenders with developmental disabilities living in the community, either on parole or probation orders. They found that there were substantial variations in how these programmes were funded and administered. There was little systematic evaluation of these programmes. Three of the programmes provided outcomes for participants. Arrest rates ranged from 6.5% over five years to a recidivism rate of 5% over 10 years, and a parole revocation rate of 25% within an unspecified time period. Difficulties in interpreting this research are immediately apparent. First, studies use different definitions of recidivism. Some programmes used parole and/or probation revocation, some arrest and some conviction. Second, the time period over which recidivism was tracked is not specified. Thus, it is not clear if reported arrest and recidivism rates were measured while clients were receiving a service from the programme, following discharge from the programme or a combination of the two. Finally, these studies did not routinely or consistently report the type and severity of the offences that resulted in revocation, arrest or re-conviction.

In their own study Linhorst et al. (2003) reported on a community case management programme for convicted offenders with mental retardation and other developmental disabilities in St Louis City and County. There were 252 participants in this study. The majority were voluntary clients on probation or parole orders. The primary functions of the programme's case coordinators were to facilitate clients' access to services and benefits and to share information between relevant organisations. Recidivism in this study was defined as arrests during the period when the clients' cases were open, and within a six-month period following case closure. During the period their cases were open, 40% of clients were arrested. During the six months following case closure 34% were arrested. The majority of crimes resulting in arrest were minor. Only 13% of arrests across both time periods were for felonies against the person. Of the clients who completed the programme, 25% were arrested during the follow-up period whereas 43% of those who dropped out of the programme were arrested. However, the recidivism rate of 25% is markedly higher than that for programmes that provided more intense levels of supervision and mandated clients' inclusion in the programmes through parole or probation order conditions. Comparisons of recidivism rates for offenders with developmental disabilities with those for general populations of offenders are very difficult because of differences in sampling methods, definitions of recidivism and time periods. However, Linhorst et al. (2003) pointed out that Langan and Cunnliff (1992) reported that the re-arrest rate was 43% for a large general population of people on probation ($N = 79,000$) and that Langan and Levin (2002) reported that 30% of 300,000 offenders were arrested within six months of release. These comparison data suggest that the high rate of recidivism for offenders with developmental disabilities is consistent, but neither higher or lower than, the general populations of offenders.

Future research regarding recidivism rates for offenders with developmental disabilities needs to include operationally defined indices of recidivism, clearly indicate study time periods, and, where appropriate, provide detailed descriptions of the components of case management and treatment programmes. Particular features of programmes that should be investigated are whether they require mandated or voluntary involvement, the minimum amount of time that clients are expected to remain in the programme, the intensities and nature of client contacts, and costs of services. It may not be feasible or ethical to randomly allocate clients to programme versus no programme conditions for comparison purposes. However, it is possible to design studies that compare outcomes for programmes that intervene at different stages of the criminal justice process, such as pre-trial versus post-conviction versus post-release parole. It is also possible to compare different intensities of supports, different kinds of supports and different established case management programmes with each other.

SOCIAL AND DEVELOPMENTAL INFLUENCES ON OFFENDING BEHAVIOUR

A fundamental research question in this area concerns the hypothesis that offenders with developmental disabilities have not progressed beyond the basic stages of social or moral reasoning. Arbuthnot, Gordon and Jurkovic (1987) suggested that most offenders have not progressed beyond the second stage of Kohlberg's (1964) model of moral development. Once again the question is raised as to what extent offenders with developmental disabilities are different in terms of moral development from offenders in general or people with developmental disabilities who have not offended. Additionally, one might ask whether offenders with developmental disabilities are at a different level of moral development than other people with developmental disabilities. This issue has important implications for assessment, treatment and management of this client group.

In Chapter 1 several models that incorporated social and economic factors in the development of criminality were outlined. Hirschi's (1969) model was the most developed, with its elements of attachment, commitment, involvement and belief. The degree to which this model applies to people with developmental disabilities may vary from other sections of the population. In relation to attachment, it might be hypothesised that people with developmental disabilities tend to be more conformist and conservative than other populations. There is some oblique evidence for this. For example, Lindsay, Michie, Staines, Bellshaw and Culross (1994) investigated attitudes towards sexuality among people with developmental disabilities. They found them to be considerably more conservative, if not indeed reactionary, than might be expected in other sections of the population. It may be that people with developmental disabilities identify strongly with the conservative values of society. On the other hand, an individual's intellectual disabilities may limit the extent to which he or she is able to commit to these values during moments of opportunity; for example, a person's understanding of the consequences of arrest and conviction may be somewhat restricted. This notion echoes ideas presented in Chapter 3 by Baroff, who developed the notion of reduced responsibility for criminal acts. In relation to the concept of involvement, it is plain that many offenders with developmental disabilities do not have jobs. Although they may be involved with occupational or educational placements, these may only be part-time, leaving greater opportunities to engage in crime. Finally, in relation to belief, the potential conformist nature of this client group would lead us to expect a greater acceptance of the laws of society without necessarily appreciating their full ramifications. It should be stressed that these ideas are simply hypotheses waiting to be tested.

In the same way, one might develop hypotheses about the effects of environment, housing, ethnicity, socio-economic status, immigrant status and delinquent peer groups. For example, it is often observed that the offender with developmental disability is the "fall guy" within a delinquent peer group; they are often the naïve gang member who is caught during the execution of a crime, perhaps unwittingly set up by their peers to be caught. Again, this observation simply suggests a hypothesis that needs to be tested systematically that these clients may relate to and identify with a delinquent subculture in a different way.

As noted in Chapter 1, Patterson and Yoerger (1997) found that child-rearing practices and developmental processes are related to early- and late-onset delinquency. It may be that similar effects occur in relation to individuals with developmental disabilities, but this again remains to be demonstrated. One would also wish to investigate the effects of upbringing in state or local government residential homes and fostering on these individuals. Rutter *et al.* (1997) found that the association between child-rearing practices and an increased probability of antisocial behaviour in children could be explained in terms of hostile parenting, rather than by parental personality disorder. This leads to a hypothesis that if an individual has parents with developmental disability, this would not in itself lead to an increased probability of antisocial behaviour. The essential component is distressed parenting (Snyder & Patterson, 1995). The relative importance of, and differences between, early- and late-onset delinquency would be another interesting avenue of investigation.

Farrington (1995) reported that a number of childhood factors significantly predicted criminality in later years. The variables of troublesomeness, uncooperative families, poor housing and poor parental behaviour will be familiar to most practitioners in the forensic field. We must assume that they are as relevant to people with developmental disabilities as they are to the general criminal population. However, this assumption remains to be tested.

PSYCHOLOGICAL FACTORS INFLUENCING CRIMINAL BEHAVIOUR

The inverse relationship between IQ and offending is well established. However, within this literature there is the interesting suggestion that this relationship may not hold at IQs at or below two standard deviations from the mean. For example,

McCord and McCord (1959) reported that those in the lowest IQ bands recorded a rate of conviction lower than that in the IQ band 81–90 and higher than that in the IQ band over 110. There was some support for this hypothesis from studies following up children who had severe reading difficulties in school (Maughan, Pickles, Hagell, Rutter & Yule 1996). If this were found to be the case, could explanations be found in studies suggested above investigating Hirschi's (1969) control theory of delinquent development?

The whole question of the involvement of psychological processes in the development of criminal behaviour remains at the stage of hypothesis development. Ward, Hudson, Johnston and Marshall (1997) suggested that our understanding of sexual offending should involve a range of complex processes, including selective attention, sensitisation, deviant sexual arousal and cognitive distortions. These processes would almost certainly apply to clients with developmental disabilities. For example, a number of additional processes were suggested in Chapter 10. Counterfeit deviance, deviant sexual arousal and cognitive distortions might be considered to be permissive of sexual offending in this client group. Similarly, in Chapter 11, a number of explanations for assaultive behaviour were outlined, including cognitive misconstruction of anger-provoking situations and high states of arousal. In relation to arson, the limited research conducted to date indicates that anger and feelings of not being listened to are frequent antecedents to people with developmental disabilities setting fires (Murphy & Clare, 1996; Taylor et al., 2002b). These cognitive and arousal processes are certainly deserving of greater experimental attention and it is to be hoped that future research will move beyond evaluation of outcomes and assessment of risk to investigating the psychological processes that are involved in the development and maintenance of offending behaviour.

Such research would also incorporate the psychological variables of impulsivity and the way in which people with developmental disabilities make decisions at critical times leading to offending. Impulsivity and sensation seeking have often been related to offending (Barratt, 1994; Moeller, Barratt, Dougherty, Schmitz & Swann, 2001). These variables have not been extensively investigated in offenders with developmental disabilities, although Glaser and Deane (1999) hypothesised that offending in this client group was related to impulsiveness irrespective of the nature of the offence. Novaco and Taylor (in press) found that extraversion, thought to be associated with under-socialisation and higher levels of aggressive behaviour, was a significant predictor of in-patient violent behaviour in male forensic patients with mild and borderline levels of developmental disability.

McGillivray and Moore (2001) compared substance use by offenders and non-offenders with mild developmental disability. They found that the offender group used larger quantities of alcohol and illicit substances more frequently than non-offenders. Furthermore, half of this group were under the influence of such substances at the time of their offence. Extrapolating this finding, it would appear that among this population, substance abuse is a common feature in offending behaviour. Out of the twelve sexual offenders included in the sample only two reported using illicit substances at the time of the offence and only one reported prior use of alcohol. This would seem to suggest that sexual offending in people with mild developmental disability can not readily be explained by the poor behavioural control associated with the use of substances. Therefore, any increase in impulsiveness that may result from the use of alcohol or substances cannot adequately explain sexual offending by people with mild developmental disability but may be involved with other types of offences. These findings would present a competing hypothesis to that of Glaser and Deane (1999) and are worthy of further investigation involving larger study samples.

Sturmey, Reyer, Lee and Robek (2003) conducted a broad review of substance use in people with developmental disabilities. In that review they found that among adolescents and adults with mild mental retardation living independently and with limited supervision were a significant minority who used a variety of substances, such as alcohol, marijuana and other illegal drugs, in a problematic way. Among these people were some who were at a greater risk of engaging in a variety of dangerous behaviours, such as violence, access to weapons, unsafe sexual practices, perhaps prostitution and unsafe intravenous drug use. They note that these people fall between developmental disabilities services, substance abuse services and mental health services. Consequently, they are a hard-to-serve group and few clinicians and services develop expertise in working with this population (Annand, 2002). A minority of these clients have contact with the justice system related to a variety of usually minor criminal acts. However, because they are a hard population to identify, relatively little is known about them. Important clinical challenges with this population include providing effective treatments, service coordination, and staff training and support (Annand, 2002.)

Impulsiveness is often considered as a personality trait (Plutchik & Van Praag, 1995). This leads us to note that personality variables have rarely been considered in relation to offending with this client group. Reid *et al.* considered this issue in Chapter 15, mainly in relation to personality disorder and psychopathy. However, they did report some pilot work in the development of personality measures and made some hypotheses about the relationship of personality variables and psychopathology to offending.

TREATMENT OUTCOME RESEARCH

Evaluating Treatment Outcome Study Results

Identifying interventions that are effective is a vexed issue for psychology, psychiatry, and social policy generally. Eysenck (1952) published his review of outcome studies of psychotherapy and concluded that psychotherapy was ineffective. Although interest in treatment efficacy has waxed and waned since then, it remains a controversial topic. Narrative reviews of outcome research in the 1970s and 1980s produced very different conclusions concerning treatment efficacy, even when these reviews included the same studies. For example, Luborsky, Singer and Luborsky (1976) concluded that, in the *Alice in Wonderland* world of psychotherapy research, "everyone has won and all must have prizes". The latter position continues to be supported today in literature that hypothesises that therapy technique is irrelevant. Rather, all therapies have common interpersonal processes, such as the therapeutic alliance or inspiration of hope, that are the true mechanisms for behaviour change. In contrast is the position that there are real differences between the effectiveness of different forms of therapy. For example, authors such as Giles (1993) have produced numerous narrative reviews of the psychotherapy outcome literature indicating the superiority of behaviour therapy for many mental health disorders

In response to these blatant disagreements between narrative reviews and charges of bias in the selection and interpretation of studies, numerical methods of summarising the outcome literature emerged in the 1980s. Meta-analysis was presented as an apparently objective approach to answer questions concerning the relative efficacy of treatments and programmes in educational, clinical and other forms of outcome research. Smith and Glass (1977) reported one of the earliest meta-analyses of psychotherapy outcome literature, and this meta-analysis generated just as much controversy as narrative reviews of psychotherapy research: authors cited the same meta-analysis as evidence of the equivalence of psychotherapies or the superiority of one form of psychotherapy over another.

Meta-analysis has now become an established method of evaluating outcome questions in psychology, medicine and education, despite the many methodological objections to it. The current movement known as evidence-based medicine or practice is an outgrowth of this approach. Cochrane Collaboration reviews, with their emphasis on systematic searches of the literature, explicit inclusion and exclusion criteria, objective measures of the quality of outcome studies, and explicit conclusions and recommendations on treatment efficacy, are an important example of this approach. Although traditional narrative literature reviews continue to be published (e.g. Matson *et al.*, 2000), several meta-analyses of outcome research in mental developmental disabilities have now been published (Brylewski & Duggan, 1999; Carr *et al.*, 2000; Corrigan, 1991; Didden, Duker & Korzilius, 1997; Kahng, Iwata & Lewin, 2002; Prout & Nowak-Drabik, 2003; Salman, 2002; Vargas & Carmilli, 1999; Wehmeyer, 1995). Indeed, this method has been used by Simpson and Hogg (2001a, b) in the specific area of epidemiology, interventions and policy for offenders with developmental disabilities.

Dependent Measures in Treatment Outcome Research

The purpose of outcome research is to allow us to conclude that there was an important and socially significant change in behaviour and that the reason for that change was caused by the therapy and not by any other factor. However, the design requirements of psychotherapy research are formidable. Let us investigate these two concerns separately. First, how is socially significant change in behaviour measured? One of the most important concerns with offenders is recidivism, especially of offences against the person, such as physical assault, sexual offences or offences against property, such as arson, that present a risk to others. How do we measure reoffending behaviour? Typically, reconviction is used as a proxy for reoffending. Obviously, only a subset of those people who reoffend is reconvicted. Thus, recidivism data may in part measure reoffending, but it also measures other factors such as likelihood of being caught, the quality of the defence and prosecution lawyers, and the vagaries of judges and juries. Reoffending data, especially on offences against other people, is among the most important and socially valid data on treatment of offenders. Yet it cannot be measured easily. Despite these limitations, recidivism data are an important outcome measure in treatment research on offenders with developmental disabilities that society values.

Although recidivism has a great deal of social validity other measures of behaviour change are often used. Merely reducing a maladaptive behaviour may leave a client at risk for relapse and with a life of poor quality. One of the most important reasons for intervention with offenders with developmental disabilities is to protect future victims from future offences. However, the therapist also has an ethical obligation to maximise client benefit (American Psychological Association, 2002; Sturmey & Gaubatz, 2002). Training in social skills, problem-solving skills, self-management, vocational skills and activities of daily living can all help minimise relapse in offenders (Hollin, 1992). Thus, the acquisition of a range of adaptive behaviours related to relapse prevention may be important outcome measures.

Outcome research on offenders with developmental disabilities has often evaluated cognitive, emotional and symptom change, such as attributions and beliefs concerning sexual offending (Lindsay, 2002). Should these measures be regarded as outcome measures or measures of the process of therapy? Without changes in other relevant variables, it might be argued that measures of cognition and attribution are inherently suspect and of questionable validity. Appearing to be cooperative and making progress in treatment may all be behaviours that lead to continued freedom, access to therapy and therapists, and sometimes perhaps even access to continued offending. Not cooperating with therapy and failure to make progress, and overt threats to reoffend may all lead to termination of therapy, more restrictive programmes and incarceration. Therapists inadvertently and unknowingly shape client verbal behaviour (Murray, 1956; Truax, 1966). In any case, saying and doing may be independent behavioural repertoires. Thus, for many reasons self-report measures of beliefs, attributions and knowledge are inherently limited as stand-alone outcome measures. They must be supplemented by more objective measures, such as recidivism, reoffending and skills acquisition data.

Outcome Study Design Issues

Conducting outcome research with offenders with developmental disabilities is fraught with problems associated with other kinds of outcome research, as well as its own specific problems. For example, behaviour change occurs slowly in people with developmental disabilities. It requires longer periods of intervention and evaluation. Also, when dealing with offending behaviour, which may be low frequency but which has severe consequences when it occurs, long follow-up periods are needed to evaluate the effect of interventions. In addition, the difficulty that low baseline rates of overt aggression in highly supervised and controlled environments create in demonstrating treatment effects has been discussed by several anger treatment researchers (Taylor, Novaco, Gillmer & Thorne, 2002a).

Most of the work in the forensic developmental disability field relies on the relationship between clinical practice and the development of research or theoretical issues. Therefore, the field is typified by a relative preponderance of studies employing case illustrations, single-case or case series experimental designs. There are only a small number of controlled studies and many are in the field of anger management and treatment (Benson, Johnson-Rice & Miranti, 1986; Rose, West & Clifford, 2000; Taylor et al., 2002a; Willner, Jones, Tams & Green, 2002). While this volume has outlined a variety of treatment approaches for a variety of forensic problems, there is obviously a dearth of controlled trials. In Chapter 8, Beail sets out in detail the relative strengths and limitations of single-case and group designs, including randomised controlled trials (RCTs). Major difficulties with conducting RCTs in this field include ethical issues with no-treatment or placebo conditions, sample size, representativeness and randomisation problems, and treatment protocol standardisation and adherence requirements. More extensive use of systematic single-case experimental designs can overcome some of the problems associated with RCTs. Herson and Barlow (1976) outlined a range of single-case designs which allow for greater experimental control than some of those already published in the field. Group designs are used to deduce generalisability through the assumption that the groups studied are representative of the populations from which they are drawn. Single-case studies induce generalisability from their replication across a series of cases and independent studies. It has to be recognised that the population of offenders with developmental disability within any specific offence category is likely to be relatively small. Therefore, even a randomly selected sample, from a local population, such as consecutive referrals to a particular clinic, may be subject to systematic biases such as referral trends to that particular service. In this case it is clear that a series of well-controlled single-case studies, utilising multiple baseline, multiple probe and changing criterion designs, may produce results that are as valid as group comparison studies.

Perhaps the greatest obstacle to evaluating outcomes for offenders with developmental disabilities is the lack of standardised measures. Issues of reliability and validity are critical in the development of an evidence base and, if ignored, can introduce random error into any outcome study. There have been some encouraging recent reports about developments in assessments related to anger and aggression (Novaco & Taylor, in press), and sex offending (Broxholme & Lindsay, 2003; Kolton, Boer & Boer, 2001). However, there remains precious little evidence that enables robust evaluation of the myriad of issues in this field that require further research, only some of which have been mentioned in this chapter. This is a crucial issue if a body of knowledge is to develop concerning the characteristics of offenders and their response to intervention.

Generalisation of Treatment Effects across Settings

There are no data available that directly address the issue of generalisation of treatment gains from secure settings. However, the high rates of relapse and recidivism in offenders strongly suggest that this is a significant problem for treatments that take place in secure settings. Changes in behaviour in one setting are often completely independent of behaviour change in another setting. Secure settings and clinics are highly characteristic environments with their own contingencies and discriminative stimuli. Many of the problems that are addressed in secure settings typically occur in other environments. Offenders' problem drinking, theft and illegal sexual behaviours also occur in characteristic social and physical environments. Stimulus control of offending behaviours in people with developmental disabilities may, like much other behaviour, be highly idiosyncratic. For example, sexual approaches to children may be elicited by specific physical and behavioural stimuli cues from the child and specific cues in the physical environment. Precisely which discriminative stimuli control the offender's inappropriate sexual behaviour will be idiosyncratic and depend on that particular client's learning history.

Fortunately, behaviour analysis has an extensive conceptual analysis of generalisation and an accompanying technology to promote generalisation (Stokes & Bear, 1977). Failure to generalise across settings is due to inappropriately narrow stimulus control of the behaviour of interest. Stimulus control can be broadened in a number of ways. These include reinforcing instances of generalisation, training using multiple exemplars of relevant stimuli, and introducing relevant stimuli into the training environment. Generalisation of treatment gains must be incorporated into therapy from the beginning, and not hoped for or planned at the end of therapy. Planning for generalisation requires an analysis and understanding at the beginning of therapy not only of what behaviour must change, but when and where and with whom the behaviour must change.

Generalisation of treatment gains from secure to community settings and maintenance of treatment gains over time cannot be left to chance. An outstanding but isolated treatment programme in a secure setting that is not integrated and contiguous with community settings is unlikely to promote generalisation and maintenance of change. Thus, research is required concerning the best service models and delivery systems to facilitate transfer of behaviour change to new settings, necessary to ensure generalisation and maintenance of treatment gains.

Treatment Acceptability Issues

What limited data there are on treatment of offenders with developmental disabilities has paid little attention to the issue of treatment acceptability. Treatment acceptability measures are typically psychometric instruments that rate the acceptability of the treatment (Kazdin, French & Sherick, 1981). These measures have been used extensively in treatment of people with developmental disabilities (McDonnell, Dearden & Sturmey, 1993, McDonnell & Sturmey, 2000; Cunningham, McDonnell, Easton & Sturmey, 2003). They have also been used to a lesser extent in treatment of people in mental health services (Newton, Hartley & Sturmey, 1993; Sturmey, 1992) and behaviour management procedures in dentistry (Newton, Shah, Patel & Sturmey, 2003b; Newton, Naidu & Sturmey, 2003a; Sturmey, Thomsett, Sundaram & Newton, 2003).

Earlier studies of treatment acceptability emphasised that more restrictive treatments are often seen as less acceptable. However, more recent studies have demonstrated that treatment effectiveness, irrespective of treatment restrictiveness, may be a more important determinant of treatment acceptability (Newton et al., 2003a, b; Sturmey et al., 2003). Demographic variables such as gender, age and disability may have a smaller effect on treatment acceptability, although in certain circumstances certain forms of intervention may be seen as particularly appropriate or inappropriate for certain populations. Offenders with developmental disabilities are doubly stigmatised by their developmental disability and often by the nature of their offences. Thus, they may be particularly vulnerable to overly restrictive and stigmatising treatments. Other recent studies have also demonstrated that changes in the frequency of target behaviours—even large changes—may be associated with poor treatment acceptability ratings. Outcomes that are less proximal to offending behaviour, such as client happiness, health issues related to the target behaviour, and perceptions of treatment effectiveness by others, may be more important determinants of treatment acceptability than changes in the frequency of the target behaviour (Sturmey, Nabeyama & Newton, in review).

Only one study of treatment acceptability for offenders with intellectual disabilities was located. Lundervold and Young (1992) presented vignettes describing various kinds of offenders, offences and treatments. The offender might have a disability or be of average intelligence. The offences included public masturbation, rape and fondling a child. Treatments included non-restrictive treatments, such as social skills training, and restrictive treatments and disposals, such as noxious odours or incarceration. Generally social skills training was most acceptable for both types of perpetrators and most kinds of offences. An exception to this was that social skills training was as acceptable as aversive treatments and incarceration for more severe offences. This study can be used as a model for future research to determine empirically what kinds of treatment are acceptable for offenders with developmental disabilities. Future research on evaluating treatment acceptability should attend to the important variable of treatment outcome. Given the very sensitive nature of some of the target behaviours, it seems likely that treatment effectiveness may be an important determinant of treatment acceptability. Future treatment outcome research should include measures of treatment acceptability in addition to more typical measures of reoffending, self-report of attributions, and cognitions and skills change.

RESEARCH ON VICTIMS OF CRIME AND PREVENTION

The majority of research reviewed in this volume has focused on perpetrators of crime (Sobsey, 1994). Relatively little attention has been paid to people with developmental disabilities as victims of crime. They may be vulnerable because of inability to recognise and report crime and because of fear of coercion and retribution, if the perpetrators of that crime are family members, care staff or peers.

One line of research that appears promising is a series of empirical studies teaching people with intellectual disabilities how to act assertively and report and prevent abuse, such as sexual abuse. Lumley and Miltenberger (1997) have noted that many previous intervention programmes in this area have been limited by the use of knowledge measures and self-report measures of behaviour change. Lumley, Miltenberger, Long, Rapp and Roberts (1998) used measures of knowledge, role play, verbal reports, and, importantly, naturalistic probes to evaluate a skills training approach to teach abuse prevention skills to women with mental retardation. The women were taught that when solicitation occurred from a stranger they should say "no", walk away and then report the incident to a person in authority. The results of the programme were quite disappointing. Although participant knowledge increased and behaviour changed appropriately in the role-play situation, there was little behaviour change in probes in the natural environment. At follow-up even changes in verbal reports did not maintain over time. Subsequently, Miltenberger *et al.* (1999) demonstrated that for the programme to be effective in changing behaviour in the natural environment, training in the naturalistic environment was necessary.

People with developmental disabilities may need a variety of skills to behave safely. To date we do not have a good database as to the most common situations that present dangers to people with mental retardation (Sobsey, 1994). Thus, it is not clear which skills are most important to teach to prevent crime. Further, many people with more severe forms of developmental disability are unlikely to be able to learn some of these skills. Future research could address prevention of victimisation of these clients through training staff and family members, and by setting up effective administrative mechanisms for crime prevention.

PARTICIPATORY RESEARCH

Most research involving offenders with developmental disabilities, like that in the developmental disability field in general, is guided by traditional experimental or quasi-experimental paradigms first developed in the natural sciences. Critics of these traditional paradigms believe that this research is carried out *on subjects*, rather than *in collaboration with participants* (Clements, Rapley & Cummins, 1999). These critics suggest that there is a power imbalance between a self-serving scientific community and vulnerable people such as those with disabilities, who are exploited by researchers pursuing their own agendas, or those of the funding institutions that represent society's establishment. This polemical analysis seems somewhat counter to the actual situation. In the field of developmental disability research—in the UK at least—there is relatively little status and kudos attained by researchers, grants from major funding organisations are virtually unknown, and there are barely any meaningful academic career pathways available for aspiring researchers. Witness the steady decline, and, in some cases, the demise, of the few UK research centres focusing on disability issues in recent years.

This is not to say that traditional approaches to research do not have real limitations in this field. These include investigation of research questions that may be of interest to research funders, service commissioners or to the researchers themselves, but may be of no consequence or immediate benefit to the subjects of the enquiry, who are quite passive within the research process. It has been suggested that traditional research promulgates the medical model of disability, which locates the problem, disorder or deficit within the individual and ignores the social construction of disability (Kiernan, 1999a). It has also been claimed that another failure of traditional approaches is their inability to effect immediate social, political or economic changes that would benefit people with disabilities (Oliver, 1992).

Critics of traditional paradigms have proposed a radical alternative in the form of *emancipatory* research (Oliver, 1992; Ward, 1997). This paradigm involves people with disabilities as equal partners, or co-researchers, at every stage of the research process. They are involved from the framing of the research question, through the development of the design and methods, the collection and analysis of data, and the dissemination of the research findings. The professional researcher is no longer the expert within this paradigm. Rather their role is to facilitate the research and be a *labourer* for the researcher with disabilities, who has the power and is in complete control of the process of research that is focused exclusively on bringing about immediate change and improvement to the lives of people with disabilities. This represents an overtly political approach: the researchers become activists. As such it has a number of limitations, including naiveté concerning the complex interaction between the impact of outputs from research on public policy and attitudes over time. It discounts the validity of research questions that others within a community concerned with disability, including families, formal and informal carers, service commissioners and providers, might have. Further, there are important questions concerning the generalisability of the findings from such studies and the representativeness of the views of researchers involved in this approach.

Kiernan (1999a, b) reviewed both these general issues and more specific limitations of this new paradigm research for people with developmental disabilities. He noted that there are obvious constraints that individuals' intellectual limitations, particularly those with severe and profound levels of disability, would have on their true involvement in all aspects of a research process that requires complex cognitive skills. Of particular concern is the extent to which this approach would have relevance, value, or be supported or allowed by the funders of services and research for offenders with developmental disabilities and the statutory authorities.

Somewhere between the traditional and the radical new research paradigms are qualitative research methodologies that have clear application and value in the forensic field. Although research questions may still be determined by the researcher, or the research funder, qualitative research grounds studies in the experience and views of participants (Kiernan, 1999a). Still further along the research continuum from quantitative approaches, participatory research requires the involvement of people with disabilities at all stages of the process, but as partners and collaborators rather than as controllers. While it is anticipated that people involved in this approach to research will be empowered personally by the process, and will benefit directly from the outputs, the goals are not overtly socio-political as in emancipatory research. Ward and Trigler (2001) review how some people with developmental disabilities have been helped to take wide-ranging roles within the participatory research paradigm. While there are some recent examples of the application of qualitative methodologies in the forensic developmental disability field (e.g. Heyman, Buswell Griffiths & Taylor, 2002), it is not clear if there have been any studies involving offenders with developmental disabilities that have used a true participatory research paradigm that has involved them setting the research agenda, developing the research design and methods, carrying out the data collection and analysis, and disseminating the findings. This approach could be seen to add value to particular aspects of research in this field, such as mapping the pathways into forensic services and increasing understanding of the impact of services' responses on clients' experiences, and ultimately on outcomes. Clearly there are significant logistical and funding challenges to this approach becoming commonplace in the short term in research with offenders with developmental disabilities.

Notwithstanding these issues, in the UK the NHS National Programme on Forensic Mental Health Research and Development (2003) has stated its commitment to the involvement of service users in all aspects of the commissioning process. It actively encourages service-user involvement in the research it supports financially, including that with people with developmental disabilities.

ETHICAL ISSUES

Ethical issues concerning research with offenders in secure settings, and in particular consent for treatment and for participation in research, are classic problem areas for professional ethics (American Psychological Association, 2002; Sturmey & Gaubatz, 2002). Offenders in secure settings have been subject to various forms of abuse, including dangerous research that has resulted in injury and harm from unwittingly participating in research without due process. Although some people with developmental disabilities can understand the elements necessary for participation in treatment, fewer can comprehend all the elements necessary for participation in research (Arscott, Dagnan & Stenfert Kroese, 1998, 1999). In any case many offenders with developmental disabilities in secure settings are placed there because they are judged to be legally incompetent. In such cases it is unclear who can consent for either treatment or participation in research. However, this is probably not very different for people without developmental disabilities. There is evidence that research participants of average intellectual functioning do not understand and are unable to recall accurately key aspects of studies that they have consented to take part in (Featherstone & Donovan, 2002). Therefore, we would want to avoid the situation where discriminatory decisions to exclude people with developmental disabilities from potentially beneficial or benign research are made on the basis of erroneous assumptions about their capacity to give consent compared with members of the general population. A balance is required in order to protect potentially vulnerable individuals and to promote self-determination.

Valid consent requires that prospective participants are provided with sufficient accurate information concerning the research, that they have capacity to make a decision about participating and to understand the consequences of the decision, and that their decision to participate is voluntary (Lord Chancellor's Department, 1999). Making information about treatment and research understandable and accessible to people with cognitive limitations is challenging for researchers, but not insurmountable (Arscott et al., 1998, 1999). One helpful approach in the case of treatment evaluations is to include a psycho-educational preparatory phase, following which participants will be better informed and able to give or withhold valid consent (Taylor et al., 2002a). Further research is required concerning assessment of the elements required for capacity to give valid consent. These elements should include the ability to comprehend information about the research, to be able to assimilate and recall the information and to be able to make a decision about participation in a specific research study (Iacono & Murray, 2003; Wong, Clare, Gunn & Holland, 1999). However, the extent to which consent-giving by offenders with developmental disabilities can ever be totally free of a degree of coercion, and therefore completely voluntary, is questionable. This is a debate that needs to be brought into the open and not avoided or ignored. In that way researchers, offenders and ethics committees can be clear about the ethical issues in this difficult area.

Treatment can be legally mandated by a court, but participation in research can not. In the United States Institutional Review Boards (IRBs) are responsible for reviewing the ethics of all research involving human subjects, including ensuring adequate consent. IRBs attempt to balance the risks of the research and the benefits of participating in that research. Note that if consent cannot be given and the client would have benefited from that research, then another ethical dilemma is the denial of the benefits of participation in research to people for whom adequate consent cannot be obtained. In England and Wales this issue is addressed in the Department of Health (2001) guidance document, *Seeking Consent: Working with People with Learning Disabilities*. This guidance suggests that individuals who do not have the capacity to give consent can be included in therapeutic research if it is judged to be in the person's best interests, and they may be included in non-therapeutic research as long as it is not against the interests of the individual.

Outcome research with offenders, including offenders with mental health problems or developmental disabilities, is an area of considerable public and professional concern. The conflicting goals to punish offenders, protect the public from offenders, or rehabilitate offenders further muddies these waters. Psychotherapy research, including treatment research in developmental disabilities, has been subject to numerous fashions and fads (Jacobson, Foxx & Mulick, 2004). Fashionable and fad treatments may *not* be harmless. They may indirectly deprive people of the benefits of known effective therapies. They waste public resources, the money and time of parents, insurance companies, public agencies and clients and may interfere with ongoing effective treatments (Jacobson *et al.*, 2004; Sturmey, 2004). Faddish and fashionable treatments may do more than deprive clients of effective treatment and waste money: in some cases therapy does positive harm. For example, facilitated communication was not merely unhelpful, wasteful and ineffective (Mostert, 2001) it resulted in the wrongful conviction of parents of sexual abuse of their children and separated children from their families. Several RCTs of psychological debriefing post-traumatic stress disorder (PTSD) have indicated that therapy results in higher rates of PTSD in the *treatment* group than in the non-treatment control groups at one-year follow-up (e.g. Wessely, Rose & Bisson, 2000). The assumption that well-intended therapy is helpful, neutral or harmless is directly challenged by these findings. In the absence of data to the contrary we should therefore be duly cautious in evaluating claims for therapy effectiveness.

CONCLUSIONS

This volume has demonstrated that in general there is increasing interest in, and work being carried out at a number of levels, including clinical, service development, criminological and legal, policy development and political, concerning offenders with developmental disabilities. Despite this heartening picture of activity and endeavour, the field of forensic developmental disability is developing from a very low baseline in terms of a research literature and evidence base. The material that is available shows promise with regard to positive outcomes. However, there is much still to be done in terms of research and development to improve our understanding of this illusive and heterogeneous population, their needs in terms of services and models of delivery, and the active ingredients of effective and sustainable clinical, educational and social interventions. Beyond these goals, we should anticipate another challenging agenda, similar to that in other human service areas with more established evidence bases. This concerns how to get what we do know, and might discover, to make a difference to the lives of clients and their putative victims; that is the conundrum of how to translate research into practice.

Alongside these issues, there are other important questions about how to secure meaningful levels of financial support for research in a field that is viewed by many, due the nature of the clients and their behaviour, to be unattractive and undeserving of more than the minimum support in terms of public funding. Closely aligned to this issue is the question of how to build a critical mass of academic and clinical researchers, with supporting organisational infrastructures, networks and career pathways, so that the field can develop. Only then will it be able to begin to compete in a concerted way for the available resources, raise the profile of this complex and challenging area of enquiry, and contribute to the twin aims of improving the chances of offenders with developmental disabilities being successfully rehabilitated, and affording the public proper levels of protection based on accurate assessments of risk and associated needs.

REFERENCES

American Psychological Association (2002). *Ethical Principals and Code of Conduct*. Washington, DC: American Psychological Association.

Annand, J. (2002). *More than Accommodation: Overcoming Barriers to Effective Treatment of Persons with Both Cognitive Disabilities and Chemical Dependency*. Beaverton, OR: Nightwind Publishing.

Arbuthnot, J., Gordon, D. & Jurkovic, G.J. (1987). Personality. In H.C. Quay (ed.) *Handbook of Juvenile Delinquency* (pp. 139–83). New York: John Wiley & Sons.

Arscott, K., Dagnan, D. & Stenfert Kroese, B. (1998). Consent to psychological research by people with an intellectual disability. *Journal of Applied Research in Intellectual Disabilities*, **11**, 77–83.

Arscott, K., Dagnan, D. & Stenfert Kroese, B. (1999). Assessing the ability of people with a learning disability to give informed consent to treatment. *Psychological Medicine*, **29**, 1367–75.

Barratt, G.S. (1994). Impulsivity and aggression. In J. Monahan & H.J. Steadman (eds) *Violence in Mental Disorder*. (pp. 61–79) Chicago, IL: University of Chicago Press.

Beirne-Smith, M.B., Ittenbach, R.F. & Patton, J.R. (2002). *Mental Retardation*, 6th edn. Upper Saddle River, NJ: Merrill Prentice Hall.

Benson, B.A., Johnson-Rice, C. & Miranti, S.V. (1986). Effects of anger management training with mentally retarded adults in group treatment. *Journal of Consulting and Clinical Psychology*, **54**, 728–9.

Broxholme, S. & Lindsay, W.R. (2003). Development and preliminary evaluation of a questionnaire on cognitions related to sex offending for use with individuals who have mild intellectual disability. *Journal of Intellectual Disability Research*, **47**, 472–82.

Brylewski, J. & Duggan, L. (1999). Antipsychotic medication for challenging behaviour in people with learning disability. *Journal of Intellectual Disability Research*, **43**, 360–71.

Carr, J.E., Coriaty, S., Wilder, D.A., Gaunt, B.T., Dozier, C.L., Britton, L.N., Avina, C. & Reed, C.L. (2000). A review of "noncontingent" reinforcement as treatment for the aberrant behaviour of individuals with developmental disabilities. *Research in Developmental Disabilities*, **21**, 377–91.

Clements, J., Rapley, M. & Cummins, R.A. (1999). On, to, for, with—vulnerable people and the practices of the research community. *Behavioural and Cognitive Psychotherapy*, **27**, 103–15.

Corrigan, P.W. (1991). Social skills training in adult psychiatric populations: a meta-analysis. *Journal of Behavior Therapy and Experimental Psychiatry*, **22**, 203–10.

Coucouvanis, K., Polister, B., Prouty, R. & Lakin, C. (2003). Continuing reduction in populations of large state residential facilities for persons with intellectual and developmental disabilities. *Mental Retardation*, **41**, 67–70.

Cunningham, J., McDonnell, A., Easton, S. & Sturmey, P. (2003). Social validation on three methods of physical restraint: views of consumers, staff and students. *Research in Developmental Disabilities*, **24**, 307–16.

Day, K. (1994). Male mentally handicapped sex offenders. *British Journal of Psychiatry*, **165**, 630–9.

Department of Health (2001). *Seeking Consent: Working with People with Learning Disabilities*. London: Department of Health Publications.

Didden, R., Duker, P.C. & Korzilius, H. (1997). Meta-analytic study on treatment effectiveness for problem behaviors with individuals who have mental retardation. *American Journal on Mental Retardation*, **101**, 387–99.

Eysenck, H.J. (1952). The effects of psychotherapy: an evaluation. *Journal of Consulting and Clinical Psychology*, **16**, 319–24.

Farrington, D.P. (1995). The development of offending and antisocial behaviour from childhood: key findings from the Cambridge study in delinquent development. *Journal of Child Psychology and Psychiatry*, **36**, 929–64.

Fass, S.M. & Pi, C. (2002). Getting tough on juvenile crime: an analysis of costs and benefits. *Journal of Research in Crime and Delinquency*, **39**, 363–99.

Featherstone, K. & Donovan, J. (2002). "Why don't they just tell me straight, why allocate it?" The struggle to make sense of participating in a randomised controlled trial. *Social Science and Medicine*, **55**, 709–19.

Giles, T. (ed.) (1993) *Handbook of Effective Psychotherapy*. New York: Plenum Press.

Glaser, W. & Deane, K. (1999). Normalisation in an abnormal world: a study of prisoners with intellectual disability. *Journal of Offender Therapy and Comparative Criminology*, **43**, 338–50.

Herson, M. & Barlow, D. (1976). *Single-Case Experimental Designs: Strategies for Studying Behaviour Change*. New York: Pergamon Press.

Heyman, B., Buswell Griffiths, C. & Taylor, J. (2002). Health risk escalators and the rehabilitation of offenders with learning disabilities. *Social Science and Medicine*, **54**, 1429–40.

Hirschi, T. (1969). *Causes of Delinquency*. Berkeley, CA: University of California Press.

Holland, T., Clare, I.C.H. & Mukhopadhyay, T. (2002). Prevalence of "criminal offending" by men and women with intellectual disability and the characteristics of "offenders": implications for research and service development. *Journal of Intellectual Disability Research*, **46** (suppl. 1), 6–20.

Hollin, C. (1992). *Cognitive Behavioural Interventions with Young Offenders*. Englewood Cliffs, NJ: Prentice Hall.

Iacono, T. & Murray, V. (2003). Issues of informed consent in conducting medical research involving people with intellectual disability. *Journal of Applied Research in Intellectual Disabilities*, **16**, 41–51.

Jacobson, J., Foxx, F.M. & Mulick, J.A. (eds) (2004). *Controversial Therapies for Developmental Disabilities: Fads, Fashion, and Science in Professional Practice*. Mahwah, NJ: Lawrence Erlbaum Associates.

Kahng, S., Iwata, B.A. & Lewin, A.B. (2002). Behavioural treatment of self-injury, 1964–2000. *American Journal on Mental Retardation*, **107**, 212–21.

Kazdin, A.E., French, N.H. & Sherick, R.B. (1981). Acceptability of alternative treatments for children: evaluations by inpatient children, parents and staff. *Journal of Consulting and Clinical Psychology*, **49**, 900–7.

Kiernan, C. (1999a). Participation in research by people with learning disability: origins and issues. *British Journal of Learning Disabilities*, **27**, 43–7.

Kiernan, C. (1999b). "Respect" in research with people with learning disabilities. *Behavioural and Cognitive Psychotherapy*, **27**, 17–124.

Klimecki, M.R., Jenkinson, J. & Wilson, L. (1994). A study of recidivism amongst offenders with intellectual disability. *Australia and New Zealand Journal of Developmental Disabilities. (Journal of Intellectual and Developmental Disabilities)*, **19**, 209–19.

Kohlberg, L. (1964). The development of moral character. In M.C. Hoffman (ed.) *Child Development* (pp. 72–95). New York: Russell Sage Foundation.

Kolton, D.J., Boer, A. & Boer, D.P. (2001). A revision of the Abel and Becker Cognitions Scale for intellectually disabled sex offenders. *Sexual Abuse: A Journal of Research and Treatment*, **13**, 217–19.

Langan, P.A. & Cunnliff, M.A. (1992). *Recidivism for Felons on Probation*. Bureau of Statistics, Special Report (NCJ-134177). Washington, DC: United States Department of Justice, Bureau of Justice Statistics.

Langan, P.A. & Levin, D.J. (2002). *Recidivism of Prisoners Released in 1994*. Bureau of Statistics, Special Report (NCJ-193427). Washington, DC: United States Department of Justice, Bureau of Justice Statistics.

Lindsay, W.R. (2002). Research and literature on sex offenders with intellectual and developmental disabilities. *Journal of Intellectual Disability Research*, **46** (suppl. 1), 74–85.

Lindsay, W.R., Elliot, S.N.E.F. & Astell, A. (submitted). Predictions of sexual offence recidivism in offenders with intellectual disabilities.

Lindsay, W.R., Michie, A.M., Staines, C., Bellshaw, E. & Culross, G. (1994). Client attitudes towards relationships: changes following a sex education programme. *British Journal of Learning Disabilities*, **22**, 70–3.

Lindsay, W.R. & Smith, A.H.W. (1998). Responses to treatment for sex offenders with intellectual disability: a comparison of one and two year probation sentences. *Journal of Intellectual Disability Research*, **42**, 346–53.

Linhorst, D.M., McCutchen, T.A. & Bennett, L. (2003). Recidivism among offenders with developmental disabilities participating in a case management programme. *Research in Developmental Disabilities*, **24**, 210–30.

Lord Chancellor's Department (1999). *Making Decisions. The Government's Proposals for Making Decisions on Behalf of Mentally Incapacitated Adults*. London: The Stationery Office.

Luborsky, L., Singer, B. & Luborsky, L. (1976). Comparative studies of psychotherapies: is it true that "everybody has won and all must have prizes"? *Proceedings of the Annual Meeting of the American Psychopathology Association*, **64**, 3–22.

Lumley, V.A. & Miltenberger, R.G. (1997). Sexual abuse prevention for persons with mental retardation. *American Journal on Mental Retardation*, **101**, 459–72.

Lumley, V.A., Miltenberger, R.G., Long, E.S., Rapp, J.T. & Roberts, J.A. (1998). Evaluation of a sexual abuse prevention programme for adults with mental retardation. *Journal of Applied Behaviour Analysis*, **31**, 91–101.

Lundervold, D.A. & Young, L.G. (1992). Treatment acceptability ratings for sexual offenders: effect of diagnosis and offense. *Research in Developmental Disabilities*, **13**, 229–37.

McBrien, J. (2003). The intellectually disabled offender: methodological problems in identification. *Journal of Applied Research in Intellectual Disabilities*, **16**, 95–105.

McCord, W. & McCord, J. (1959). *Origins of Crime: A New Evaluation of the Cambridge-Somerville Youth Study*. New York: Columbia University Press.

McDonnell, A.J., Dearden, R. and Sturmey, P. (1993). The acceptability of physical restraint procedures for people with learning disabilities. *Behavioural and Cognitive Psychotherapy*, **21**, 255–64.

McDonnell, A. & Sturmey, P. (2000). The social validation of physical restraint procedures with people with developmental disabilities: a comparison of young people and professional groups. *Research in Developmental Disabilities*, **21**, 85–92.

McGillivray, J.A. & Moore, M.R. (2001). Substance use by offenders with mild intellectual disability. *Journal of Intellectual and Developmental Disability*, **26**, 297–310.

Macmillan D.L., Gresham, F.M., Siperstein, G.N. & Bocian, K.M. (1996). The labyrinth of IDEA: school decisions on referred students with subaverage general intelligence. *American Journal on Mental Retardation*, **101**, 161–74.

Mason, J. & Murphy, G. (2002). Intellectual disability amongst people on probation: prevalence and outcome. *Journal of Intellectual Disability Research*, **46**, 230–8.

Matson, J.L., Bamburg, J.W., Mayville, E.A., Pinkston, J., Bielecki, J., Kuhn, D., Smalls, Y. & Logan, J.R. (2000). Psychopharmacology and mental retardation: a 10 year review (1990–1999). *Research in Developmental Disabilities*, **21**, 263–96.

Maughan, B., Pickles, A., Hagell, A., Rutter, M. & Yule, W. (1996). Reading problems and antisocial behaviour: developmental trends in comorbidity. *Journal of Child Psychology and Psychiatry*, **37**, 405–18.

Miltenberger, R.G., Roberts, J.A., Ellinson, S., Galensky, T., Rapp, J.T., Long, E.S. & Lumley, V.A. (1999). Training and generalization of sexual abuse prevention skills for women with mental retardation. *Journal of Applied Behavior Analysis*, **32**, 385–8.

Moeller, G.F., Barratt, E.S., Dougherty, D.M., Schmitz, J.M. & Swann, A.C. (2001). Psychiatric aspects of impulsivity: perspectives—reviews and overviews. *American Journal of Psychiatry*, **158**, 1783–93.

Mostert, M.P. (2001). Facilitated communication since 1995: a review of published studies. *Journal of Autism and Developmental Disorders*, **31**, 287–313.

Murphy, G.H. & Clare, I.C.H. (1996). Analysis of motivation in people with mild learning disabilities (mental handicap) who set fires. *Psychology, Crime and Law*, **2**, 153–64.

Murray, E.J. (1956). A content analysis method for studying psychotherapy. *Psychological Monographs*, **70**(13), 420.

National Programme on Forensic Mental Health Research and Development (2003). User involvement http://www.doh.gov.uk/research/rd3/nhsrandd/timeltdprogs/fmh/fmhrd.htm (accessed 5 June 2003).

Newton. T., Hartley, P. & Sturmey, P. (1993). Treatment evaluation for eating disorders by clients with eating disorders. *Behavioural and Cognitive Psychotherapy*, **21**, 371–4.

Newton, J.T., Naidu, R. & Sturmey, P. (2003a). The acceptability of the use of sedation in the management of dental anxiety in children: views of dental students. *European Journal of Dental Education*, **7**, 72–6.

Newton, J.T., Shah, S., Patel, H. & Sturmey, P. (2003b). Non-pharmacological approaches to behaviour management in children. *Dental Update*, **30**, 194–9.

Novaco, R.W. & Taylor, J.L. (in press). Assessment of anger and aggression in offenders with developmental disabilities. *Psychological Assessment*.

Oliver, M. (1992). Changing the social relations in research production. *Disability, Handicap and Society*, **7**, 157–69.

Patterson, G.R. & Yoerger, K. (1997). A developmental model for late onset delinquency. In D.W. Osgood (ed.) *Motivation and Delinquency* (pp. 119–77). Lincoln, NE: University of Nebraska Press.

Plutchik, R. & Van Praag, H.M. (1995). The nature of impulsivity: definitions, ontology, genetics and relations to aggression. In E. Hollander & D. Stein (eds) *Impulsivity and Aggression*. Chichester: John Wiley & Sons.

Polloway, E.A. & Smith, J.D. (1983). Changes in mild mental retardation: population, programmes, and perspectives. *Exceptional Children*, **50**, 149–59.

Prout, H.T. & Nowak-Drabik, K.M. (2003). Psychotherapy with persons who have mental retardation: an evaluation of effectiveness. *American Journal on Mental Retardation*, **108**, 82–93.

Rose, J., West, C. & Clifford, D. (2000). Group interventions for anger in people with intellectual disabilities. *Research in Developmental Disabilities*, **21**, 171–81.

Rutter, M., Maughan, B., Meyer, J., Pickles, A., Silberg, J., Simonoff, E. & Taylor, E. (1997). Heterogeneity of antisocial behaviour: causes, continuities and consequences. In D.W. Osgood (ed.) *Motivation and Delinquency* (pp. 45–118). Lincoln, NE: University of Nebraska Press.

Salman, M. (2002). Systematic review of the effect of therapeutic dietary supplements and drugs on cognitive function in subjects with Down syndrome. *European Journal of Paediatric Neurology*, **6**, 213–19.

Simpson, M.K. & Hogg, J. (2001a). Patterns of offending among people with intellectual disability: a systematic review. Part I: methodology and prevalence data. *Journal of Intellectual Disability Research*, **45**, 384–96.

Simpson, M.K. & Hogg, J. (2001b). Patterns of offending among people with intellectual disability: a systematic review. Part II: predisposing factors. *Journal of Intellectual Disability Research*, **45**, 397–406.

Smith, M.L. & Glass, G.V. (1977). Meta-analysis of psychotherapy outcome measures. *American Psychologist*, **32**, 752–60.

Snyder, J.J. & Patterson, G.R. (1995). Individual differences in social aggression: a test of a reinforcement model of socialisation in the natural environment. *Behavior Therapy*, **26**, 371–91.

Sobsey, D. (1994). *Violence and Abuse in the Lives of People with Disabilities*. Baltimore, MD: Paul Brookes.

Stokes, T.F. & Bear, D.M. (1977). An implicit technology of generalisation. *Journal of Applied Behaviour Analysis*, **10**, 349–67.

Sturmey, P. (1992). Treatment acceptability for anorexia nervosa: effect of treatment type, problem severity, and outcome. *Behavioural Psychotherapy*, **20**, 91–3.

Sturmey, P. (2004) . Ethical dilemmas and the most effective treatments. In J. Jacobson, F.M. Foxx & J.A. Mulick (eds) *Controversial Therapies for Developmental Disabilities: Fads, Fashion, and Science in Professional Practice*. Mahwah, NJ: Lawrence Erlbaum Associates.

Sturmey, P. & Gaubatz, M. (2002). *Clinical and Counselling Psychology: A Case Study Approach*. Boston, MA: Allyn & Bacon.

Sturmey, P., Nabeyama, B.C. & Newton, J.T. (in review). The effects of reduction in frequency of target behaviour and nonspecific outcomes on treatment acceptability ratings.

Sturmey, P., Reyer, H., Lee, R. & Robek, A. (2003). *Substance-Related Disorders in Persons with Mental Retardation*. Kingston, NY: NADD Press.

Sturmey, P., Thomsett, M., Sundaram, G. & Newton, J.T. (2003). The effects of method of behaviour management client characteristics, and outcome on public perceptions of intervention acceptability in paediatric dentistry. *Behavioural and Cognitive Psychotherapy*, **31**, 169–76.

Taylor, J.L., Keddie, T. & Lee, S. (2003). Working with sex offenders with intellectual disabilities: evaluation of an introductory workshop for direct care staff. *Journal of Intellectual Disability Research*, **47**, 203–9.

Taylor, J.L., Novaco, R.W., Gillmer, B. & Thorne, I. (2002a). Cognitive-behavioural treatment of anger intensity among offenders with intellectual disabilities. *Journal of Applied Research in Intellectual Disabilities*, **15**, 151–65.

Taylor, J.L., Thorne, I., Robertson, A. & Avery, G. (2002b). Evaluation of a group intervention for convicted arsonists with mild and borderline intellectual disabilities. *Criminal Behaviour and Mental Health*, **12**(4), 282–93.

Truax, C.B. (1966). Reinforcement and nonreinforcement in Rogerian psychotherapy. *Journal of Abnormal Psychology*, **71**, 1–9.

Vargas, S. & Camilli, G. (1999). A meta-analysis of research on sensory integration treatment. *American Journal of Occupational Therapy*, **53**, 189–98.

Ward, L. (1997). Funding for change: translating emancipatory disability research from theory to practice. In C. Barnes & G. Mercer (eds) *Doing Disability Research*. Leeds: The Disability Press.

Ward, T., Hudson, S.M., Johnston, L. & Marshall, W.L. (1997). Cognitive distortions in sex offenders: an integrative review. *Clinical Psychology Review*, **17**, 479–507.

Ward, K. & Trigler, J.S. (2001). Reflections on participatory action research with people who have developmental disabilities. *Mental Retardation*, **39**, 57–9.

Wehmeyer, M.L. (1995). Intra-individual factors influencing efficacy of interventions for stereotyped behaviours: a meta-analysis. *Journal of Intellectual Disabilities Research*, **39**, 205–14.

Wessely, S., Rose, J. & Bisson, J. (2000). Brief psychological interventions ("debriefing") for trauma-related symptoms and the prevention of post traumatic stress disorder. *Cochrane Database Systematic Reviews*, **2001**(2): CD000560.

Willner, P., Jones, J., Tams, R. & Green, G. (2002). A randomised controlled trial of the efficacy of a cognitive behavioural anger management group for clients with learning disabilities. *Journal of Applied Research in Intellectual Disabilities*, **15**, 224–35.

Wilson, D., Gallacher, C.A. & McKenzie, D.C. (2000). A meta analysis of corrections based education, vocation and work programmes for adult offenders. *Journal of Research in Crime and Delinquency*, **37**, 347–68.

Wong, J.G., Clare, I.C.H., Gunn, J. & Holland, A.J. (1999). Capacity to make health care decisions: its importance in clinical practice. *Psychological Medicine*, **29**, 437–46.

INDEX

Note: Abbreviations used in the index are: ADHD = attention deficit hyperactive disorder; DDs = developmental disabilities; MIETS = Mental Impairment Evaluation and Treatment Service.